Robin Barker is a registered nurse midwife and pediatric nurse practitioner with twenty-five years experience working with the under-threes.

As toddlers never doubt their place at the center of the universe Robin is very much aware that living with them is both a delight and a challenge for the parents in the thick of it—and for the "experts" who attempt to guide them through the blurry maze. After years of spending time with toddlers and hearing and talking about them, Robin suspects it is the toddlers who have the last laugh.

The Mighty Toddler follows her first book *Baby Love*. Both books are based on many hours spent one-on-one with parents discussing things like temper tantrums, sleep hassles, not eating, biting, the inevitable poo, and strange habits. Mad and wonderful hours full of laughter, amazement, and sometimes tears (not always just the parents').

Robin's detailed knowledge arises from these experiences and focuses on the practicalities of being a parent today. Bearing in mind the avalanche of advice and information now available, she offers safe options for care whenever possible.

Robin has two spectacular children who once were toddlers. She lives and works in Sydney.

Other books by Robin Barker

Baby Love
Australian Baby and Toddler Meals
The Baby Love Guide to Crying
The Baby Love Guide to Feeding
The Baby Love Guide to Sleeping
The Baby Love Guide to the First Three Months

THE MIGHTY TODDLER

ROBIN BARKER

M. EVANS AND CO., INC.
NEW YORK

NOTE TO READERS

All care has been taken to provide accurate, safe information, but it is impossible to cover every situation, so please consult a competent health professional whenever you are in doubt about your toddler's health or behavior. A book can never be a substitute for an individual professional consultation. The author and the publishers cannot accept legal responsibility for any problems arising out of the contents of this book.

M. Evans and Company, Inc.
216 East 49th Street
New York, New York 10017

ISBN 0-87131-986-1

First published 2001 in Macmillan by Pan Macmillan Australia Pty Limited
St Martins Tower, 31 Market Street, Sydney

Illustrations by Tim Snowdon

"The Flames" by Kate Llewelyn, from *The Selected Poems*, published by Hudson Hawthorne, Australia, 1996, reproduced with permission from the author.

Printed in the United States of America

9 8 7 6 5 4 3 2 1

To all the toddlers in my life, both past and present, especially Adam, Kate, Amy, Emma, Danny, Bobby, Angie, Gabriel, and Indigo. And those still to come . . .

He, she, and so on

In this book the mother is she, the father is he, and the toddler is he because in the interest of equal exposure in my books it is time for the boys to take center stage.

You used to lean
on that cot rail
and wait
with the vigour of a flame
to leap into my arms
two feet tall and two years old
a sagging nappy
archless feet soft as cats' tongues
and trodden underneath
a thick and clammy waterproof
warm from sleep
the sheet ruched at the end
toys heaped confused
neglected as the dead
a duck stuck in the corner
I could see the basket of your ribs
your hands were opened
and all your bones and life
leapt up to mine.

Kate Llewelyn, "The Flames"

Contents

About This Book   xi

One to Three—the Toddler Years   1

part **one**
UNDERSTANDING HOW YOUR TODDLER GROWS AND DEVELOPS
1. Growing   9
2. Developing   18
3. Milestones and Their Many Variations   38

part **two**
THE QUESTION OF BEHAVIOR
4. What's Behind Toddler Behavior?   73
5. Discipline   99
6. The ABC's of Typical Toddler Behavior   127

part **three**
THE BASICS
7. Day-to-Day Toddler Care   189
8. Sleep   221
9. Food   257
10. Play   295
11. Safety and Immunization   322

part**four**

WHY IS HE ALWAYS SICK? TODDLER MEDICAL
CONDITIONS AND ILLNESSES

12. Coughing, Mucus, and Poo   347
13. Skin Problems   357
14. An Ailment or Two   372
15. Infectious Diseases   393
16. Infestations   407

part**five**

FOR PARENTS

17. Your Toddler's Fine—How About You?   415
18. The Vexed Topic of Childcare   452
19. Room for More?   481

The Last Word . . .   504
Sources and Resources   507
Resources and Helping Organizations   509
Recommended Reading   517
Endnotes   520
Bibliography   521
Acknowledgments   522
Percentile Charts   525
Index   527

About This Book

At the end of *Baby Love,* my book about the first year after birth, I said that the end of the first year was really just the beginning of a never-ending story. Turning from a baby into a child is another step in that story. Small in time but mighty in accomplishments for you both, it will touch your heart and stay in your memory forever.

Like *Baby Love, The Mighty Toddler* contains practical down-to-earth information built from my years of talking to mothers (mostly) and some fathers in my work as a pediatric nurse practitioner. Safe options for care are offered whenever possible, and it is not recommended that the book be read from cover to cover like a novel (heaven forbid)—it is intended as a parent's working manual and information is repeated when relevant.

We are unfortunately living in a time when everyone is obsessed with outcomes. Consequently much information about child rearing today focuses on optimal things to do when children are young to ensure a good outcome when they are older. Toddlers, however, are not too much interested in outcomes. They live very much in the present. My information is intended as a guide to help you enjoy your time with your toddler in the here and now rather than to encourage you to strive to be the perfect parent raising the perfect child. It is not intended to solve every problem that comes your way. Nor does it come with promises to make your toddler more optimistic, happier, more intelligent, more musically talented, or more physically coordinated.

Rather it is written with the aim of helping you understand this time in your child's life and to offer a practical framework for you to work within should you need one. Not all toddler problems are solvable—many disappear as the toddler years pass—but just knowing what is normal and having a few ideas of what is helpful and what is not can be comforting.

The Mighty Toddler is intended for all parents, including same-sex couples and sole parents. Regardless of their situation, the ideal of stable and functional family life is something most parents strive for. And it is possible to care for children and offer them love and protection in a variety of family structures. However, it takes guts and determination when there is only one parent and, to a lesser extent, when there are two parents of the same sex. As the vast majority of same-sex parents are women, one of the bonuses for them is that the care of the babies and toddlers is much more likely to be evenly shared. But, as with sole parents, same-sex parents face tougher challenges than do traditional parents.

It is difficult when writing to include the many variations of family settings, but I assure all parents who are living in nontraditional family structures that the information is here for you too—I certainly had you in mind when I wrote it.

I have used the word *parents* so consistently throughout the book that readers may wonder if I am aware of the difference between mothers and fathers. I assure you I am.

The decision to follow the trend and address readers as parents rather than mothers (as once was the case in childcare manuals) was not taken lightly. It is done with some reluctance because statistics repeatedly show that less than ten percent of couples share equally the household tasks and the nitty-gritty of baby and toddler care. Mothers still undertake most of the hard work of caring and nurturing babies and toddlers.

However, it is impossible to refer to mothers and fathers separately according to how *I* might think each role should work. Apart from being difficult from a writing perspective, it is likely to cause even more dismay than addressing only mothers and thus ignoring fathers. Besides, I think that it is important to acknowledge the ten percent of families where shared care is a reality.

Finally, I use *parents* with a certain amount of hope and optimism that sharing the hard work of the baby and toddler years equally between parents will increase in substantial ways in the future.

As I sit writing about such serious matters, I suddenly hear the sound of busy footsteps on the pavement outside my window and a voice shrill with excitement.

"Mommy, I've just done the biggest poo."

Welcome back to the present.

I hope this book helps you make some sense of the comical, magic, and enchanting world of your toddler.

One to Three—
the Toddler Years

The toddler years are a time in life when babies not only become mobile but also start to separate from their parents and find their own identities emotionally and socially. Anytime from eight months onward your baby will begin to realize that he is a separate person from you. He will find it exciting to be able to move away from you, but scary when you move away from him.

It's a time of tremendous development when babies discover they are able to use their minds and bodies to make things happen, giving them a sense of power that is both exhilarating and frightening. It's also a time, similar to adolescence, of coming to terms with the urge to become self-reliant while still needing and wanting parental affection and protection.

Toddlerhood encompasses the whole range of development that takes place as babies become children. It is a transition so dramatic that it cannot happen without arousing very mixed feelings for most parents, not to mention some rather uncomfortable emotions. While there is much to relish, there's also a certain amount of dismay and frustration living with a toddler as he rackets around trying out his new skills and learning how the world works.

It's a time in adult development when we have to learn tolerance, patience, and how to deal satisfactorily with the intense feelings our toddler may provoke in us.

The toddler years bring a lot of pleasure. The curl of an eyelash on the fat cheek of a sleeping child, a chubby, dimpled little bottom, sturdy legs chasing seagulls along a beach, and the first sloppy kisses all give us passionate moments of knee-weakening

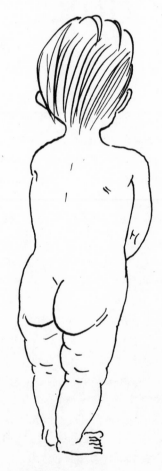

A chubby, dimpled little bottom

love. We exclaim with amazement as each day brings a new accomplishment. We laugh at the funny things toddlers do and the hilarious conclusions they come to as they try to make sense of what's going on around them. We are entranced by the magic they bring to the ordinary things in life.

The toddler years also bring a lot of hard work, particularly between fourteen months and two years. This is the time most commonly referred to as the terrible twos. It is an unfortunate term as it suggests it is an entirely negative phase rather than a crucial stage of development that transforms babies into children.

During this stage toddlers need a lot of attention and super-vision to make sure they are safe and that other people and valued possessions are safe from them. It is widely acknowl-edged that the combination of their self-assertiveness and lack of ability to reason tests the goodwill of their parents a lot of the time. Nevertheless, there are aspects of the toddler years that are delightful despite the difficulties. The achievements of this par-ticular stage are so immense that the only way to understand just how spectacular they are is to experience them firsthand. So much so that even if you are relieved when it's over, it's an essential part of your history together which you will value highly. And talk about, laugh about, and remember for the rest of your life.

What's important?

It's easy to lose sight of the basics in today's world. In some ways the explosion in research and technology has given us more infor-mation than we really need, especially in relation to babies and toddlers.

It's true it has given today's parents many more options and much more information, so they are not stuck in the rigid standards parents of previous eras were. However, freedom is not always liberating. It can be quite scary and raise all sorts of anxieties, particularly when it comes to deciding the best way to bring up your children. The predictions of future success or failure arising from the choices that parents make can at times seem to be as much of a burden as the rigidity and restrictions of past eras. When you're feeling confused, it's helpful to get back to the basics and work on them—if the basics are there, a lot of the other stuff either falls into place or melts away.

What are the basic things a toddler needs?

- Someone to be responsible for caring for him and who is passionately in love with him and always available. Obviously this is easier when there are two people, but there is no reason why several interested adults cannot all contribute to caring for a toddler. Shared care of toddlers makes a lot of sense as the expectation that the total care should be the responsibility of one person (read the mother) is unrealistic and unfair.

- Security to explore and test himself and his experiences in a stress-free environment where consistent limits are set. He needs to know that he can rely on the adults in his life to provide a sanctuary for him to return to when he has finished exploring.

- Good adult role models. Toddlers are great imitators, and modeling the kinds of behaviors you want your toddler to learn is a powerful way of making your attitudes and personal values as important to him as they are to you.

Living with a toddler is exhilarating, exhausting, fascinating, tedious, surprising, rewarding, passionate, depressing, and full of loving moments. Toddlers need available, firm, energetic, fun-loving, confident parents with realistic expectations of themselves and their children.

Trust your own judgment and look for options rather than easy solutions. And never forget to remind yourself that you *are* doing the most vital job in life. Even if it is unpaid, unacknowledged, unappreciated, and often unsupported by the society in which we live, the person your toddler will become will be a tribute to your skill and commitment. Truly amazing when you think that we learn it all on the job, isn't it?

part **one**

UNDERSTANDING HOW YOUR TODDLER GROWS AND DEVELOPS

chapter **one**

Growing

What is growth?

Growth refers to an increase in size. (I like stating the obvious!) The physical growth of a baby is very reassuring to his parents. It is tangible evidence of the baby's well-being at a time when he seems so vulnerable and has very limited communication skills. As the baby continues to grow rapidly in that first year, growth becomes much less of an issue. Early feeding problems get resolved and the majority of babies thrive even if they become fussy eaters.

It is normal for many babies' weights to level out between nine and twelve months, especially if they are breastfed. This is a time when many babies start to become mobile, drink less milk, and often lose interest in eating big spoonfuls of baby food. After the first year, the weight gain slows right down and you are likely to see only modest increases every three months or so.

However, increases in height continue, so babies now start to look longer and thinner. Some do stay quite chubby, but for most the rounded baby look starts to disappear, though toddlers still tend to have funny little pot bellies until some muscle tone develops.

Measuring length, weight, and head circumference and plotting the results on a percentile chart is the way growth is assessed.

Percentile charts

Percentile charts are based on measurements of children from a certain population (for example, all the babies in the United States in a certain year). As normal variations in height and weight are considerable, the charts are drawn in percentile measurements to allow for the variations. If you look at percentile charts, you will see that the lines represent the fifth, tenth, twenty-fifth, fiftieth, seventy-fifth, ninetieth, and ninety-fifth percentiles for weight, height, and head circumference. Most toddlers' weight and length fall somewhere between the fifth and ninety-fifth percentiles.

Weight and height are often around the same percentile (for example, fiftieth percentile for weight and height). However, the normal range includes the thinner toddlers who weigh one or two percentiles below their height and the chubbier ones who weigh one or two above.

It is not necessary to routinely assess the weight, height, and head circumference of healthy toddlers unless you want to. If you do want to, three-monthly assessments are quite sufficient unless you have reason to be worried or your toddler has a particular problem that needs monitoring.

Measuring and weighing toddlers between ages one and two years is often a challenge. Toddlers do not like being held down on a table to be measured and it's usually very difficult to persuade them to stand nicely against a wall. They hate strange people wrapping tape measures around their heads and generally bounce gleefully around on the scales, frightening the wits out of everyone before trying to leap off. I've never been too sure why some parents and health professionals insist on this rather stressful ritual when it is quite obvious that the toddler is bright-eyed, full of energy, and growing out of his clothes and shoes at a great rate.

Once your toddler is old enough to understand and cooperate, it's fun to measure him from time to time on a special spot on the wall at home where he can see his own progress.

Weight—when to worry

Concern about a toddler's weight is generally centered on thinness rather than fatness, although excessive weight gains are sometimes of concern. Thoughtless comments by onlookers or well-meaning relatives can be very upsetting—"What a fat/thin, tall/short child," and so on. These are inevitably false perceptions, but if you are worried, it's worth the hassle to have your toddler's length, weight, and head circumference taken by someone reliable and plotted on a percentile chart. Weight without length is meaningless, and allowances have to be made for premature babies. Nine times out of ten, weighing and measuring are all that is required to put your mind at rest.

If your toddler's weight percentile is a long way below his height percentile, there may be a problem.

Common reasons for problematic low weight in toddlers

Medical illnesses

Medical problems are nearly always accompanied by signs other than just low weight, such as strange-smelling poo, apathy, fevers, delayed development, irritability, or constant unhappiness.

Runs of acute minor illnesses, which are a part of many toddlers' lives until they build up a good supply of antibodies to fight

11

infection, are a common cause of continuing stationary or small weight gains. Viral diarrhea, upper respiratory tract infections, and ear infections are the main offenders. Once these pass, the toddler should start gaining weight again.

Medical problems such as urinary tract infections or other rarer conditions are sometimes diagnosed. A small number of toddlers are found to have problems with absorbing food. They need accurate diagnosis and treatment.

Diet

The healthy, active "noneating" toddler who is offered a wide range of nutritious food is unlikely to be seriously underweight.

Sometimes, with the best intentions in the world, parents restrict their toddler's diet for unsound reasons. Limiting the range of food they have access to is problematic for small people with fussy appetites. If you have been advised to restrict your toddler's diet or you wish to follow a vegan diet, make sure you talk to a dietitian to ensure your toddler's dietary intake is adequate. Many dietary restrictions have no scientific basis and are unlikely to stop your toddler's tantrums or his endlessly runny nose.

Breastfeeding into the second year and beyond has many benefits if it suits you and your toddler; however, breastmilk alone will not meet his growth requirements. Toddlers who exist on umpteen dozen breastfeedings around the clock and virtually no food continue to grow in height, but their weight gradually declines. Opinions vary as to how much of a problem this is. I have seen enough seriously skinny eighteen-month-old toddlers with despairing mothers to believe that it is a problem and recommend dramatically cutting down the breastfeedings to two every twenty-four hours or weaning completely. This is easier said than done. See page 289 for suggestions. Once the breastfeedings stop or are reduced, the toddler inevitably starts eating—often quite well—and gains some weight.

Emotional and social problems

Tragically there are homes where children are physically and emotionally abused or where parents are so burdened with their own problems that their children's needs are neglected. These experiences, however, are outside the scope of this book. If you think this may be the case in your own home, I urge you to seek professional help.

Toddlers in general will occasionally respond to disruptions to family life by not eating and losing weight.

Occasionally mealtimes become such a battle that the toddler is more interested in the drama than the food. Many families have periods where food dramas happen, but occasionally the dramas go on for months, resulting in the toddler weighing considerably less than would be expected for his height. Taking off the pressure and being more realistic about toddler eating usually results in more food going in and more weight going on.

Having said all this, be reassured that the majority of "underweight" toddlers have nothing wrong with them and it's likely that anyone will ever know precisely why they are underweight. The difficulty is in deciding when the reasons for being underweight need investigating. The approach of health professionals varies tremendously, so parents often find that they receive conflicting advice. Techniques to diagnose possible medical causes are invasive, often expensive, and should not be embarked upon as a matter of course.

Often being underweight seems to be a family trait. I frequently see parents pursuing every avenue with their first underweight healthy toddler only to cease worrying with subsequent toddlers who all follow the same pattern.

When your toddler is bright and active, lives in a loving home, is offered an adequate diet, does normal poos, and continues putting on some weight every so often, there's unlikely to be anything wrong.

Premature babies of very low birth weight tend to stay small for the first year or two but follow a steady growth pattern of their own. Like full-term babies, those born prematurely may put on weight sporadically in the toddler years.

What about the overweight toddler?

As with the toddler who is underweight, it is important to first assess whether there is really a problem. Some toddlers look lean, others look chubby, but when weighed and measured, they are found to be fine. If your toddler's weight is more than two percentiles above his height, it could be said that he is overweight (depending on his age).

Is it a problem?

In these days of obsession with weight and the accompanying high incidence of eating disorders in adolescents, I am somewhat reluctant to start talking about the problem of the overweight toddler. However . . .

Here is some information about obesity

- A lot of twelve-month-old babies/toddlers are plump, especially the ones who enjoy their food and are still not moving around much. Many lose this chubbiness as they become mobile and find other interests apart from food. So being overweight becomes more significant the older the toddler is.

- It is believed that the longer a toddler stays overweight, the more likely the trend will continue into adolescence, so an overweight four-year-old is more of a concern than an overweight one-year-old.

- It is also believed that obesity in children relates to the parents' weight. If both parents are significantly overweight, there is a great possibility that their children will also be overweight; if one parent is overweight, the possibility is much less, and if neither parent is overweight, there is only a small chance that their children will have a weight problem. Whether this is heredity or environmental is unclear, but it is probably a combination of both.

- It is also recognized that some people appear to be genetically more predisposed to becoming overweight than others, and this tendency may start in early childhood.

- A minuscule number of toddlers have medical conditions that cause obesity.

However, as we all know, the main reason for being overweight is usually too much food and too little exercise.

Great care has to be taken diagnosing and treating obesity in the toddler years. Weight-reducing diets used by adults are not safe for toddlers. Nor are low-fat diets or high-fiber diets.

If toddlers continue to be overweight after they have become active (some toddlers don't start to walk until eighteen months or even two years), it's best to look at some simple strategies first.

- Endless bottles of milk and fruit juice contribute to excessive weight gains. Say farewell to the bottles.

- Some toddlers will sit and allow the food to be spooned in for as long as someone is prepared to do it. And indeed it is a joy to see bowls full of food disappearing into an open mouth. So much easier than living with a picky eater who throws food all over the room; however, it also increases the likelihood that the toddler is eating more than he needs. If your toddler is a "good eater," stick to basic healthy foods and avoid desserts, deep-fried food, and junk food. Encourage him to feed himself, particularly by about eighteen months, and don't insist on everything in sight being eaten when he is not interested.

- If your toddler eats three good meals a day, one light snack in between is plenty.

- Food is also often used for social reasons that have nothing to do with nutrition—to keep the toddler occupied, head off a temper tantrum, and so on. We all do this from time to time, but when it becomes a routine part of every day it's time to call a halt, especially if the foods are of the sweet and junk food variety.

- Once toddlers become active, they need plenty of time outdoors running, jumping, walking, and playing.

Height—when to worry

Most toddlers grow within the wide range of normal.

Growth disorders occur if there is a hormone imbalance, one of a range of rare genetic and medical conditions, a severe or long-lasting illness, inadequate nutrition, or psychosocial circumstances detrimental to good health. Inadequate nutrition refers to situations where the toddler does not have access to good food. It does not refer to the healthy "non-eating" toddler living in a home where plenty of food is available.

Growth disorders are confirmed by documenting a slowing of growth rate and failure to maintain a height percentile on the growth chart.

When assessing height, it is essential to remember the strong influence heredity plays. Short stature tends to run in families. The critical factor is not only a short toddler but also his *documented growth failure over time.*

Assessing and treating growth disorders is a specialized area of pediatric medicine. If you are concerned about your toddler's height, the first step is to have an accurate weight and height measurement taken. If there appears to be a reduced rate of growth, seek an assessment with a pediatrician. Regular measurements over a period of time may be required before any conclusions are reached or any further action is taken.

Medical treatment is available for children who have a growth hormone insufficiency. Treatment is expensive and involves regular injections over long periods of time.

Healthy premature babies generally experience catching-up growth between three and eighteen months. By school age, the height of most premature babies is within the normal range.

chapter two

Developing

It is impossible to write a book about the toddler years without looking at development in some detail so that you are able to view the things toddlers do in the context of their development rather than seeing them as egocentric, tantrum-throwing, negative little people.

Having an insight into how development unfolds over time, especially the emotional, cognitive, and sensory-motor development, gives meaning to what seems like illogical behavior. It will help you respond to your toddler with more pleasure, greater self-confidence, and less angst.

Development involves the accumulation over time of all the complex skills that enable us to live and function in the society to which we belong. Development continues throughout life, but the rapid development that takes place in the first three years is so conspicuous and dramatic that parents (who themselves are in a new stage of development) frequently use words like *miraculous* and *amazing* to describe their baby's progress.

Milestones

Sequence of development (the order in which babies and toddlers move along the developmental path) is based on close, detailed observations of babies, toddlers, and children over long periods of time. The results are then described in a systematic fashion. Developmental sequences tend to be the same in all children and are linked to the maturing of the central nervous system. These sequences are what are commonly known as milestones, and most parents are familiar with them.

Although the *sequence* of milestone achievements is similar for all children, the *rate* at which they achieve them varies from child to child and may be affected by prematurity, culture, environment, health and disability, availability of opportunity, genetic potential, and so on. Sequential development is considered under the following areas of interrelated development:

Gross motor: Refers to the control of large muscles. These skills enable your toddler to walk, run, skip, and jump.

Fine motor: Refers to the ability to control small muscles. These skills enable your toddler to feed himself, draw, thread beads, turn a light switch on and off, and pick his nose.

Vision: Refers to the ability to see near and far and interpret what is seen.

Hearing and speech: Hearing is the ability to hear and receive information and listen (interpret). *Speech* is the ability to understand and learn language and use it to communicate effectively.

Social skills and play: These skills enable your toddler to learn how to eventually look after himself (feeding, dressing, bathing); how to interact with his world through play; and how, through experience, to make discoveries for himself.

The observation and description of sequential development have given us the tools to assess normal development, to identify potential problems early, and to help parents anticipate what's ahead and thus prepare for safety issues.

Unfortunately parents and health professionals often use

19

milestones in a one-dimensional manner. Milestones are sometimes viewed as boxes to check off in the production of an assembly-line product.

Although development in the first three years has many conspicuous and dramatic moments, it is mostly a gradual, continuous progression involving a number of closely related things all happening at the same time. Achievements in motor development (walking, running, climbing), emotional and cognitive development (thinking, communicating, and understanding), and social development (sharing, showing affection, increasing competency in self-care) are all intertwined. For example, a toddler has to develop manipulative skills and hand-eye coordination before being able to learn to use a pencil.

Developing toddlers are intensely curious, constantly active and want to be in good relationships with other people, especially their parents (truly, even though it doesn't seem like it after a whiney day of no's).

Cognitive (intellectual) development

Having some understanding of the way your child develops intellectually is extremely helpful throughout childhood but is especially so during the toddler years when the dramatic development of his mental processes parallels the dramatic increase in his physical skills.

Cognition refers to the way in which we get to know the world, its objects, its people, and how they all work. Children absorb information through their senses and come to understand the relationship between objects, people, the world, and themselves. They acquire the ability to reason, believe, remember, and perceive what's going on around them. Although we must never forget that all children are different, there are similarities in the way they develop intelligence. As children grow, the maturing of their central nervous system and sensory organs in combination with their experiences help them deal more effectively with the world. Understanding a new experience grows out of what was learned from a previous experience. The child himself is an active participant in the process, not just a passive being, bowled along by external forces.

The toddler years are a time of continuous investigation, repetition, and deliberate trial and error to find out how things and people, including himself, work. Add this to the task of mastering physical skills and the belief that everyone sees the world the way he does, and you start to have some idea of why this period can be so turbulent.

Development of memory

Memory is a highly complicated process that is an important part of cognitive development: an intimate relationship exists between learning and memory. Cognitive (thinking) development relies partly on being able to understand a new experience from remembering what was learned from a previous one.

Memory has at least three important systems commonly agreed upon—sensory memory, short-term memory, and long-term memory. These are not separate and isolated but rather all part of the same process.

Sensory memory refers to a lingering of something heard, seen, or smelled (a whiff of summer in the air) and only plays a small part in everyday activities.

Short-term memory is our working memory—what we are currently paying attention to. Humans can only deal with a limited amount of information at any given moment. This applies especially to toddlers and often to their mothers as well.

Long-term memory is the stored knowledge we have about the world we live in. This vast store includes knowledge of language and information to help us deal with our daily life experiences, as well as plans for what we intend to do in the future. What is stored in our long-term memory depends largely on our previous experiences.

Memory involves not only storage capacity but also the ability to represent things in a symbolic fashion. Symbolic thought is like holding a picture record of objects, people, and events. It is thought that babies start to do this at nine months. It is difficult to know for sure until they are around eighteen months old, but most parents have stories that demonstrate their baby's memory of events, objects, and people before this age.

By eighteen months, a toddler is capable of symbolic representation of familiar objects and has a working memory that stretches from day to day. By three years, a child has a fully developed short-term memory within the limitations of his language development at that age.

Memory development—the practicalities

Parents often mistakenly believe that their baby or toddler has no memory because adults generally do not remember much before the age of three. No one is too sure why this is so. A major contributing factor is probably the immature language abilities of babies and toddlers. It is not until children have developed the full repertoire of language skills that they have the ability to encode and symbolize thoughts, a necessary ingredient for memory development.

Another reason for not remembering much before the age of three or four may be that the way we think prior to three is radically different from the way we think as adults. In their book *How Babies Think,* Gopnik, Meltzoff, and Kuhl suggest that toddlers don't seem to understand the difference between past and present thoughts and don't seem to recollect past thoughts when they conflict with current ones.[1] This explanation, as well as the vital role language plays in memory development, contributes a great deal to understanding many aspects of toddler behavior (for example, not remembering from one day to the next why he can't touch the stove or eat the dog's food).

The other mistake parents often make is to rely too much on their toddler's memory when it becomes obvious to them that he can remember some things. Bear in mind that his developing memory is competing with a limited understanding of cause and effect, his driving curiosity to explore, his desire for independence, and his compulsion to do the things you don't want him to do so that he can test his boundaries and figure out how you work. By the time he is three, the combination of the increasing efficiency of his memory and the flowering of his speech, body skills, and mental abilities means that you can rely on his memory to a much greater degree (within the limitations of his language development).

Development of speech and language

Language describes the way human beings communicate by using a system of symbols. Symbols of language are speech, writing, drawing, miming, or using signs. The symbols carry meaning, which humans have to be able to receive, express, and understand whether the object of what the symbol represents is present or not. Language can come from many different sources—people speaking to each other, books, theater, radio, TV, and movies. Language that comes directly to babies and toddlers from parents or other people is the best way for them to learn.

Speech is one of the symbols of language and refers to the ability to communicate by speaking.

Speech and language development is the golden gateway for communication between the toddler turning into the child and the adults in his life. It gives the toddler and his parents much more opportunity for seeing into each other's minds and getting to know each other's personalities. It's an incredible experience for parents to hear how their toddler's thoughts and understanding are growing and it's lots of fun as well—think of all the amazing things they come up with.

The ability to understand language and learning to speak progress at different rates. Speech is but one of a complex set of steps involved in the development of language. Babies and toddlers have to identify sounds correctly, string them together, learn to understand what they mean as well as the concepts behind them, and how to use them appropriately. When you consider all the fine distinctions in language that are signaled only by intonation or emphasis, as well as the subtleties of the overall intent of a sentence, the apparent ease in the way children learn language is miraculous.

How do they do it?

There are lots of theories, one of which is that babies are born knowing a great deal and possess powerful learning abilities that allow them to add to their innate knowledge. The ability to hear and input from adults is a crucial part of the process.

Language development and cognitive development go together. Early words often start when toddlers are extending their knowledge and abilities in other ways, so suddenly a word makes sense to them because of a new experience. Saying a new word does not just involve the sound but grasping the sense of the word, taking it in, making it yours.

Babies' and toddlers' language development is to a large degree about "getting it." Toddlers often "get it" and understand many words and concepts before starting to form words.

The speech and language development of normal babies, toddlers, and children moves predictably from one step to another, but the rate at which this occurs varies.

In the beginning, parents learn to follow their baby's cues—sounds, expressions, and actions—while the baby learns about his parents by their cues and responses. Sometimes the parent controls the turn-taking, but often it is the baby who initiates the communication by making a sound or expression which the adult copies. Speech develops from the sounds the baby enjoys making. He is responded to and thus prompted to make the same sound again, which he then practices repeatedly. Gradually he builds up a large range of sounds which develop meaning and eventually become words.

By two months (often much earlier), a baby will look at an adult and smile. The first cooing noises, those lovely expressions of pleasure, also start around this time, and it's delightful seeing the way babies move their mouths and concentrate as they try to converse. By three months, they are making a range of tuneful vocalizations which start to take the place of crying when they wake, especially first thing in the morning. At eight months, babies are producing a huge range of speech patterns and combinations and starting to use consonants before vowels—"ma," "da," "ga," and so on. They also make lip and throaty sounds.

No one knows what determines when a baby first speaks—it remains a mystery. Around twelve months, babies start to understand that certain things have certain meanings, so between this and their constant babbling practice (at this age called "jargoning" because it tends to sound like a foreign language), the first words start to emerge.

When toddlers start to talk, they do not sound like us. They may say things like "nana" for banana, "do" for dog or "amma" for hammer. Sometimes adults don't realize that their toddler is talking to them because of the odd-sounding words and language structure. Language is invented as much as learned. Mimicking is part of the process, but toddlers also restructure language to suit their own purposes; so even if words are not clear to you, they have meaning for your toddler. Instead of correcting, it's better to repeat the word back so that he can hear how the word is made. Try to listen to *what* is said rather than *how* it is said so that your toddler feels encouraged, not criticized. Remember that toddlers have much more understanding of language than their use of language indicates, so try to avoid talking about your toddler or other issues related to him in front of him as if he were not there.

Around eighteen months, parents notice that their toddler understands many more words, such as names for things and people, action words, and words for body parts. They also understand location words such as *in, on, up* and describing words such as *big, little, hot.*

By the time they are using approximately fifty words, they are usually close to putting two words together. At this stage (between eighteen months and two and a half), you might find that your toddler wants to talk a lot, tugging at you to get your attention and wanting you to tell him the same things over and over again. It's likely to drive you a bit crazy, but like other bothersome toddler behavior, it will pass as his knowledge and speaking skills grow.

The things that toddlers talk about most relate to emotions (*hurt, sad, crying*), desires (*want, no, give me, don't*), and perceptions (*look, finish, all gone*).

Between two and three, most children learn to use the right words in the right order and the right form surprisingly quickly. While it seems they are genetically programmed to do this, it is crucial for them to have an adult model to provide them with the speech patterns of language and consistent feedback to let them know that they are getting their message across.

Ways to encourage your toddler's speech and language development

- *Talk to him:* Tell him who you are, where you are, what you're doing, all about the people and things you can see, hear, smell, and touch. It is important for your toddler to have someone to listen to. Never underestimate how much he can learn from listening.

- *Listen* to the noises he is making and to the kind of talking he is doing.

- *Copy* the noises he makes and take turns at making noises.

- *Talk in simple short sentences,* pitching the language at his level. Some adults are under the impression that toddlers should be spoken to as though they were adults, but simplifying language and repeating phrases now and then helps toddlers learn more easily.

- *Play with him:* Sing songs, play peek-a-boo, clap hands, play tickling games, make funny faces, look in the mirror.

- *Let him help you with some of the household chores (when you can):* For example, folding the laundry, putting away shopping, washing a few dishes or sloshing around with a mop (lovely thought). Doing jobs that have a beginning, a middle, and an end, help him to develop the ability to explain, talk about things that have happened in his world, and tell stories.

- **Look at books with him every day:** Don't worry if he can't sit still long enough to listen to the whole story; just talk about the pictures. Look, too, at the colors, shapes, numbers, and letters.

- **Tell him stories:** Invent your own—he especially likes stories in which he is the protagonist or which include events from his day-to-day life.

- **Sing to him:** Songs and nursery rhymes.

- **Take him to the library:** Spend some time there and find new books to read.

- **Provide recorded stories and music:** To listen and dance to.

Why do some children talk earlier than others?

There is a wide normal range for speech and language development, and when the child has no other developmental, social, or emotional problems, nobody knows for sure why some children talk earlier than others. It may be partly genetic.

There is a difference between the onset of speech and the onset of language. The first words may be spoken anytime between nine and eighteen months. There is often a dramatic increase in words around the second birthday. The onset of understanding words (sometimes called the inner language) occurs around nine months and should proceed in a consistent way from that age on. For example, a toddler of eighteen months may only have a few words; however, if when asked, he can feed his doll, point to pictures in books, scribble with a pencil, and so on, he is demonstrating that he has inner language development expected for his age.

There are times, however, when help is needed for delayed speech and/or development. This is complicated because learning to talk involves many different areas, such as efficient anatomy coordination of body systems as well as a supportive environment. Finding the best way to help a child who appears to have problems is not easy, and usually a speech-language pathologist and perhaps other specialists will be involved.

A speech-language pathologist with experience in child-development can assess, diagnose, and treat all aspects of communication skills. Speech-language pathologists provide services in schools, colleges and universities, hospitals, clinics and private practices. For a complete list of professional services in audiology (hearing tests) and speech-language pathology in your state write or call:

American Speech-Language-Hearing Association
10801 Rockville Pike
Rockville, Maryland   20852
800-638-8255 (Voice or TTY)
301-897-8682 (Voice or TTY)

Affordable testing and treatment are available for developmentally delayed babies and toddlers. Check with your state or county health or education programs for information on what's available.

When should parents start worrying? Here is a basic guide if you are wondering whether your toddler has a communication problem. Seek help if:

- You have a feeling something is not right—that any aspect of your toddler's development is delayed beyond what you think is normal. Even if it turns out that your fears are unfounded, it's still better to make sure.

- You are ever concerned about your toddler's ability to hear (see next section). Optimum hearing is crucial for speech, language, and overall development.
- Your toddler is not using single words by eighteen months.
- Is not using two-word sentences by two and a half.
- Is so hesitant when trying to speak that it makes you anxious.
- Is very nasal, jerky, or hoarse.
- Has periods of not being able to hear, stops talking, or imitates without speaking spontaneously.

Stuttering

Stuttering has many variations. It is now believed that early intervention is beneficial even when the stuttering is what is commonly referred to as "normal" stuttering.

The current recommendation is to seek advice for any of the following:

- Stuttering because the ideas burst forth quicker than the tongue can manage. This happens a lot and is what is called "normal" stuttering.

    In my opinion, recommending parents seek advice for normal stuttering is a little over the top. Many families do not have easy access to speech-language pathologists, and such advice is likely to cause an undue amount of stress.

    Many toddlers do this sort of stuttering between two and two and a half. It is usually a combination of too many ideas for the tongue to manage, habit, and experimentation. It can also be an attention-seeking device in association with the arrival of a new baby or other life changes (childcare, divorce, and so on).

Certainly if you have easy access to a speech pathologist with whom you can discuss this, please do. Otherwise, here are some suggestions:

- Monitor it for three to six months. Initially you might find that the stuttering increases before it starts to disappear.

- If you are concerned, you can keep a diary and put check-marks down every time the stuttering occurs each day. That way you can keep track of the number of times the stuttering is happening.

- If you think it is necessary, you can remind your toddler to make his words "smooth" rather than "bumpy."

Other forms of stuttering when it is advisable to seek help from a speech pathologist

• Repeating whole words and phrases

• Repeating sounds

• Repeating parts of words

• Prolonging sounds or syllables in words

• Blocking (unable to produce a sound/word while trying to)

Development of hearing

Hearing involves both listening and hearing. Hearing is an awareness of sound and is made possible by the complex hearing system we are born with.

Listening means making an effort to hear something with the intent of working out the significance of its meaning.

The importance of good hearing for optimum development

Hearing loss is associated with language and general developmental delay, so it is vital that detection is made as early as possible.

Disorders of hearing are identified according to the location of the problem.

Conductive hearing loss results from interference of the transmission of sound to the middle ear. It is the most common cause of hearing loss in babies over six months, toddlers, and children. It can be caused by anomalies in the structure of the middle ear, but it is usually the result of a buildup of fluid behind the eardrum. The degree of hearing loss from this condition may be mild to moderate and can appear, disappear, and reappear.

Ear infections, which cause the fluid buildup, are very common in the toddler years in association with repeated upper respiratory tract infections. Not all ear infections are associated with hearing loss and not all episodes of hearing loss are associated with developmental delay. But if the infections and hearing loss are persistent, it may be recommended that the toddler has small tubes placed in his eardrums to facilitate optimum hearing.

If you are ever concerned about your toddler's hearing following an ear infection, it is important to have his hearing tested by an audiologist and perhaps to have a consultation with a pediatric ear, nose, and throat specialist. Your family doctor can arrange this for you.

Fluid behind the eardrum can sometimes cause hearing loss without any other symptoms being present. It is often difficult to know whether a toddler is hearing everything he is supposed to because of his stage of development—particularly between the ages of one and two. If you are ever concerned about your toddler's hearing, see your nurse, or practitioner/pediatrician.

Sensorineural hearing loss (nerve deafness) involves damage to the inner ear structures and/or the auditory nerve. It is generally present at birth unless acquired later through injury, infection, or drugs.

Mixed conductive/sensorineural hearing loss is a combination of both of the above.

Every year approximately 24,000 babies are born with significant hearing impairment and the American Academy of Pediatrics wants every parent to know that early detection of hearing impairment is crucial for optimum language development. Every newborn should have their hearing tested. The cost for an accurate test is around $30–$40, covered by state funding or most insurance carriers. In most states, hearing testing is now mandatory.

Development of vision

Like hearing, vision is an essential part of child development. Through sight, toddlers learn about spatial relationships like distance and size. Vision is essential for learning about the environment, and during the baby and toddler years much is learned by staring and watching. Vision is intimately linked with motor activities—climbing, going up and down steps, drawing, picking up tiny objects, and so on. Unlike hearing, serious visual problems tend to become obvious in the first three months if they are not picked up soon after birth, so most serious visual problems are identified early. However, there is a range of common problems that may not become apparent until the second year or later.

General indications of possible problems

Bear in mind that scrunching up of the face and constant blinking can be habits that are unrelated to eyesight.

- Crossed eyes, turned eye ("lazy" eye)
- Constant holding of the head to one side
- Constant blinking
- Constant squinting, screwing up of face, unrelated to being in bright sunlight
- Difficulty seeing small objects

Toddlers are unable to say when they can't see properly because they are unaware that they have a problem. If you are ever in any doubt at all about your toddler's vision, especially if there is a history of eyesight problems in the family, speak to your nurse, practitioner, or pediatrician, who will refer you to the appropriate specialist.

Emotional development

Emotions are the moods, feelings, and values that drive and motivate us and are a major factor in how we react to people and events. Emotions confirm our existence. They are the threads running through our lives which give our experiences depth and color, texture, and intensity. During the toddler years, a lot of complex activity is happening at once, which for the toddler is fun, scary, annoying, puzzling, and often shrouded in uncertainty. Toddlers are deluged with new sensations and feelings they can't understand. Their behavior and emotions are often bewildering, to themselves as well as to the adults who love them. As they grow older and gain new information from their life experiences, they modify their emotions and the turbulence passes (until adolescence).

Emotional development integrates feelings and values with knowledge, reasoning skills, and experience. Emotional development is the process of learning how to manage our own emotions in a reasonable way (most of the time) and being able to identify and understand the emotions of others. It enhances our personal enjoyment of life while still producing the ethical behavior preferred in the society in which we live.

Different ages or stages in our development are associated with peaks in emotional responses. The toddler years, starting school, adolescence, childbirth, becoming a parent for the first time, the death of someone close, and menopause are some examples of emotional milestones. At the current time in Western society, other peak emotional times for children must include separation and divorce, and childcare for the under threes.

Optimum emotional development requires that humans have the time and opportunity to work out what's going on with their emotions and to learn from their emotional experiences. They need emotional space. They need support and understanding from the humans who care deeply for them and support from the society in which they live. This is particularly true at the peak times mentioned previously.

Development of sexuality and gender awareness

From the moment of birth, babies enjoy pleasurable feelings from being stroked and touched in a loving way. They experience sensual feeling through their body senses—smell, touch, hearing, taste, and sight. They learn that they are loved and valued by their parents from the way they are spoken to and touched.

It's common and quite normal for baby boys to have erections and baby girls to have vaginal lubrication. As soon as they are able to, babies like to touch themselves, play with and stimulate their genitals.

From six months onwards, babies rapidly develop a natural curiosity about their bodies, which flourishes between the ages of two and four as they discover how they are made and how other children and adults are made. The fun and lovely feelings associated with their genitals are a source of great pride and pleasure for toddlers. Examination, masturbation, and, as toddlers' communication skills expand, an increasing number of questions about what body part does what are to be expected.

Gender identification

From about eighteen months, toddlers start to define themselves as boys or girls in relation to the way their parents and other people respond to them. Apart from body differences, there are many ways that toddlers become aware of their gender. Clothes, toys, and the differences between their mothers and fathers—how they talk, look, the way they behave, and the things they do from day to day—all give them clues to their own gender.

Between two and three, they start to identify with the parent who is the same sex as they are. If there is only one parent or same-sex parents, they will identify with other adults who are the same sex as they are.

Between the ages of three and six, children explore bodies, speculate about how things work, and use role-play (doctors and nurses) in response to their natural interest and as a practical way of sorting out questions. They imitate both parents, but more so the one they spend the most time with (it's common for boys to breast-feed dolls).

One aspect of emotional sexual development that parents often find surprising is the erotic behavior of a three-year-old. Behaving like a passionate lover towards one or both parents is very common at this age. This is probably due to the toddler trying out his gender identification and also realizing that his parents are truly separate people with their own thoughts and feelings and maybe even other loves apart from them.

chapter **three**

Milestones and Their Many Variations

Over the next two years, you will see your toddler gradually inte-
grate his physical movements with his increasing cognitive and
social abilities, sometimes with breathtaking ease, sometimes with
a certain amount of grief.

It's useful and interesting to have some idea of the developmental milestones and the age at which your toddler is likely to
reach them, but remember that they are not set in concrete at a particular age but spread across an age range. I have listed cognitive,
emotional, social, and play milestones separately because these
areas of development give us some idea of the link between the
toddler's inner and outer worlds. However, as I said in chapter two,
specific areas of development cannot be isolated from development as a whole—everything is a fundamental part of everything
else.

So please don't use the information as boxes to be checked off.
Rather see it as a guide to understanding the range of behavior that
comes with your toddler's developmental journey. If you look

something up and it appears that your toddler has not yet reached that particular milestone, look back or forward three or six months.

Seeking help

Many avenues are available for help if you are ever concerned about any aspect of your toddler's development. They are listed in the Resources section at the back of this book.

Twelve to fifteen months

Twelve to fifteen months is a time when your toddler is beginning to discover that he is a separate being distinct from you and that he can explore and discover things for himself. At the same time, he is starting to match names to many of the important things around him. He can recognize himself in a mirror and knows how to get you to help him with things when he can't do them himself or when he wants something. Some toddlers are not mobile until eighteen months or occasionally even later, but they still develop well in all other areas, so do not panic. The word *toddler* relates to a state of mind as much as to the physical ability to move. Many nine-month-old babies start to show signs of wanting to make their own decisions and become self-reliant long before they are mobile.

TWELVE-MONTH MILESTONES

Gross motor (big movements)
- Sits well for long periods (some babies are still just sitting at twelve months).
- Pulls himself up onto furniture and may "cruise" around the furniture.

39

- Crawls on hands and knees (styles vary), bottom shuffles, or may walk alone with or without assistance.
- Can move from a lying position to a sitting position.

Fine motor (manipulation) and vision

- Uses his thumb and tip of finger like pincers to pick things up and has a fine eye for detail (dust on the carpet, crumbs, and string).
- Points with index finger (constantly).
- Drops and throws objects deliberately and watches where they fall. Investigates things by pushing, pulling, and banging.
- Stares at and watches movement of people, animals, cars, wind in the trees, airplanes, birds, and so on. Likes looking out of windows to see what's going on.
- Recognizes familiar people from a distance.

Hearing, speech, and language

- Understands simple instructions such as "Come to Mommy," "Bring me the cup," "Where's the dog?," "Say bye-bye," and "Wave to Daddy."
- Knows his own name and turns immediately when called.
- Looks for people he knows when they are named.
- Understands and uses "no."
- Talking noises contain vowels and consonants. Lots of loud conversational noise (called jargon).
- Imitates sounds.

Cognitive (thinking and understanding)

- Starting to imitate actions of other people (particularly parents).
- Uses gestures to get messages across because his language is limited. Many toddlers get frustrated and annoyed when they are not understood.

- He can probably stack one or two blocks. He can certainly deliberately (and joyfully) knock things down.
- Starting to enjoy books for limited period. Points to pictures.
- Looks in the right places for toys that roll out of sight.
- Interested in sounds.

Emotional

The range of the emotionally driven behavior toddlers are so well known for will be experienced in different ways at different ages with varying degrees of intensity. Overall the most emotionally tumultuous time seems to be from about fourteen months to two years. This is the most likely time for what is commonly referred to as the terrible twos. Many toddlers steadily become much calmer and more predictable from two onward.

- Starting to show a blossoming sense of humor.
- Stranger anxiety and/or separation anxiety (fear of strange faces and places and being separated from his mother) are common in varying degrees.
- Starting to show increasing assertiveness and frustration with diaper changing, being dressed, and being fed (wants to do it himself).

Social

- Shows affection. Some toddlers are more "cuddly" than others. The active explorers would sooner be off and out than engaging in prolonged cuddle sessions.
- Deliberately seeks help from you to do things (for example, puts your hand on a toy he can't yet "work").
- Starting to do things for approval (waving bye-bye, clapping hands).
- Pretends to talk on a toy telephone.

Play

- Likes pop-up toys and toys that make sounds.

- Loves collections of small objects to examine, suck, bang and drop.

- Loves emptying contents out of containers (often one at a time) and putting them back and then starting again.

- Likes playing peek-a-boo and pat-a-cake.

- Likes banging and waving things around.

- Most toddlers of any age love anything to do with water, but some are frightened of the tub.

- Starting simple make-believe games (pretending to talk on a toy telephone or drive a car).

FIFTEEN-MONTH MILESTONES

Gross motor

- May do any of the following:
  Crawl well or bottom shuffle
  Stand
  Cruise around furniture
  Walk with uneven steps, arms outstretched for balance, on automatic drive like a clockwork doll
  Walk well.

- Get from standing to sitting by collapsing with a bump. Can get back up to standing alone.

- Beginning to climb.

Fine motor and vision

- Has busy fingers—handling, touching, poking, squeezing, feeling everything in reach using both hands.

- Makes demands for things that he wants by pointing.
- Can drop a small object into a narrow opening.
- Loves throwing things around (especially food).
- Grasps a pencil with his whole hand and scribbles on whatever is available (this is a warning . . .).
- Shows preference for one hand when scribbling.

Hearing, speech, and language

- May have a few words which he uses with lots of jargon (strings of conversation-like noises) but shows that he understands lots more.
- Tries to sing.
- Understands and obeys simple commands such as "Open your mouth," "Give me the teddy," "Go to Daddy" and so on.
- Enjoys imitating noises of things like animals and cars.

Cognitive

- Turns pages of books and wants to know the names of pictures.
- Places large circle shape into the right space on a puzzle board.
- Gestures and understands "up" and "down."
- Is comforted by the sound of his mother's voice even when he can't see her.
- Enjoys putting one object into another and pulling it out again.
- Likes throwing or rolling a ball or a car along the floor, then finding and retrieving it.

Emotional

- Differences between your toddler and other toddlers are becoming obvious (active, shy, more intense, less intense, excitable, calm).
- Enjoys games with parents and shows sense of fun, pleasure, excitement.

- Looks to you for praise and delight when he achieves something tricky (climbs up stairs, pushes a wagon).
- Anger outbursts (temper tantrums).
- Sudden mood changes for what appears like no logical reason (that an adult can understand anyway).
- May be showing anxiety about events (going to the doctor, swimming classes, baby gym, and so on).
- Very dependent on being near beloved adults. He may be treating each parent differently, which sometimes causes anxiety for what appears to be the less favored parent.

Social

- Still more an explorer than a socializer but uses his beloved adults as a safe haven when he is feeling vulnerable.
- Will bring you items of clothing (for example, shoes) on request.
- Helps when being dressed (holds arm out, foot out, and so on).
- Likes watching other children.
- **Beginning** to understand and learn about simple rules (this doesn't necessarily mean he is going to do what you request—constant supervision is essential).
- Drinks from a cup when an adult holds it. Has the **ability** to chew well but may not (see page 279).
- Manages a covered spout cup on his own.

Play

- Can push a wagon with a handle along the floor.
- Loves getting in and out of things (big boxes, small spaces, cabinets).
- Adores opening and shutting doors.
- Is almost obsessive about twisting knobs and dials.
- Likes messing around with water.

Suggestions for toys at twelve–fifteen months

Pop-up toys (toys with a surprise element, now you see it, now you don't)

Wooden blocks, various shapes and colors, and toys to pull and/or push

Balls of various sizes

Wooden hammer and nail set

A variety of bath toys

Water toys (watering can, buckets, squirters)

Plastic containers with lids

A beanbag

Nesting bowls, cups

Board books, plastic books

Conventional books with large, lifelike pictures

Bells, buzzers

Toy telephone

Pots and pans

A sturdy ride-on vehicle

Simple puzzles

Stacking toys

Small cars, trucks, vans, and so on with wheels for zooming across the floor

An outdoor swing

A sandbox

When to get help at twelve–fifteen months

- If you are worried about any aspect of your toddler's development or behavior.

- If you have any concerns about your toddler's ability to see or hear.

- If your toddler is not showing curiosity and interest in his surroundings.

- If he is not babbling tunefully.

- If he can't stand upright beside furniture.

Developmental concerns at twelve to fifteen months

Bottom shuffling

Bottom-shuffling babies are normal late walkers. They move about in a sitting position, keeping their trunk, head, and shoulders upright, not forward, and extending their legs. They propel themselves around by bending and straightening their legs and pushing from behind with their hands.

Babies who move around like this are late to pull themselves up onto furniture as it's much harder to pull up onto furniture from a sitting position than from a face-down hands-and-knees crawling position (try it yourself). This means they are also later to walk (eighteen months or sometimes later), but this is no cause for concern.

Noncrawlers

A number of babies bypass crawling altogether and go straight to pulling themselves up, cruising and walking. There is no scientific evidence supporting the theory that babies have to crawl in order to be able to develop well in other areas. A proven relationship between crawling and reading skills has never been established. Such claims are based on circumstantial and anecdotal evidence, so take them with a big grain of salt, especially if they come via a commercial baby gym class.

And what about walking on tiptoe?

Walking on the toes is a normal variation when toddlers first start to walk. When they are otherwise developing normally, it appears that they probably do this because they prefer it. The use of baby walkers encourages toe walking because babies push back with the tops of their feet to propel themselves along—one of the many reasons the use of walkers is not recommended.

If your toddler is still toe-walking after he has been walking for a couple of months, consult a pediatric physiotherapist for some advice.

A note on pointing

Pointing is a fascinating developmental milestone. It is a way of communicating and connecting with others. Pointing is how toddlers recognize (often with great glee) that they share visual and emotional experiences with other humans. They become aware that they will see something by looking at what other people point to and that other people will see something they point to.

It takes longer, though, for young children to understand that what they can see is not necessarily what others can see. I can still remember assembling all my presents in front of the radio when the presenter of a popular children's program asked her young listeners what they got for Christmas, in the firm belief that she could see them.

Not all toddlers go through the endless pointing stage. If your toddler is otherwise developing normally, don't worry if he shows no inclination to point.

Handedness (right- or left-handed?)

The use of the preferred hand is evident between one and two years; however, babies and toddlers do remain largely ambidextrous until sometime between two and three when a marked preference will be revealed. Even so, handedness is not firmly established until school age.

Some children remain ambidextrous, using one hand for throwing and one hand for writing, and as we all know, some children are left-handed. The favored hand is genetically determined, and if both parents are left-handed, there's a fifty percent chance that their children will also be left-handed.

Trying to change left-handed children into right-handed children is an outdated practice that caused a lot of grief and harm and is a good example of a childhood development theory being proven wrong over the passage of time.

Feet that turn in or out, bow legs, knock-knees, and flat feet

Parents are often concerned about one or more of the above once their toddler starts to walk. However, they are usually normal variations and right themselves over time. The tendency nowadays is for minimal interference, but if you are at all worried, the best person to consult is a pediatric physiotherapist. If you don't have access to one, see your nurse, or practitioner/pediatrician.

Here's some general information:

FEET THAT TURN IN

Feet that turn in may be caused by a problem with the foot, the lower leg, or the hip, or sometimes a combination of all three. If it is very noticeable and particularly if your toddler is constantly tripping and falling over, seek help. Treatment, *if* it is needed, varies from stretching to splinting to plastering (if severe) for a period if the problem is in the foot, to changing the toddler's sitting and sleeping position if the problem is located in the hip. In-toeing caused by a slight twist of the lower leg rights itself once the toddler spends more time walking than crawling.

FEET THAT TURN OUT

Out-toeing is not as common as in-toeing and becomes noticeable once the toddler starts pulling himself up and standing. Both feet, or sometimes only one foot, point out like a ballet dancer. Turned-out feet are usually due to the position the baby was in when he was in the uterus. It is also something that toddlers do to help keep their balance as they totter around when they first start to walk. Out-toeing rights itself in time and usually requires no treatment.

Note: Swapping shoes (that is, left shoe on right foot, right shoe on left foot) is not recommended as a way to treat either in-toeing or out-toeing. And if anyone suggests that your toddler needs prohibitively expensive "special" shoes to treat in-toeing or out-toeing, seek a second opinion.

BOWLEGS

Bowleggedness is very common from the time walking starts until the toddler is about two and a half. It is much more extreme in some toddlers than others. Treatment is not needed unless the bowleggedness is the result of some other condition (unusual). Bowleggedness rights itself by about three years, sometimes to be replaced by knock-knees.

KNOCK-KNEES

Knock-knees are common in toddlers two years and older and are often associated with flat feet. There is no treatment for knock-knees—most right themselves by age seven.

FLAT FEET

Flat feet are very common in toddlers because the long arch of the foot is not fully developed and the hollow in the arch is filled with a large fat pad. As the toddler grows, the fat pad gradually disappears, and by four to five years of age, most children have developed a longitudinal arch.

Physiotherapy and exercises don't help flat feet, nor is it advised to get special arch supports for the shoes of flat-footed toddlers.

Shoes

Toddlers need shoes for warmth and protection, not for development or support. They learn to run and walk more efficiently in bare feet, so leave your toddler barefoot whenever it's warm enough and he is not in danger of hurting his feet.

Wait until he has been walking for seven or eight weeks before you buy him shoes. Slipping and sliding can be a hazard while he is mastering walking—bootees with a nonslip sole are good. *Buy the shoes you can afford. Bear in mind that they will not fit him for long.*

- The fit should be the same size and shape as the foot, with sufficient room for the toes.
- Shoes should be flexible and not too heavy. Ankle support is not required. The only advantage of expensive leather ankle boots is that they are more difficult for toddlers to keep removing.
- Make sure socks are large enough and do not restrict the feet.
- Sneakers are fine, as are plastic, canvas, or leather sandals and thongs.
- Good, quality hand-me-down shoes are fine as long as they fit well. Busy feet soon mold the shoes into their new owner's shape.

Speech and language worries

You might find that after learning one word your toddler might learn a few more quite quickly, then seem to plateau out. This is likely to be because he is too busy mastering his walking and climbing abilities to concentrate on learning to talk.

Fifteen to eighteen months

Life with your toddler is now probably fast-paced, and for many families it is a wild combination of hilarity, endless battles, and a sense of exhausted wonderment at their toddlers' amazing abilities. Many parents find it is a time when there is a considerable amount of conflict. They may often feel stressed and burdened dealing with their toddler's increasing determination as he works out a balance between how much power he has and how much he loves and needs his mother and father.

EIGHTEEN-MONTH MILESTONES

Gross motor

- Most toddlers can now walk well; however, if your toddler has only just started to walk, he might be still tottering around like a clockwork doll. If your toddler is a bottom shuffler, chances are he may be still bottom shuffling. If he is otherwise developing normally, be patient and ignore comments from others. Naturally, if you are concerned, consult with your family doctor, nurse practitioner, pediatrician or pediatric physiotherapist.
- Can take a few steps backward.
- Runs but has to be careful, falls are still common, and he is likely to bump into things in haste (it's very common to see a few colorful bruises on toddlers' foreheads around this time).
- Can now carry one or two things around with him while he is walking (favorite doll or toy).
- He can kneel, and notice how he squats to pick things up rather than stooping—that's how we should all do it.
- Walks up and down stairs with help.
- Is obviously going to go into the furniture removal business—pushes and pulls things around all over the house.

Fine motor and vision

- Picks up tiny objects easily and delicately.

- Can sometimes put three blocks one on top of the other but is still more interested in knocking them down.
- Points to interesting faraway things when outside.
- Uses crayon or pencils—sometimes in preferred hand, sometimes in the other hand, and sometimes with both hands to do energetic scribbles and dots. He is now starting to hold the crayon down near its point with his thumb and four fingers rather than grasping it like a weapon to stab someone with.
- Feeds self with spoon and gets most of it in when he's interested in eating rather than playing.
- Can handle a cup of fluid by himself, but here's a warning—the spilled-drink syndrome of early childhood lasts until adolescence (as does the attention-seeking behavior the minute you start talking on the phone).
- Likes looking at books and recognizes and points to objects in the pictures.

Hearing, speech, and language

- Listens when you speak to him (when he's not distracted or upset or choosing to ignore you).
- Uses six or seven clear words (or more). Understands much more.
- Talks loud but tuneful nonsense to himself that sounds like conversation while he's playing and often when he wakes in the morning.
- Enjoys bopping around to familiar music and tries to sing. Likes nursery rhymes and rhythmic sounds in books.
- Echoes some words after you have spoken to him.

Cognitive

- Knows his own nose and his teddy's nose and your nose.
- Hands you familiar objects when you ask for them.
- Says no a lot even when he means yes.
- Remembers where objects belong.

- Can put puzzle pieces in round holes. Increasingly enthralled with his hands and what they can do.
- Very interested in body products and functions (poo, urine, what's inside the nose, farting, spit).

Emotional

- Possessive with toys and objects he likes.
- Becoming choosy about clothes, food, and people.
- Constantly demanding attention; whining is common.
- Temper tantrums for many (not all toddlers have temper tantrums).
- Wants to be near his favourite adult(s) for large parts of the day. Eighteen months is the height of separation anxiety for many toddlers.
- May be developing some fears.

Social

- Plays alone but enjoys the company of other children (for limited, supervised periods).
- Shows affection spontaneously (kisses and hugs and cuddles—gorgeous).
- Shows when he's annoyed or irritated by something you're doing.
- Has a sense of humor—enjoys showing off, being the clown, and making you laugh.
- Very good at taking off shoes and socks.

Play

- Still mastering physical movements and very interested in climbing up on things and exploring.
- Imitates everyday activities; for example, sweeping the floor, feeding his doll, hammering, making cakes (with playdough or mud and water).
- Likes walking and pulling toys along behind.

- No longer sucking and chewing everything in sight, although care has to be taken when he is playing with very small objects as the mouth is still used to test things (playdough and crayons are particular favorites).

- Enjoys simple puzzles.

Suggestions for toys at eighteen months

Dump truck, wheelbarrow

Doll and stroller

Music box, mechanical or electronic book

A growing library of suitable books

Musical toys/instruments

Large Lego blocks (or similar construction blocks)

Suitable music on tape/CD

A safe flashlight

A stairs and slide set for outdoors

Take-apart toys (very large beads, ball inside ball, objects that fit in round holes)

Shape-sorting box and pieces

Washable nontoxic crayons and markers and plenty of paper

Table and chairs set

Small broom, toy lawnmower, plastic tools

When to get help at eighteen months

- If you are worried about any aspect of your toddler's development or behavior.

- If you have any suspicion your toddler might not be able to see or hear properly.

- If there is no speech or minimal speech, particularly if he doesn't appear to understand what you are saying.

- If he is always irritable and has no interest in what is going on around him.

- If he is still mouthing everything.

- If he never plays constructively—throws things aimlessly, bashes things together in an unthinking manner.

- If there is any sign of a limp.

Eighteen to twenty-four months

This six months might be called interesting by some parents, difficult and stressful by others, maybe a challenge or even delightful and rewarding. I'm trying not to be too negative here as I am aware that every toddler is different and that every parent's experience of each stage of their child's development is also different. The reality is that most parents will probably find it's a combination of all four. From the toddler's point of view, it must seem like the world is full of wonder and endless possibilities as he learns to run, climb, make things happen, and talk. But this six months is also a peak time for tension and clinginess as his drive to understand the world and the people in it often conflicts with his need to live happily and close to his parents.

His language ability is limited and he still does not have the capacity to see anyone else's point of view or put himself in the place of another person. On the other hand, it is a joy to witness his natural enthusiasm for learning and his boundless energy. And to experience his unconditional, passionate love for you which never wavers even when he's furious with you. Toddlers never want a slimmer mom or a dad with bigger muscles—they really do love you just the way you are.

TWENTY-FOUR-MONTH MILESTONES

Gross motor

- Runs and walks with greater skill—much fewer catastrophes from falling over and bumping into things. Walking is now something he does to get somewhere or to do something rather than a novelty in itself.
- Climbs onto furniture to get to things he wants, to open doors, or to look out of windows.

Many of his natural positions are yoga postures which he
gets into with grace and ease

- Walks up and down stairs with two feet to a step, holding the wall or railing for balance.
- Can jump off a step.
- Squats to play or pick things up (if you are a yoga fan, notice how many of your toddler's natural movements are yoga positions which he gets into with a grace and ease that is beyond most adults).
- Can throw a small ball overhand and kick a large ball.
- Starting to show an understanding of his size in relation to the size and shape of things around him (whether things are bigger or smaller than he is and whether he can fit into the cabinet or under the stairs or squash in between Mommy and Daddy).
- Can sit on a wheeled toy, steer, and propel himself around but cannot use pedals yet (wheely toys without pedals are best at this age).

Fine motor and vision

- Easily removes wrapping from a small object.
- Can pour water from one cup to another.
- Can draw a vertical line if you show him how, and does vigorous circular scribble as well as scribble and dots. Holds the pencil with thumb and three fingers well down the shaft.
- Recognizes people he knows well in photographs but perhaps not himself.
- Builds a tower of six or seven blocks.
- Turns pages of books one at a time and notices the fine details in the pictures.
- Can screw and unscrew lids that are not too tight (safety warning) or wind a key on a toy.

Hearing, speech, and language

- Many toddlers have anything from fifty to a couple of hundred words and obviously understand many more. Many are using simple sentences of two or more words.

- Matches sounds to animals and makes noises ("moo," "meow," "oink-oink" and so on).
- Refers to himself by his name.
- Answers simple questions—"Where is the book?," "Where is Daddy?"
- Has long conversations with himself as he plays, some of which is comprehensible and much of which isn't (lots of it is hilarious).
- Carries out simple instructions—"Bring me the paper," "Put the toys in the tub" and so on.
- Understands "big," "little," "on." For example, "Put the book on the table."

Cognitive

- Uses the word "mine."
- Can be told what is happening next. Has some understanding of "now," "soon," and "later."
- Very interested in knowing how to use things.
- Asks for help.
- Notices small details and inconsistencies.
- Can plan and carry out activities that require a few different steps (for example, watering the plants, bringing a chair to the table and equipment needed for drawing).
- Knows where objects are and will often know where he left them.
- Little understanding of common dangers (will drink strange liquids, fall into pools, run on the road, get fingers caught in the car door, pull hot things on top of himself, and so on).

Emotional

- Often radiates charm and affection.
- Overall more confident and secure than at eighteen months.
- Temper tantrums and whining when tired and frustrated.

- Often wants to do more than he is capable of.
- Finds it difficult to choose between two alternatives—wants it all or wants nothing.
- Gets upset with sudden change of plans, likes routine and ritual ("Uh-oh, we forgot to tell you we are going out tonight" is likely to cause a drama).
- Fears and phobias are common.

Social

- Feeds himself with a spoon, drinks from a cup, and has the ability to chew well.
- He can put his own hat on and remove unfastened clothes.
- Likes to "help."
- Uneasy with people he doesn't know.
- Not yet ready to share—defends his possessions with great determination.
- Doesn't really like sharing his parents' attention with anyone else either.
- When he wants something, he wants it now—has little understanding of any need to postpone his immediate requirements or to compromise about what he wants.

Play

- Likes playing near other children but not so keen on playing with them unless they are a lot older.
- Two-year-olds have developed a lot socially and emotionally in the last six months, but they still don't have the thinking skills and emotional restraint for extended periods of play with other toddlers, especially without close adult supervision and participation.
- Likes listening to music, dancing.
- Plays more involved make-believe games which imitate the things that go on in his world and the family around him. These games involve things like

playing doctor, feeding his dolls and stuffed animals, baking a cake, and so on. Is very keen for parent participation in his games.

- Loves playing with water—especially turning taps on and off.

Suggestions for toys at twenty-four months
Stick horse
Dress-up clothes (hats, gloves, bags, shoes, very large beads, glasses, and so on)
Play kitchen
Doctor/nurse set
Bubble blowing
More books, more puzzles, more music
Playdough, modelling clay
Trucks, scoops, diggers

When to get help at twenty-four months

- If you are worried about any aspect of your toddler's development or behavior.
- If you have any suspicion your toddler can't see or hear properly.
- If there is no speech or minimal speech, particularly if he doesn't appear to understand what you are saying.
- If he is always irritable and has no interest in what is going on around him.
- If he is still mouthing everything.
- If he never plays constructively—throws things aimlessly, bashes things together in an unthinking manner.
- If there is any sign of a limp.

Twenty-four to thirty months

In this six months your toddler will become truly familiar and involved with the objects and people in his world. By the time he is two and a half, he will be showing a certain amount of reason-ableness about many things but is still likely to lose control easily. Temper tantrums remain a feature of many toddlers at this age but are often less frequent and less intense. Increased competence in all areas of development makes most two-and-a-half-year olds eas-ier to live with and a lot less work. Your toddler has mastered running, jumping, feeding himself, and many manipulative skills. He can remember things from yesterday, can look forward to things happening soon (as long as they are not too far off), and is starting to acknowledge how others feel. Fears are surfacing, imagi-nation is blossoming, rituals are important, and he is starting to be able to put ideas into words. He is starting to give as well as take. He is on the road to childhood.

THIRTY-MONTH MILESTONES

Gross motor

- All walking, running, and climbing skills improving rapidly.
- Can stand on tiptoe (show him if he doesn't know what you mean).
- Can throw and kick a ball (awkwardly and not far).
- Pushes and pulls large toys/objects around but may bash into things.
- Walks up and down stairs confidently, two feet to a step (may still like to hold wall or railing for balance).

Fine motor and vision

- Sees tiny objects (a thread, a grain of rice, a cookie crumb) and picks them up easily.
- Cuts with scissors.
- Draws a straight line and a circle if shown how.
- Recognizes himself in a photo.

Hearing, speech, and language

- Knows his full name.

- Talks aloud to himself while he plays about things that are going on in the present. Repeats things a lot.

- Gives an intelligent running commentary about the activities of the people in his game (most entertaining).

- Stuttering sometimes when his words can't match the speed of his thoughts.

- Asks for help.

Cognitive

- Identifies objects in pictures when asked to.

- Understands the concept of two.

- Can copy a circle and cross horizontal and vertical lines.

- Points to fingers, heels and toes, stomach, knees, and chin.

- Knows where teeth and fingernails are.

- Likes to talk about opposites (hot/cold), parts of the body, and time words (yesterday, tomorrow).

- Enjoys looking at books on his own.

- Enjoys puzzles with large, simple pieces suitable for his age.

- Developing an interest in why and how.

- Recites a few nursery rhymes.

Emotional

- Tantrums still common.

- Separation anxiety mostly past (depending on individual toddlers and circumstances—when we are sick, we all want our mothers).

- Still needs you to define his emotions, to help put into words how he is feeling.

- Sudden changes in mood and behavior still normal. Cuddly one minute, rejecting you the next. Full of confidence in the morning, insecure in the afternoon. In charge at breakfast, a baby at lunch.
- Gets frustrated when he can't do something.

Social

- Is now much more interested in the wider world and people other than just those he lives with.
- Is starting to understand the concept of sharing, but it remains difficult for some years to come (some people have a problem with it all their lives).
- Enjoys being with other children, but most toddlers of this age still have a limited capacity for extended play and need close adult supervision and participation. One-on-one play is usually more manageable for them.
- Eats well with a spoon; may also use a fork.

Play

- Likes dressing up and role-play but still needs a friendly adult nearby to refer to.
- Loves collecting things, storing them, and carrying them around in small handbags, backpacks, containers, and pockets.
- Many toddlers are insistent on being joined in their play by their best adult friend.
- Still enjoys climbing, swings, and water play.
- Likes banging toys such as drums (can you stand it?); hammer and pegs and a beanbag to bash help relieve frustrated feelings (good for parents as well).

Suggestions for toys at thirty months

Dress-up clothes and props

Simple craft equipment—safe scissors, glue, colored paper, stickers, drawing equipment, finger painting

Any scenario toys with little people and objects—garage, hospital, home

Puzzles, books, music

Skipping rope

Ride-on vehicle with pedals

When to get help at thirty months

- If you are worried by any aspect of his development or behavior.

- If you have any suspicion your toddler can't see or hear properly.

- If he cannot communicate by speaking.

- If he cannot communicate by body language.

- If he plays aimlessly and repetitively, showing no imagination or thought.

- If his general behavior is more like that of an eighteen-month-old.

- If there is any sign of a limp.

Thirty to thirty-six months

One of the most conspicuous and dramatic developmental leaps in early childhood is the transformation of the toddler into a child at around age three. I am a little hesitant to use the frog into the prince analogy, but for many parents this is exactly how it seems. However, I do think it's important to acknowledge that each developmental stage is special and unique for every parent despite any associated rough patches. Some people love the baby and toddler eras; others feel more comfortable when they have a small person they can communicate with. I have always found the tendency everyone has to keep warning parents about the next "worst" stage depressing in the extreme, since each stage is a building block to the next, and how parents find each one is very subjective. Many three-year-olds are delightful, relatively easy people, but some will continue to be a challenge. I believe that most adolescents are interesting, fun, and quite wonderful people, but this is another stage of human development that constantly gets bad press. By the time your child has grown up, every part of his life will have its own special memories and each stage will have contributed in a major way to your own development, perhaps the difficult stages most of all.

A three-year-old has considerable control over his own body (this doesn't necessarily mean he is going to poo in the toilet, as knowing that he has control over his own body means he knows that such an event is entirely up to him). He is full of humor and delightful originality. He is self-confident, charming, and a wonderful conversationalist. It seems that the skills and information he has been accumulating over the last two years have all come together at once. He takes pride in achieving things and being praised for his accomplishments. He is happy to be away from his parents in the company of people he knows for extended periods.

Aha, but he is still a child, if not a toddler. He still thinks differently from adults, may have the occasional tantrum, might snatch and grab or push and bite other kids. Or call you in the middle of the night. And whine, get frightened and anxious, be uncooperative, tired, and cranky.

But generally life *is* easier with a three-year-old.

THIRTY-SIX-MONTH MILESTONES

Gross motor

- Walks upstairs the way we do—one foot on each step.
- Jumps off one step—both feet together.
- Now gives a ball a good kick and sends it far.
- Runs fast, missing obstacles. Can run and pull large toys with ease; no longer bumping into things.

- Climbs playground equipment with ease.
- Can ride a bike using pedals, steering it well.
- Can walk on tiptoe.

Fine motor and vision

- Builds a tall tower with blocks.
- Good control with a pencil, holding it near the point with thumb and two fingers.
- May know the names of some colors.
- Threads large wooden beads onto a shoelace.
- Cuts with scissors.

Hearing, speech, and language

- Speech is much clearer, and unfamiliar listeners are able to understand what he is saying most of the time.
- Sentences are becoming longer, and he makes good attempts to tell about past events and stories without too much prompting.
- Grammatical errors are common.
- Asks simple questions—What?, Where?, Why?.
- Sings simple songs.
- Still having long conversations with himself about what is going on in the present in both his real and make-believe life.

Cognitive

- Attempts to retell stories from favorite books.
- Tells own sex, full name, and age.
- Knows "bigger" and "smaller."
- Counts by rote, up to ten or more, but only understands quantity in terms of two or three.

- Understands simple cause-and-effect sequences, although still believes that simultaneous events have a cause-effect relationship.
- Has a fully developed short-term memory and understands "last week," "yesterday," "tomorrow," "after three sleeps."
- Beginning to accurately observe objects and how they work, people and how they behave, and quickly picks up on inconsistencies and irregularities (fascinating for parents but often embarrassing too).
- Starting to anticipate consequences in simple ways; for example, if one more block is added to the tower, it will fall over; if more water is put into the cup, it will overflow.
- Now has the ability to focus on more than one thing at once.

Emotional

- The extreme negativity of the toddler years is fading; he is now more eager to please.
- Is able to express emotions in simple ways: "I love you," "I feel sad," "I don't love you anymore" (or similar expressions when he's annoyed with you), and "I like/don't like Isabel [a friend]."
- Still expresses emotions physically and theatrically, squealing, stamping, yelling, sobbing loudly.
- Stubbornness is common.
- Shows feelings of pride in accomplishments but gets frustrated when he can't "do things right."
- May be starting to see someone else's perspective in a limited way depending on the situation and how it affects him emotionally.

Social

- Companionable and confiding with close adults. Complies with simple requests.
- Flushes toilet purposefully, not just for fun or experimental purposes. Washes hands purposefully.

- Removes and replaces pants/underwear, puts on shoes. Probably needs help to fasten shoes (certainly can't tie laces yet).

- Eats with a fork and spoon.

- Increasing interest in being with other children—socializing (visiting, staying overnight) and playing more complicated games (being a leader and a follower).

- Looks forward to and enjoys events much more now (birthday parties, religious festivals and holidays).

Play

- Vivid make-believe play, inventing characters and objects. Is starting to be able to organize materials and ideas with another child to play games that combine dressing up, building something, and being someone (a firefighter, a storekeeper, a teacher).

- More idea of sharing.

- Likes building, filling and dumping, water play and anything messy, little containers of small things, riding a bike, swinging, climbing, jumping.

- Likes excursions, picnics, swimming, and the great outdoors in general.

- Can now imaginatively use resources to make boats, airplanes, and spaceships.

Suggestions for toys at thirty-six months

Dress-up clothes and props
Simple craft equipment—safe scissors, glue, colored paper, stickers, drawing equipment, finger painting
Any scenario toys with little people and objects—garage, hospital, home
Puzzles, books, music
Skipping rope
Ride-on vehicle with pedals

When to get help at thirty-six months

- If you are worried by any aspect of his development or behavior.
- If you have any suspicion your toddler can't see or hear properly.
- If he cannot communicate by speaking.
- If he cannot communicate through body language.
- If he plays aimlessly and repetitively, showing no imagination or thought.
- If his general behavior is more like that of an eighteen-month-old.
- If there is any sign of a limp.

part two

THE

QUESTION OF

BEHAVIOR

chapter four

What's Behind Toddler Behavior?

Toddler behavior is fascinating, is often difficult to understand, and can be exhausting to live with. A toddler's rapidly developing skills will have his parents applauding him one minute and tearing their hair out the next. Until his language skills are proficient, his behavior is his main form of communication, and it is often confusing working out what he wants or what he is so upset about.

Common ways parents describe their toddler's behavior

- Attention seeking (has temper tantrums, screeches, uses naughty words, whines)
- Selfish (does not understand sharing, fond of the word *my*, has great difficulty in taking turns)
- Aggressive (bites, pulls hair, pinches, smacks)

- Antisocial (shy, does not enjoy playgroup, fights with other toddlers, refuses to kiss Grandma)
- Impatient and demanding (wants a drink *now*, interrupts phone conversations, asks questions constantly)
- Self-centered, no understanding of anyone else's feelings (is ungrateful for lovingly prepared nutritious meals, shows preference for one parent, squeezes baby's arm)
- Irritating, sometimes repulsive habits (picks nose, bangs head, bites nails, sucks thumb, pacifier never out of mouth)
- Fascinated with his or her genitals and those belonging to others (masturbates, takes great interest in body parts of friends, animals, and parents)
- Fascinated with body products (smears poo, examines and plays with mucus and spit)
- Obsessive (will only wear the same pants every day, wears boots to bed, wants the same story every night and a Band-Aid every day)
- No common sense (runs barefoot in the snow, wants to wear a thick sweater in the tropics, gives himself a haircut, eats dog poo)
- No understanding of common dangers (climbs onto cabinets, jumps into a swimming pool, fascinated with fire, drinks detergent)
- Negativity rules (*no* and *don't* are the favorite words)
- Uncooperative (doesn't want to get in the bath, doesn't want to get out, hates being rushed, dawdles, refuses food, won't sit in the stroller or on the potty chair).
- Difficulty in adapting to changes (the arrival of a new baby, starting childcare, a change of breakfast cereal or brand of yogurt)
- Difficulties in separating from close adults—mother in particular

(clings around the house, sleeping is a hassle, miserable at being left with a babysitter, unhappy at childcare)

- Emotionally as changeable as the weather (gives you a cuddle, squeals with excitement, and collapses in a distraught heap all in the space of five short minutes)
- Illogical fears and anxieties (of the tub, of the hairdresser, of dogs, of things in the night, of a model in a shop window, of the dark)
- Limited attention span (needs to flit from one activity to the next after a short space of time—excursions and treats can be disappointing when boredom sets in after half an hour at the zoo)
- Unreliable memory (does not remember that fingers can get caught in the door, that hot water comes out of the kettle, or that he's going to get into trouble when Daddy gets home)
- No respect for other people's possessions or property (destroys books, hammers furniture, turns out cabinets and drawers, draws on walls)

What a formidable list! In adult terms this sort of behavior would be an indication of serious psychological problems. But we all understand, up to a point, that in toddler terms it's more or less normal; however, what is less clear is why toddlers behave in the way that they do.

Another way of describing their behavior

Toddlers function in the present, find it difficult to wait for things, and view the world only through their experience of it. They have an inflated sense of their ability to make things happen and a limited understanding of how other people might feel or think.

Their feelings *are* as changeable as the weather. Sometimes they can tell you how they are feeling, but mostly they express their feelings through their behavior.

Day-to-day life for toddlers is generally a constant round of exploration. They test things and people repeatedly to find out how they work, how they are made, and how they can affect them.

Toddlers are interested in finding out about

- **Themselves:** What they are capable of, how they can get what they want, how they can get other people to do what they want and how they can affect things around them.

- **Other people:** How they work. Where they are going. What they are doing. How they are feeling—especially as it relates to them. When they are returning.

- **The physical world:** How objects look, feel, and work. What objects they are allowed to touch, feel, and make work, and what things their parents are allowed to touch, feel, and make work. What makes objects do the things they do? What happens when a packet of flour gets tipped onto the floor?

- **Labeling:** What are things called? What colors are they? How many of them are there? What goes with what?

- **Predictability and control:** What things stay the same? What things change? How do their parents respond to the things that they do? What can they control? What do Mommy and Daddy control? Are there some things Mommy and Daddy can't make them do?

Getting a grip on predictability and control is an important part of a toddler's surge toward independence and is the reason for many of his exasperating behaviors. Like us, a toddler likes to feel in control. In order to feel in control, he needs to master some basic independent living skills and know how others will respond to him in a variety of situations. Unlike us, he doesn't yet have our understanding of the world or know what steps to take to gain control over many aspects of his life. And of course he is still mastering communication and body skills, which adds to the frustration.

Most toddler behavior originates from the following

Temperament

Temperament describes the individual differences we are all born with. Personality traits in toddlers and children have been described by researchers and put into complicated categories of temperamental types. All parents are aware of their toddler's particular personality or temperamen— full-on, active, shy, placid, easy, difficult and so on.

The most useful outcome from the research into temperament is the acceptance nowadays that babes or toddlers contribute in a major way to the interaction that goes on between them and their parents. A difficult toddler has the capacity to deplete his parents' confidence and energy no matter how developmentally aware they are or how realistic their approach. It can be a relief for a mother to know that her toddler's antics are not necessarily her fault.

Less useful aspects of emphasis on temperament include labeling a toddler difficult or shy for life.

How much of a toddler's behavior is dictated by the temperament he brings with him from birth and how much is learned from his environment remains the subject of much debate, but it seems likely to be a combination of the two.

Temperament explains the wide variations in development. For example, why one toddler is clingy and another one isn't (often in the same family where the environment is the same), why some toddlers eat anything and others are picky, why some toddlers settle quickly into childcare and others don't.

It's easy, especially during the toddler years, to get bogged down and start to believe that you might be a better parent if some of the negative aspects of your toddler's personality would disappear. However, it's interesting to note how many seemingly negative personality traits in the toddler years turn into positive attributes in the adult (for example, stubbornness into determination, sensitiveness into artistic talent, high activity levels into sporting prowess, and so on.)

Important points about temperament

- Parents need to recognize and understand their own toddler's temperament and work out the best plan for their family without being influenced by what other families down the road are doing with their toddlers. This is often easier said than done and takes time and confidence.

  An example: Having an extremely active toddler may make it impossible for you to visit friends indoors for any length of time. You may wish it were otherwise and even envy your friend because she can take her toddler anywhere. Accepting this and avoiding situations doomed to embarrassing disruption is a way of recognizing your toddler's temperament.

- Most toddlers have difficult aspects to their personalities as they emerge from babyhood into childhood, but some are more difficult (or, to put it more politely, challenging) than others. It is not uncommon for parents to wish their toddler was different— that is, quieter, less shy, more active, less active, and so on. Needless to say, a toddler who constantly hears negative things about himself will start to view himself negatively, which is not a great start to his life. Try to understand, respect, and be positive about tricky aspects of your toddler's personality even if you wonder where on earth they came from. Chances are that your toddler wonders about some of the strange things you do and say too.

- Most parents have times when they can't work out whether it's them, their toddler's temperament, or his current stage of development that's causing them grief.

  An example: You may wonder if your toddler is waking at night because of his temperament, because he's learned to stand at the side of the crib, or because you allow him into your bed at night. It's probably a little of all three. The most important thing in situations like this is to work out what you are going to do about it. Aspects of your own temperament and your toddler's may dictate what you are prepared to do. Sometimes these may conflict and compromises have to be made.

- Temperament is something that for the most part can't be changed, but it can be modified, magnified, or changed in intensity over time. Many active, noisy, and tantrum-throwing toddlers become relatively calm school-age children.

  Other things related to temperament are unchangeable. Trying to turn an active sports lover with no interest in academia into a brain surgeon is probably going to lead to disaster. While it is important to be mindful of temperament and your toddler's stage of development, an overall approach that provides heaps of love combined with appropriate limit setting and as much consistency as you can manage is the basis for caring for all toddlers.

Types of temperament

While variations on temperaments and personalities are endless, I find the *shy* toddler and the *superactive* toddler to be among the most common temperament types to cause parents concern.

SHYNESS

The dictionary definition of shy lists the following negatives, "uncomfortable with others, diffident, reserved, timid, cautious, unwilling to trust, fearful of new experiences, and wary of strangers." Hmmm, no wonder we often overreact to signs of shyness in our toddlers.

Shyness as part of development

Most toddlers are shy in certain situations. Being timid in public but assertive at home, slow to warm up, reluctant to join in, clingy, and cautious when confronted with unfamiliar circumstances are all normal ways for toddlers to behave and do not indicate a lifetime of shyness ahead. Most shyness in the early years is developmental and gradually diminishes as the child grows; however, shyness can come and go—how many of us have memories of the paralyzing shyness of the teenage years?

Shyness as an inborn trait

For some children the shyness is not developmental but an inborn trait, and they go on to become shy adults. This can cause problems, but many adults learn ways to deal with or overcome their shyness.

Living with a shy toddler

When considering shy behavior in your toddler, it is best not to get out the crystal ball but to accept him the way he is now and to help him learn to deal with situations he finds difficult. Above all, avoid burdening him with the shy label, as such a tag tends to be self-fulfilling.

The behaviors that are associated with shyness in toddlers are things like:

- Being wary or nervous of strangers or unfamiliar situations.
- Being reluctant (often refusing) to try new things or to join in.
- Preferring one-on-one with a familiar friend than being with a group.
- Being quiet and slow to warm up in unfamiliar circumstances (but when comfortable with people and surroundings may be quite capable of being noisy and adventurous).

There are times when this sort of behavior is disappointing ("We thought he would love the clown"), irritating, even embarrassing for parents, but accepting it, allowing for it, and taking time to prepare the toddler for new experiences is the only sane approach.

The trick is to introduce your toddler to the great unknown in gradual non-stressful ways while avoiding overprotection. Be content with small gains over relatively long periods.

Here is a framework to work within

- Prepare your toddler for new experiences. Tell him where you are going, who will be there, and what will happen.
- Stay with him until he warms up and starts to enjoy himself.
- Step back and remain available, but don't hover.
- Resist the temptation to rush in the minute he calls or looks uncertain. Wave reassuringly and chat to someone.
- Accept without anger that there may be times when he never enjoys himself and panics. You might have to leave (keep your sense of humor).

- It may be better (especially between fifteen months and two years) to concentrate on one-on-one sessions with another suitable toddler before trying groups.

- Toddlers often love and respond well to older children (around six years and up) who are more predictable and patient but are still children. Spending time with an older child if one is available gives them a positive experience to build on.

- During quiet times at home with books and toys, teach children what to say and what to do in social settings.

- Extreme shyness that doesn't seem to respond over time can be modified with professional help.

SUPERACTIVITY

Superactive toddlers have a higher level and intensity of the normal range of activity. They are more restless than most toddlers, less interested in sedentary activities (being read to, playing with puzzles, blocks, and so on), and have a constant urge to explore and try out their physical skills. They invariably like climbing, jumping into things, jumping off things, and indulging in wild activities they don't have the necessary skills for. They do not like being in a restricted environment and are difficult to take anywhere they cannot have free roam. All toddlers have a short concentration span but superactive toddlers have even shorter ones, which makes them difficult to occupy and keep from being bored. Restriction and boredom lead quickly to tantrums, aggression, and destructive behavior.

Whew! Superactive toddlers are not easy.

The intensity of their behavior usually wanes by three years as they develop and start to gain the skills they need to be able to channel their energy into more constructive outlets.

Is It Attention Deficit Hyperactivity Disorder?

Parents are often concerned that their superactive two-year-old is over the top and wonder if he may be hyperactive or have Attention Deficit Hyperactivity Disorder (ADHD). A detailed discussion of ADHD is outside the scope of this book. An abundance of information covering the spectrum of opinion about the condition is widely available.

The majority of superactive toddlers do not go on to have ADHD. A formal diagnosis of ADHD is usually not possible until the school years; however, if your toddler's active behavior is out of control and you are finding it very difficult to manage, it is advisable to seek help.

Here is a framework to work within

Having had my share of experience with superactive toddlers, I would like to give you hope for the future along with the dot points. It does come to an end. You will go on to have many happy times together, and the outrageous stories will be part of your family history forever.

- Firm, confident, consistent limit setting (about major things) is essential if any of you are to have a life during this time. Set up a routine, particularly in relation to bedtime and night sleeping, and stick to it. Active toddlers may resist routines and limit setting more than other toddlers, but they feel more in control and secure within firm limits.

- Give him simple concrete reasons for the way you want him to behave. Lecturing and nagging is counterproductive for any toddler but particularly for the superactives.

- Reward him for periods of calm behavior, particularly if he spends ten minutes at Great Aunt Freda's without breaking anything. Catching them being good is especially important for superactive toddlers, who are so prone to being at the center of calamities.

- Avoid as many potentially disastrous situations as possible until he is calmer (the supermarket, restaurants, afternoon tea parties, long telephone conversations when he's around, and so on).

- Concentrate on what is important. Let him win a few arguments.

- Avoid boredom as much as possible. Wear him out— swimming is excellent, but any outdoor activity helps.

- Toddlerproof your home as much as you can so that he can move freely without the need for a lot of supervision.

- Above all, try to arrange some regular time off for yourself via your partner, a relative, friend or babysitter, preschool or occasional care. Or perhaps by going back to work for a day or two.

Egocentrism

This is a tricky concept as it implies a negative trait rather than a normal state of development, but it goes a long way to explaining a toddler's attention-seeking behavior as well as his impatience, his apparent selfishness, and his unwillingness to share.

Egocentrism is not a character flaw in toddlers to get their own way but rather what they believe based on their experiences up to date. They understand only what they have experienced themselves and believe that everyone in the world sees things in exactly the way they do. Their reaction to events tends to be centered on how the event affects them. For example, if your toddler wants to get up at 4 a.m. and start the day, he expects everyone else in the house will want to as well.

Your toddler genuinely believes that the only reason you are there is for him. It is a monumental developmental leap for him to learn that other things may require your attention and that he has to share your affection.

In the same way, toddlers believe that everything in the world belongs to them. Their developing sense of self is largely through their possessions (similar to many adults), which is why, although you can begin to teach the concept, there is little point in expecting your toddler to share until he is nearer to school age.

Causality (how things affect other things)

In simple terms, causality resembles logical thought, essential for the ability to reason. A lot of your toddler's behavior is associated with his strong exploratory drive and his innate curiosity about how things work. His life is a constant round of research and experimentation to find out the relationship between actions and consequences.

Your toddler is very interested in your responses to his life's work. What will you do if he throws food on the floor? What will you do if he smacks your face? What is your response when he draws on the wall?

By eighteen months, toddlers are starting to understand quite complicated ideas about how objects affect each other and the consequences of certain actions. However, it takes a while before they are able to transfer that knowledge to new situations, so they must keep reinvestigating things like the switch on the TV and the flush lever on the toilet. This inability to transfer knowledge is one of the many reasons why toddlers under three are so vulnerable to unintentional injuries. It is also a reason why time concepts such as "soon," "next week" and "when Daddy gets home" are lost on toddlers, which has implications for daily living, discipline, and limit setting.

From an adult's point of view, a toddler's research, and his rapidly expanding abilities arising from it, veers from being exciting and extraordinarily clever to exasperating and tedious.

By the time toddlers are three years old, they have learned many of the complex ways in which the things in the world can influence one another.

But until they are much older, they often believe that cause and effect is directly related to their own capacity to make things happen.

Classifying, cataloging, sorting

Like other "thinking" developmental concepts, this is a complicated theory, but it also gives us insight into why toddlers do the things they do.

Here's a very simple version

Classification is the grouping of objects by similar properties; for example, flowers, food, receptacles, cars, houses, round shapes, buttons, heavy objects, light objects and so on. Obviously it is a much deeper and more intricate process than this since each object exists individually and has its own properties. Exactly how humans classify objects and use the information remains a bit of a mystery. Classification also goes beyond objects, to include all manner of experiences and behaviors.

Children start to learn to discriminate between categories from babyhood, and the ever-evolving process continues more or less throughout life.

A toddler's early classification of objects is mostly by appearance and function. For example, the tub, the toilet, and the diaper bucket are all containers of water, and to him they potentially all have the same purpose. He is allowed to throw toys into the tub and play in the water, so he is likely to do the same with the toilet and diaper bucket. Expecting him to know the difference before age two is unrealistic—it's better to make sure he can't get to the diaper bucket, the toilet, or into the bathroom unsupervised.

Sometime between two and three years old, toddlers go beyond the superficial appearance and function of objects and start to get into the deeper implications of what it means for objects to belong to categories.

For example, diaper buckets are not the same as baths even if they do both contain water, and there is a similarity between the function of the diaper bucket and the toilet which is different from the function of the tub. Or Daddy is a man, but not all men are daddies. Or Daddy is a man, but not all men are my daddy, and so on. Are you beginning to see how complicated it all is? No wonder three-year-olds never stop asking questions.

Object permanence (what on earth is that?)

Apologies for sounding so technical, but object permanence is an important cognitive (thinking) skill. It refers to the ability to know that something still exists, although it can't be seen. Adults take this for granted, but children have to develop the concept over time as they build on their knowledge and experience.

Until object permanence is acquired, your toddler doesn't realize that objects can still exist when they are not in sight. Not having a sense of object permanence contributes to clingy behavior and separation anxiety, which is common in older babies and toddlers up to age two. The mystery is that while all toddlers have to acquire this skill, not all toddlers experience separation anxiety and not all toddlers cling to their mother's legs as she goes from room to room. Other things such as temperament, life events, and other developmental experiences also contribute to these behaviors.

Sometime between eighteen months and two years, your toddler will grasp the fact that although he can't see something, it still exists. To be able to do this, he has to develop a mental symbol (a bit like an image) to represent an object or person. A symbol is something in his mind that represents the object he is thinking about even when that object is not present. As using symbols is the basis of language, it starts to become obvious why the concept of object permanence is such an important thinking skill.

Between twelve and eighteen months, toddlers move from finding things hidden in front of them to becoming increasingly aware of the existence of interesting things hidden behind closed doors, in cabinets and drawers, and in out-of-the-way places like under beds. By the time they reach eighteen months, they will search for a hidden object in a few potential hiding places other than just the original one.

Play ideas to help develop object permanence

- Play peek-a-boo games, making toys and objects disappear and reappear. Cover your face and say "Peek-a-boo," then reveal your face. Cover his face with his hands for him and say "Peek-a-boo," then reveal his face.

- Hide a favorite toy or book under something (a towel or a container) while he watches, then ask him to find it. Next, move it to a new hiding place while your toddler watches and see if he will find it. And finally try hiding it somewhere without him seeing and see if he can find it. Don't move on to each step until he has done the previous ones many times with different covers and objects.

- Go looking for things together around the house. For example, "Where are the clothespins, Bronte? Aha, here they are, behind the basket." To avoid a drama, stick to things he can play with when they are found.

Abstract and concrete thought

Abstract thought is another complex cognitive ability and covers a broad range of thinking from understanding letters and numbers to the ability to reason and develop theories about freedom or justice or childhood development. Abstract ideas are based on speculation, theories, or assumptions, which are worked out in the head rather than from something concrete.

Simple abstract thought first appears around age two (sometimes earlier), and you will become aware of it when your toddler expresses an idea or gives a reason for his actions.

Here's an example: After spending a miserable morning at playgroup, Robin asked Kate (age two) why she hadn't enjoyed herself.

"Sad," was her reply.

"You were sad?" Robin asked.

Kate nodded.

"Why were you sad?"

"The people," said Kate.

"You didn't like the people?"

Kate shook her head. "No."

Concrete thought is based on something solid that exists in reality, not just from an idea. It can be seen and touched (using fingers for counting is an example of concrete thought).

Even though toddlers begin to have a reasoning ability from a young age, they are still mostly concrete thinkers, and their thinking depends a lot on their own perceptions and instincts based on their life experiences so far. They are predominantly oriented to the here and now and can communicate best about things they can feel, see, and touch. Reasoning with toddlers much before age three is likely to be frustrating and pointless unless it's kept very simple and basic. So is expecting them to understand why you're so tired or to do something for you based on your relationship. For example, "Pick up your toys—for Mommy." Toddlers do best when they are shown what is required of them and when they have parents who model for themselves the sort of behavior they want to see in their toddlers. Toddlers are great imitators and learn a lot from observation.

Magic

Until toddlers start to understand some of the complex ways in which the things and people in the world influence one another, life for them is a bit like a magic show where things just seem to happen. This is both good and bad as it encourages toddlers to think that they can control the world in a magical way (great for them, not so great for parents). And that anything is possible (I can fly to the moon). But the magic might also include a hairy monster under the bed (not so good).

Putting yourself in someone else's place

We adults find it hard enough to put ourselves in someone else's place—think how difficult it is for us to see things from our toddler's point of view—so it must be extremely difficult for a toddler or a child to see any perspective other than his own when his experiences of life are so new and few and he is so busy getting to know himself. Some toddlers do show a limited ability to put themselves in another's place by age three, but this skill develops very gradually over many years, if not over a lifetime.

Helping toddlers understand how other people feel

- Talk in general terms about feelings and point out how things appear to others when a suitable occasion presents itself.
- Discuss the characters in books—where they are, what they are doing, and how they are feeling.
- Encourage play and make-believe—children start to develop empathy when they take on the role of the mother, the teacher, or the baby.
- Here are some concrete examples to start children thinking of

how it might feel to be someone or somewhere else:

- "Oscar, look at that man right up there on top of that building. Doesn't he look small? I wonder how he feels. I wonder if he can see more than we can? I wonder how big we look to him? How would you feel if you were up there? Frightened, brave, excited?"
- "Look how easily you can fit into that box, Edward, and curl up snug as a bug. Let's see what happens when I try . . . Oops, impossible . . . Ouch, it squashes my arm."
- "Look at that baby in the pram, Natasha. I wonder what she can see from where she is. Do you think she wants to get out and run around like you can? She looks happy/sad/mad/tired."

Negativism and the "no" word

No is the favored word of most toddlers between fourteen and twenty-four months.

Some people think (before they have children) that if they avoid using *no* and *don't*, their toddlers will bypass both the negative stage and the words that go with it. Unfortunately this is generally wishful thinking. It's true that some toddlers are not as negative as others, but this is more likely to be due to their temperament than the result of a planned strategy.

Negativism is a normal part of your toddler's developing self-awareness and appears between twelve and eighteen months. It starts to lose its intensity around age three (earlier for some, later for others). In the second year, your toddler becomes increasingly aware that he is his own person and has the capabilities to make his own decisions and to be "in charge." He doesn't quite know how much power he has in relation to this heady feeling of omnipotence and will continually test you to find out. He does this by resisting requests and becoming choosy about food, what to wear, what toys to have in the tub and so on. Deliberately touching forbidden objects is part of the general picture, and by the time he is two, doing this is often more to see what your reaction will be than out of curiosity about the object.

Staying safe, learning to live and obey the rules of our home, workplace, and the culture in which we live involves *not* doing a whole range of things. Toddlers are exposed to many *no's* and *don't's* whether their parents actually use the word or indicate the concept in some other way. It stands to reason that at some stage they will start using a few no's themselves one way or another, even if it isn't by actually using the word.

Naturally when the *no* word is overused by adults, the less significance it has for the toddler and the more frustrated he is likely to get. It is very easy for parents to get bogged down with *no's,* and for most of us it takes a concentrated effort to ignore the things that don't matter and to remember to turn the negatives into positives as often as is reasonably possible.

Fears and phobias

Toddlers between one and three years have many reasons to be afraid.

- They are still working out that temporary separation from their parent is not forever and doesn't mean that they have lost his or her love.
- Discovering about their own bodies and the way they work can be frightening at times.

- They have yet to learn by experience that strange people, strange objects, and strange sudden noises are not life-threatening. And that in fact these events often not only turn out to be harmless but give life its colour and zip.

- Toddlers can't explain what they want and what exactly is bothering them.

- Their expanding memory, imagination, and fantasy life lead to new fears surfacing.

- The intensity of their burgeoning emotions can be very scary for them.

Fears are normal and actually help toddlers sort things out in their heads as they grow mentally and physically. Experiencing fears also seems to be a way of getting attention and help from parents during developmental spurts when they need extra emotional support to work out what is going on.

Fears are a part of life for all of us. Old fears replace new as we develop and face the challenges that are thrown at us. How often do we find, even as adults, that when we are frightened we still long for the sort of protection and reassurance our parents (in particular our mothers) gave us when we were young.

Some fears are universal and easy to understand, but people's idiosyncratic fears can sometimes seem irrational or even laughable. Some toddler fears are perfectly understandable and bring back our own memories of monsters under the bed or being frightened by dogs. Some of the fears are funny (for the parent, not the toddler) and some have the capacity to drive parents mad because of their irrationality and the inconvenience they cause (fear of the bathtub being a common one in this category). To make it even more confusing, toddlers who shriek at the sight of the bathtub are likely to have no fear at all of attempting truly fearful acts that leave parents quivering wrecks (running onto the road, jumping into a swimming pool, drinking paint thinner, and so on).

Helping and supporting a toddler through his fears

- Accept that the fears are real and talk openly about them without ridiculing him and without overemphasizing the fear. Overreacting gives the toddler the impression that the fear is very serious indeed and inhibits his ability to learn to deal with it himself.

- Help him put his fear into words without introducing new ideas and subsequently a host of new fears that had not yet occurred to him.

- Help him respond less dramatically by exposing him gradually to the feared situation or object without a lot of fuss.

- Avoid talking endlessly about his fear(s) with all everyone within his earshot.

Anxiety

A certain amount of anxiety is to be expected during all ages of childhood. It is often hard for parents to deal with this fact because the expectation today is that children should be happy all the time, and that if their home life is secure and stable, then they have nothing to be anxious about. Anxiety is an emotion that is part of living, and toddlers and children need to feel anxiety in order to learn how to deal with it. Anxiety accompanies new stages of development at all ages (starting school and becoming a new parent are examples of this).

The right amount of anxiety encourages toddlers to use their own resources to deal with disappointment and distress. As long as their parents are available to support them, toddlers learn to manage anxiety themselves. They gradually discover that many anxiety-provoking situations turn out to be harmless and, a lot of the time, fun. Parents can help their toddler by making sure he is not overwhelmed by new experiences without interfering unnecessarily or going out of their way to change reasonable arrangements, for example, having a haircut or being left for a few hours with a babysitter. He may cry and have a tantrum but with support he will learn that such feelings can be tolerated.

The way toddlers respond to anxiety-producing situations varies tremendously according to their temperaments. It can be difficult for parents to know whether to do "control crying" (page 232) or not. Or when to continue swimming lessons or childcare in the face of their toddler's upsetting protestations as there is a fine line between healthy anxiety and unhealthy anxiety that has the potential to cause psychological and emotional damage.

I think most of us are aware in general terms of the sorts of situations that induce harmful anxiety. They are the same for toddlers as they are for all humans (and, if it comes to that, other living creatures too).

Harmful anxiety is likely to result from the following:

- Constantly being unsure of the outcome of your own actions or the actions of people around you and having to live with the feeling that the outcome will always be negative.

- Never knowing what's going to happen next.

- Being in situations in which you never have any personal control and no one you are close to treats you with respect.

- Being constantly blamed for things outside your control.

- Having things expected of you that you can't possibly deliver.

- Being made to feel inferior to others around you.

- Being made to feel a fool.

- Constantly being given things to do that are outside your capabilities.

- Being pressured for no good reason.

- Not being given emotional support or being rejected by those you love.

- Constantly feeling, isolated and frightened.

In terms of caring for a toddler, the following things lead to chronic, unhealthy anxiety:

- Threats of withdrawing love and leaving him or sending him away.

- Telling him that he is "bad," "dumb," "unreliable," and so on.

- Chaos and unpredictability in day-to-day life, with the toddler often being left with people he doesn't know or have any emotional connection with.

- Exposing him to long, sudden, and frequent separations from beloved adult(s) without him being in the care of a known and trusted substitute.

- Constantly blaming the toddler for the parent's state of health: "You make me sick," "You give me headaches," and so on.

- Constant harsh punishment or threats of harsh punishment (spanking, locking in room).

- Constant ridiculing that makes him lose face.

- Excessive demands on him in relation to ensuring "optimum" development.

- Overly anxious parents with very little self-confidence themselves who hover and warn of inevitable disaster in every step their toddler makes and every single breath he takes.

Goodness, what a heavy list—it sounds like a description of the home from hell. Thankfully most parents don't behave in such a ghastly fashion. But there are times when all of us fall through the cracks and say and do things that make our children anxious. Even if they are not as dire as the above list, they are likely to be minor variations on the themes. It's highly unlikely that occasional thoughtless actions are going to cause damaging lifelong anxiety. It's when they take over that serious thought needs to be given to changing what we are doing.

So, you see, it's not surprising to find that adult and toddler behavior is at odds so much of the time. When you consider the reasons behind your toddler's behavior, it's really quite amazing how much of the time his behavior is in fact quite reasonable (especially from his point of view). We'll look further into specific toddler behaviors in chapter six, but first a look at that tricky topic most closely related to a toddler's general behavior—discipline.

chapter **five**

Discipline

This subject is of great interest to parents once babies turn into toddlers, but what is actually meant by discipline?

Common feelings and beliefs

- Discipline is sometimes viewed with trepidation because in many parents' minds it means punishment—"Should I or shouldn't I spank?"

- Discipline is often thought of solely as crisis intervention for serious problems. "His biting's getting out of control. It's time we got some discipline going around here."

- Or as an instant solution to stop whatever behavior is causing the current grief. "How *do* I stop him from throwing food?"

- Many parents believe that discipline is about moral issues, about teaching children to be "good"—that is, to be honest, to consider the feelings of others, to tell the truth, to respect their parents, and so on.

So what is discipline?

The simplest definition of discipline is to lead, teach, guide, and influence. Discipline is not about stopping bad behavior so much as encouraging desirable behavior. It is primarily about teaching children how to behave and, more importantly, to *want* to behave in an acceptable way according to the personal standards and cultural norms of their family and society.

At its best, discipline teaches children inner control. It teaches them how to regulate their own behavior, how to predict how others will behave and what the consequences of their own behavior will be.

Because of the strong association of discipline with punishment it's common to hear children referred to as being disciplined or not disciplined: "It's plain to see that child has had no discipline at all. If he were mine, I'd give him a good smack. That would straighten him out."

In truth there is no such thing as no discipline—some children are taught well and some are taught poorly. The spanking issue is a minuscule overemphasized part of the whole process.

All your responses teach your toddler something, whether the response is positive, negative, or no response at all. It is my belief that a large part of the discipline process comes naturally to committed parents who love their children and want the best for them. A few saint-like parents (and I am excluded from this category) teach well and effectively all of the time. And sadly some parents teach badly and ineffectively all of the time. Most of us do well a lot of the time and poorly some of the time.

What role does punishment play?

Since the 1950s, research has repeatedly shown that punishment is ineffective in reducing misbehavior. Given often enough and severely enough, punishment actually motivates children to behave badly and encourages hostile and devious behavior. It also teaches children that tough, bullying behavior is okay. Consequently they are likely to behave like that toward others and eventually toward their own children.

In both practical and philosophical terms, it has been found that giving attention to positive behavior (positive reinforcement) and minimizing attention to negative behavior (negative reinforcement) is a far more effective way of encouraging children to behave in an acceptable way. Unfortunately this has been interpreted as "no punishment means no discipline," with the perception that if we went back to the good old days we would not have the child behavioral problems we have today. This is a very simplistic way of looking at things—the parents of every generation for thousands of years have had troubles with the behavior of their children in one way or another. It is normal for children to misbehave, it's how they learn about themselves and the world they live in.

Punishment is needed sometimes, but it should be used as a teaching strategy so that eventually the child will change his behavior not in order to avoid punishment but because he feels *inside* that it's the right thing to do.

Punishment is ineffective when it is used as a fear tactic or as a way for the parent to get his or her revenge. In order to avoid overemphasis on punishment, many experts refer to discipline as setting limits and boundaries. Effective discipline does not punish children. It protects them. It helps them grow socially and emotionally and builds their self-esteem.

None of this means condoning unacceptable behavior. It is vital for parents to set limits, have ideas about right and wrong, and communicate this with words and actions in as fair and reasonable a way as possible.

101

Real-life discipline

I find it interesting in my work to discover how many parents read books and attend seminars on discipline techniques. They proclaim how fantastic they are, but when pressed on the issue, admit to only "sort of" doing what is suggested. Or saying things like, "Well, it worked with Lisa, but Emily is a different child." It is generally conceded that spanking is not only potentially dangerous but also an ineffective discipline technique, yet many parents continue to spank. Most parents have a great deal of trouble staying consistent day in and day out. Most parents succumb to delivering threats without following through; many admit to shouting sometimes or acknowledge that there are times when they pay more attention to negative behavior than is helpful. Quite a few parents admit to nagging or using bribery in desperation, and still more confess that they give in to their toddlers' demands to avoid scenes. However, in my experience, although most loving parents do some of the above, their threats never include the threat of withdrawing love or of desertion, their spanks are occasional, and shouting and nagging are not their usual ways of communicating.

When I ask my friends with grown-up children what they did about discipline, they are all very vague and can't really remember an overall philosophy. They do remember specifics like, "I think I waved the wooden spoon once or twice," or "We did send them to their rooms," or a gruff "We didn't put up with any nonsense." I don't know how their children (or my own, come to think of it) view the discipline they received. Like most children, I dare say they think they can improve upon it when their turn comes. However, they have all grown up to be responsible people and are good friends with their parents.

I have always known that there is a hidden element to discipline that goes beyond understanding behavior and actively managing it, important as this might be; something else that sustains parents' and children's relationships through the disasters as they grow and learn together.

I recently found what I believe is this hidden element articulated in Peter Williamson's book *Good Kids, Bad Behavior*, now unfortunately out of print but available in some public libraries.[2] Williamson says that it is not necessarily what we actively teach our children that has the greatest impact on them but the more indirect things like the background mood of the family and the indescribable, ever-present atmosphere of the home. The parents' attitudes contribute to this, but it is also communicated through the family's regular rituals and routines which give security and rhythm to daily life and provide a predictable sense of safety. There is an orderly flow to meals, bedtime routines, holidays, visiting friends, grandparents, and so on. All families go through their share of turmoil and all parents experience problems raising their children, but when family life provides children with a strong sense of certainty and safety, it will enrich their lives and make a lasting positive impact whatever individual discipline methods are put in place.

The basics of discipline/limit setting

You will find that there is a heap of information around about discipline or, if you prefer, limit setting. The core concepts are similar, but the information can appear to be conflicting because in the end no one can tell each individual member of each individual family exactly how they should conduct their lives.

Every parent's personal feelings vary about what he or she is prepared to tolerate and how much he or she is prepared to bend when specific problems arise. Only you can decide where that limit lies.

Discipline for toddlers involves

- Giving them a sense of organization. Making their outside world more predictable and controlled helps them regulate and understand their inner world.
- Helping them learn social skills—how to get along with others, how to cooperate.
- Helping them to know what to expect of others, especially their parents.
- Letting them know that you care for them and that you are on their side even when you have to show them why their behavior is unacceptable.

Dealing with conflict

All parents at some time vacillate about setting limits because of the inevitable conflict that will ensue. While it is unhealthy to base family life on conflict, it is healthy for toddlers to experience some conflict so that they can test themselves and their limits. And as unpleasant as it may be at the time, learning to handle family disagreements strengthens parents' abilities and increases their confidence. This is far more positive for toddlers than having their demands given in to by a nervous parent for the sake of some temporary peace and quiet or because the parent is scared that the toddler won't like him or her.

Minimizing unnecessary conflict

Prevent and avoid as many problems as you can. Here are some suggestions how:

1. TRY TO HAVE REALISTIC EXPECTATIONS

Are your expectations reasonable? Because so many of us have little to do with babies and toddlers before we have our own, it's easy to assign adult expectations to toddler behavior. Most parents don't expect an eighteen-month-old toddler to get the dinner, but it's easy to fall into the trap of expecting too much in subtler areas.

For example:

- To play quietly while you write your novel
- To enjoy hours of socializing with other two-year-olds
- To sit at the dinner table and enjoy a relaxing three-course meal and adult chatter
- To enjoy a camping trip to see the Grand Canyon
- To not interrupt you on the phone when you're doing an important business deal
- To pick up the toys because he loves you and you're so tired

2. TRY TO WORK OUT IF THE BEHAVIOR IS ACTUALLY A PROBLEM

Before you label the behavior a problem you need to ask yourself how often and how intensely the behavior is occurring. The seriousness of the problem will dictate your approach. You are the only one who can decide how irrelevant, disruptive, or irritating the behavior is. You may tolerate things that others find intolerable, which might be fine in your own home but raise difficulties when he is further afield.

Try to think of the possible reasons for the behavior in the context of your toddler's life and stage of development rather than as a single issue that needs fixing.

It is important to look at his health, any life events that might be affecting him, and how you are responding to him before declaring his behavior an unmitigated disaster.

3. ANTICIPATE POTENTIAL PROBLEMS AND MAKE SUITABLE ADJUSTMENTS

Potential trouble is predictable in a range of situations, for example:

- In restaurants
- Long lines at the bank
- Shopping (especially the dreaded supermarket)
- Too long playing with Ella (you know they always end up bashing each other)
- Rowdy games with sticks
- Transitional times of the day, particularly the evenings

4. DISTRACTION

As every parent comes to learn, distraction is a handy strategy for avoiding some temper tantrums, helping toddlers to recover quickly from minor mishaps, and redirecting toddler interests away from the garbage bin to playing with some saucepans.

Distraction is most effective in the second and third years when the toddler's short-term memory is still developing and he is intensely curious about anything and everything around him. As his memory and cognitive development expands, distraction is not as easy, but it is still a good tool on and off until children are three (as long as they are not overtired, hungry, or sick).

5. RITUALS AND ROUTINES

The positive contribution that routines and rituals make to how toddlers behave should never be underestimated.

Rituals are similar to but different from routines. Rituals are customs that have social, emotional, or psychological significance and help humans to feel that they belong to a special group of people. Rituals are calming and reassuring and give order to a toddler's life at a time when his inner world tends to be somewhat chaotic and uncertain. Rituals between a toddler and his parents strengthen their bond and help them connect (and reconnect after a bad day). They are also a part of teaching a toddler how to look after himself and how to behave in the family and the culture in which he lives.

Rituals are things like story time before bed or perhaps the same song every night. Having a bath with Daddy and playing with special toys might be a ritual in some families. Or coming into Mommy and Daddy's bed in the mornings, then getting dressed and eating breakfast from the same plate.

On the other hand, routines, although they are also important for many families, are more a way of organizing life into a convenient and efficient structure. Although I acknowledge that routines are optional and that it's up to parents to decide whether their family life is going to run on a schedule or not, if families live in a state of constant turmoil and disorganization the little things become magnified and out of all proportion. In contrast, a predictable but flexible routine not only prevents and reduces the intensity of many behavior problems but enables parents to have some time for themselves to recharge their batteries.

Behavior management techniques

Discipline advice is usually presented in the form of specific behavior management techniques to prevent or correct problematic behavior. Behavior management techniques are also called behavior modification, behavioral therapy, or disciplining strategies.

You will find them in this book too. But although such techniques are very helpful, they tend to oversimplify the concept of discipline and the ease of solving problems. It is best to view them as guides or tools to help you problem-solve rather than as solutions that will miraculously change the behavior overnight.

After you work out how serious the problem is, it is advisable to try the mildest and most positive strategies first—things that involve showing your toddler what to do and encouraging him to do it. Move on to more interventionist strategies as needed.

Here, then, are the basics of behavior management techniques for toddlers.

Positive reinforcement

Rewards versus bribes

Rewarding behavior you want to encourage is the cornerstone of discipline for any age group but especially toddlers.

The difference between rewarding and bribing is confusing and in some ways subtle. It is very common for rewards to end up as bribes despite that not being the original intention.

WHAT IS THE DIFFERENCE?

- A reward comes unsolicited *after* the behavior, the bribe is offered *before*.

    "I see that you have put your toys away, Jack. Thank you. Would you like me to read you a story?"

    as opposed to

    "Stop yelling and I'll give you a lollipop."

    In the first example, the toddler is being acknowledged positively for doing something that has his parents' approval. In the second, the toddler is being acknowledged positively for doing something that has his parents' *dis*approval.

- Rewards contribute in a major way to positively changing a toddler's behavior *over time*. They gradually encourage the toddler to want to do things that have his parents' approval because it makes him feel good inside. It may take a while for him to work this out, which is why positive reinforcement is a long-term strategy, the immediate benefits of which are not always obvious.

- Bribery is an offer made by a parent to a toddler when the parent wants the toddler to do something to help her. It is usually given at times when the parent is desperate and the toddler indifferent. It can have immediate satisfying results, but constant bribing is a form of blackmail that gives the parent the burden and the toddler the control. As an ongoing strategy, it turns into a bottomless pit, has no long-term positive effect on behavior and if it becomes the major tool in the parent's repertoire, actually increases parental stress levels.

- Rewards for toddlers mostly center on your attention—things like hugs, smiles, and warm voices. We all like to be noticed and acknowledged in positive ways, and this is especially so for toddlers. Most parents underestimate the power their approval has on their toddler's behavior.

- Rewards can also be tangible such as a special treat, an outing, reading a favorite story, or wearing Mommy's special necklace.

- Rewards are something you can walk away from without grief: "Oh well, I guess you don't want me to read that story after all."

  A bribe, on the other hand, is usually an act of desperation: "Please do this for me and I'll buy you a doll." What do you do when your toddler says he doesn't want the silly old doll and he'd sooner have a dump truck?

- Rewards for toddlers must be immediate and accompanied by a short, explicit reason for the reward: "Oscar, I am going to read you two stories tonight because you got in and out of the tub without a fuss."

- Inappropriate rewards for toddlers include noisy clapping, loud phony-sounding praise, money, star charts, and promises of treats sometime in the future.

Praise versus acknowledgment

All toddlers grow to love praise, and praise is an effective way to encourage desirable behavior, but there are some conditions on the best ways to use praise.

The more exaggerated, loud, and phony praise becomes, the less its value. And depending on the temperament of the toddler, a constant flow of loud, extravagant hand-clapping praise can even have the reverse effect. Some toddlers find such attention too much to deal with and collapse in an emotional heap or have a mammoth tantrum. Others find the pressure of the expectation of a continued performance too much to bear and regress (particularly in relation to potty training).

What most of us, including toddlers, want on a day-to-day basis is genuine but quiet acknowledgment of our small achievements by those near and dear to us.

"You're managing so well now, Bronte, drinking from a cup. Look at that, it's nearly gone. Good girl."

"I do appreciate it when you sit still while I put your boots on, Gabriel. It makes it so much easier for me."

High praise is best reserved for significant accomplishments (and in my opinion pooing in the potty chair is not as significant an event for the toddler as it is for the parent) and should be paired with an explicit reason for the praise.

Negative reinforcement

We all unwittingly negatively reinforce undesirable behavior in toddlers. It's easy to get into a rut where the toddler gets the most attention when he is doing the things we don't want him to do. Then, when there is a break in the negative behavior and he is being quiet or "good," we retire in exhaustion and end up ignoring the behavior we want to encourage.

Consequently, to our dismay, the undesirable behavior grows and the desirable behavior shrinks.

Some examples of negative reinforcers

- Smacking, shouting, bribery, and inconsistent responses to undesirable behavior such as whining, tantrums, wanting access to forbidden objects, and night sleep issues.
- Endless conversations to other adults about the toddler's exploits and failings within his hearing.
- Overreaction behavior driven by developmental stages (biting, lying, using rude words, and making messes).
- Laughing at behavior you wish to discourage.
- Constant nagging and exaggerated threats on which you haven't any intention of following through.
- Being overly protective and accommodating for every minor mishap and upsetting moment in daily life.

Remember that toddlers have trouble telling the difference between positive and negative ways of getting attention. Minimize the negative reinforcers as much as you can.

Warning versus threats

Warnings

As toddlers find change difficult, warnings are important to help them adjust to the idea that something new is about to happen. They are a way of letting your toddler know what will happen next. *Warnings are given to alert him to a change in his activities rather than as a prelude to a consequence for misbehavior.*

An example: "Grace Pearl, after you have been down the slide two more times we will go home." Count one, two in a loud voice as she comes down the slide, catch her, and go home.

Effective warnings need to be prompt and exact and to be followed through. This way toddlers develop a sense of predictability and also a concept of time.

What about threats?

Threats often pop out in the heat of the moment. They tend to be irrational and nonconstructive and are not going to teach your toddler anything useful. Threats encourage power struggles and battles you can't win, especially in relation to eating and potty training.

Threats are often not followed through. If they are, they inevitably have consequences that are more serious for the parent than the toddler.

An example: "If you don't eat your lunch, we are not going to go to the park." If you carry this threat through, it means you now have another two hours hanging around the home front with a whining toddler. On the other hand, not following it through negatively reinforces the behavior you are trying to change.

Consistency

The importance of consistency is emphasized in every book written about discipline, yet most parents simply cannot maintain consistency twenty-four hours a day, seven days a week, particularly the parent (usually the mother) who is with the toddler the most. Consistency is an ideal to aim for, but there is always going to be a discrepancy between the ideal and the reality.

Complete consistency is impossible, and the extent to which parents can be consistent depends on their circumstances, their temperaments, and perhaps most of all, the temperament of their toddler.

If you are finding it very difficult to maintain consistency, think of a few things that are important and aim for consistency in those things. Is it important that your toddler is in bed by 7 p.m. every night and stays in his bed all night? If so, be consistent about that behavior.

Discipline related to your toddler's personal safety is very important and requires consistency, but whether he eats his veggies every day doesn't really matter, does it? Just because it was important to your mother doesn't mean you have to be consistent about the family tradition.

And yes, your response to a tantrum is going to be different at home, where the potential for embarrassing escalation is far less, from your response in the middle of a restaurant. If you try hard for consistency in relation to the tantrums at home, eventually you will find that they are less troublesome when you are out.

The level of consistency for specific behavior will vary from family to family. Do not be discouraged if you find other parents see things differently you. Stick to what you think is important.

Consequences for misbehavior

Consequences for undesirable behavior are a necessary part of discipline, as toddlers need to start to feel the contrast between negative and positive responses to their behavior.

A consequence for undesirable behavior should be short, immediate, and respect, the toddler's feelings. A toddler needs to learn over time that consequences will be predictable, consistent, and immediate.

The main aims of consequences are

- To calm things down.

- To discourage negative attention-seeking behavior (the irritating stuff).

- To encourage the toddler to be aware of what he's done wrong.

- As he grows older, to be willing to put things right.

The most effective consequences for toddlers are things that limit their access to their parents and limit their parents' attention to them.

Consequences that have a deterrent value (removal of privileges, no dessert, not allowed out to play) are inappropriate for toddlers, who still do not understand cause and effect, time, or the relationship between actions and their consequences.

It's also helpful to allow toddlers to learn about the natural consequences of their actions whenever possible. For example, "Throwing the apple out the window means that it's gone—no more apple."

Depending on the behavior you have a choice from a number of consequences. Here they are.

Pretending to ignore the undesirable behavior

By withholding your attention, many toddler behaviors modify and even disappear over time. This is because toddlers gravitate toward attention—any attention, even if it is negative. Ignoring removes the reward the toddler is receiving for the negative attention-seeking behavior.

However, ask any parent, this is easier said than done.

Successful ignoring is an art that requires practice. It is also important to know when it is appropriate and when it is not. Ignoring has its limitations. The extent to which a parent is able to ignore also depends on things like the toddler's temperament and her own, the sort of day it's been so far, and how much she is being undermined by other adults around her.

THE TECHNIQUE OF IGNORING

Very few parents can completely ignore a whining toddler pulling on their skirt or having a supertantrum on the kitchen floor. So, the aim is to **pretend to ignore.**

- Avoid eye contact, hide your true feelings, and pretend to be calm. Above all, do not laugh (I know that, generally, laughing is not going to be your first response, but there are some undesirable toddler behaviors that are funny . . . for a while).

- Busy yourself with some activity. Perhaps hum or put on the headphones. Think of greener pastures.

- When he stops whining or throwing the tantrum, offer him a reward—smile, hug, play briefly with him.

- Resist the temptation to act annoyed or to nag.

Pretending to ignore is hard work—at first.

If the toddler has been receiving attention for the behavior for some time, changing your tactics and pretending to ignore it will take a lot of resolve and stamina, as the behavior will almost certainly escalate before it diminishes. Changing *your* behavior will take some energy and commitment, but for certain behaviors the result is worth it.

When is pretending to ignore appropriate?

Pretending to ignore is suitable for low-key attention-seeking behavior. It is particularly successful with toddlers who are still at the experimental stage of learning how to behave. It is good for things like rude words, refusing to eat, temper tantrums, nose picking, nail biting, refusing to go to bed, and whining. It is also a necessary strategy for weaning a reluctant toddler from the breast.

When is pretending to ignore not appropriate?

Pretending to ignore is most successful in an environment in which the toddler has a limited capacity to escalate the behavior and where the parent is not pressured to take action. Restaurants, someone else's home, and the supermarket are not always conducive to successful ignoring. However, practicing pretending to ignore as consistently as you can on the home front eventually filters out to further afield.

Irritating behavior tends to escalate before it wanes, so ignoring is unsuitable for behavior that is likely to escalate to the point where people (including the toddler) and property might be hurt. For example, biting, throwing objects, hitting.

It is also inappropriate for serious behavior. Toddlers need plenty of positive attention for desirable behavior because if the only way they can get attention is by doing something serious, then eventually they will do something serious. For example, running onto the road, jumping out of a window, smashing a vase.

It is also important to look at reasons behind the behavior you are ignoring to make sure that your toddler is not ill or upset by life events. Self-destructive behaviors should not be ignored.

Reprimands

A reprimand is a clear statement delivered in three parts:

1. A command to stop the behavior
2. A very short reason why (younger toddlers will not respond to the reason but to the tone of your voice)
3. A simple alternative

An example for a younger toddler:

1. "Stop hitting my face."
2. "It hurts."
3. "Sit and play on the floor."

And an older toddler:

1. "Please don't take the toy from Samuel."
2. "He had it first."
3. "Please give it back and drive the truck instead."

Toddlers need to be shown as well as told. Calling across a room is not as effective as being with them and showing them how to redirect their activities.

Timeout

Most parents today are familiar with the concept of timeout but are less familiar with the philosophy behind it and why it must be carried out correctly to get positive results.

Let's look first at what timeout is **not**

- Timeout is *not* punishment. It has no deterrent value. The aim of timeout is to remove the toddler from any attention, positive or negative, for a short period.

- It's value as a threat is negligible—if timeout is continually used as a threat, eventually the toddler will grow into a child who will say he couldn't care less about timeout, threaten all you like.

- It is not meant to humiliate or make the toddler feel bad about himself.

- Timeout is commonly thought of as the last resort for a furious parent who needs to separate herself from her toddler for fear of succumbing to spanking him or doing something she might regret. This is a valid course of action that most of us take from time to time and is recommended for heated moments, but it is not timeout.

Now let's look at what timeout **is**

- Timeout gives parents something concrete to do when they cannot ignore what is going on.

- It is a formal way of removing a toddler from his parents' attention.

- It is used to let the toddler know that his parents have noticed a particular behavior they don't want to continue.

Reasons why parents say timeout doesn't work

- They have an expectation that timeout will stop the behavior right away forever.

- They have an expectation that the toddler will be upset by the timeout (in a similar way to being spanked).

- They report that the toddler has a good time playing with his toys in the bedroom, or he trashes his room.
- They find that when he comes out of timeout, he goes right back to the same behavior.

All the above are common experiences but many parents discover that timeout is worth persevering with. Spanking and yelling can be more satisfying and sometimes have an immediate desirable effect, but constant attention in this manner is a dead end. It negatively reinforces the behavior you want to change and doesn't teach the toddler anything except that it's okay to hit and yell. The initial satisfaction the parent feels turns into guilty feelings and in a short space of time the toddler becomes immune to the treatment.

Here are some suggestions for more successful timeout.

The aim of timeout is to remove all attention from the toddler for a brief period

Thrusting a toddler into timeout in a fit of anger provides attention. Talking to him while he is there provides attention.

For timeout to have the desired effect, the parent, after giving the toddler a very short reason for the timeout, must stay bland, colorless, disinterested, and temporarily unavailable.

Where should the toddler go during timeout?

Opinions differ as to whether timeout should take place in the bedroom, in another room, on the stairs, in a corner of the living room, or sitting on a chair by the door.

Training children to use a chair or a corner means that younger toddlers may have to be held in place (hold them firmly, avoid eye contact, and give them no attention), but by avoiding the bedroom, the room wrecking that sometimes happens with older children is avoided.

I don't think it really matters where timeout happens as long it is always in the same place, there is no loss of face for the toddler, and there is no attention directed to him while he is there. Decisions about the best location will also vary with the temperament of the toddler.

How long should timeout last?

The duration of timeout is relatively short. A rule of thumb is one minute for every year, but for a toddler under two, thirty seconds is probably sufficient. Using an egg timer can be quite successful for older toddlers (from three years).

When timeout is over, what then?

When the timeout is over, the parent needs to change from being bland and disinterested to being warm and welcoming.

Once the toddler has the language skills and understanding of cause and effect, have a brief discussion about why timeout was necessary and allow him to make amends.

After timeout, toddlers *must* be redirected into a new activity or given a change of scenery. Allowing them to come out and continue on where they left off is just asking for more trouble.

What about when he trashes his room in timeout?

This is more likely to happen when a child beyond the toddler age is given timeout as a punishment and is left in the room for a relatively long period. Or when he is sent to his room by a very angry parent in full flight. Timeout is best used for only a short period and ideally should be presented in a low-key and bland manner by the parent.

If the room does get turned upside down, ignore it and wait

until you are calm before addressing the issue, which may take a day or two.

When you are calm, reinstate order together. Remember, the bigger the impact the trashing of the room has made on you, the more likely it is that it will happen again.

Timeout is not for everyone

Timeout is not for all families. Some families simply don't feel the need to use it. Others find even when they use it correctly, it is still ineffective or inappropriate for their situation. It is up to individual parents to decide which limit-setting strategies work best in their homes.

Last but not least

Like anything else, if timeout is overused, the effectiveness declines. Timeout should be saved for important situations.

If you find every day is a constant round of threats and ineffective timeouts, it's time to rethink what you are doing. Use other strategies for minor misdemeanors.

Remember, too, that toddlers need variety in their days, a reasonable routine, and supervision when they are with other toddlers. Most importantly, they need sufficient positive time-in with their parents to ensure that they are not forced to get attention through undesirable behavior.

Spanking

The issue of whether or not to spank is particularly intense in the first five years, as this is a time of tremendous developmental changes in children which most parents find exhausting and frustrating at least some of the time. Despite the growing belief that physical punishment is wrong and the piles of research showing that it is ineffective as a disciplinary tool, spanking is still used by large numbers of parents.

Many feel guilty and embarrassed about the fact that they spank; others believe that used sparingly and as a last resort it is an acceptable, effective deterrent to serious misbehavior, or that it is okay when it is limited to drawing children's attention to their safety and survival.

Why do parents spank?

- Because they have reached the end of their rope.
- Because they feel pressured by other parents to spank, for example, their toddler bites another toddler at playgroup.
- Frightened parents spank when their child narrowly escapes some life-threatening event.
- Some parents spank as a planned consequence for certain misbehavior because they believe it is more effective than pretending to ignore or using timeout.

How effective is spanking?

- Spanking may have an immediate and satisfying effect for the adult in times of stress, but it is unlikely to teach toddlers different behavior in the long term.
- The emotional impact of spanking may change things momentarily (the tantrum or the biting or the hitting may stop), but it has been shown over and over again to be an ineffective way of teaching toddlers, or anyone else for that matter, to adjust their behavior.
- It's hard to believe that the rare spanking is harmful in the context of a loving family, but escalation of physical punishment can

be abusive, dangerous, and gives toddlers messages such as "Bigger and louder is better," "I'm really bad" and "If they can do that, so can I."

- Constant spanking increases a toddler's anger, humiliates him, and usually makes his parents feel guilty, which the toddler will soon be aware of. Guilty feelings decrease confidence. Lack of confidence stops parents, believing in themselves. Their toddler is the first to notice, which then decreases the effectiveness of his parents' overall discipline and limit setting.

Final words on spanking

Discipline aims to *teach* long-term desirable behavior in positive ways which will help children decide that they want to behave in an acceptable manner because it makes them feel happier, not because they are frightened they might get spanked.

Here's a summary of the way to encourage desirable behavior

- Reward desired behavior; give minimal attention to undesirable behavior.
- Have realistic expectations of yourself and your toddler, remembering that toddlers have places to go, things to do, and messes to make.
- Consider your toddler's developmental level—there is a lot of difference between a fifteen-month-old and a toddler who is nearly three years old.
- Consider your toddler's temperament.
- Consider daily variations in your toddler's behavior (good days, bad days).
- Consider your own temperament and lifestyle:
    How far you are willing to bend?
    What things really matter to you?
    How high are your energy levels?

What are your work commitments?

How much help do you have?

- Try to see things from your toddler's point of view. Having some understanding of why he's behaving the way he is helps you to be his ally rather than his opponent—much more helpful in the long run even if you are temporarily furious.

- Look for reasons for misbehavior—developmental experiences, a new baby, illness such as an ear infection, any disruption to routine or a sudden developmental spurt (for example, learning to walk).

- Pretend to ignore.

- Distract when possible.

- Set up some structure and routine, especially in relation to meals and sleep. This is usually an achievable goal, and it's amazing how many other things fall into place if your toddler has a predictable routine for activities, eating, and sleeping.

- Anticipate potential problems and think about ways to avoid them. This is not always possible, as toddlers have many hidden surprises and there is always the chance of the unexpected, but it is possible a lot of the time.

- Consistency is highly desirable, but sometimes it's necessary to adjust a routine or to change the environment to avoid misbehavior. Being consistent doesn't mean being rigid.

- Avoid doing things that your toddler doesn't care too much for when he's tired and hungry.

- Let him do things for himself as often as possible.

- Sometimes perceived behavior problems are better solved by a simple practical change. For example:

    If he won't eat mushy food from a spoon, give him finger food.

    If he keeps leaping out of the highchair, change to small table and chairs.

    If he keeps climbing out of his crib, put him into a bed.

    If he hates swimming lessons and putting his head under the water, give them up until next summer.

And here are the specific things you can do to encourage and teach your toddler to behave the way you'd like him to

- As often as possible, tell your toddler what you would like him to do, not what you don't want him to do.

- Let him know it's his behavior you don't like, not him. "I don't like it when you . . . " rather than "I don't like you when you . . . "

- Make sure you get your toddler's attention and give him your full attention when you are speaking to him.

- Use very short sentences. If you want to explain something, give a short explanation first, followed by what you want done. Avoid confusing him by phrasing what you want done as a question when he doesn't have a choice in the matter. For example:

    "How would you like to get out of the tub now?" is better expressed: "It's time to get out of the tub."

    "Would you like me to buckle you in the car seat now?" is better expressed: "Hold your doll while I do the buckle up."

- It is, however, excellent to offer specific choices when appropriate. Remember, though, that open-ended choices don't work. "Which shirt do you want to put on?" is better expressed: "Would you like to wear your blue shirt today or the yellow t-shirt?"

    Limit choices to two and make sure you are prepared to accept the child's decision, which in this case might be "both."

- Avoid vague abstracts; for example, "Be good," "Be nice," "Don't make a mess." Toddlers need concrete messages accompanied by associated actions. "Please give me the jar of hand cream. I don't want it smeared all over the bathroom mirror." "I want you to empty the sand out of your dump truck and come inside."

- Give warnings before a change of activities. Use simple time devices when appropriate. Count slowly and clearly; an egg timer for an older toddler is useful (for when to get out of the tub, for example). Songs, a short video, or a short piece of music are other ways.

125

- When you are teaching your toddler specific activities (picking up toys), stay with him and watch him.

- Practice what you want him to do at home where there are fewer distractions and it's easier to ignore things like tantrums, negativity, and whining.

- We all fall into holes at times and behave badly. Toddlers, bless them, tend to forgive us and love us anyway. It's nice to apologize to your toddler and let him know that the way you behaved is not his fault. This is how they learn to apologize sorry themselves.

- Be a role model. Practice what you preach. Toddlers are great imitators.

chapter six

The ABC's of Typical Toddler Behavior

How to use this part of the book

This section looks at the main behavior problems parents encounter during the toddler years but doesn't include potty training, sleeping, or eating, which all have a section to themselves as they tend to assume mammoth proportions at this time in life.

Although the specifics vary, most families with toddlers experience a similar range of behavior problems and similar concerns about those problems. Parents are usually looking for very specific information that relates precisely to their particular circumstances and to what their toddler is doing.

"Is this normal?"

"How long will it go on for?"

"What can I do to make it go away?"

"What's the recommended strategy?"

They are often looking for a magic solution to make things right. But there are no magic solutions in this or any other book.

Eventually parents have to work out their own ways of dealing with the specifics of their toddler's behavior.

It is impossible in any book to cover every scenario as there are potentially a million "what if's" and "yes, but's" because of the range of individual situations and the complexity of human behavior. There's also the endless creativity of toddlers as they think up new ways to test their limits and exercise their control.

The information in this chapter should be used as a stepping stone to working things out for yourself rather than read and applied as an instant solution to an irritating problem.

I think that the *biggest* asset of reading a book like this or talking over strange toddler behavior with someone else is the comfort factor: "Oh, so my toddler is not so unusual." "Well, I didn't realize that other parents felt like this too."

I realize I am at risk of causing outbreaks of panic by including the most common ages during which these behaviors occur, but some of them are more common with younger toddlers, others more common with older toddlers. Sometimes this is very clear-cut. A fifteen-month-old toddler is not going to be telling lies. And it would be very unusual for a three-year-old to smear poo.

However, many of these behaviors do spread right across the toddler spectrum and beyond; for example, temper tantrums and, gosh, at what age does masturbation and curiosity about everyone else's bits and pieces end? So please do not panic if your toddler is still doing something that I have put in a younger age bracket. All these behaviors are normal for toddlers, though occasionally, under certain circumstances, they can indicate a more in-depth problem that may need professional help. If you are in any doubt, please consult a reliable health professional.

Getting help for your toddler's behavior

In general, the main concerns parents have during the toddler years relate to their toddler's behavior. Things like temper tantrums, not eating, not sleeping, potty training, biting, hitting and shyness give most parents pause for thought. The majority find the information they need by talking to other parents, extended family members and friends, and by reading books. Nurse practitioners and doctors are also available for reassurance and guidance.

Parent groups and parent education programs that focus on toddlers and discipline are often available through local organizations such as churches, pre-schools, hospitals, and county health services. Look in your local newspaper or phone book, or if you have access try the Internet, via www.google.com

Some parents, however, find that they are caught up in endless behavior struggles with their toddlers which never seem to get resolved, and advice from professionals who specialize in helping with behavior can be very useful. The health professional may be a psychologist, a social worker, a psychiatrist, a pediatrician, or a pediatric nurse practitioner. Many parents find that one or two visits can make a big difference to their skill and confidence.

Sometimes finding the right person and the right help is a matter of trial and error, but if help is needed, it is worth persevering because the right help at the right time can make the world of difference to family life.

Power struggles

Power struggles with toddlers inevitably end up in a lose–lose situation, so it's best to avoid them whenever you can. Here are two suggestions to help circumvent as many as possible.

1. Work out what matters

Part of dealing with toddler negativity and their resistance to doing what you want them to do is working out what really matters. It's easy for parents to lose perspective because of the many external pressures they have to deal with. For the sake of your sanity, it is sometimes advisable to step back and ask yourself how important the issue is and why you are insisting. Everyone has different ideas on these matters, so it is up to you to decide. The fewer the absolutes, the less the stress.

For example, it may be important to you to have your toddler in bed by seven-thirty each night—fine. But does it really matter if he keeps the pacifier another year? It would be excellent if he went to preschool three mornings a week, but is it worth the ongoing drama? Next year he may really enjoy it. And just because little Ben is using the potty chair does not mean that your toddler should be as well.

2. Brick walls

Whenever you come up against a brick wall, which can be a frequent occurrence with toddlers, ask yourself the following questions:

"Why am I so distressed?"

"Will it really matter in twenty years?"

Often concerns for many toddler problems are based on unsound reasons.

"Because that's what my mother did."

"Because everyone else's toddler is doing it."

"Because I'm so embarrassed."

"Because I read it in a book."

"Because I'm worried that he will never learn."

In many situations it's wise to step back and lose the urgency. When you are distressed and your toddler is comfortable, indifferent, or determined about whatever the issue is, he is unlikely to change. Toddlers tend to come around to doing many of the things we want them to do when they are ready.

And now, in alphabetical order for easy reference:

Puzzling behavior, frustrating but normal

Aggressive behavior

Biting, pulling hair, hitting, kicking, throwing toys at people.
Most common from nine months to three years.
Aggressive behavior is another of the less attractive features of the toddler years and can have parents despairing. But be reassured,

antisocial behavior in normal, healthy toddlers is not permanent and passes in time as their development expands and they are taught other ways of behaving. Learning the subtleties of standing up for one's rights in an effective way is a skill that takes years.

Aggressive and violent behavior cannot be ignored, but it is also wise to remember that hitting and biting are not always aggressive acts from the toddler's point of view. Biting may be the only way he feels he can deal with the situation. Sometimes, particularly with younger toddlers, it is experimental: "Hmm, what happens if I do that?"

Why?

- Experimentation (pulling mother's hair, biting mother's shoulder, throwing a toy in a fellow toddler's face, and so on). Experimental behavior of this nature is common in older babies and younger toddlers. There is no premeditation and no malice is intended.

- All the usual developmental reasons:
    Egocentricity
    Living in the present
    No understanding of cause and consequence
    Limited communication skills

- Remember, too, that temperament makes a difference to how toddlers respond to the situations they find themselves in.

- Overstimulation.

- Boredom.

- Being in social situations the toddler cannot handle (for example, where there are too many other toddlers, being somewhere for too long, inadequate adult supervision).

- Hunger, overtiredness.

- As a defense when feeling threatened or afraid (for example, a doctor's visit, immunization, having a bath, going for a haircut).

- Too many sudden changes to deal with (new baby, childcare, marriage breakup, chaos and unpredictability on the home front).

A FRAMEWORK TO WORK WITHIN

It is sometimes hard to work out whether it is more stressful being the mother of the aggressor or the mother of the victim. Both situations pose challenges.

A lot of aggressive behavior can be prevented or headed off at the pass

- When younger toddlers playfully nip your shoulder, pull your hair, pull your earrings out of their sockets, pat then slap your cheek, treat it seriously. Sit the toddler on the floor, give him a brief timeout and tell him firmly, "I don't like it when you do that." After thirty seconds, redirect him to another activity. Above all, don't laugh at behavior you want to discourage.

- Have realistic expectations about how long your toddler can be with other toddlers without resorting to grabbing, hitting, biting, or pushing. Take into account his age and personality when you arrange playtime with other toddlers, playgroup sessions, and, if possible, childcare arrangements.

- Make sure toddlers are adequately supervised. There is much more likelihood of aggressive acts when you leave toddlers playing alone while you write your novel or when all the adults at playgroup leave the toddlers and disappear into the kitchen for coffee and a gossip. The younger toddlers are, the more hands-on supervision they need.

    Supervision usually requires that you actively participate by talking to the toddlers from time to time and by redirecting their activities when necessary—but you also need to know when to stay out of things (tricky, comes with practice).

- When confronted with continuous conflict between toddlers, sometimes the only way to change things is to divert their attention to something new involving you—for example, a story, water play, music, a change of setting (off to the park)—or to take drastic action and call it a day and take your toddler home.

OTHER SUGGESTIONS

- During calm times, give older toddlers (eighteen months onward) ideas for alternatives to hitting, biting, throwing or punching. Teach your toddler to say, "I don't want to play any more," or "Stop throwing, it's my turn."

- Give attention to and reward nonaggressive behavior. Remember to pair the reward with an explicit reason: "I was very proud of you today, you played with Sam without hitting or throwing."

- Be a role model. Hitting, throwing things and losing it yourself teaches your child how to be aggressive.

- Look for reasons for the aggression. For example, lack of social technique to get what he wants, illness, tiredness, hunger.

Consequences

- Consequences for aggression must be immediate. Depending on the situation, use a reprimand first. A reprimand tells the toddler to **stop:** "Don't throw"; gives an **alternative:** "Come to me if you feel cross"; and gives a **reason:** "Throwing is dangerous." If the behavior continues, repeat the reprimand and give the toddler two or three minutes of timeout depending on his age.

- If another toddler has been hurt or the behavior continues despite the reprimand, comfort the hurt toddler, distract her with another activity or toy, and take your toddler aside. Give him a reprimand and timeout. Shaming him, humiliating him, or using physical violence is counterproductive and only encourages aggressive behavior. It is also counterproductive to endlessly go on about how upset the victim is is also counterproductive—your toddler is more concerned about your approval or disapproval than about how the other toddler feels.

- When he comes out of timeout give him a chance to fix things, but do not force him to apologize. Once toddlers are more familiar with one-on-one relationships and are given good examples at home of sharing and caring, apologies will eventually be given spontaneously, at which stage they mean much more than when they are repeated parrot fashion on demand.

- Once the episode is over, redirect your toddler to another activity. Avoid nagging and lecturing. Move on.

- Avoid putting pressure on other parents to take stronger action when their toddler is aggressive or allowing yourself to be pressured. Parents often end up spanking and verbally humiliating their toddler to make him apologize against their better judgment because of the disapproving mutterings and body language of other parents.

A few words about biting

From a toddler's point of view, biting is no worse than hitting, kicking, pushing or punching. From an adult's point of view, biting is a particularly heinous crime and many parents secretly think that biting is a sign of a serious flaw in the toddler and his parents. Panic about biting has increased in recent times with the tendency to overstate and exaggerate the potential risk of HIV and Hepatitis B from a toddler bite.

Biting other toddlers is the preferred action of a percentage of all toddlers when they are angry, frustrated, thwarted, jealous, or just generally upset. The framework for dealing with this is the same as for aggression, but if you know your toddler is likely to bite under certain circumstances, here is some additional information:

- Contrary to popular opinion, biting is not a sign of "teething" but an intentional experimental/defensive/aggressive/emotional action common among toddlers. Biting tends to disappear over time, but preschool children and even older children sometimes bite when antagonized.

  Occasionally biting is an emotional response to weaning from the breast, the arrival of a new baby, or any sudden life change the toddler finds difficult to adjust to, but mostly the reasons are similar to any of the other aggressive acts toddlers are prone to.

- Younger "bitey" toddlers, who may be missing the breast, may be helped to stop biting by being given something to bite on when they need to. They still need to be reprimanded and given timeout when they bite other humans.

- Let other parents know your toddler may bite and remain ever vigilant to avoid it whenever possible. Sadly, biting has the potential to break up even the closest of friends, which is more an indication of the shortcomings of adults than toddlers.

- Biting discipline does *not* require hysterical outbursts, humiliation of the biter, or spanking. Nor does it require biting back which is demeaning for the parent and teaches the toddler that biting is okay if you get mad enough.

Aggressive with toys

Most common age from fifteen months to two years (preverbal).
Toddlers sometimes take out their anger and frustration on their toys. It can be quite alarming to see your toddler bite dolly or beat teddy's head on the floor, but acting out their feelings with toys is one way toddlers come to grips with managing some of the powerful emotions they are experiencing.

A FRAMEWORK TO WORK WITHIN

- Paying attention to the behavior is likely to escalate it, so pretend to ignore.

- Redirect his activity when you can: "Put dolly to bed now. We are going out."

- Give *mild* attention—a comment in passing—when dolly is being treated nicely: "Lucky dolly, getting a kiss."

Occasionally aggressive behavior with toys is an indication of something the toddler has witnessed at childcare or some other venue. It can be difficult pursuing such possibilities, especially before the toddler has much speech, but if it seems this might be the case, it is probably a good idea to make some discreet inquiries.

Badly behaved for parents, well behaved for others

Most common from one year to four years, but common on and off forever.
Most parents have tales of how well behaved and compliant their toddlers are for others and how uncooperative they are for them.

"He always sleeps at daycare but never will for me."

"He eats all his lunch for my mother but won't eat a thing for me."

"He was so good for Sally, then the minute I appeared, he threw a monumental tantrum."

It's extremely frustrating but normal.

Why?

Toddlers have a unique emotional connection with their parents. You are the most important person in your toddler's life, and it is from you that he learns what to do. You are the one he relies upon to protect him and to help him through the hard times as he learns to regulate his behavior. With you he does not have to be on his guard. He can experiment with ways of communicating that are both pleasant and unpleasant, knowing that he will always be accepted even if his behavior is not. Most of the time he has nothing to gain from testing other adults he is with for relatively short periods and who do not have an emotional investment in him. He does not know whether he can trust them the way he trusts you.

A FRAMEWORK TO WORK WITHIN

- Ignore unhelpful comments that question your abilities as a parent: "I don't know why you have so much trouble, William always eats his lunch for me, even the brussels sprouts."
- Remember that your toddler needs to be able to behave badly with someone who loves him dearly and whom he trusts in order to learn the difference between acceptable and unacceptable behavior.

Breath holding

Most common from around twelve months to four years. Peak time for blue attacks (type 1) is during the second year.

Why?

About five percent of toddlers hold their breath; however, there are two different types of breath holding with a different reason for each.

1. THE BLUE ATTACK

Three-quarters of all breath holding is a response to being thwarted, a mostly soundless tantrum where the toddler gives a few loud screeches, then passes out, going blue and silent. Very scary.

Fortunately, the breathing switches to automatic and continues. The toddler returns to consciousness within twenty seconds.

A FRAMEWORK TO WORK WITHIN

- Blue attacks in a healthy toddler as part of a tantrum do not cause damage unless the toddler hurts himself on the way to the floor.

- If necessary, help him avoid injury by moving him somewhere safe before he lands; otherwise pretend to ignore it. Stay nearby, but as soon as he gains consciousness, move away and go about your business.

- When he comes to, refrain from discussing it. Blue attacks are essentially a rather dramatic attention-seeking device. The less attention they receive, the fewer there will be.

- Do not change your limit setting or house rules to accommodate blue attacks.

- If you find you are very anxious after the first episode, take your toddler to have a thorough medical check with a pediatrician. Blue attacks are easier to ignore when you are assured of a clean bill of health.

- Blue attacks cease around four years.

2. THE WHITE ATTACK

A quarter of breath-holding attacks are in response to fear or injury.

The toddler will go limp and pale and fall to the ground as if in a faint. Unlike the blue attack, he does not screech or hold his breath. It is thought that toddlers who have white attacks may grow up to be adults who faint easily at the sight of blood, when having minor surgical procedures, or when having injections.

A FRAMEWORK TO WORK WITHIN

- Leave him lying flat until he recovers. Recovery is quick.

- If the attack is the result of a genuine fear or of being hurt, cuddle and reassure him, but don't overcompensate for his sensitivity.

- Have a thorough medical checkup if you are unsure of the reason for these attacks.

Car-seat refusal

Most common between nine months and four years (can be an on-again off-again behavior).

Why?

Who knows exactly why?

Toddlers don't enjoy being strapped down and immobilized. The precise reason probably varies from toddler to toddler.

THERE ARE MANY DEVELOPMENTAL REASONS

- His expanding physical skills mean that he wants to be constantly on the move. Staying in one place for any length of time is difficult for him; it is also a threat to his blossoming independence.

- He has no real understanding of why he has to be restricted in such a fashion.

- Limit testing is at its peak. He figures if he protests a lot, you might give in.
- He doesn't have any idea how long this restriction is going to be imposed upon him.

Other reasons might include:

- He doesn't like the smell of the car.
- It's boring sitting strapped down for any length of time.
- He gets carsick.

As cars are so much a part of our daily life, toddlers eventually adjust to car travel and to being strapped in. It is an area where no options are available, so parents must remain firm and consistent (remember, patience is a virtue!). Sometimes car journeys have to be restricted until toddlers can manage to sit without protesting for a reasonable length of time.

Temperament plays a large role in how toddlers take to car travel. Some will sit happily for hours, which makes long drives possible; others start to complain loudly after they have been sitting for twenty minutes. As it is difficult to drive safely for any length of time with a crescendo going on in the back seat, long-distance travel sometimes has to be avoided until the toddler adapts.

A FRAMEWORK TO WORK WITHIN

- Check that he is as comfortable as possible and that the car-seat, straps, and buckle are correctly adjusted and not too tight or rubbing on bare skin.
- Have realistic expectations. Factor his resistance into your daily living and holiday plans. Waiting for a miracle to happen means it is more likely you will become frustrated and angry. Accept that for an undetermined time there will nearly always be a struggle. Plan your movements as much as possible to avoid last-minute flurries. The more flustered you get, the worse the struggle becomes.

- State a simple rule every time you buckle him in: "Gabriel, you must always have your seat belt on before we can drive." Say it again when you put your belt on (even if it is with gritted teeth).

- Tell him what you want him to do, not what you don't want him to do. "Gabriel, I want you to hold teddy while I do the buckle up."

- Avoid the use of punishment, threats, or bribery. They will only escalate the behavior, make you very tense, and will not encourage him to behave differently.

- Reward him every time he doesn't struggle and sits quietly. Always accompany the reward verbally, telling him exactly why he is getting the reward. A reward might be a cuddle and a warm acknowledgment. For example, a big hug and "I'm so proud of you sitting still in the car seat while I buckled you up. Thank you, Gabriel."

Clinginess—the excessive kind

Most common from nine months to two and a half years.
Some older babies and toddlers up to age two (at which time it usually starts to diminish) are clingy in a way that makes them very hard to live with. If they are not receiving constant attention, they whine, want to be picked up, or scream.

Why?

As well as all the reasons given for fear of separation on pages 152–3, excessive clinginess may also be due to:

- Illness, so it's always a good idea to have your toddler checked by your family doctor—especially his ears.

- Temperament.

- Late walking or delayed development. Late walking (eighteen months to age two) in otherwise normal toddlers is within the normal range, but the toddler's lack of mobility is sometimes a cause of excessive clingy behavior. If you are concerned about your toddler's development, seek advice.

- A new baby, childcare, family turmoil, or a sudden change of environment.

A FRAMEWORK TO WORK WITHIN

Excessive clinginess is hard to live with. Sometimes parents unwittingly do things to encourage the clinginess because it is the easiest and most peaceful option at the time. The toddler is given lots of attention for being clingy, such as being picked up, taken to the toilet with his mother where he is allowed to sit on her lap, carried from room to room, and, even if it is in a negative way, constantly acknowledged for the clinginess. The mother is so fed-up that very little time ends up being spent doing positive things together, such as reading a story or playing with the blocks. The trick is to reverse the situation. It is not easy, but it is not impossible.

Here are some suggestions

- It is often helpful to think about the reasons why you feel you cannot do anything about some of the most burdensome aspects of the clinginess. Usually it comes down to a lack of confidence arising out of a fear of damaging your toddler psychologically. Maybe it's because of something you read about attachment or bonding or perhaps because of something related to your own childhood. Perhaps it's because of your lifestyle or because you have no support. These are only suggestions. Sometimes it helps to talk things over with a professional.

  In the meantime, here is a pep talk.
- It is normal for toddlers to experience problems with separation,

but that does not mean your toddler has to be with you and on you every minute of the day. You are the parent and in charge. In as fair and reasonable a way as possible, it is fine to take the initiative in helping your toddler to understand what is acceptable and what isn't in your daily life together.

Teaching him to separate will involve some conflict. It is tempting to do anything to avoid conflict, but, in the end, you will become increasingly resentful and your toddler will become increasingly clingy. He needs you to show him what to do.

- Try to identify one aspect of the clinginess that you find particularly hard to live with and start by working on that.

For example, having to take your toddler with you when you take a shower or when you go to the toilet because he screams blue murder when you leave him is very tedious. It is something you can change. Tell him that he cannot come with you, you won't be long, and if he wants to scream, that's okay. Put him somewhere safe and do what you have to do. If necessary, warn the neighbours about the yelling. Stay calm and above all stay consistent once you have decided on your plan of action. When you emerge, give him a hug and tell him again that this is how it is going to be from now on.

Give him a reward the first time he lets you go without a fuss. Build on your achievement.

- Ignore as much of the clinging behavior as you can and give lots of positive attention and a reward when he plays alone for a while.

- Try to arrange for some time off for yourself, even if it's only for an hour every few days. He will not be damaged psychologically if he is left for an hour with someone suitable, even if he does yell the whole time you are gone (this may not be the case for the caregiver though!).

- Eventually he will learn that you always come back, and he may even start to enjoy himself in your absence.

Destroying books

Most common from nine months to two years.

Why?

They enjoy it. They have access to books they can destroy. It passes with time as parents teach respect and love for books.

A FRAMEWORK TO WORK WITHIN

- Provide board or plastic books for your toddler to play with.
- Always supervise when your toddler has access to other books.
- Give a brief reprimand. Show your toddler how to mend the book with sticky tape.
- Encourage older toddlers (over three) to mend books themselves when there is accidental damage.

Pacifiers

Most common from birth to age five (even the most committed pacifier-users give them away once school starts).

Why?

They enjoy having a pacifier; it gives them comfort.

A FRAMEWORK TO WORK WITHIN

Parents are often pressured to make their toddler throw away the pacifier but persuading a reluctant toddler to relinquish the pacifier is easier said than done. As it is unlikely to be without some drama, it is advisable to consider why you think the pacifier has to go.

Sometimes the benefits of being pacifier-free outweigh the

trauma of bidding it goodbye, but at other times the benefits are negligible and do not warrant the heartache.

LET'S LOOK AT THE INVALID REASONS FIRST

- Because of pressure from relatives and friends.
- Because you don't like the look of it.
- Because you think it will look funny when he graduates from college.
- Because it will push out his teeth (see thumb sucking).
- Because you are sick of buying new pacifiers (live with it).

AND NOW SOME VALID REASONS

- Prolonged use of pacifiers in a small number of toddlers contributes to excessive dribbling late into the second year as the posture of the mouth with the pacifier in situ interferes with optimum muscular development around the mouth and encourages tongue thrusting. Part of the treatment to stop the dribbling involves removing the pacifier. This is discussed in more detail on page 208

- The pacifier is causing ongoing night sleeping problems because it comes out every few hours and you have to go and put it back. This is more likely to be the case for younger toddlers (twelve to fifteen months), as older toddlers can put their own pacifiers back. For more information on your options for night waking, see page 228.

- The pacifier is starting to seriously affect your sanity—you can't stand the endless looking for it and the emotional dependence your toddler seems to have on it. You feel so strongly about it that you can't ignore it, and the constant nagging is making your toddler more attached to it. Scenes are common because it keeps getting lost and everyone is paralyzed until it is found. Any advantages it may have once had are now grossly outweighed by its disadvantages.

How do you do it?

There are two main ways of bidding the pacifier farewell: **nicely** and **not so nicely**. Both methods require you to mean what you say and stay consistent. Remember, it is never a good idea to remove pacifiers in association with the arrival of a new baby, major changes in daily life such as childcare, parental separation, or in time of illness. Do it before or well after the event.

If it is in association with night waking, see page 239.

1. Nicely

Swap the pacifier for a prearranged reward at a department store. Plan the event and make it into a little growing-up ceremony. The toddler is presented with the reward after the pacifier is handed over to the nice store attendant. After the event, the pacifier *never* returns. This is suitable for older toddlers (two and a half to three) whose thinking abilities have expanded enough to understand the plan, think ahead a little, and know what is entailed.

2. Not so nicely

It is not ideal to seize the pacifier, angrily cut it up, and throw it out in front of a screaming toddler as it will make the event much more significant than it deserves to be. It will also make you feel guilty and go out and buy six brand-new top-of-the-line pacifiers.

Plan the removal ahead of time. Pick a time when your toddler is well and you and your partner are available to keep him occupied.

Give your toddler a simple explanation, make the pacifiers disappear at a suitable time, and never let them return.

Avoid making a big issue of the event, ignore whining as much as possible, and stay confident. Mean what you say; you are in charge. Your toddler will follow your lead. After a few busy days, the pacifier will be forgotten.

And you can enjoy your pacifier-free life.

Endless questions

Most common from two and a half to four years.

Why?

- The toddler's insatiable need to figure things out and find out how things work and what goes with what.
- A way of practicing language skills.
- Attention seeking.

A FRAMEWORK TO WORK WITHIN

- It's usually obvious when the questions are genuine and when they are merely being used as an attention-seeking device.
- When it's attention seeking, answer once, then pretend to ignore. If the questions relate to a disciplinary matter, avoid getting into convoluted circular conversations. "Because I said so" is a good enough answer to "But why?" if your first short but clear answer fell on deaf ears.

Fears

The specific fears listed below are the most common ones experienced by toddlers between one and three years (see pages 93–95 for general information about fears). Most fears of this age disappear with maturity. For night terrors and nightmares, see the section on sleep on page 245.

There could well be a host of other fears which I have not included in the list of specific fears, as the potential range is endless, but there are some general guidelines for all fears:

- Acknowledge that the fears are real to your toddler. Even if you feel that they are ridiculous and irritating, brushing them off, making fun of them, or pretending they don't exist will increase the fears and make your toddler more anxious. Until his memory and cognitive abilities expand, the fears are real and reasonable to him.

- If your toddler's language development permits, ask him to talk about his fears. Use direct questions so that you don't introduce the possibility of another round of separate fears. "Are you scared?" "What are you scared of?" "Sophie, tell me what happened to frighten you."

- Give a very simple explanation of the fear and if possible a demonstration of the mechanics when you and your toddler are both calm; for example, show him that the rubber duck can't fit down the drain in the bathtub. Talking openly about the fear helps toddlers see the difference between fact and fantasy.

- Think before you indulge in Halloween tricks or birthday novelties that go bang, and consider the effect household gadgets might have on toddlers when they are suddenly exposed to them without warning.

- Monsters in the bedroom are a common fear. Searching the room to demonstrate that there is nothing there is not helpful as it negates the toddler's experience. It is better to acknowledge the monster exists but that Mommy and Daddy don't allow monsters inside and they have asked him to leave.

- Encourage your toddler to use his teddy or security object as protection against the fear.

- Accept that there are going to be times when things have to proceed despite the fears. For example, immunization, visits to the doctor, having hair washed, or being left with a babysitter. Avoid sounding anxious and behaving in a fearful manner. Stay confident while giving support and comfort, but do what has to be done.

- When the fear involves things like fear of the tub, the toilet, the vacuum cleaner, or dogs, the best approach is to gently and gradually desensitize the fear over time.

Specific fears

1. Bath refusal

Most common from age twelve months to two and a half years.
A very common occurrence that passes with time.

Why?

- They are frightened. Fear of the bathtub is a common toddler fear, quite irrational to us but very real to the toddler. Until his thinking skills develop, he doesn't know for sure that he won't disappear down the drain with the water.
- Other reasons may include a bad experience with soap in the eyes, slipping and falling, bumping his head on the faucet or water too hot or too cold, but it's usually not as clear-cut as this.
- Attention seeking (occasionally).
- Testing limits (occasionally).

A FRAMEWORK TO WORK WITHIN

- Forcing a frightened toddler to have a bath is counterproductive. Try and treat it as no big deal and wash him from a bowl or a bucket. Some toddlers will shower with a parent. Gradually see if you can persuade him back to the bath, but stay low-key. All toddlers eventually get back into the bath, and the less fuss and attention that is brought to bear, the sooner it will happen.

- Avoid long conversations with others about your toddler's bathing habits within his hearing.

- If he is using bathtime to test limits or seek attention, be firm and consistent about what you want him to do. Give positive attention when he cooperates.

- Make sure you have everything ready for a smooth operation. Let him choose a bath toy or a special soap. Remember to keep choices to one out of two or he will spend all evening working out which towel he wants from the linen closet.

- Give him plenty of warning before you start.

- Use a positive voice and tell him what you want him to do, not what you don't want him to do.

2. Hair-washing refusal

Most common from fifteen months to two and a half years.

A very common occurrence that passes with time.

Why?

- They are frightened or have had a previous bad experience with soap in their eyes or their head under the water.

- Resistance to something they don't enjoy.

A FRAMEWORK TO WORK WITHIN

- Unfortunately hair has to be washed *sometime*. Once a week is sufficient.

- Make it quick. If you think his hair needs conditioner, use an all-in-one conditioner and shampoo.

- Keep his hair short (if he is not frightened of having it cut, of course).

- Maybe try a shampoo guard (like a sunshade) and if possible a handheld water spray.

- If you have to wash his hair over the sink because he is afraid of the bathtub and the shower, wait until you have another person there to help you.

- Prepare everything before you start and give a running commentary on what you are doing as you proceed, even if he is yelling his head off.

3. Fear of separation

Most common from twelve months to two years. Fear of separation from one or both of their parents is normal for all toddlers in varying degrees from around seven months to age three, occasionally even beyond. Separation anxiety can start as early as three months, but the height of the fear is between nine and eighteen months.

Temperament plays a large role in the intensity and extent of the anxiety. Some babies and toddlers appear to breeze through this stage with barely a murmur, while others are noticeably distressed. The level of distress varies from manageable levels to the clingy toddler who can't bear his mother being out of his sight for a minute. He follows her from room to room, accompanies her to the bathroom, winds himself around her legs, and constantly wants to be picked up.

Rumor has it that if you leave babies with other people from a young age and give them plenty of experiences of new faces and places it is possible to avoid separation anxiety. I find in my work that while this might help avoid separation fears to some extent, it doesn't necessarily make a great deal of difference to how toddlers react to separating from their parents. In the same family where the environment is similar for all children, one toddler may be incredibly clingy and another one may be fine.

Fear of separation reveals itself in a variety of ways

- Clingy behavior—not letting you out of his sight.
- Wanting to be carried, to hold your hand, to sit on your lap.
- Wary of other people.
- Regresses in some areas, baby behavior.
- Whines a lot.
- Night waking, wanting to be with you.
- Difficulty going to bed.
- Distress or even panic at mother or father's absence.

Why?

- Limited memory (until around eighteen months, he does not understand the concept that an object still exists even if he can't see it).
- Lives in the present. Cannot grasp the fact that he will see you again later.
- Egocentrism—believes that you exist for him.

- His increased independence gives him feelings of exhilaration on the one hand and insecurity on the other. His increasing mobility makes him aware that if he can move away from you, then you can move away from him. This is potentially alarming for him and explains the increase in clinginess, tantrums, and whining that often accompanies a spurt in gross motor skills.

- His cognitive development has expanded enough for him to tell the difference between places and people and to compare and judge them, so he knows when things are not the way he wants them to be.

A FRAMEWORK TO WORK WITHIN
Accept the inevitable

- Fear of separation is a part of life for many toddlers and is a normal developmental process which they (and you) have to go through. You can't make it painlessly disappear. You can support and encourage your toddler while he comes to terms with the inevitability of separation by keeping his environment stable, giving him plenty of positive attention when you are together, and remaining confident and firm while he adjusts.

- Fear of separation is *not* a signal to stop leaving your toddler with other people if you want to (for social reasons, time off, appointments, shopping, part-time work or study). The repeated experience of your absence and return teaches him that he can adapt.

- Nor should separation fears night and nocturnal visits if you want to change your methods of handling.

- Nor should it discourage you from weaning a reluctant toddler if that is what you want.

Plan the first separation beforehand

- Acknowledge your own feelings—"I can hardly wait," "I'm not sure I want to do this," "I feel really guilty," or "I feel really anxious about this"—so you can get used to the feelings and, on the surface at least, be cheerful, calm, and confident when the time comes. Tell your toddler clearly and simply what is happening. Use short sentences.

- Help your toddler familiarize himself with the caregiver and the surroundings before you leave him.

When you leave

- Remind him what you will do together when you are reunited—"I'll pick you up and we'll go home and have a bath together."

- Avoid being hesitant or sounding doubtful when you leave. Do not linger; leave confidently.

- Never disappear without saying goodbye and telling him that you are leaving. It may seem easier in the beginning but disappearing in a puff of smoke will destroy his trust and make him more anxious.

- Avoid leaving your toddler abruptly and unprepared in unfamiliar surroundings with unfamiliar people unless it's an emergency.

Prolonged separations need to be given serious consideration, but there is no doubt that many toddlers can be happily left for a few days or a week with a familiar relative (grandma again) in familiar surroundings. A lot depends on the toddler's temperament and the intensity of his separation fears. It's not a good idea to leave toddlers who are having a difficult time separating for long periods until they are happier about the idea. Some toddlers are around three before this happens.

155

What about the toddlers who experience intense distress at being separated?

- Great patience is needed and, if possible, flexibility in relation to childcare for work purposes.

- It is better to try leaving him for short periods (an hour or so) frequently rather than leaving him less often for a whole morning or afternoon.

Unfortunately the perception in today's society is that it is somehow abnormal for a toddler to be very reluctant to separate. I acknowledge that a clinging, upset toddler who doesn't want to be with anyone other than his mother can be irritating and restrictive for the parents; however, all things being equal, it is normal. Expecting toddlers to be joyful about the opportunity to socialize and have time away from their parents is more about the hopes of adults with busy lives than the toddlers' preference.

Most of the normal, healthy toddlers in secure homes who do experience intense anxiety will separate by around three if they are allowed to do it gradually, in their own time.

Getting his own back—the cold shoulder or the emotional collapse on your return

It's not unusual for toddlers to greet their parents' return with disinterest (pretending to ignore) or even anger after their "abandonment." Increased clinging, increased tantrums, and perhaps later the surfacing of other fears (the bath, bedtime and night waking) may follow temporarily. Some toddlers simply collapse in a heap of tears, and others have a joyous reunion with no aftereffects. All these responses are normal.

- Acknowledge your toddler's feelings and tell him how much you missed him. Give him extra hugs and attention, but avoid transferring your guilty or anxious feelings to him.

- At home be available, but continue with your normal routine and limit setting—don't let the system collapse. Remember that routine, structure, and firm, reasonable limits help toddlers to feel secure.

Head banging

Most common from nine months to two years.

Why?

Head banging is often associated with developmentally delayed toddlers and toddlers who are emotionally deprived, so parents tend to view it with some alarm. However, most toddlers who indulge in head banging are normal in every way and bang their heads for the following reasons:

1. As part of a temper tantrum when thwarted.

2. To attract attention.

3. Out of habit.

4. As a soothing technique to get off to sleep.

5. Sudden head banging and a restless toddler may indicate illness (ear infection, for example).

Head banging passes in time.

A FRAMEWORK TO WORK WITHIN

1. As part of a temper tantrum

Most toddlers do not hurt themselves when they bang their heads as part of a temper tantrum. However, if your toddler is in danger of hurting himself, tell him that you can't let him hurt himself, move him to a safe spot, then pretend to ignore. Stay calm yourself.

2. To attract attention

Pretend to ignore. Minimize boredom. Give positive attention to behaviors you want to encourage; for example, looking at books, playing with toys, listening to music, drawing, and so on (depending on age).

3. Out of habit

Pretend to ignore. Divert to other activities. Remember to give positive attention to behaviors you want to encourage.

4. As a soothing technique to get off to sleep

Pad up the crib and pretend to ignore.

5. Sudden head banging and a whining toddler

Consult your pediatrician. Have the toddler's ears checked.

It is very unusual for a normal, healthy toddler to harm himself from head banging when the behavior stems from these listed reasons. Occasionally, however, head banging is a genuine expression of frustration, even despair, and will go on until the toddler hurts himself. Ignoring this sort of head banging is inappropriate and it is advisable to seek help.

Interrupting conversations and phone calls

Most common from fifteen months until the child leaves home (in my experience).

Why?

- A powerful attention-seeking device
- Egocentrism
- Boredom

A FRAMEWORK TO WORK WITHIN

- Have realistic expectations. This is normal behavior for toddlers and to some extent children of any age. Long conversations with other adults, whether it's on the phone or over lunch, are not possible with toddlers around unless they have something riveting to occupy them or they are asleep. Unfortunately when you get off the phone you may find that what kept him so occupied was not worth the phone call.

- Plan for interruptions, particularly if you are visiting a child-free home. Rather than try to converse over the toddler, arrange to go for a walk to the local park where the toddler is more easily distracted.

- Child-free friends who visit you should understand that as long as the toddler is around and busy, he will take center stage and it is no longer possible to have the one-on-ones you once enjoyed until he goes down for his nap. Some people need reminding of this—friendships have dissipated over less.

- If you are invited to a daytime function in a child-free house, it is polite to check whether your toddler is welcome. Groups of adults are not always happy about the constant attention most toddlers expect as their due.

- Make your lengthy phone calls when your toddler is asleep or not around.

Masturbation, sexual curiosity

Most common from six months and forever more.

Parents usually become aware of their toddler's sexual curiosity around eighteen months to four years. During these years, toddlers are uninhibited and up-front about their sexual activities. They explore and play with their own genitals, and ask questions and compare their equipment with their friends' and their parents'.

Why?

They want to know more about these parts of their bodies and what they can do. They are especially curious about the difference between girls and boys. And masturbating feels nice—toddlers often use it as a way to comfort themselves.

A FRAMEWORK TO WORK WITHIN

People are more comfortable these days about sexual behavior, thank goodness. Most parents know, in theory at least, that it's best to stay relaxed about it and not get too upset when they stumble across the odd game of doctors and nurses.

But often there's still that little twinge of doubt, and some parents have trouble accepting that it really is harmless if their daughter keeps riding the rocking horse in a state of wild excitement, obviously rubbing her clitoris on the horse's back as she rocks. Or their son has his hands down his pajama pants and is playing with his penis as he watches *Playschool*. Or they find their daughter and the neighbor's son naked in the playhouse, playing doctors.

Is it really all right? Yes.

Here are a few suggestions

- Answer any questions about body parts simply and honestly without providing any more information than your toddler has asked for. Call body parts by their correct names.

- Avoid overreacting to masturbation, games with friends, and experiments with body parts (little girls sometimes like to put things into their vaginas). If you think it is appropriate, redirect their activities in a matter-of-fact way.

- Try not to sound nervous, disapproving, or flustered when you answer questions or interrupt masturbation or sexual games.

- Teach your toddler about privacy and the best places to do things. For example, jumping and running feels great, but it's best to do that outside. Or playing with your penis feels nice, but it's best to do that in your bedroom. And picking your nose is best done in private too.

- Excessive masturbation may be caused by:

  An overload of stress and excitement. Think of ways to reduce it.

  Too much negative attention being paid to the habit.

Nail biting

Most common from three years onward.

Why?

- They enjoy it.
- It becomes a habit.
- Guarantees attention from adults.

A FRAMEWORK TO WORK WITHIN

- Many children bite their fingernails on and off during the school years. It is not usually a sign of anxiety or insecurity in itself.

- Doing nothing and pretending to ignore is the only sensible course of action. Constantly drawing attention to the nail biting reinforces the behavior, as does putting nasty stuff on the nails and gloves on at night.

Nose picking

Most common from two and a half onward.

Why?

- Because they enjoy it.
- Because it becomes a habit.
- Because it guarantees attention from adults.
- Occasionally excessive nose picking may be due to an irritation of the lining of the nose due to allergic rhinitis (hay fever). If you're worried, talk it over with your pediatrician.

A FRAMEWORK TO WORK WITHIN

- All toddlers and children pick their nose and do disgusting things with the contents (so do some adults).
- Overreaction encourages the habit.
- Divert or redirect activity when appropriate or suggest they do it in private.

Preferring one parent

Most common from eighteen months to four years.

It is very common for toddlers to treat their parents differently and at times to show a preference for one or the other. The preference shifts from time to time, so don't panic if it seems your toddler loves his dad more than you or vice versa. Sometimes the preference is for the one he spends less time with (novelty value) and sometimes it's for the one who does most of the day-to-day caring (usually the mother). Or it might be for the exciting parent who rides the motorbike. Or perhaps for the one who reads the best stories.

Toddlers often give the hardest time to the parent they feel they can depend upon most because they are more familiar with and confident of that parent's response when they test the limits and behave in challenging ways. Try not to take it personally and keep a united front. It passes in time.

Sometimes parent preference becomes exaggerated and starts to cause major difficulties when toddlers refuse to be left with one parent, won't go to sleep or eat for one parent, and so on.

Why?

- Attention seeking.

- Emotional manipulation (don't panic; experimenting with emotional manipulation is a normal way for toddlers to try to get the people they love to do what they want).

- Novelty factor (the toddler suddenly realizes that the other parent exists and has his/her own particular charms).

- One parent is responsible for *all* the care.

- One parent is never around.

- Overreaction by the parents—the toddler is being rewarded for the behavior.

A FRAMEWORK TO WORK WITHIN

- Remain a team and try not undermine each other. Anger and disagreement over the issue will escalate the behavior.

- Don't take your toddler's yelling or comments to heart. Remember, toddlers have a limited capacity for expressing themselves, and yelling "I want Daddy" is the only way they know how to communicate what they want.

- Arrange for the toddler to have special time with the preferred parent, but also arrange for routine tasks to be shared more evenly and consistently by both parents, even if there is a fuss initially.

- Stay calm, especially if you are temporarily the unpopular parent. Think of ways to make your time with the toddler in the other parent's absence more fun. Refrain from long stories of disaster within your toddler's hearing range, when your partner returns from tennis.

Pulling out hair (trichotillomania)

All ages.

Why?

A common habit among babies, toddlers, and children of all ages, the cause of which varies from a self-comforting, enjoyable habit (similar to nail biting) to stress and developmental reasons in older children and adolescents.

Hair pulling in toddlers is usually a self-comforting habit that accompanies thumb sucking and which may have started in babyhood.

A FRAMEWORK TO WORK WITHIN

- In otherwise happy, healthy toddlers, the more attention paid to the hair pulling, the more likely it is to continue. Pretend to ignore as much as possible. Hair pulling does not cause permanent hair loss.

- Hair pulling is more likely when your toddler is bored, watching television, tired, or just before falling asleep. It may help to give your toddler something that feels like hair to hold between his fingers; for example, satin ribbons, a feather, a piece of velvet, or a soft hairy animal (not a real one . . .).

Resistance to teeth cleaning and nail cutting

Most common from twelve months to two and a half years.
Passes in time as development expands.

Why?

The usual developmental reasons:

- Negativity, assertion of self.

- No understanding of the "why," only appreciates what is happening right now and knows that he doesn't want to cooperate, thank you very much. The possibility of grubby teeth, bad breath, and black nails does not worry him in the slightest. The problem is entirely yours.

A FRAMEWORK TO WORK WITHIN

Teeth cleaning

- Yes, ideally teeth should be cleaned as soon as they arrive, but the reality of cleaning a struggling toddler's teeth properly twice a day before the age of two, even two and a half, is daunting for most parents. But if the teeth cleaning starts to assume nightmare proportions, consider once a day instead of twice a day—perhaps even once or twice a week until age brings more reason.

- It may help to demonstrate by showing him what good fun it is when you do it.

- If he is very resistant to allowing you to do it, let him do it himself without taking over. I realize that from a cleaning point of view this is next to useless, but it may help him see reason eventually.

- Perhaps allowing him to "clean" yours before you clean his might encourage him to cooperate. Can you stand it?

- Cleaning his teeth in the bathtub might work.
- The more urgent you become and the more attention you pay to his resistance, the more important it will become to him not to cooperate. Stay cool.

I'm on a roll here—how many more dot points do you want? Here's one more . . .

- The main line of defense against black teeth in the first two years is the right diet. Sugar is the main offender. Remember sugar is sugar whether it is brown, "natural" (whatever that means), honey, or white. Other forms of sugar are found in milk and fruit juice. Pacifiers dipped in sweet things and around-the-clock bottles cause dental decay. Apart from water, all other drinks in bottles are a potential problem when they are sucked for a large part of the day or night. This includes fruit juice. Other major contributors are sticky "natural" fruit bars, soft drinks, and so on . . . you know what they are.

For more info and tips on the actual cleaning, see page 209.

Nail cutting

- Do it when he's asleep.

Screeching and screaming

Most common from nine months to two years.

Why?
- They enjoy it.
- To test their voices and their range of sound.
- To attract attention.
- Because they are bored.

166

- Because they are excited.
- Because it becomes a habit.

It passes with time.

A FRAMEWORK TO WORK WITHIN

- Be a role model; resist screeching and screaming yourself.
- Ignore behavior you wish to discourage.
- Teach your toddler what a whisper sounds like.
- Teach him about indoor and outdoor voices.
- Give positive acknowledgment for screech-free periods.
- Minimize boredom.

Security objects

Most common from one year up to school age. Peak time is between one and two years.

It's common for many toddlers to have a special comforter (blanket, cuddly, teddy, piece of mother's clothing) which they take to bed and carry around with them. An object they can touch, feel, and smell links them with their parents even when they are not present. Not all toddlers use comforters, so it's not a sign that something's wrong if your toddler doesn't have one. Nor is it a sign of lack of love and attention from you if he does.

Comforters are used in many different ways. They can be played with and slept with. Or dropped and forgotten and reclaimed when needed.

Why?

- As well as helping toddlers feel secure, security objects are a part of their lives they can control.

- Comforters are a concrete way of helping toddlers reconcile their urge to be independent with their need for love and security. Armed with their blanket or teddy, they can face the world.

A FRAMEWORK TO WORK WITHIN

- It can be inconvenient if your toddler insists on the comforter being with him every second of the day, so encourage him to leave it behind or in the car when you are out somewhere where there are plenty of other things for him to think about.

- It's also a good idea to get him used to a cuddly or a blanket being washed at regular intervals and to have a few identical comforters around for replacement purposes when the originals get worn out or lost.

- Pacifiers and bottles are also comforters, but sometimes there are problems with their use. Use of pacifiers and bottles during the toddler years is discussed in various sections throughout the book.

Sharing or refusing to

Most common from fifteen months to three years; but let's face it, sharing is something most of us have to work at all our lives.
Once toddlers are more familiar with one-on-one relationships and are given good examples of sharing and caring at home, the abrupt refusals to share and the feeling that everything in the world belongs to them fades—up to a point.

Why?

All the usual developmental reasons:

- Egocentricity.

- Inability to put themselves in the place of another; cannot understand another's feelings or see their perspective.

- Initially humans develop a sense of themselves through their possessions—that is why everything is "mine."

- Concrete thinking predominates (the concept of sharing requires abstract thinking).

- Individual temperaments contribute to the degree of possessiveness toddlers feel during these years.

A FRAMEWORK TO WORK WITHIN

- Be realistic. Toddlers do not understand the concept of sharing. It starts to form around two and a half to three years and remains a difficult area for quite some time after that.

- In order to learn to share, your toddler needs to learn what things are his and to feel secure about them ("his" mommy and daddy, for example, "his" special spoon, "his" blanky). It is reasonable for him to have one or two special toys which he does not have to share (put them away when visitors come).

- Toddlers can be encouraged to share, but it should not be forced upon them. The long-term goal is to help the toddler feel less possessive and ready to share *inside*. Sharing, like apologizing, is best when it becomes more or less voluntary (a little nudging here and there is to be expected).

- Have a few rules about toys when conflict occurs. If there is no conflict, do not intervene.

Sample rules

- The toddler who has the toy first keeps it to play with.
- Time for the toy is limited if other toddlers want that toy (often toddlers only want a particular toy because someone else has it—when they get it, they lose interest).
- Ongoing unresolved conflict over a toy might be best managed by removing the toy.

• Playtimes with other toddlers have a tendency to become emotionally fraught when outbreaks of possessiveness occur and may not be the best times for teaching about sharing. The most successful lessons come from within the home in calm situations. Parents should model the sharing behavior they want to encourage and teach toddlers in concrete ways. "Let's share this apple." "Would you like to wear my necklace for a while, Indigo?" "One for you and one for me, Matthew." "This belongs to me and this belongs to you." "Edward, the bike belongs to Daddy, not you, but you can have a ride on it."

Smearing poo

Most common from fifteen months to two years.
Passes quickly with simple strategies.

Why?

- They enjoy it.
- Fascination with body products.
- Attention seeking.
- Boredom.

A FRAMEWORK TO WORK WITHIN

Poo smearing is repulsive but thankfully is usually a one-time occurrence as long as parents take a few precautions to prevent it from happening again.

- It is most likely to happen when a toddler is left in his crib to amuse himself and doesn't feel like sleeping. The most common times are the afternoon nap and in the early hours of the morning.

The afternoon nap

It is sometimes hard for parents to persuade themselves that the afternoon nap has to go. But if there comes a time when the older toddler will not sleep in the afternoon and the poo in the diaper becomes a pleasant diversion, you may have to think seriously about stopping the nap.

The early hours of the morning

Many toddlers wake at the crack of dawn and some are cooperative enough to stay in their cribs playing until a more reasonable hour. But an entertaining diversion may present itself if there is a poo in the diaper. Early morning waking may require that you get up and check on the state of the diaper.

- Use suitable clothing to prevent hands, getting into the diaper area (overalls and creative use of safety pins).
- Hard though it is, make your distaste apparent without a huge amount of attention. This is definitely a behavior you don't want to escalate.

Stroller refusal

Most common from nine months to three years (can be an on-again off-again behavior).

Why?

Some toddlers have times when they will stay in their strollers and times when they will not; others adamantly refuse all the time. The reasons are similar to car-seat refusal and center around development.

- The toddler's expanding physical capabilities make walking and pushing the stroller himself much more exciting than being strapped in and pushed by someone else.

- His drive for independence makes him want to be in charge.

- Remember his egocentrism? He has no understanding that it is easier for you if he stays in the stroller.

- It's boring sitting so restricted with all those things around to touch and explore.

- He might not like being at street level where he can't see anyone's face and catches the gasoline fumes at every street corner.

A FRAMEWORK TO WORK WITHIN

- Have realistic expectations. Again, you might have to fit your daily life around this rather major inconvenience until it passes. Sometimes it is possible to use a backpack carrier instead of a stroller, depending on the age and size of the toddler and the strength of the mother.

- Tell him what you want him to do, not what you don't want him to do. "Matthew, I want you to sit in the stroller until we get to the park. Then you can get out and walk."

- Avoid the use of punishment, threats, or bribery. They will only escalate the behavior, make you very tense, and will not encourage him to behave differently.

- Reward him every time he stays in the stroller. Always accompany the reward verbally, telling him exactly why he is getting the reward (a cuddle, a warm comment). For example, a big hug and "I'm so pleased with the way you stayed in the stroller while we were in the store. Thank you, Matthew."

Swear words

Most common from four to six years, but interesting words will pop up in the toddler years once toddlers have some verbal skills.

Why?

- Between two and four years of age, swear words arrive with all the other words toddlers are exposed to—that is, of course, if they hear swear words. It is often a mystery as to where the swear words come from as they *never* hear them at home. Toddlers are also fascinated with words related to excretion; for example, "pooey bum," "smelly bottom', "wee-wee head" or similar expressions are all popular and satisfying.

- Four-to-six-year olds use swear words as a powerful attention-seeking device, which they are, especially when used in front of a suitable audience as you say blushingly, "I don't know where he heard that."

A FRAMEWORK TO WORK WITHIN

- Between two and three, toddlers, are still learning to distinguish one word from another, so using swear words means nothing at this age. As much as it horrifies adults, it is not a huge problem, so it's best not to turn it into one.

- Pretend to ignore is the best strategy. Above all, try not to laugh at the first swear words. They can take you by surprise and usually pop out, parrot fashion, at a most inappropriate moment (when you are backing out the car).

- Try not to give nonverbal messages through body language or facial expressions either. Hum and look out the car window, if you haven't run into something with the shock of it all.

- Suggest replacement words or phrases such as "oh gosh, goodness me."

- Older children (three-to-six-year olds) should be ignored, quietly asked not to say things like that, or given timeout depending on the age and the circumstances.

- Swearing is very common on TV now. Television should be supervised and the use of swear words discussed if necessary.

- And if you don't want your toddler to swear, don't swear yourself (and doesn't that sound preachy)!

Telling lies

Most likely from four years onward.
Lying in the sense of intentionally concealing what a child believes to be a wrongdoing does not occur until around four. However, children under four can appear to tell lies. Sometimes parents overreact and misjudge the reasons behind the lies.

Why?

- Inventive lies are often the first indication that a toddler is starting to use abstract thought and experiment with ideas. For example, "How did your shoe get into the drain, Ben?" "The wind blew it there" is a response a two-year-old might give after having thrown his shoe into the drain. He is still not old enough to realize that from your point of view this is ridiculous; however, he is old enough to create an idea and work out a scapegoat for his own actions.

174

- Lying in toddlers is associated with wish fulfillment (if I say it is, so it will be), forgetfulness, exaggerations ("I visited you in the night because the biggest dog in the world frightened me"), magic, imagination, and tall tales.

A FRAMEWORK TO WORK WITHIN

- Avoid yelling and frightening toddlers for misdemeanors. Come to terms with the fact that mistakes happen, toddlers are clumsy, and the temptation for them to try things is ever present.

- Focus on solutions, not blame. Rather than: "Did you draw on the wall?," try: "Hmm, Ella, I see that you have drawn on the wall. Now I want you to help me clean it up."

- Be a role model. Let him see you dealing with tricky situations without lying.

Temper tantrums

Everyone agrees that tantrums are common during the toddler years (and beyond), but everyone has a different view about the peak tantrum age. Potentially tantrums can start as early as nine months and continue throughout life. In my work I find that parents report the most difficult time as being from fourteen months to around two and a half years.

Tantrums and negativity are the hallmarks of the era commonly described as the terrible twos, but by the time many toddlers reach two, the intensity of these behaviors is on the wane.

The variations on temper-tantrum behavior are wide. Some toddlers don't have them, others have them occasionally, and others seem to never stop having them. Most tantrum behavior is minimal once children reach school age, although tantrum throwing can become an unfortunate habit that persists throughout life. Some professional athletes have turned it into an art form. England's King Henry II was renown for throwing extraordinary, down-on-the-ground-beating-the-castle-floor tantrums, in best toddler tradition, all his life.

A continual round of tantrums by a negative toddler can be exhausting, depressing, and debilitating for his parents, especially for his mother, as she is usually the one who bears the brunt of the performances.

Tantrums are a normal and necessary part of development. It helps to know why they happen and the things that can be done to minimize the fallout. There are no cure-alls for tantrums, but be reassured that as the toddler becomes more skilled in all areas of development, and particularly as his cognitive and language abilities expand, the tantrums tend to disappear or at least become fewer and more manageable.

Why?

GENERAL REASONS (DEVELOPMENTAL)

- Conflict between wanting to be independent and not having the necessary skills to do the things he wants.
- Reconciling his drive toward autonomy with his need for security and his need for his parents' love and approval.
- Difficulty in communicating because of his immature language skills. A toddler has a limited capacity to identify what he is feeling and to describe those feelings with words, so he does it with actions instead.
- It is difficult for him to regulate and distinguish between his intense emotions—a reason why a toddler can veer wildly between excitement and anger. Hysterical laughter one minute, a temper tantrum the next.

Tantrums teach children that anger and frustration are part of the human experience and not the end of the world

- His limited understanding of time means that he functions in the present and finds it difficult to wait for things. His desires are immediate and concrete.

- Remember egocentrism? His experience of life only allows him to see things from his point of view. And from his point of view, urgent matters ("I want it now") require urgent action.

- Sometimes throwing a tantrum is a response to a potentially frightening situation. For example, a visit to the doctor, his first haircut, being left with a babysitter, having a bath, having his hair washed, and so on. A tantrum can be a way of defending himself from harm.

SPECIFIC REASONS

- Attention seeking.
- A rewarding habit—it gets him what he wants.
- As a way of testing limits. A tantrum is a powerful device—"Do you really mean it?"
- The temperament of the toddler.
- Too many "no's" and "don'ts" in his life.
- The transition times of the day are always wobbly. Getting dressed in the morning, waking after daytime sleep (see page 253), and in the evening.
- Overstimulation.
- Understimulation (boredom).
- Hunger, overtiredness.
- Minor illnesses.
- Too many sudden changes to deal with (for example, new baby, childcare, marriage breakup, chaos on the home front).
- Occasionally, as with head banging, tantrums indicate a more

serious problem if they are endless and the toddler keeps hurting himself out of unresolved frustration and despair rather than for any of the reasons given above. It can be hard as a parent knowing when behavior has gone beyond the "normal," so if you are worried about your toddler's development or finding it very difficult to manage, it is advisable to seek help.

A FRAMEWORK TO WORK WITHIN

1. Avoid as many tantrums as you can

- Try not to expect too much of your toddler when he is hungry, tired, has a minor illness, or has to make a significant change in his life. Warn him in advance when you are about to change his activity; for example, getting into the bathtub, getting out of the bathtub, leaving his cousin's house when he is happy, and so on.

- Bear in mind his particular temperament and adjust his daily life accordingly. Resist comparing him with Sophie down the road who never throws tantrums.

- Avoid overstimulation and unrealistic expectations of his socializing abilities. When he has reached his limit at playgroup or at a friend's house, go home.

- Think carefully, about and perhaps avoid tantrum triggers such as unsuitable toys or special activities that frustrate your toddler. He may not have the temperament for Suzuki violin lessons.

- As much as possible, avoid the supermarket, shopping for your winter wardrobe, waiting in the doctor's office, long car trips, plane trips, restaurants, and spending time in the child-free homes of friends or aging relatives.

  Obviously avoiding these things is not always feasible, so planning needs to take into consideration the possibility of a tantrum and what you might do if/when it happens (see below).

Other planning should include things to take to amuse your toddler while you visit or wait (see suggestions for activity bag on page 214) and working out a reasonable time for your shopping/visit/doctor's consultation. You know your toddler's temperament and breaking point— most toddlers are okay for a limited period at any of these venues, but beyond a certain time things can fall apart. If your toddler gets easily frustrated by shopping, make other arrangements for him if you can and avoid the stress.

2. Simple intervention

- There are times when simple things like shifting your toddler's attention to another activity or removing him from the frustration work quickly and well to stop the tantrum.

- At other times a handy diversion will do the trick. "Where's the plane, James?"

- If the tantrum is the result of being frightened or unwell, holding and rocking is a way to reassure him.

   Note: Some experts suggest holding and rocking as the best way to handle all tantrums. I speak to some parents who agree with this and say it works best for their toddlers. However, while this may be so in some cases, the hold-and-rock plan doesn't work too well for the majority of tantrums where the toddler is out of control and the stressed parent is also in danger of losing control.

3. Pretend to ignore

- This is very difficult, but with practice you will get better at it.

- Stay calm (deep breath, count to ten).

- Acknowledge that you are angry, frustrated, and that you feel like having a tantrum too. Remind yourself that your toddler *needs* you to stay in control so that you can show him what to do. His inner world is in collapse; his outer world needs to remain intact.

- Tell him that you understand why he is upset, but stay firm about whatever is causing the tantrum. If you are bathing, dressing, or otherwise attending to his care, continue if the struggle is not too difficult. Get some help if your partner is around. If it is too hard to continue or if the tantrum, is about a limit-setting issue, don't give in, leave him to get on with his tantrum and busy yourself with something. Move away. Hum, or perhaps turn the music up a little. Think of greener pastures.

- When the tantrum is over, avoid recriminations or lectures. Move on.

4. Timeout or separation

- Depending on the intensity and extent of the tantrum, timeout as described on page 117 can be used as an intervention if the tantrum cannot be ignored.

- If, in the course of the tantrum, the toddler is at risk of hurting himself or if you are feeling very angry and stressed and need to separate yourself from your toddler, put him somewhere safe (usually the bedroom is the best place) until you both cool down.

5. Reward your toddler

- Give warm acknowledgments, hugs, smiles, or a small tangible reward for nontantrum behavior in tricky situations. And for the times when he gets the tantrum under control before it goes into full flight.

- Remember to accompany the reward with a short, clear reason for your pleasure.

6. Unhelpful tantrum tactics

We all indulge in these from time to time, but they are best avoided whenever possible because they escalate the number and intensity of the tantrums.

- *Losing control*

  This is always a disaster as the parent inevitably ends up doing something he or she regrets. Guilt and remorse follow and inevitably the toddler gets overcompensated for his parent's sins after the drama has died down. The toddler ends up receiving a massive amount of attention for the very behavior his parent wishes to reduce.

- *Bribery*

  Occasionally a bribe has an immediate and positive effect, especially when trying to avoid a public tantrum. Mostly, though, bribery is an act of desperation by an anxious parent, which gives the toddler positive attention for *having* tantrums, rather than for *not having* them.

- *Lengthy explanations*

  As to why you have made the decision which has led to the tantrum. Your toddler will neither understand nor care, so keep it simple.

- *Shouting, spanking, stamping foot, banging saucepans, name-calling, and threats*

  Gives a toddler the message that having a tantrum is the best way to deal with anger and frustration because Mommy's having a humdinger of a tantrum in the kitchen.

7. Tantrums when out and about

The public tantrum makes parents feel embarrassed, vulnerable, agitated, foolish, and upset. It can also be a trigger for the most irrational thoughts:

"Is this how the rest of my life is going to be?"

"It's not fair that I have to put up with this."

"I think I might walk away and leave him here. I don't care if I never see him again."

"If I can't get on top of this now, what's it going to be like when he's a teenager?"

It's hard to know how to react. If the tantrum is ignored, onlookers make unsolicited comments and suggestions that are bound to be unhelpful if not downright rude. If the parent loses it and vents his or her anger in a very public display of fury, the toddler increases the noise, the unhelpful people intervene, and someone calls the police. A public tantrum is potentially a lose–lose situation for any parent.

However, it is a common event and is almost an obligatory rite of passage into parenthood. In fact, I am tempted to propose that no adult human has ever been put to a basic test of maturity until they have had to deal with a tantrum-throwing toddler in public. It is one of nature's great equalizers and can be viewed as a stepping stone to adulthood.

Here are some suggestions

- Think before you act. The more attention the toddler gets, the more intense the tantrum will become and the more attention you'll attract from onlookers. The calmer you stay, the more confident you will become.

- Acknowledge how you feel. It's perfectly understandable to feel angry, embarrassed, and letdown.

- Remember that temper tantrums are a normal part of early childhood behavior.

- Sometimes simple intervention works. For example (depending on where you are), brief timeout (in the nearest rest room, in a corner somewhere), distraction ("When we get home we will have lunch/watch a video/play in the wading pool . . .") or shifting attention: "Look at that little boy over there sitting so nicely. I guess he might get a treat because he's being so quiet."

Realistically it's quite likely that none of these tactics is going to have much impact on the full-fledged tantrum, but they are always worth a try.

- The only other alternative is to leave your toddler to perform, quickly finish what you are doing, and make an orderly retreat as quickly as possible with your dignity intact. Once you are away from the scene, the intense feelings you are having will diminish.

- Sometimes dealing with curious onlookers is more difficult than dealing with your toddler's tantrum. Again, if you can stay calm and confident, this is easier too.

Here are two options depending on the circumstances

1. Completely ignore the people around you. Avoid looking at their faces and do not make eye contact. Focus on helping your toddler, doing what you have to do, and leaving as soon as you can.

2. Brightly enlist their support: "My little boy has totally lost it. Could you let me go ahead?"

- Public tantrums decrease as toddlers mature and parents learn how to deal with tantrums at home.

8. The positives of tantrums

There are some—believe it or not.

- Tantrums teach children that anger and frustration are part of human experience and not the end of the world.

- Through tantrums children have opportunities to learn better ways of dealing with life's disappointments and uncertainties.

- But perhaps more importantly, toddler tantrums help adults learn to think things through, develop their own self-control, adjust their expectations, become more tolerant, and never again look down their noses at someone else's toddler performing in a supermarket.

Thumb sucking

Most common from birth to eight years. Some continue beyond this age.

Why?
They enjoy it.

A FRAMEWORK TO WORK WITHIN
Thumb sucking is a normal activity. It does not indicate stress and has no effect on the toddler's progress if it is continued throughout early childhood. Nor does it affect teeth until the permanent teeth are through, at which time ten percent of children who continue to suck their fingers or thumbs push their teeth up and out and require orthodontics. I can't help noticing how many children have orthodontic treatment anyway for a whole range of reasons, many of which do not include thumb sucking, so it's not an issue I see as highly significant.

It is very difficult to persuade a committed thumb or finger sucker to give it up. Best to pretend to ignore it.

Some toddlers are so enamored of their thumbs that they suck them while they eat. This is a harmless habit and stops sometime before age two.

Whining

Most common from nine months to two years but easily becomes a habit when rewarded (that is, given plenty of attention) and can continue well into the childhood years and indeed throughout life.

185

Why?

Whining is usually used as a rather effective attention-seeking device. Sudden uncharacteristic whining in a toddler can be an indication of illness (especially ear infections).

A FRAMEWORK TO WORK WITHIN

- Make sure your toddler is not sick.

- Teach him what the word *whining* means by demonstrating the difference between asking for something pleasantly and whining for it.

- Pretend to ignore. This is very difficult, which is why whining is such an effective tool. If you have been responding to the whining, you will find that when you start to consistently ignore it, it will escalate before it starts to wane.

- Try to distract yourself; headphones can be useful.

- Bored toddlers whine more. Avoid long days at home where you both get irritated and fed up with each other.

- Timeout for whining can be used. Some parents find using a whining corner or a whining chair helps.

- Give positive attention to significant periods of nonwhining behavior.

- Think about how much you complain and what it might sound like to your toddler. If you are in a bad mood, rather than complaining endlessly, give your toddler a short, simple explanation of why you are unhappy (obviously not the intimate details of why you're upset with your mother) and try to move on.

part three

THE BASICS

Day-to-Day Toddler Care

Watch a mother out and about with two or three spruced-up toddlers in tow. She makes it look so easy. Yet the number of woman-hours involved in just getting everyone out the front door is mind-boggling. Let alone the time spent from sun-up to sundown changing and dressing, washing and wiping, dressing and grooming. Just like mother bear getting her cubs into shape.

The daily care of your particular cub is likely to be complicated by his opposition to aspects of his grooming. Resistance to hair washing, nail cutting, teeth cleaning, face washing, nose wiping, and getting dressed and undressed will almost certainly be the order of the day. There are no solutions—you will find some days are worse than others. Try to stay calm and do what you have to do as swiftly as possible. When practical, allow your toddler to do as much for himself as you can. Sometime between two and three, most toddlers become much more cooperative and even start to enjoy some of the grooming rituals. For more information on dealing with the daily struggles, look for specifics in chapter six.

Here is some information to help with the day-to-day care of toddler cubs.

Babysitting

Employing babysitters is part and parcel of life with a toddler unless you have available family or friends close by. Lucky for you if you do, but if you don't, it is great if you can find a sitter who will remain with you for a few years, as toddlers are more comfortable with people they know.

A good way of finding a babysitter is via friends and neighbors or sometimes through local high schools. Babysitters are also available through agencies, but like most parents, you will probably prefer to employ someone you know personally. If you are employing someone you have no personal knowledge of, it is important to ask for references (and to check them) unless the person has come via a reputable agency which runs appropriate screening procedures before putting people on their books.

Agencies have a set fee schedule and conditions of employment which you will be informed of, but if *you* are employing your babysitter, it is very important to discuss conditions of employment and make a firm verbal contract before the babysitting begins.

Here is a checklist

- Rates of pay must be negotiated, which includes allowances for taxi fares home if necessary.
- You should be confident that your babysitter will be reliable in times of stress and that she is aware of your toddler's needs. It is advisable to employ a babysitter who has energy and experience with young children. He or she needs an understanding of the emotional needs of toddlers and the best ways to play with and comfort them, particularly if the babysitting involves times when the toddler is up and about.

- It is a good idea to write down the toddler's routine for the babysitter and include information on food, fluids, TV, nap time, bath time, favorite stories, any medication, bedtime, and diaper changing or potty regimes.

- Discipline is a vital issue which needs clear-cut guidelines and plenty of discussion so that your babysitter knows what is expected of him or her, especially in relation to things like spanking.

- Activities apart from babysitting, such as cooking and housework, should be negotiated and agreed upon before employment.

Babysitting safety

- Show your babysitter how to use equipment such as the stove, thermostat, and so on.

- Make sure he or she knows where the emergency phone numbers are (see page 329).

- Always leave your phone number and the address and phone number of a reliable friend or relative in case the babysitter can't locate you.

- Your babysitter also needs to know, in writing, what to do in an emergency and where the first-aid kit is kept (see page 329).

- Leave your babysitter a reliable flashlight.

Genitals

Boys

Care of the uncircumcised penis

The uncircumcised penis needs the same care as the elbow (thank you, Jann Zintgraff). The foreskin should not be pushed back. Forcing it back before it is ready causes bleeding, scarring, and damage that may require surgical treatment. Sometime between three and seven years, the foreskin will slip backward and forward quite easily.

Girls

Labial fusion

If you find that you can't part the labia (the folds of skin on a girl's genitals), see your pediatrician. It is quite common for the edges of the labia to adhere to each other in babies and toddlers. This is because the skin is relatively thin and estrogen levels are low. Once babies are over twelve months, the usual treatment is to apply some estrogen cream regularly for a few weeks. The estrogen cream thickens the skin, helping it to separate.

It is important to treat the condition because urine can pool behind the fusion and cause other problems.

Potty training

It's best to view potty training as no big deal even if you are longing for the day when you don't have to face another messy poo.

Toilet training is simply one of the many basic daily tasks that parents and children have to work out together.

Unfortunately potty training, whether it's early or late, is often seen as a test of a parent's skill or a child's intelligence rather than a small part of normal development that will happen automatically with a little help. Most children become potty trained for the daytime between eighteen months and three and a half years; some in a matter of days, others in an on-again off-again sort of way which takes a year or more. Variations in age depend not only on the ability to recognize the sensations that warn of an impending pee or poo but also on a willingness to participate in the process.

Some toddlers are interested enough in the proceedings to cooperate at around eighteen months, but it's pointless to push those who aren't. Between fourteen and twenty-four months of age is the peak period of toddler negativity and a time when they are very busy working out the extent of their own newly emerging powers and capabilities. Potty training presents them with many opportunities to gain attention and test their personal control, so it's not a good time to push an issue that is not important enough to warrant so much attention.

Pick a time somewhere between eighteen months and three when you think the time is right.

But when is the right time?

- The most important indicator of the right time is when your toddler is *generally* cooperative and responsive to verbal rewards. And when he is free of illness, not upset by life events (new baby, starting childcare, moving to a new house, and so on), and is able to understand and follow instructions.

- The right time is also when you have the time, patience, and a good attitude. The age by which you, your partner, your other children, or your friends' toddlers were trained is irrelevant. It's also unrealistic to expect to train a child to a deadline, such as before the new baby arrives or in time for preschool, unless that's what he wants too. The pressure on an unwilling toddler in such situations is invariably a recipe for disaster.

- Many potty-training experts talk about the signs that indicate a readiness to start training. These might include the toddler announcing when there is a poo or a pee in his diaper. He may show signs of discomfort when the diaper is wet or dirty. He might ask to sit on the potty or toilet. Or even start to stay dry for a few hours at a time.

  Certainly if your toddler is showing signs of readiness it's worth giving potty training a trial run, but it's advisable to have realistic expectations because unfortunately signs of readiness are not necessarily an indication that the toddler is ready to cooperate with the idea. Parents often become very frustrated when they observe the "signs of readiness" and know that their toddler knows when he wants to go but continues to refuse to do what's required. This is something you may have to live with until he is prepared to cooperate. You might find that some days he will cooperate and some days he won't—that's the nature of the toddler.

- Warm weather is preferable as accidents are easier to manage and there are fewer clothes to have to bother with.

Tips for a trial run

- Show your toddler what happens when you use the toilet. It does not matter whether he uses a potty or a toilet as long as he is comfortable and not frightened. If you use the toilet, make sure it has a special seat so that he doesn't fall in and has something to rest his feet on. The advantage of a potty is that you can move it around and take it with you when you go out.

- Try removing his diaper in the day when an accident is not going to cause a major catastrophe.

  If you go out anywhere where an accident is likely to create a problem, put him back into diapers. It's quite all right to go in and out of diapers until you are confident there will be no more accidents. No one likes urine-soaked car seats and people tend to get upset about poos on their carpets.

  Once toddlers are fairly reliably potty trained, they still need reminding to go at regular intervals (without driving them crazy). And immediate attention when they announce the urge to pee or poo, no matter where you happen to be.

- If he is prepared to cooperate, sit him on the potty or toilet at various times throughout the day—before going out, after meals, or when you arrive home. Just before the bath in the evening is a good time to see how he takes to the idea. Give him a book to look at while he sits (boys as well as girls often sit down to pee initially).

- If it looks as though you are on the road to success, dress your toddler in clothes that are easy to get on and off. Give normal fluids – restricting fluids does not train the bladder to hold good amounts of fluid.

- Use a positive tone when discussing excretory products and try to avoid too many negative words ("dirty," "whew," "smelly" and "yucky") unless they are expressed with an air of pride and satisfaction.

- Try to stay calm and tolerant when there are accidents (easier said than done!).

- It helps to positively acknowledge success and to give quiet encouragement to keep going. However, overdoing the praise (carrying on at length, calling Daddy, providing gifts of lollipops, dolls for rewards, and so on) in the early stages of potty training can put too much pressure on toddlers. Too much attention and praise in the early stages often have the reverse effect. In my opinion, extravagant praise also overemphasizes the importance of potty training in family life.

- If after a week your toddler has no inclination to do what is being asked of him and the accidents are too hard to live with, put him back into diapers and try again in a few months.

- As hard as it may be, ignore friends and relatives who question your methods or skill as a parent because of the stage of your child's potty training. Try not to jump from one scheme to another on the advice of friends (a typical piece of advice being, "Once they are out of diapers, leave them out") as you will end up feeling confused and inadequate. All parents have to find their own way.

- Avoid battles and constant long discussions about potty training with all others within the child's hearing range. Young children are very aware that they cannot be forced to use the potty. In the end it is their decision, so if it becomes a battle, the parents will always lose. When your child's increasing knowledge and experience help him to see the advantage of using a potty he will do so.

- It's normal to lose it occasionally over a pee or a poo deposited in the wrong place. As long as you are not in a constant state of stress and conflict over potty training, there's no harm done. Try not to let your anger lead you into punishing your toddler (spanking, withdrawing affection, and punishing verbally), as you will find in the long run that such a response impedes the process.

- The intriguing thing about potty training is that no one knows exactly what pattern their toddler will take. There is no universal system. What works for someone else may not work for you. Your job is simply to show your toddler the ropes, gently encourage, and leave it up to him.

What about twins?

All the parents of twins I speak to advise waiting until both twins are ready if there are differences in each toddler's attitude to being potty trained. Apart from the extra work involved training one, then the other, it appears it is easy for the one being trained to be the subject of too much positive attention and the other twin gets too much negative attention. Comparisons are almost unavoidable. As potty training, in the big scheme of life, is of such relative unimportance, it's best to avoid turning it into a competition destined to make one twin feel good and the other feel bad.

Two variations on the potty-training theme

1. It's common for some children to ask for a diaper to do a poo in rather than be prepared to sit on the potty, a state of affairs that sometimes lasts until school age. Some toddlers who do not wear diapers during the day will wait for the night diaper to go on before doing their daily poo—very frustrating.

   From time to time, you can let your toddler know what you would prefer him to do and try some gentle persuasion with the possibility of a tangible reward, but overall it is best to take a relaxed approach about this. If constant pressure is put on your toddler, he is likely to start to hold onto the poo and become

197

very constipated. This can spiral into an extended period of poo distress, both for the toddler and the family, which can be quite difficult to resolve. When he is ready, he will change from the diaper to the potty or toilet.

2. Some toddlers even after being potty trained continue to insist that one of their parents remains with them while they do their business. Once again this is related to their development. It could be a combination of attention seeking and egocentrism (not having any notion that their parent may not enjoy hanging around with them or might have other things to do). Or it may have something to do with the irrational fears that toddlers experience (of being left alone or of falling into the toilet).

Here is a framework to work within

- Make sure there is nothing scary around to contribute to his fears (wobbly toilet seat, dark room, or an isolated area).
- Provide books, music, and a toy or two.
- Try to gradually withdraw over a period of time. For example, move from the room to the doorway, then in small increments move further away each day.
- And as usual give positive reinforcement for gains (a small reward) and minimal attention to the demand—do not engage in conversations, games, or songs if he insists that you accompany him while he sits.

Night training

Control of the bladder at night won't happen until your child has control during the day. About eighty percent of children are mostly dry by four years of age, but the remainder will continue to wet the bed until age eight or even older, and this is viewed as common and normal.

Children from the age of three who suddenly regress after having had both bowel and bladder control for six months or longer usually need help for either medical or psychological problems.

Routines

Food, sleep, and play form the basis of day-to-day living for toddlers. Setting up some structure and routine in these three areas can reduce the frequency and intensity of many of the hassles that come with living with a toddler. If the basics are in place, many of the minor but recurring irritations are eliminated or at least minimized.

All toddlers and parents are different; some need more structure than others. Very active toddlers (sometimes called "difficult") do best in a well-ordered, predictable family environment where there are firm limits. Other easier-going toddlers who have less trouble adapting to change and can occupy themselves may not need their lives structured to the same extent. Some parents live happily in chaos, but many find they enjoy family life more when there is predictability to the rhythm of daily life.

Routines do not have to be set in concrete—flexibility is essential. Once the basic structure is in place, slipping out of routine does not cause major catastrophes. All families have times when routines are inevitably disrupted. Toddlers and parents sometimes get sick, have bad days, go on vacations, and have special treats. Release from daily routine can sometimes be liberating, but getting back into it provides familiarity and safety which most of us look forward to.

How parents choose to structure their lives is a personal matter, and any suggestions for routines are not intended as a prescription for all families but rather as a guide for those who are looking for one.

For a toddler eating routine, see page 272.

For a bedtime sleep routine, see page 227.

Soaps, shampoo, moisturizers, sunscreens

The market is afloat with baby and toddler products for grooming and skin care. Unless your toddler has sensitive skin or a skin condition that requires special care, basic products are all you need.

Soap is fine for washing the gorgeous toddler body and any of the no-tears shampoos quite satisfactory for hair washing.

Hypoallergenic Moisturizing Lotion or Cream is recommended (for example, Moisturel products), although younger toddlers may not be too happy to lie while you massage it in. It can be used as a soap substitute in the tub, but you might find you still need soap for the ground-in dirty spots.

Having seen too many negative effects on the skin from bubble baths, I think that it is wise to give them a miss until toddlers are over three. Talcum powder is messy, has no benefits, and is potentially dangerous if the toddler inhales it.

Toddler clothes can be washed in with everyone else's.

Teaching sun protection to children is now as routine a job for parents as teeth
cleaning, crossing the road, and encouraging healthy eating

Sun protection

Sun protection is crucial in preventing permanent skin damage. It is said that there is no such thing as a healthy tan. Nearly eighty percent of skin cancers in adulthood are a result of sun damage before the age of eighteen. It is estimated that for each one percent drop in the ozone layer, there will be a corresponding two percent rise in the incidence of skin cancer.

Teaching sun protection to children is now as routine a job for parents as teeth cleaning, crossing the road, and encouraging healthy eating. It can be frustrating and tiresome, but by keeping on working away at it, the message does get through and you are laying the foundations for sensible skin care in young adulthood.

The *first* line of defense against sun damage is to keep out of the sun as much as possible. The sun's ultraviolet light is at its most intense between the hours of 10 a.m. and 2 p.m. (11 a.m. to 3 p.m. in areas where there is daylight saving). When there is a choice, outdoor activities between May and October should be planned for early morning or late afternoon. Remember that dull days or sitting in the shade out of doors are not a protection from sun damage in themselves, and suitable protective clothes and sunscreen are still needed.

The **second** line of defense is to cover up as much of your toddler's skin as possible when out of doors—ideally a shirt with a collar and a hat that provides shade over face, neck and ears. Toddlers are renown for continually pulling hats off but will eventually get used to them and leave them on as long as the hat is replaced every time it comes off. And be a role model—wear one yourself.

The *third* line of defense is to generously apply a sunscreen to exposed areas of skin whenever your toddler is out of doors. Ideally sunscreen should be applied ten or fifteen minutes before sun exposure. It is wise to apply it again after swimming or vigorous towel drying.

202

Lips also need sunscreen protection, and it is now recommended that babies, toddlers, and children of all ages wear sunglasses when out in the sun. The sunglasses need to be approved by the American National Standards Institutegh (ANSI), both for their safety (shatter-proof safety lenses) and effectiveness to absorb ultraviolet radiation.

About sunscreens

Do not let the endless array of sun protection products confuse you. It is simple to pick one that both you and your toddler can use.

Some sunscreens work by absorbing ultraviolet radiation; others work by reflecting the ultraviolet away and may be less likely to cause allergic reactions to the skin.

Sunscreens have a sun protection factor (SPF) which ranges from 4 to 30. The higher the SPF, the longer the sunscreen protects. A 30+ SPF gives toddlers the most effective protection. Sunscreens that protect against both ultraviolet A and B are called broad spectrum, and a toddler's skin needs this protection.

Specially formulated toddler sunblocks are combinations of ingredients thought to be less allergenic and so less likely to irritate a baby or toddler's skin. The chemical PABA is a sunscreen additive, which causes problems for sensitive skins, so is not used in a number of sunscreens. Some sunscreens have an alcoholic base, which may sting a toddler's skin.

When choosing a sunscreen for your child

- Read the label carefully
- 30+ sun protection factor
- No PABA

- Nonalcoholic base
- Water-resistant base
- Broad-spectrum base

Many brands are available which comply with these recommendations, so don't go to the added expense of buying a toddler sunscreen if the one you have already fits the bill. If you are unsure of your toddler's sensitivity to a sun protection product, do a skin test by applying a small amount on his forearm—if there is no itch or sting within a few hours, the product is safe to use.

The growing of teeth (my favorite topic)

Readers who are familiar with my book on a baby's first year, *Baby Love*, will be aware of my often unpopular views about teething which, disappointingly or even annoyingly for some of you, have not changed.

After observing many babies and toddlers for many years, I am still convinced the perception that growing teeth causes problems in babies and toddlers is primarily due to the fact that babies and toddlers cannot communicate clearly. Once a toddler's communication skills (verbal and otherwise) are proficient enough to explain what his problems are (between two and a half and three), the belief that teething causes everything from sleep problems to whining attacks and loose poo fades away.

Teething is a convenient, quick explanation for busy health professionals who wish to avoid lengthy consultations about sleep, whining, not eating, biting, mysterious fevers, endless mucus, and poo, which are so much a part of the toddler years. Most experienced health professionals, when pushed, acknowledge that it is unlikely growing teeth causes anything other than new teeth.

I am aware that my approach is unsatisfactory, even objectionable to some people, and has perhaps even cost me a few book sales. Nevertheless, undaunted I continue my mission to rid the world of the myths of teething.

Why am I being so stubborn?

I believe it is more useful for parents to understand the many more rational reasons relating to their baby's development, behavior and health than to be treated like children and brushed off with teething fairy stories.

The term *teething* implies a medical condition rather than a natural growth process (similar to growing bone, hair, and fingernails). As babies grow twenty teeth sometime in their first three years, there are always going to be times when the emergence of a tooth coincides with developmental changes, normal but strange toddler habits, diaper rash, and the round of illnesses so common in the toddler years as their immunity builds up.

Emerging teeth, however, do not cause fevers, diarrhea, colds, coughs, ear infections, smelly urine, or diaper rash. Persisting with these myths means, at best, effective treatment is delayed or, at worst, a serious illness is missed. Nor are sleep problems caused by teeth emerging, and if your toddler's sleep patterns are causing you grief, constantly blaming teeth will not change anything.

Why the myths?

The historical fascination and obsession surrounding the emergence of teeth during the baby years, originally fostered by ignorance and superstition, has somehow been carried, largely unchanged, into the present time.

Until around 1880, scurvy was a common disease among infants, and a symptom of scurvy is red swollen gums, it was presumed that the problem was "teething." Gums were often lanced in order to get the teeth through and so, it was thought, improve the baby's health. Teething (or dentition) was frequently given as a cause of death on death certificates when in fact babies were dying of scurvy, diphtheria, measles, scarlet fever, and so on. At the turn of the twentieth century, teething appeared in dental textbooks as a cause of epilepsy.

Science has made us realize how ridiculous these notions are, but to a lesser degree we are still being ridiculous. When seven- and eight-year-old children are growing teeth (some teeth at this age grow for the first time), scant attention is paid. Teething is never a suggested cause for illness or misbehavior in this age group because older children communicate more effectively and behave more predictably, so it is easier for adults to identify exactly what the problem is.

Let's look at the growing of teeth

Growing and losing teeth is normal for all humans and happens on and off for twenty years or longer.

The first tooth appears sometime between fourteen weeks and sixteen months of age. It announces its presence by simply appearing, though sometimes a small lump comes first. No secret signs herald the arrival of a tooth, so a health professional cannot peer at a toothless gum and announce that a tooth will or won't appear next week!

After the first tooth arrives, others pop up at varying intervals. The first twenty teeth arrive during the first two and a half years. They are lost and replaced by thirty-two permanent teeth between the ages of six and twenty years.

Does growing teeth cause toddlers discomfort?

Who knows? The preverbal toddler cannot tell us.

By the time he can, it's interesting to note that the subject of his teeth is something he never much talks about until they are getting wobbly and starting to come out, at which time his main interest centers around the tooth fairy.

Certainly discomfort for three months before they are visible is highly unlikely! Nor do they cause pain by moving around under the gum. An uncomfortable sensation just before the tooth emerges may worry some toddlers, and if you decide an emerging tooth is causing a problem, a single dose of acetaminophen is the safest medication to use. Avoid giving it for weeks on end and avoid teething gels that contain salicylates (aspirin). If your toddler is very distressed and behaving in an unusual way, never assume the problem is simply teething. Look further and if necessary seek a second opinion.

Drooling

Drooling is a normal feature of the first year and continues until babies or toddlers learn how to swallow their saliva. Drooling is not related to teething. Most toddlers stop drooling sometime in their second year but a few persist indefinitely. Excessive prolonged drooling is associated with developmental delay, but when this is the case there are other indications of developmental problems. For example, toddlers with cerebral palsy and Down's syndrome.

Prolonged drooling in otherwise normally developing healthy toddlers is usually due to low muscle tone around the lips and mouth and a protruding or slack tongue. Occasionally the drooling is exacerbated by an overabundance of salivary glands under the tongue, which can be surgically treated.

Prolonged use of pacifiers contributes to drooling as the posture of the mouth with the pacifier in place interferes with optimum muscular development around the mouth and encourages tongue thrusting. The saliva pools under the tongue and falls out instead of being swallowed.

Treatment of prolonged or excessive drooling in toddlers includes checking for any underlying problems, removing the pacifier, and consulting with a speech pathologist on the best ways to strengthen the muscles around the mouth and to stop the tongue thrust.

Other teeth tidbits

- A bluish swelling is often present when a tooth is emerging. This is normal and not painful for the toddler.
- Growing teeth is not a developmental milestone and the stage at which they appear has nothing to do with whether the toddler will grow up to be a brain surgeon.
- Toddlers do not need a full set of teeth for eating a variety of

foods; for example, bread, fruit, cheese. Until they learn to chew effectively (around three years), they break the food down into digestible lumps with their gums and teeth. Although unchewed foods such as carrots and peas turn up in the poo, beneficial nutrients are leached out of them on the way through, so don't panic about malnutrition.

Care of teeth

Teeth cleaning should be started once a day as soon as they arrive. Use a soft toothbrush without toothpaste. Once the toddler is able to spit the toothpaste out, use a very small amount of fluoride toothpaste. Too much fluoride toothpaste can cause chalky-looking permanent teeth.

My family's teeth are cared for by the best husband-and-wife dental team the world. Here is their recommended approach to cleaning toddler teeth.

- If possible, conduct the teeth cleaning in a brightly lit place.
- Position yourself behind your toddler, both either standing or sitting, whichever you prefer.
- Encourage the toddler to look up at you and to "open up."
- Start with the back teeth because that is all you may have time to do (the back teeth remain until age ten to twelve, the front teeth only until six to eight).
- Clean teeth twice a day if possible. If not, try for once a day. Missing a day occasionally is acceptable.

Did you know that children do not have the manual dexterity to clean their teeth properly until they are around eight to ten years old? The American Academy of Pediatric Dentistry recommends that parents make a point of cleaning their children's teeth twice a day until that age.

As many parents soon come to realize, however, cleaning a toddler's teeth is easier said than done, especially between one and two years of age (see page 165 for resistance to teeth brushing). The majority of parents are fully aware of the need to clean toddler teeth, but when the daily battle becomes too tedious, they tend to give up, which in my opinion is perfectly understandable.

Three interacting factors have the potential to cause decay—tooth decay bacteria, all sugars (including lactose, which is found in milk), and an individual's inherent ability to resist the decay. So, without wishing to minimize the importance of daily brushing, I think it is reasonable to live with an erratic cleaning regime until the toddler is more cooperative as long as the other lines of defense against tooth decay are in place.

Let's look at them:

1. An individual's ability to resist decay

The predisposition of individuals to tooth decay varies. Some toddlers will not get tooth decay despite lack of teeth cleaning and a sugar-laden diet. However, as it is best not to rely solely on genetic inheritance, it is also vital to eliminate the dietary risk factor and to use fluoride.

2. The dietary risk factor

The main line of defense against black teeth is attention to diet, especially during the toddler years when effective teeth cleaning is so difficult and when prolonged use of bottles is so prevalent. As noted, sugar is the biggest offender. That means brown, "natural" and honey too. Other forms of sugar are found in fruit juices, so don't be fooled into thinking these are harmless.

Pacifiers dipped in sweet things or sucked by parents before being placed into the toddler's mouth can cause decay. Apart from water, all drinks in bottles are a potential problem when they are sucked for a large part of the day or night. Other foods that contribute to tooth decay are "natural" fruit bars, cookies, soft drinks, and so on . . .

3. Fluoride

Fluoride protects strengthens teeth internally, under the gums in the jawbone, and externally by strengthening the enamel on the surface of the teeth. Two of the most common sources of fluoride are tap water and fluoridated toothpaste. Water fluoridation is the safest and most cost-effective way to prevent tooth decay. Fluoride is added to the water in most major municipalities, however, there are areas in the U.S. where the water is unfluoridated or where the water supply comes from wells. There are also many families who rely on bottled or purified water for drinking. These do not provide enough fluoride for tooth decay prevention when used as the primary source of drinking water.

When this is the case, it is recommended to start fluoride supplements at 12 months of age by way of fluoride drops, vitamins or tablets. While fluoride is safe and necessary, it is very important to check on the amount of fluoride in the drinking water before starting supplements as too much fluoride can cause permanent tooth discoloration. This is harmless but of cosmetic concern.

The American Academy of Pediatric Dentistry advises parents to schedule their baby's first dental appointment when the first tooth appears or not later than the first birthday to determine risk factors and evaluate fluoride requirements.

Grinding teeth

Most toddlers and young children have bouts of teeth grinding, especially in their sleep. At this age nothing need be done. Chronic grinding (bruxing) of teeth in adults needs dental advice and treatment in order to avoid serious long-term damage.

Cosmetic appearance of toddler teeth

Wide spaces, crooked teeth, and so on are not treated during the toddler years. If you are concerned about the look of your toddler's teeth, check with your dentist.

Traveling with toddlers

It's difficult for me to be positive about traveling any distance with toddlers, especially those between one and two years old. However, I acknowledge that there are parents who make very ambitious journeys with babies and toddlers and not only live to tell the tale but seem to enjoy it. The perspective taken very much depends on the temperament and attitude of the parents (it's easy to tell where I sit) and the temperament and behavior of the toddler.

A certain amount of traveling with toddlers is unavoidable, being a necessary part of seeing family or having vacations. And of course the alternative of never going anywhere during the toddler years is going to deny you the opportunities of getting away and enjoying new places, experiences, and people, which most of us look forward to.

So don't let me put you off!

Here is some general information

As you are almost certainly aware by now, traveling with a toddler is quite different from traveling on your own. It can be rewarding and exciting, but it is hard work.

Developmental issues such as their lack of concentration, limited attention span, and dislike of being contained in small spaces, combined with the lack of physical activity, complicate traveling with toddlers. The innate ability of the toddler to throw up at the drop of a hat and do a huge sloppy poo at the most inopportune moment also contributes to making travel with them an adventure.

To ensure as smooth a trip as possible, planning is essential. Planning includes mental preparation so that you don't have too many unrealistic ideas of what's ahead. Leisurely meals, shopping expeditions, fishing trips, extensive sightseeing, late nights, and long drives without stopping tend not to be compatible with toddlers. Be mentally prepared for the unexpected so that you don't feel too let-down when things go wrong. Illness, screaming attacks, and diarrhea are all possible toddler events when you're on the road.

Many babies and toddlers find travel disrupting, which doesn't hurt them in any way, but you might find their eating, sleeping, and behavior patterns change temporarily.

Sedatives

You may wonder about using a sedative for your toddler, especially if you are traveling overseas. Some parents do take a mild sedative with them in case of difficult times, but most find they don't use it. If you need to, talk it over with your family doctor or pediatrician.

If you do use a mild sedative, remember sometimes these drugs have the reverse effect and make toddlers more alert (woop-dedoo); so ask your doctor about giving your toddler a trial dose a week or so before leaving.

Sedating toddlers for a long car trip may be necessary occasionally, but sedatives should never be given as a matter of course for car trips and should never be used on a daily basis for the duration of a long trip.

Activity bags and snack boxes

Whether traveling by car, train, or plane, an activity bag with some novelty items is a useful distraction. To get the most out of your activity bag, it is advisable to delay delving into it until it is needed, and then hand out the items one at a time.

Obviously attention has to be paid to the age of the toddler and safety aspects (choking and so on) when assembling the activity bag for your trip.

Here are some suggestions

THE ACTIVITY BAG

- An assortment of colored snap-together blocks in various shapes and sizes
- Plastic measuring spoons, small plastic jug
- Other small cooking utensils (toy or real)
- Small plastic tool set
- Card collections, deck of cards
- A good supply of books, especially those with moveable parts and pop-ups
- Coloring book, crayons
- Bubble-making equipment
- Simple puzzles

- Modelling clay
- Stickers
- Box of Band-Aids
- Calculator (large), stopwatch, egg timer with bell (will drive the other passengers mad)
- Musical toys (ditto)
- Flashlight
- Special photo album prepared for traveling
- Funny hats, sunglasses, scarves for dressing up
- Set of keys, magnet
- Toy telephone
- Small toys—soft toys, cars, finger puppets, tractors, dolls, and so on

THE SNACK BOX (FOR DISTRACTION AND HUNGER PANGS)

- Small boxes of raisins
- Dried apricots, apples
- Small sandwiches
- Bread
- Cheese slices, cubes, small packets
- Unsalted pretzels
- Crackers
- Bananas
- Cut-up fruit (watermelon)

But no matter how creative and varied your activity bag is or what gourmet delights are in your snack box, don't be surprised to find that *you* will be at the center of most of your toddler's entertainment during his waking hours (depending on his age).

Plane trips

Short trips don't cause too many difficulties; however, strollers are generally not allowed on board domestic airlines, posing difficulties when there are stopovers and if you are hanging around an airport with an active toddler for any length of time. Some airlines have strollers available to borrow while you wait; it's always worth asking. Domestic flights also do not have a supply of disposable diapers on hand, so make sure you have some with you.

Long flights overseas with babies and toddlers are becoming more and more common for families.

Here are a few tips

- Book well in advance. Try to travel during off-peak times.
- Book nonstop flights where possible so that you can avoid extra landings and takeoffs and hanging around airports.
- Order special meals when you book.
- Ask whether the airline has change tables in the economy class bathrooms.
- Are you able to take an umbrella stroller on board? If not, are they available to borrow during stopovers?
- When you get to the other end, you might find your toddler comes down with a minor illness (cough, cold, or diarrhea) which unfortunately often seems to happen when toddlers leave their usual environment.

Reorganizing sleep patterns might be tricky for a short time. Get your toddler back into his normal sleeping patterns as soon as you can by keeping him up at his normal times during the day rather than letting him sleep for long periods.

Car trips

Some toddlers travel well in their car seat for long stretches. Others only manage two-hourly stints without becoming irritable. And a small number go into full roar straight after departure and continue until the car stops and they are taken out. It's very hard to know why some toddlers do this—one of mine carried on in this fashion until she was nearly three, which meant our car travel was quite limited during that time.

Have your toddler comfortably dressed, well fed, and if possible ready for a sleep before leaving. Make sure he is protected from the sun. Long car trips are tiring for everyone. Plan to stop every two hours for a break.

What do you do if your toddler has a sudden screaming attack and you can't pull over?

- Sing a song, play a tape, or turn up the radio.
- Try to distract him with a toy, finger food, or a drink.
- Obviously stop as soon as you can if he doesn't settle and the noise is too distracting to drive safely.

Traveling experiences with toddlers and young children are many and varied and it's always worth asking well-traveled friends for tips when you are looking for information.

Happy travels . . .

Understanding death

Most toddlers will not have to deal with the death of someone close to them in their day-to-day life. However, by the time they

217

are three or four, many may be exposed to death by way of the death of a pet or perhaps seeing a dead bird in the yard. Older toddlers may use the word *death* but they do not understand the concept. They respond to the effect the death has on other family members, particularly their parents, and to any changes that directly affect them. They will feel great loss if the death is of someone they are close to because that person will no longer be around, but they do not understand that death is forever.

The loss of the person and the upheaval surrounding the death are likely to cause a regression in aspects of the toddler's behavior, with an increase in things like temper tantrums, whining, clinging, fussy eating and so on. As the toddler's routine is reestablished and his environment becomes more stable, his behavior will return to normal—for him (bearing in mind the wide range of what is considered normal for toddler behavior).

Developmental issues relating to death

- His rudimentary understanding of cause and effect and his egocentrism will make him associate death directly through his own experiences. For example, "If Grandma left, then maybe Mommy will leave too"; "Grandma left because I wouldn't eat the dinner she cooked"; and so on.

- Having just mastered the concept that people and things have not gone forever even if we can't see them, and that Mommy and Daddy always come back when they go away, it is impossible for toddlers to now grasp the idea that some people (or animals) never come back.

- Their lack of verbal communication abilities means they are

218

likely to act out scenes of dying by pretending to be dead themselves or playing with "dead" dolls. This might happen months
after the event.

Here are some ways to help your toddler

- Avoid using terms like "going to sleep" or "gone for a rest." It is
  better to simply use the word *died*. If you talk about "going to
  heaven" it is important to stress that the person (or animal) is not
  coming back.
- Tell your toddler as much as you think he can understand. Toddlers need simple, short explanations. Tell him why you are
  upset. It is quite all right for him to see you crying. Reassure him
  that your grief is not caused by anything he has done and that
  you love him and that *you* are not going anywhere.
- Talk about the person (or animal) when the toddler brings it up.
  Reminisce about past times if your toddler shows interest. If your
  toddler has good language skills, expect the topic to pop up out
  of the blue from time to time.
- Get him back into his routine as quickly as possible – remember,
  routines and rituals are very comforting for all of us especially
  toddlers.
- Let staff know at childcare or preschool.

If help is needed

Toddlers are very much tuned into their parents' reactions and
emotions. They will deal with the loss as long as their parents are
available and supportive and life more or less goes on as normal.

If you find your grief is preventing this, it is advisable to seek help. Talk to your nurse practitioner about the availability of grief counseling in your area.

chapter **eight**

Sleep

Volumes have been written about sleep in the first three years in response to the fact that how babies and toddlers sleep (or don't sleep) is of primary concern for large numbers of parents. Anxiety about baby and toddler sleep seems to have reached epidemic proportions in Western society. I don't know for sure about *other cultures,* but the perception is that the sleeping habits of *their* young do not create the same urgency for their families as for *ours*.

Health professionals who work with families and babies quickly become aware that, one way or another, the focus of most consultations inevitably turns into long discussions about sleep in all its minuscule and endless variations.

Obviously it's in everyone's best interests to get regular and sound sleep. One of the shocks of parenthood is the amount of time it takes to properly care for babies and toddlers. Add to that the possibility of three years of very little sleep and it's no wonder parents become somewhat obsessed with finding out how to get as much as possible.

Why has sleep become such a big deal in our society?

- When both parents are working it becomes crucial that the toddler sleeps well at night, since allowances for parental exhaustion in the workplace are rare.
- Many families have no support or backup for troubled times.
- Work commitments and family lifestyles are organized on the assumption that after three months the baby will sleep through for the rest of his life.
- Many other baby and toddler problems seem to evaporate if their sleeping patterns are compatible with those of their parents.
- Research shows a relationship between lack of sleep and post-partum depression.
- As with childcare, the way babies and toddlers sleep and what the parents choose to do about it is now firmly in the public

arena. Sleep now comes with its own propaganda, factions, and political messages.

It is no wonder parents today worry and agonize about sleep so much when it is given such a high profile. The most negative aspect of the volume of material on the topic and the growing public nature of the debate is the erosion of parents' confidence to make their own sleeping arrangements. And to make their own decisions about how they are going to respond to their babies and toddlers in the middle of the night.

My approach

I endeavor to present sleep information in as practical and uncomplicated a way as possible and to offer a few safe options. My approach will not suit every parent, as the information I provide is, to a large extent, no frills—a result of many years of helping parents in a busy well-baby practice center where routine sleep problems take up large portions of each day. I do not provide guaranteed solutions or promises to solve all problems.

Routine sleep problems are very common

Without wishing to minimize the impact that years of disturbed sleep can have, dealing with sleep problems in healthy babies and toddlers is a routine part of family life in the first three years. It should be treated as such.

When it's about more than just sleep

There are times when toddler sleep problems are an indication of more deep-seated family problems, or perhaps the personal problems of one parent, which need to be addressed before there is likely to be any way of dealing with the sleep problem from a practical level. It is impossible when writing a book to address the experiences of every individual reader, so if you are aware of such a possibility in your household, seek further advice.

A quick rule of thumb is that *if you find that you are continually distressed* about your toddler's sleeping or bedtime routine and you can't put a teach-to-sleep plan into action or come to a suitable compromise, then further help is advisable. This usually involves counseling to resolve issues that may be affecting your ability to deal satisfactorily with the sleep hassles.

Why are there so many sleep hassles?

1. Sleep patterns—a simple explanation

Humans of all ages have brief waking periods during the night following a light sleep and dreaming phase before moving into a deep sleep phase. Toddlers who continue to disturb their parents at night become fully awake at this time, are unable to put themselves back to sleep, and eventually start to want attention. At this stage, they are given a breastfeeding, a pacifier, a bottle, are rocked and patted, or are brought into bed with their parents.

Apart from the fact that a bottle of anything other than water is a risk factor for tooth decay, there is nothing wrong with nighttime attention per se, as long as parents are happy about the situation. However, by the time the first year is over, many parents are wondering why the night waking is still happening and how much longer it might continue.

Why does it continue?

Because the toddler associates sleep with certain conditions, and unless they are present, he is unable to put himself back to sleep after waking briefly as a part of his normal night sleep patterns.

Some toddlers stop calling for attention by themselves sometime during the second year, but in my experience the majority of nighttime wakers don't. The longer the night waking continues, the higher the possibility that it will carry on until sometime between three and five years. ***This is not necessarily a problem for all families.***

2. Constant illness

The toddler years are renown for the never-ending rounds of viral infections, ear infections, diarrhea, and so on which have the capacity to play havoc with night-time sleeping. (Teething is not a medical illness and is unrelated to night waking.)

3. Developmental issues

Many things related to normal toddler development have the potential to interfere with sleep.

- Nightmares, night terrors and fears of the dark, monsters, and so on.

- The development of fantasy and imagination around twenty months.
- Separation anxiety.
- New experiences (childcare, moving to a new house, separation and divorce, new baby, holidays, visitors).
- Negativity, testing limits, and working out how much control they have.

Most of the time constant illness and developmental issues are not the primary reason for constant night waking and bedtime hassles. If an overall structure is confidently put in place, these things can be managed so that they do not turn into years of disturbed nights.

Bedroom safety

Whether your toddler sleeps in your room or in his own, as soon as he is mobile and able to move out of his bed or crib, it is important to make sure his room is safe. Apart from your toddler's welfare, knowing his room is safe will help your confidence should you decide to take a firm approach to bedtime and nighttime shenanigans.

- If your toddler is still in a crib make sure:
  There is no bumper.
  The mattress fits snugly.
- Once he is out of a crib, a low bed is advisable. For higher beds, a bed guard might be a good idea depending on the amount your toddler moves around during the night. A quilt or blanket on the floor by the bed might be all you need.

- Make sure he can't fall or climb out of a window.

- Remove all breakable objects (for example, mirrors, vases and framed glass).

- Check on potential climbing apparatus that might lead to trouble (for example, a cabinet or a change table).

- Remove any toys that are a safety hazard when your toddler is unsupervised (for example, small objects that can be swallowed, string that can be wound around the neck, and plastic bags of any description).

A basic bedtime routine

As every family will have their own bedtime ritual and routine, please use this as a guide only. The message here is that the likelihood of easy bedtimes and undisturbed nights is enhanced by consistent, predictable routine and special family rituals. The optimum time to set this up is between nine months and two years.

- Allow enough time in the evening for a relaxed dinner, quiet play, bath, and story before bed. Give your toddler plenty of positive attention during this period. Turn off the TV.

- Try to follow the same routine and order of activities as often as you can.

- Give warnings before each change in activity. If necessary, use an egg timer to herald the imminent end of bathtime. Encourage older toddlers (two and older) to use a clock that marks the start of bedtime—"When the big hand is on six and the little hand is on . . . etc.."

- Tuck in teddy, dolly, clowny, or whoever is the night companion, then tuck in your toddler.

- Read a story together.

- Sing a lullaby or special song (I can still remember my mother doing that until I was quite old). As your toddler gets older, give him a choice between two songs.

- Say a special goodnight—a goodnight ritual might include a humming hug, a butterfly kiss, rubbing noses, light kisses on forehead, cheeks, and nose. Phrases might be "Nighty, nighty, sleep tighty," "Hoo-roo boo-boo," "God bless." Make it the same every night. Rituals are comforting and give toddlers a great sense of being special and of feeling secure.

- Keep the time short but positive. When you leave, do so decisively. A night-light is fine if you think it is needed. The door can be left open or shut.

- If your toddler is used to sleeping with a closed door from a young age, it makes it easier to discourage night visitations and helps minimize fear of the dark and of being alone. If, however, your toddler insists on having the door open, leave it slightly ajar.

Night waking—your options

Part of working out whether to do anything about your toddler's night waking is to decide whether what is happening is a problem or not. It's easy to feel pressured by those around you. Learn to ignore unwanted advice. ***If you are happy with what's happening, there's no need to do anything.***

Options are limited, and despite a multitude of variations on the theme, when you peel back all the layers there are only three.

1. ***Live with it (sharing your bed is the main option here).***

2. ***Leave your toddler to his own devices ("control crying" is the main option here).***

3. ***Sedation (a very limited option and only appropriate under certain circumstances).***

Solving or living with your toddler's nighttime sleep habits always involves one of these options.

Option 1: Living with what's happening

Readers who are familiar with the sleep section in *Baby Love* will be aware that I put this option third there and teach-to-sleep first. Now I am changing them around.

Why?

It's a trick to confuse you.

No. I believe that the longer a toddler is used to behaving in certain ways prior to going to bed or during the night, the harder it is to change what is happening. By the time the toddler is two years old, preventing him from sharing your bed and/or getting him to go to bed alone at 7 p.m. instead of lying on the couch to go to sleep requires a great deal of resolution and commitment from parents. Changing the routine is unlikely to happen without considerable pain and probably noise. If the parents remain firm, consistent, and calm, the pain is short-lived and a change is achieved.

However, many parents who have lived with the situation for this long have difficulty facing the pain and find themselves more distressed making the change than the situation warrants.

This is why it is very important to think carefully about why you want things to be different and how far you are prepared to go to achieve the change. There is usually a lot of crying, and once a toddler is in a bed or can climb out of his crib, a barrier of some sort has to be put in place to prevent him from leaving his bedroom. Older toddlers with language skills will often say some truly distressing things: "Why are you doing this to me?," "I don't love you anymore," and so on (these are a few of the milder ones).

I am not trying to discourage any parents who wish to follow the teach-to-sleep plan, nor to give the impression that I disapprove of my own information—far from it—but to make the point that it is not easy. I frequently talk to parents for whom the potential drama of doing the "control crying" is far worse than living with a toddler crawling into bed at 4 a.m. every morning for a few hours. Or putting up with a toddler going to sleep on the couch before being carried to bed at 10 p.m.

Co-sleeping and the family bed have many adherents, and if that is what you want, fine. Even if it is not what you originally planned, you may find that sharing your bed with a toddler or two is preferable to the alternative (getting in and out of bed all night or doing the dreaded "control crying").

Not all sleep problems can be solved, and sometimes learning to live with a toddler's sleep patterns is a matter of changing your expectations of what is normal and achievable and how life with a toddler should be. Sadly, boasting by other parents about how good their toddlers are at night can lead those who share beds into negative thoughts about themselves and their babies. Over the years, I have talked to many families who come to terms with night waking and bed sharing when it becomes apparent that, for them, it is the only option. And of course for some parents bed sharing is a very positive experience.

Be as consistent as possible

If you allow the bed sharing one night, then leave your toddler to cry the next, only to succumb after an hour, nighttimes are always going to be stressful.

If your toddler normally sleeps in his room, in his own bed, avoid allowing him into your bed on a whim, when one partner is away, after a bad dream, or when he is sick if that is not what you want to do the rest of the time.

Option 2: Teaching-to-sleep

Teaching-to-sleep, "control crying," "control comforting," "crying down" or "leaving to cry" are all different names for what is essentially the same thing—changing the toddler's conditions of sleep to exclude the external aids he needs in order to get to sleep or get back to sleep. The different names reflect creative attempts to make parents feel better about leaving their toddlers to cry. Techniques vary according to the health professional giving the advice and the parents' feelings on the matter.

Some programs are simple, others more complex. Some favour (as I do) a direct jump-in-at-the-deep-end approach; others prefer softer, more gradual withdrawal of the parents' attention. In my experience the latter approach often does not achieve a great deal apart from more exhaustion for the parents and mixed messages for the toddler, who ends up without a clear idea of what it is his parents want him to do.

The advice from those who view all such strategies as wrong is inevitably to learn to enjoy the bed sharing and take comfort in the fact that you are an "attached parent" (and so, presumably, somehow superior to other parents). And I guess that is consolation of sorts for years of disturbed sleep.

One of the problems faced by parents who would like to change things is the fear that "control crying" is harmful. The term has become blurred with overuse and now has a negative if not sinister aura around it, so before launching into the Barker version, let's put it into some perspective.

What is "control crying?"

Control crying means that the toddler is left to cry until he puts himself to sleep instead of being rewrapped, given a pacifier, or a bottle, breastfed, rocked, patted, rolled over, or allowed to come into the parental bed.

The parent visits the toddler at varying intervals, briefly comforts him, then leaves again.

Success rates

Consistent reliable research supporting the unqualified success of this method for older babies and toddlers is hard to find. But anecdotal evidence from hands-on practitioners reports a high degree of success. Unfortunately it is not always permanent, but even when it's not, just trying it often contributes to helping parents work out what they want to do in relation to their toddler's sleep patterns.

Proof of harm

Conversely it is also hard to find any concrete evidence that doing the various forms of control crying causes permanent emotional and psychological damage to healthy children in loving homes. And in one form or another, it has been done regularly throughout the world at least since the 1960s and almost certainly for decades prior to that. Though not, apparently, by *other cultures*, who I'm sure have their own child-rearing practices that we would view with a certain amount of distaste.

The critics

The critics of strategies to leave older babies and toddlers to cry are invariably people who do not have the day-to-day experience that hands-on practitioners have. They do not have to come up with suitable, practical ways of helping all parents rather than just some. Critics include parents who feel it is not right (for them), as well as some health professionals, journalists, researchers, and academics whose opinions are based on personal experience with their own children and lots of theory but on limited wide-ranging practice.

Sadly many critics present their point of view in a way designed to make many responsible parents, particularly mothers, feel guilty and alarmed. Suggestions by some, with no evidence to support their claims, are that "control" crying leads to suboptimal brain growth, a diminishment in relationship skills and serious personality glitches. Others believe that parents are forced to do "control crying" by experts and are thus turned away from trusting their own instincts.

Parents learn as they go and are highly unlikely to be pushed into a strategy like control crying unless they decide for themselves that this is what they want to do. In a basic framework of being loved, respected, wanted and cared for, I am convinced it is drawing a wide bow to suggest that trying control crying for a limited period is going to be a crucial factor in determining the outcome of the average twenty-one-year-old.

Sleep-deprived parents must be given the option

Health professionals with the day-to-day experience of a never-ending flow of sleep-deprived parents always feel it is an option

233

they must offer if parents are to be fully informed. And if offered, parents must be confidently supported should they decide to follow the strategy.

The parents' perspective

Naturally for those parents who suddenly get some sleep for the first time in a year, and in the process find that their enjoyment of their toddler increases dramatically, such a technique can seem like a miracle. For others, the thought of doing such a thing is an anathema.

When making the decision to try control crying, parents must bear in mind that, apart from the toddler changing himself over time, it is the only safe way of bringing persistent nighttime disturbances by a healthy toddler to an end when other milder strategies (taking the toddler back to bed when he appears, pretending to ignore his nighttime demands, and so on) have had no impact. And that it doesn't always work and good results are not always permanent.

A plan for teaching your toddler to sleep

As leaving toddlers to cry is never easy, it's best to teach your toddler to sleep in the most efficient way possible so that it's all over quickly and everyone can start enjoying a good night's sleep. This means planning—the more haphazard you are, the more exhausting and drawn out the whole thing becomes, with little chance of anything changing.

Before you begin

- Your toddler must be in a room on his own. This may mean a temporary moving around of family members.

  If your toddler shares your room and there is no other bedroom, I suggest you and your partner sleep in the living room for a week. Once your toddler is sleeping all night, move back. Unfortunately shared accommodation sometimes means a return to disturbed nights, but if you're getting desperate for sleep, it's certainly worth a try.

  If you are about to move into a new house, wait until you've moved before teaching your toddler to sleep.

  If your toddler shares a room with a baby or an older sibling, arrange for him to sleep on his own for a week.

- If your toddler can climb out of his crib or is in a bed, a barrier must be placed at the door of his room to prevent him from leaving.

  What sort of barrier?

  If your toddler is accustomed to having the door closed, shut the door. It may be necessary to fasten it from the outside so that he cannot leave. Alternatively, if the idea of locking him in is distasteful or if he is used to having the door open, use a safety gate (which he can't climb over) or something creative that will keep the door ajar enough for him to see out but will prevent him from getting out. Ideas include a chest of drawers, or something jammed under the door. Use your imagination—I'm sure you'll come up with something.

- Double-check the safety of the room (see page 226).

- You and your partner must cooperate; talk it over well in advance so that you both agree on your plan of action.

Teaching your toddler to sleep is so much easier when partners agree and both take part; however, this is not always possible. When one parent is prepared to follow the plan and the other isn't, the nonparticipator must either bury his or her head under the pillow and ignore or, if this is too difficult, sleep somewhere else for three to five nights. Listening to yelling and calling out, is not easy but it's doubly difficult when one partner undermines the other's actions, creating extra *unnecessary* stress for the participating parent.

- If you have close neighbors let them know so that they don't give you a hard time. Impress upon them that you are up with your toddler—he is not being left to cry on his own—and that you would appreciate their patience for a few nights.

- Pick a time that suits you, bearing in mind things like work commitments, visitors, holidays, and moving into a new house. It's important to make sure your toddler continues to sleep in the same bed in the same room for at least a month afterward.

- Your toddler must be well (ignore teething).

- You and your partner must be well and not trying to handle an undue amount of other difficulties at the same time. Toddlers respond well as long as their parents stay calm and confident—if you become visibly upset and worried, your toddler picks up your distress signals and there is less chance of a positive result.

The basic principles of teaching-to-sleep

Going to bed

1. Decide upon a suitable bedtime (anytime from 6:30 to 7:30 p.m.).

   Work out a bedtime routine. Make sure your toddler does not sleep too long in the afternoon. Have him up by 3:30 p.m. or, for some eighteen-month to two-year-olds, perhaps think about omitting altogether. Depending on the toddler, omitting the afternoon sleep can sometimes contribute in a positive way to fuss-free bedtimes.

   Dress him in warm clothes if necessary, since he may fall asleep on the floor the first night or two.

   Tell your toddler what is now going to happen at bedtimes. Keep it clear and simple: "After your bath I will read you a story/sing you a song, then it is bedtime. I am not going to stay with you while you go to sleep. I would like you to go to sleep on your own. I would also like you to stay in your room after you go to bed. I am going to fix the door of your room to help you stay in your room." Show him how you intend to fix the door.

   You must then do exactly what you said you would do, calmly and confidently.

2. After the final goodnight, leave decisively.

   Now comes the hard part.

   Your toddler will probably come to the door and start to call out, cry, and so on. Leave him for a few minutes. If it continues, go to him and put him back into bed. Leave the room.

He will almost certainly come to the door again.

Leave him for a time that you elect (anything from five to twenty minutes).

This time go to the door only and talk to him briefly.

"I understand that you are upset, but this is how it is going to be from now on. I don't mind if you stand and cry at the door. When you are ready, go back to bed."

Leave.

Continue in this way until he goes back to bed—or goes to sleep by the door. Obviously do not go to the door at the point where it sounds as if he is winding down.

If you think you can put him back to bed without waking him, do so; otherwise leave him.

3. I cannot emphasize enough how important it is for you to keep calm, firm, and consistent. If you vacillate, lose it, look anxious and guilty and beat your chest, there is no point in continuing.

   It is also crucial to do exactly the same thing every night for a month, and even then not to vary the routine apart from illness, outings, or holidays.

What about during the night?

1. Again it's important to tell your toddler before he goes to bed what the new arrangement is and to show him what you are doing to the door.

2. When he wakes in the night, he will get to the door, find that he can't get out and cry, call out, or yell.

3. You must get out of bed, get dressed, and go to your toddler. Go in, give brief attention, and put him back to bed. Remind him of

the new regime and leave him.

4. Do not go back to bed. Make a cup of tea. Repeat the bedtime procedure. Do not go into the room. Talk to him briefly through the door at ten, fifteen, or twenty-minute intervals. Stay up until he goes to sleep.

5. Continue in the same way each evening and/or night.

6. And . . . ?

Usually within a week (sometimes it can be within a night or two) the toddler starts going to bed without too much of a fuss and the night waking and wandering ceases.

Tips

• The pacifier

If the main reason you are getting up at night is to replace the pacifier then it makes sense to bid it farewell as part of the plan. Pacifiers are more likely to be a night-waking issue for younger toddlers (twelve to fifteen months). By the time they are older, they can find their own pacifiers and put them back in.

• Throwing up

What if he throws up? A good vomit is certainly distressing, but remain calm, clean your toddler up with a minimum of fuss, and continue where you left off.

Whatever you do, don't get frazzled over a vomit.

Unlike healthy adults, healthy toddlers vomit very easily (especially if they have a big bottle of milk prior to bed). *Providing they are otherwise well*, it is not a sign of anything drastic. Toddlers who throw up when left to cry as part of teaching-to-sleep stop quickly as long as their parents stay calm and consistent so that the toddler gets a clear message. Stopping the bottles of milk also helps.

Common questions

What about twins?

The variations in twins' sleeping patterns follow the same variations of any siblings. Both might sleep through, both might call for room service, or one might sleep through and one might want attention during the night. Some twins sleep together in the same bed, some in the same room, and some in separate rooms, depending on their parents' feelings on the matter and the available space.

When both toddlers are waking, follow the teaching-to-sleep for one toddler. Leave both toddlers in the same room, plan things carefully around work schedules and so on, and be mentally prepared for a stint of night duty as undoubtedly you will find it harder than parents with one toddler do. However, if you can see it through, both toddlers will learn to sleep within the same time frame as one toddler.

If only one toddler is waking, the decision has to be made whether or not to separate them while the teaching-to-sleep takes place. This is not an easy decision, as twins often not only sleep in the same room but in the same bed until school age, so it is up to individual parents to work out the best strategy for their own family situation. Try getting advice from other parents of twins.

And sole parents?

Sorting out sleep problems is harder for sole parents because it is much easier for them to slip into the shared-bed routine and much harder for them to take action and see it through on their own. If, after having read through all the information in this section, you decide you wish to do the teaching-to-sleep, try and plan it very carefully, and if possible arrange for someone to be with you throughout. (your mother, another close family member, a good friend). It is important that your helper understands exactly what you want to achieve and supports you totally in what you are doing. It is best to enlist someone who agrees with the concept of control crying.

Once your toddler is sleeping in his own bed, in his own space, try not to succumb to sharing the bed in times of illness, nightmares, holidays, or loneliness if that is not what you want to do on a regular basis.

How long do you let him cry for?

As long as it takes. Remember that the more attention you give, the longer the crying is likely to go on for.

What if it takes longer than a week?

Obviously letting toddlers shriek for nights on end is not appropriate. If at the end of a week there is no improvement, it's time to rethink everything. The main reasons for endless crying include:

- Inconsistency (ignore one night, cuddle the next, losing the routine).
- Lack of support from partner.
- Lack of confidence by the parent for a variety of reasons, which may include:

  Disapproval from extended family members.

  Fear of doing the wrong thing after reading of the dangers of control crying.

  Worry that the toddler won't love them anymore—that the attachment is threatened.
- Inadequate planning—wrong time (sick toddler, moving to a new house, visitors, attempting to change things in conjunction with the

arrival of a new baby, separation of parents or the first week in childcare).

- Doing it for the wrong reasons—"because it is time that I 'control-cried' him."

- A basic child-rearing philosophy that is at odds with this strategy.

- Insecurity in the toddler because of social and emotional family problems which need attention.

- Unknown (it doesn't always work).

Will my toddler be upset and clingy during the day?

Possibly. Initially it is a major change for him; however, the clinginess will not last long. He will feel more rested and you will enjoy your days with him more because your sleep has not been disturbed. Overall, when sleep problems are resolved, toddlers and parents enjoy renewed pleasure in each other's company.

My toddler is so erratic. Sometimes he sleeps all night. At other times he wakes up and makes a fuss and I bring him into our bed.

A tricky situation. Teaching to sleep is more a strategy for a toddler who has never slept without disturbing his parents and needs to be taught how to do it. In this case it really is a matter of how much of a problem you feel it is. You've read the plan. You know what is involved. Is it worth the drama for the nights he disturbs you? Is it really a problem to share your bed with him some nights?

Will it last forever?

As previously noted, many things disturb toddlers' sleep and it is easy to get back into old habits in times of illness or because of night terrors, bad dreams, and so on. Suggestions for dealing with these things are given in the next few pages, but essentially:

- *If you do not want your toddler in your bed, do not allow him to join you.*
- *If you want your toddler to have an evening and bedtime routine, stick to it.*
- *You are the parent. You are in charge. Your toddler will follow your lead.*
- *Toddlers want to please their parents but they have to know what it is you want them to do.*

Option 3: Sedatives

Sedatives do not solve toddler sleep problems but must be included as an option so parents are fully informed.

Busy health care professionals often suggest sedatives as the only option. When parents are exhausted and at their wits' end a sedative does seems like an easy, peaceful solution. But giving a sedative does not teach a toddler how to sleep – it's a bit like an adult taking diet pills to lose weight rather than changing his or her eating and exercise habits.

Parents are often advised to slowly decrease the dose over a certain period, at which time it is suggested that the toddler will sleep without the sedative.

I have never seen this work—once the sedative is stopped, the night waking returns.

Apart from the fact that sedatives do not teach toddlers to sleep, there are difficulties associated with using them.

- Sedatives have the reverse effect on some toddlers, so rather than calming them, they stimulate them.
- A safe dose often only promotes sleep for about four hours, so

it's a dilemma deciding whether to repeat the dose again during the night or to go back to the external aids. A dose which makes toddlers sleep all night may be outside the safe zone and, apart from anything else, keep them in a zonked-out state during the day—not the best way to promote optimum growth and development.

Occasionally when a toddler is sick or recovering from jet lag, a short-term use of a sedative may be appropriate. When using a sedative at times like this, giving the sedative the first time the toddler wakes in the night, rather than at bedtime, usually works best.

Other sleep dilemmas

Bedtime hassles

Some toddlers do not disturb their parents once they are asleep but are difficult about bedtime. They might refuse to go without tantrums and fuss. They might go down quite happily, only to keep reappearing until midnight. They might insist on going to sleep in one parent's arms or having a parent lie with them for an inordinate length of time.

The basic principles for putting reluctant toddlers to bed are the same as for night waking. See page 237.

Should I go in when my toddler wakes in the night?

If your toddler was well when you put him to bed, don't rush into his bedroom at the first sound. Wait. Sometimes toddlers call out in their sleep, cry briefly, and resettle.

Obviously if it continues or your toddler sounds very distressed, go to him.

If he is well, give him minimum attention, brief comfort, and leave. If he continues to call or cry and you are confident that it is for attention only, leave him. Do not bring him into your bed if that is not what you want to do, as it potentially sets up a pattern that is difficult to change. It is tempting when you are tired and have to go to work the next day, but each time you succumb and bring him into your bed, the habit is positively reinforced. Remember that your toddler understands things mostly through actions. If you say you don't want him in there but take him anyway, what conclusion is he likely to come to?

If he is unwell, stay with him and do what is necessary (comfort, perhaps give him fluid—in a cup is best—or medication if appropriate). You may need to stay up until he settles again.

Toddlers who are used to sleeping in their own beds can have odd nights in the parental bed when they are unwell without it turning into a regular feature.

Nightmares and night terrors

It's very easy to confuse nightmares and night terrors in the toddler years, especially before the toddler can explain what has upset him. From the parents' point of view, the toddler is frightened and crying for a reason that is hard to determine.

As the courses of action are different, it is worth knowing the difference.

1. Nightmares

Nightmares are frightening dreams that occur in the light dreaming phase of sleep. Nightmares happen in the early hours of the morning when there is much more light sleep and dreaming.

Nightmares are most common between two and the adolescent years. Fifty percent of all five-year-olds have regular nightmares.

WHY THE NIGHTMARES?

- Most nightmares have no obvious cause and are not an indication of a more serious problem. Developmental causes such as separation anxiety, expanding memories, imagination and fantasies, and new experiences can contribute.
- Medication, fever, TV, overheating (too many clothes or covers) or frightening events are sometimes the cause.
- Sometimes nightmares can be traced to specific causes such as stress over potty training, the arrival of a new baby, separation of parents, temporary absence of one parent, or childcare.
- Occasionally nightmares are a symptom of family dysfunction which needs addressing. The same nightmare night after night can be an indication of this.
- And nightmares can be a powerful attention-seeking device once the toddler realizes the effect his distress has upon his parents who take him to their bed to comfort him.

WHAT HAPPENS WHEN A TODDLER HAS A NIGHTMARE?

- It occurs in the second half of the night.

- He becomes fully awake, cries, shrieks, and calls for help after the nightmare is over.
- He continues to cry and show distress after waking while his parent is with him.
- He clings to his parent and is aware that his mother or father is with him.
- It may take a while for him to be soothed back to sleep.

A FRAMEWORK TO WORK WITHIN

- If you think there is something in your toddler's life that is contributing to frequent nightmares, try to address the issue. Sometimes more positive attention during the day and less focus on the potty training does the trick. Or, if appropriate, limit the TV and avoid scary stories or boisterous play before bedtime.
- When your toddler wakes up distressed from a bad dream, go to him and comfort him. Use the same special ritual words you use at bedtime.
- When he is calm, resettle him. Leave the room as soon as you can. Do not lie down with him or take him back to your bed if that is not what you want to do.

2. Night terrors

Night terrors occur in the early part of the night. They are not associated with dreaming and happen when someone is partially aroused from very deep sleep. The toddler might thrash around, cry, and yell but does not become fully awake. If his parents try to comfort him he does not recognize them or understand what is going on. If he wakes up, he is not frightened and has no idea what has been going on. The next day he has no recollection of the event.

WHY THE NIGHT TERRORS?

Night terrors in healthy toddlers living in loving environments are usually a normal part of deep nondreaming sleep patterns with no underlying significant causes. They may be exacerbated by over-tiredness or overheating (too many clothes or covers).

A FRAMEWORK TO WORK WITHIN

* Night terrors can sound and look alarming, but it is best to do nothing. They may last for a few minutes or up to half an hour. If you want to, stay in the room and watch over your toddler until the night terror passes.

* It is advisable to do nothing. If your toddler wakes up, speak to him briefly, settle him, and leave.

Fears

Fears of the dark, of monsters, and of being alone are more common between four and six than during the toddler years, but all children occasionally feel frightened at night.

Why the fears?

See pages 93–95 for developmental reasons.

It is normal for healthy toddlers to occasionally fear the dark and the possibility of monsters, especially after they start to develop imagination and fantasies (from around twenty months).

Badly chosen TV, stories, and games before bedtime exacerbate such fears, as does anxiety about life events such as childcare, parental separation, a new baby, inappropriate punishment, and so on.

Older toddlers who are not used to being alone at night are more likely to experience fears if their sleeping arrangements are suddenly changed.

A FRAMEWORK TO WORK WITHIN

- A dim night-light can be helpful.

- Acknowledge his fear of the monster (or the chipmunk or the bad dolly or whatever) in a matter-of-fact way without ridiculing it, but reassure your toddler that you will always be there to look after him and keep him safe.

- Most fears are fleeting. Doing big searches under beds and in cabinets to prove that nothing is there draws too much attention to the fear. It gives your toddler the impression that you too have concerns that something might be lurking.

- Encourage your toddler to use teddy or his blanky for comfort and protection against the monster.

- Address any underlying issues which you think may be contributing to excessive fears in your toddler.

Night-time attention-seeking devices

Nightmares, night terrors, and fears can all turn into attention-seeking devices to avoid going to bed and/or to get attention through the night.

It is up to you how you wish to deal with these things.

If your toddler is used to coming into your bed and you do not mind, then carry on.

If your toddler has never been allowed to share your bed and that is how you want to continue, then do not start now. If he comes into your room, take him back to his own bed. If he cries or calls for you, go to him.

Give your toddler a clear, consistent message: "I am really sorry you had a bad dream, Matthew, and I will stay with you until you are calm, but then I would like you to go off to sleep again in your own little bed in your own room."

Other attention-seeking devices are things like the endless drink of water, frequent requests for the potty, and calling out. Everyone's tolerance of these tricks is highly variable. I suggest one drink, one trip to the toilet, then pretend to ignore.

Most parents get to know the difference between attention-seeking behavior and genuine fears. The more positive reinforcement given to attention-seeking behaviors, the longer they will continue.

Where should the toddler sleep?

By now you probably know what you want. From your toddler's point of view, it really doesn't matter as long as his sleeping arrangements are consistent and everyone is (more or less) happy.

All the following are fine:

- Own room, own crib or bed; door open, door closed
- Own room, mattress on the floor; door open, door closed
- Your room, own crib or mattress on the floor
- Your room, your bed
- Shared accommodation with sibling(s); door open, door closed

Moving from crib to bed

Hmm—the things we agonize over.

The move can happen anytime from the first birthday to the third. It depends on the toddler, the available accommodation and space, the parents, the current sleeping arrangements, and what sleep problems are being encountered.

Cribs have the great advantage of containing the toddler, and if he is happy, sleeping well, and is still comfortable in the crib, leave him be.

If there are sleeping problems, moving the toddler from the crib into a bed is not likely to solve them. If the toddler is inclined to climb out of the crib and is in danger of hurting himself, it is probably best to bid the crib farewell and move him into a bed.

If there is another baby on the way and the crib is needed, it makes sense to change the toddler over well before the baby arrives.

Some toddlers are enamored of their cribs and are not happy about giving them up. Diplomacy, imagination and the right timing are required to make the change. Move a bed in and encourage him to lie on it during the day. Put his teddy or clowny into the bed. Read him a story on the bed at night and eventually see if you can persuade him into it. One weekend when you go away, arrange for someone to remove the crib, which will then not reappear until the baby needs it, by which time your toddler will have forgotten all about it.

I believe that security rails on beds are not needed unless the toddler is very young and the bed is very high.

If you are nervous about nighttime catastrophes when the toddler first moves into the bed, put a temporary thick blanket or mattress alongside the bed.

Safe Sleepwear

Toddlers should never be put to bed in oversize cotton garments such as T-shirts or sweats as these garments catch fire easily and are associated with 200–300 emergency room-treated burn injuries to children annually. Buy sleepwear that meets federal safety standards. Children's garments sold as sleepwear must be labelled **Flame Resistant** or **Snug-fitting**. Flame resistant garments do not continue burning when removed from an ignition source. Snug-fitting garments are made to fit closely around a toddler's body.

Daytime sleeping

Daytime sleep in the toddler years varies according to the toddler's temperament, the time he goes to bed at night and rises in the morning, and sometimes the amount of physical activity he has.

Whenever the daytime sleep pattern changes (that is, from two sleeps to one or from one sleep to none), there is usually a wobbly period of three to four weeks while the toddler adjusts to the new regime. He is often more irritated and tired and will need extra attention until he adjusts.

Some toddlers stop having anything other than quick catnaps in the day from an early age (twelve to fifteen months), which is hard to do much about. Little or no daytime sleep from a young age does tend to make the day longer for mothers (or fathers), but it is not harmful for the toddlers.

A general guide to daytime sleeping—if it's not appropriate, please either ignore it or adapt it to suit

CHANGING FROM TWO SLEEPS TO ONE

This happens anytime from nine to eighteen months. Toddlers who wake early (5 a.m. to 6 a.m.) are more likely to keep having two sleeps for longer. Eventually the morning sleep stops, the toddler stays up until lunchtime, then has a sleep for one, two, or three hours after lunch. If you want bedtime to be around 7:00 or

7:30 p.m., it is advisable to have your toddler up by 3:30 p.m.

CHANGING FROM ONE SLEEP TO NONE

This happens anytime from two and a half to three and is mourned by the parent who is at home with the toddler. However, it also usually means that the toddler is ready for bed nice and early in the evening and goes down without a fuss, which can be a bonus.

How do you know when to drop a sleep?

Usually the toddler simply refuses to go down. He plays in his crib for a while, then screams and performs. Or entertains himself by tearing his diaper apart or by smearing poo. After a week or so of this behavior, the parent usually reluctantly acknowledges that it is a worthless exercise. The morning sleep is usually the first to go, but if he is an early riser, he may continue to sleep in the morning and miss the afternoon sleep.

What about stopping the sleeps?

The main reason for stopping the daytime sleep is because suddenly the toddler won't go to bed until 9 p.m. A choice has to be made—continue the day sleep and live with the late bedtime, or miss the day sleep and have the toddler in bed by 6.30 p.m. If you live in Italy, the choice is probably going to be the former; if you live in the U.S. it's probably going to be the latter. It's up to you.

RESTING

Sometimes toddlers are happy to have a rest period where they do not actually sleep but play quietly in their cribs or their rooms for half an hour or so after lunch, especially if they have had an active morning. This is fine.

The mammoth tantrum on waking

This is quite common and can be frightening the first time it happens. The toddler wakes suddenly after sleeping for an hour or more and goes into a total frenzy. It is perhaps more common on hot summer afternoons or when the toddler is woken rather than wakes naturally—but it can happen regardless.

WHY?

I'm not sure, but it probably relates to the stage of sleep the toddler suddenly awakens or is woken from.

A FRAMEWORK TO WORK WITHIN

- If it helps, hold him, but sometimes this makes things worse.
- Put him gently on the floor where you can see him and verbally reassure him that everything is okay.
- If the frenzy continues, try putting him in the stroller and briskly wheeling him around the block. By the time you return, he should be over it.

Early morning waking

This is part and parcel of the toddler package. Not all toddlers wake at the crack of dawn, but lots do, and the quick answer is that there's not much you can do about it.

Leaving toddlers to cry from 5 a.m. onward doesn't usually teach them to sleep longer, and when they have been asleep since 7:00 or 7:30 p.m., it's not really a fair or reasonable thing to do.

Should I put him to bed later?

It's not a good idea for younger toddlers (twelve to eighteen months), as they tend to wake at the same time regardless of when they go to bed. Keeping them up means that they get less sleep and you miss out on time to yourself in the evening.

However, as toddlers get older, it's worth seeing what happens if you keep them up an hour later (especially if they have been going to bed around 6:30 and when daylight saving is in place), as they may sleep in a little longer.

Other strategies (good luck)

- ***Stop one of the daytime naps (if he is having two).***
  Toddlers only need a certain amount of sleep (ten to fourteen hours, and fourteen hours might be too much for some). Stopping the morning nap and giving your toddler one sleep later in the day *may* eventually impact favorably on the early morning waking (no promises).

- ***Try slowly extending the time by going in five minutes later each week.***
  I'm going to be honest here—I've never seen this work. But you never know.

- ***Here is what most parents have to do:***
  Avoid going in at first call. Wait until you can't ignore him then, unless you can give him a drink and persuade him, to stay in his crib or room for a while, get up and start your day.

  It's unfair when it's always the same person, so some sort of roster system should be worked out so, both parents get a chance to sleep in at times. If you're a single parent, there's not much you can do—unless you've got a friend or a relative who will step in sometimes.

- Sometimes bringing the toddler to bed with you for a while works, but usually the wriggling, snuffling, and finger up your nose and in your ear is more trouble than it is worth.

- Go to bed early.

  Try not to despair . . . Early morning waking becomes less of an issue as the toddler gets older. Many toddlers start sleeping a little longer between two and three. As they get older, they are more capable of looking after themselves safely (reading books, listening to a tape, or playing) and you can start laying down a few rules about being disturbed—"Not until the big hand is on the twelve and the little hand is on the seven."

When your toddler becomes an adolescent and you can never get him out of bed in time for school, you will think back to this time of his life, longingly perhaps.

chapter nine

Food

General guidelines for feeding your toddler

These days we are constantly bombarded with nutritional information, and although I acknowledge it is helpful, even essential, in today's climate of fast food, it can also cause great anxiety to conscientious parents with fussy toddlers. Many parents seem to be in a constant state of despair about the possibility of grave nutritional deficiencies in their otherwise very healthy, active toddlers because the toddlers do not eat everything that is recommended from the five food groups.

The best way to view nutritional guidelines for toddlers is as a guide for sensible *family* eating. Toddlers will frequently not comply with nutritional guidelines. But if they are living in a family where there is a variety of good food offered most of the time (most of us enjoy the pizza occasionally and a reasonable example is set by their parents, they will be fine.

Build up to a variety of foods

Toddlers often have periods when they are very selective about what they will and won't eat, but offering them a variety of foods makes it much less likely that they will consume excessive or inadequate amounts of any one food.

Toddlers need fat in their diet

Fat is an essential part of babies' and toddlers' diets. They need it as a concentrated source of energy and for brain development. Forty to fifty percent of a toddler's energy intake should come from fat, decreasing to about thirty percent at age five and twenty-five percent after puberty. Always use full-fat dairy products and include a range of dairy products in the food you offer your toddler.

Cholesterol

Cholesterol is a fat used by the body to make certain hormones as well as nerve and brain cells. We do not need to eat cholesterol because the body makes its own and, as we are aware, an over-supply in adult life usually caused by a diet high in saturated fats and/or hereditary factors can lead to problems.

However, limiting food such as eggs, meat, and dairy products in toddlers' diets may be harmful as they contain valuable nutrients for proper growth and development. Cutting back these foods in early childhood does not prevent high cholesterol in adult life. It *is*, however, advisable to reduce the intake of saturated fats such as butter, cream, margarine, fried food, and fatty meat at any age.

Provide plenty of fruit, vegetables (including legumes) and grains

These foods provide essential nutrients such as vitamin A and vita-min C as well as carbohydrates, fiber and essential minerals. Combinations of these foods provide good family meals that tod-dlers can share and are excellent as finger foods and snacks. For some snack suggestions, see page 274.

Provide only a moderate amount of sugar and food containing added sugars

Excessive sugar in toddlers' diets can cause problems such as tooth decay, diarrhea, and a reduction in their appetites for nutritious food. It also interferes with establishing good eating habits in childhood. One of the most common ways toddlers get too much sugar is from fruit juice. One juice a day is plenty. Try to give it in a cup instead of a bottle and offer water in between.

Choose low-salt foods

Salt (sodium) is currently a somewhat confused issue; a relationship between sodium intake and high blood pressure in children has not been established. High blood pressure in adults is associated more with a family history of the condition, obesity, and alcohol consumption than with sodium.

It is agreed that sodium intake should be low in the first six months of life because babies have a limited capacity to excrete excessive sodium, which has the potential to cause kidney damage in susceptible babies. However, family meals that have the occasional pinch of salt for culinary purposes are fine for toddlers. Excessive salt is much more a problem in relation to processed food, fast food, and takeout food. A high intake of these foods is not recommended.

Your toddler's nutritional requirements

Here are the five essential nutrients your toddler needs for optimum health and growth. Remember that many combinations of different foods can supply all five nutrients, which is why diets can vary considerably and still be healthy.

1. Carbohydrates (complex, sugars, and dietary fiber)

Carbohydrates provide fuel, energy, and fiber. Examples include:

- avocado
- bananas
- carrots
- pasta
- rolled oats
- baked beans
- bread (white and whole wheat)
- flour (white and whole wheat)
- potatoes

Examples of natural **sugars:**

- apples
- dates
- oranges
- white grapes
- bananas
- dried apricots
- raisins

2. Protein

Proteins are needed for growth and repair of body cells. Toddlers need much more protein for their size than adults do.

In general, if toddlers are offered a variety of food from the five food groups, they are unlikely to be deficient in protein.

Examples of **animal protein** (animal proteins work well on their owna toddler only needs to eat one type of animal protein to grow properly) include:

- cheese
- eggs
- liver
- milk
- chicken
- fish
- meat
- yogurt

Examples of **plant protein** (plant proteins need to be combined to provide nourishment for proper growth; in the right combinations they are as useful as animal proteins) include:

- brown rice
- bread
- cooked pasta
- dates
- wheat germ

- breakfast cereals
- cooked green beans
- cooked lentils
- flour

3. Vitamins

Vitamins are needed in tiny amounts to help absorb other nutrients or to speed up chemical reactions. The body cannot produce them, so they must be supplied by food. Vitamins are classified as fat-soluble (A, D, E, and K) or water soluble (the B group and C). Fat-soluble vitamins are found in food fats and are fairly stable. Water-soluble vitamins are found in vegetables, grains, meat, and milk and are sensitive to heat and overexposure.

The question of vitamin supplements

Most toddlers do not need vitamin supplements. Occasionally supplements may have a place for toddlers who have serious medical conditions.

Toddlers having a vegan diet need a vitamin B_{12} supplement, since as B_{12} is only found in animal foods.

Generally vitamin supplements are unnecessary and a waste of money.

4. Minerals

Minerals are important for the formation of healthy blood, proper growth, and strong bones. Like vitamins, minerals have to be provided by the diet. Eating a variety of foods generally ensures that your body gets all the minerals it needs. The important ones for toddlers are *iron* and *calcium.*

Iron

Iron is needed for the formation of healthy blood and muscles. There is some concern at the current time that iron deficiency is a problem for some groups of babies and toddlers.

Foods that supply iron include:

- breastmilk (iron levels diminish between six and twelve months)
- dried apricots
- iron-fortified cereals (check labels)
- pasta
- beans
- dark green vegetables
- dates
- lean meat
- liver
- peas and lentils
- whole-grain cereals

THE QUESTION OF IRON SUPPLEMENTS

Healthy toddlers who are offered a wide variety of food do not need iron supplements; however, toddlers who consume large amounts of cows' milk and eat very little food are at risk of iron deficiency. Continuing bottles into the second year and beyond is the biggest cause of excessive milk intake, so the first line of treatment in this scenario is to stop the bottles. If the iron deficiency is serious, iron supplements need to be given until the toddler's appetite for food improves.

Toddlers on vegan diets do need iron supplements. Serving some food containing vitamin C with as many meals as possible enhances iron absorption. Vitamin C is found in fresh fruit and vegetables.

5. Calcium

Calcium is needed for good bone growth and strong teeth.

Milk and dairy products such as cheese and yogurt are the best sources and the most easily absorbed by the body.

Fortified soy milk is a good source of calcium; unfortified soy milk has very little.

Calcium is also found in the following foods but in much lesser quantities than in milk or dairy products:

- broccoli
- brussels sprouts (mash bones well)
- canned fish with bones
- nuts and seeds, but whole nuts should never be given to toddlers, nuts and seeds need to be offered in a paste form (e.g., tahini, smooth peanut butter, almond paste).
- oranges
- baked beans
- legumes
- tofu

A word about water

Water is a vital nutrient.

It is an excellent idea to encourage your toddler to drink water rather than fruit juice for the following reasons:

- Water is self-limiting (the toddler only drinks to relieve thirst) and so it doesn't interfere with appetite for other foods.

- Juice is a common cause of diarrhea when consumed in large amounts.

- Large amounts of juice contribute to tooth decay. Fruit juice is useful for constipation and as a source of vitamin C for toddlers, but one drink of juice a day is sufficient.

Vegetarian diets for toddlers

Many families now choose not to eat meat. It is relatively easy to provide adequate nutrients for toddlers from a vegetarian diet that includes fish, eggs, and dairy products.

Vegetarian diets that exclude fish and eggs are also fine but need some thought and planning.

Vegan diets (plant foods only) pose potential nutritional problems for toddlers which can be hard to solve.

Tips for vegetarian toddlers

- Enhance iron absorption by including food rich in vitamin C (fresh fruit and vegetables) with meals as often as possible. Other vegetarian foods that contain iron are baked beans, cooked lentils, dark green leafy veggies, and iron-fortified products such as breakfast cereals, some cows' milk, and soy milk.

- Vegetable protein needs to be paired to provide the right balance of protein. This is not as complicated as it sounds, as it is often something we do without thinking. For example, cereal and milk, peanut butter on bread and refried beans on tortillas.

  Here is a guide for pairing protein:

  lentils or beans with grains (rice, semolina, wheat)

  nuts (ground for toddlers) or seeds with grains

  dairy products with any plant proteins

265

- Sometimes toddlers on vegetarian diets get a little skinny (skinnier than toddlers normally are) because these diets tend to be high in fiber and low in fat. This is easy to fix by adding high-fat food to meals; for example, cheese sauce, white sauce, grated cheese, white bread, white rice, full-fat yogurt, sour cream, and so on.

- Vegan (plant food only) diets pose problems for toddlers, as they tend to be bulky and offer a very limited choice at a time in life when food refusal is common. A continuing shortage of protein, vitamin B$_{12}$, iron, calcium and fat in vegan diets, as well as an overall shortage of calories, can put the toddler's growth at risk.

    Some of the problems can be overcome by continuing to breastfeed or using soy formula beyond the first year (one of the rare times infant formula is of some advantage after the first year). Mixing liberal amounts of smooth peanut butter and tahini (sesame seed paste) into dishes before serving and giving a vitamin B$_{12}$ and iron supplement is recommended.

    If you wish to give your toddler a vegan diet and you are uncertain about any aspect, it is advisable to see a pediatric dietitian to make sure his nutrition is adequate for proper growth.

Food allergy and intolerance

Concerns about the possibility of food causing allergic responses in babies and toddlers have markedly increased. Unfortunately there are now many misconceptions about which foods might cause allergic reactions, as well as the symptoms, diagnosis, and treatment of those allergies.

What is an allergy?

It's the body's adverse reaction to foreign antibodies. Food allergies usually only involve one or two foods and are most common in babies and children under five who come from families with histories of eczema, hay fever, and asthma. Overall the incidence of food allergy in children is very small—a little over one percent.

The main foods that cause allergic reactions are milk, eggs, peanuts, wheat, fish, and soybeans. Medication, chemicals, dust, smoke, insect bites, pet hair, or pollutants also cause allergic reactions.

Allergic reactions may be immediate (two hours or less) or delayed (up to forty-eight hours) after the food is ingested. Common allergic symptoms include swelling around the eyes and mouth, flushing of the skin, rashes, and hives. Other symptoms include vomiting, excessive mucus, abdominal cramps, diarrhea, and vomiting.

Laboratory tests are unreliable in diagnosing allergic reactions. The results are often used inappropriately to restrict diets in ways that are of no defense against the allergy and, in fact, put the toddler's nutritional status at risk. Other tests that are of no use include hair and saliva testing and kinesiology—save your money.

The only reliable way to test for a food allergy is to exclude the food for a set period, then reintroduce it—this is known as a food challenge. A food challenge is not as simple as it sounds because milk, egg, or peanut proteins are found in many foods. Guidance from a suitable health professional is advisable to find out exactly which foods should be avoided and what substitutes should be used in order to ensure a nutritionally adequate diet.

What is food intolerance?

Food intolerance is much more common than food allergy. Food intolerance describes an adverse reaction to chemicals in food. The chemicals may be those found naturally in the food or those added commercially, and they appear to irritate the nerve endings in different parts of the body.

Food intolerance can occur at any age, and reactions usually depend on the amount of a particular food that has been eaten. A toddler may show no symptoms after eating the food in small doses or a single dose but may react after eating or drinking a larger amount or following a buildup of the chemical(s) over time.

Food intolerance does not include reactions to food caused by psychological or physical factors, called food aversions. Food aversions are caused by things such as stress, anxiety, seasickness, or pregnancy and can result in physical symptoms like nausea or vomiting. Most people suffer from food aversions at some time in their lives.

Commonly recognized symptoms of intolerance are not that different from allergy symptoms and include rashes, migraines, irritable bowel, asthma, nasal congestion, nausea, abdominal cramps and diarrhea, lethargy, and limb pains.

The issue of allergy, food aversion, and food intolerance becomes very confusing in relation to toddlers becase they can't explain what their problems are. All toddlers at some time or another suffer from the endless runny nose, the eternal cough, attacks of diarrhea and mysterious rashes. Toddlers also tend to behave in quite unpredictable ways, eat like birds, and poo like elephants—none of which are symptoms of anything other than being a toddler.

Allergy and intolerance to food is more common in young children because their immune system is not fully developed. Most toddlers grow out of their allergies. Various foods sometimes cause mild reactions, which are not serious. It's simply a matter of waiting a month and trying the food again. If your family has a proven history of allergies or intolerance, there's a much higher chance that your toddler will have the same. The chances are doubled if both parents suffer from the allergy or intolerance.

When problems are suspected, it's important to get specialist help so that you are not eliminating food needed for proper growth and development. Results of research into the relationship between food and common childhood ailments such as eczema, asthma, and hay fever are conflicting and the success of dietary restrictions varies tremendously with individuals. As these conditions tend to come and go spontaneously, it can be very hard to work out how much of a part food plays.

What about hyperactivity and the toddler diet?

Most toddlers by nature have high levels of activity compared to adults. That, along with all the developmental factors I constantly refer to, means the majority of toddlers will behave in uncontrolled ways when they are tired, hungry, excited, overstimulated, or scared.

Some toddlers have what has been identified as a difficult temperament. Difficult (a most unfortunate word) toddlers have troubles adapting, do not like new situations or people, have intense emotional reactions, and are hard to please.

Other toddlers have been identified as active. They are impulsive, constantly on the move, cannot bear being restricted, and fiddle with everything that crosses their paths. Active toddlers inevitably leave a path of devastation and destruction in their wake.

Toddlers with these temperaments are usually within the normal range, tricky as it might be for parents to know the best way to manage their daily lives. What degree of activity and/or difficult behavior is considered a problem is very subjective from family to family. In a quiet family, a very active toddler might be seen as abnormal. In another more boisterous family, the same level of activity might pass almost unnoticed.

A tiny number of toddlers with more intense levels of activity and/or difficult behavior, as well as a history of other distinctive behavioral patterns, are eventually diagnosed with Attention Deficit Syndrome with Hyperactivity. This diagnosis is not made until the school years, and before it can be made, all other causes of hyper-active/difficult behavior must be ruled out (emotional stress, medical problems, hearing disability, developmental delay/disability, autism, and so on).

When the level of an otherwise normal toddler's activity causes continued disruption to family and social life, despairing parents often wonder how much his diet may or may not be contributing to the behavior.

And . . . ?

Dr Ben Feingold proposed the connection between hyperactivity in children and diet in 1975. His elimination diet, which attempted to remove all artificial food additives, including coloring and preservatives, as well as the naturally occurring salicylates and amines, was claimed to have dramatic effects on hyperactivity in children.

Salicylates are naturally occurring plant chemicals found in many fruits, vegetables, nuts, spices, herbs, jam, yeast extracts, and tea and coffee. They are also present in some medications (aspirin is a member of the salicylate family). Amines are products that come from the breakdown or fermentation of protein. Large amounts of amines are found in chocolate, cheese, yeast extracts, and fish products.

Many studies have since found that there is no significant ben-efit in Feingold's diet. However, although research has not shown benefits for most children, a small number do respond to the Feingold diet modified to reflect up-to-date food composition data.

Following the modified Feingold diet requires guidance from an experienced pediatric dietitian to ensure that the correct foods are being excluded, behavioral records are kept, and foods are reintroduced in the correct manner. A haphazard approach (like cutting out the Kool-Aid) is not going to be useful if your toddler has a confirmed abnormal degree of hyperactivity.

The diet is complicated and needs great commitment from parents. It also places restrictions on the toddler's social life and is sometimes viewed by the toddler as punishment. Generally in relation to toddler behavior the stress involved with strict elimination diets is disproportionate to the results achieved.

It must be emphasized that the majority of "hyperactive" or "difficult" toddlers are behaving normally for their age and stage of development. Before embarking on complicated diets, it is advisable to seek professional advice and, if appropriate, have a developmental assessment.

Behavior and sugar, artificial coloring, and preservatives

The evidence demonstrating the relationship between sugar and tooth decay is undisputed. The evidence connecting sugar and behavior problems is nonexistent. Sugar has no effect on behavior, but it is bad for the teeth, so it's sensible to restrict it.

Sensitivity to preservatives and food coloring cannot be gauged solely by an overexcited toddler's response to a few birthday parties, but only over time, through properly conducted food challenges.

What can toddlers eat?

Just about anything within the healthy food range mentioned previously. It is advisable to restrict whole nuts, chunks of celery, apple, and carrot until around three because of choking hazards.

Mealtime guidelines

Please see the chart on the next page for a toddler diet plan if you are looking for one.

Here is some general information

- Provide regular meals and snacks.
- Try to ensure a relaxed atmosphere at meal and snack times. Make it a social occasion. Minimize rules and distractions – turn off the TV.
- Decide on a set duration for the meal – allow about twenty minutes for a meal (but be prepared to cut it short if the food throwing starts) and about ten to fifteen minutes for a snack.
- Give drinks after meals.
- Finger foods play a big part in the toddler diet, especially in the second year.

A BASIC FOOD ROUTINE

If it suits you, continue breastfeeding. Otherwise, use full-fat cows' milk. Replace the bottle with a cup ("cup" means a straw or spout cup, whichever suits your toddler). One cup of juice a day is sufficient. Offer water at other times.

4.30am to 6am (how uncivilized):	**breastfeed or bottle (and hopefully back to sleep)**	
Some babies/toddlers continue early morning waking into the second year. Once they start sleeping longer, this early morning feeding stops. In general, bottles are not needed past twelve months. Breastfeeding continues for as long as you are both happy.		

	Breakfast Ideas	
The usual cereal/oats	Eggs boiled, poached, or scrambled	Grilled cheese, avocado, ham,
Muffin or bagel	(an egg a day is fine)	or tomato
Breakfast smoothie	Omelette	Yogurt with fruit
	Cup of milk/juice or water	

	Morning Snack	
Snack and cup of milk or water	Fresh fruit, dried fruit, small sandwich, scone, pikelet, tomato, cucumber, cheese slice, cracker, biscuit	

	Lunch Ideas	
	(the main meal can be now or in the evening)	
Pasta, couscous, or rice dishes	Avocado/tomato/lentil salad	Instant pizza
Sandwiches	Fish sticks	Basic salad
Basic frittata	Tuna salad	Salmon and veggies
Falafel	felafel	Fruit or fruit salad
	Cup of milk, water or juice or a breastfeeding	

	Afternoon Snack	
Snack and cup of milk or water	Muffin, slice of raisin toast, vegetable sticks, fresh fruit, fruit juice popsicle frozen yogurt	

	Evening Meal Ideas (family food)	
Noodle and veggie stir-fry	Stir-fry chicken and rice	Fish sticks
Macaroni and cheese	Steamed fish	Roasted chicken pieces
Meatloaf and	Lasagna	Fresh fruit, yogurt, rice
Tacos	Veal or chicken fillet	pudding, or steamed fruit and custard.
	(All of the above with steamed veggies, rice, pasta, or salad)	
	Cup of milk, water, or juice (or a breastfeeding)	

Despite your best intentions, you may find your toddler only wants the same old thing day in and day out. Don't search endlessly for variations. Accept his limited tastes at this time in his life. Offer new things from time to time.

Some examples of finger/snack foods

Fish and meat

- bone-free fish
- slices of cooked meat and chicken
- chicken wings/nuggets
- well-drained cooked bacon

- meatballs
- fish sticks
- veal fillet
- stir-fry meat and chicken with noodles, veggies

Fruit and veggies

- lentil patties
- little mounds of grated carrot, apple, and cheese
- fruit—cantelope, watermelon, oranges, strawberries, papaya, kiwi fruit, and so on (the bigger the variety the better)
- stir-fry veggies
- partially steamed veggies

- felafel
- spring rolls
- zucchini slice
- frozen fruit
- fruit salad
- wedges of tomato and cucumber
- fruit juice popsicles
- dried fruit

Bread, pasta, rice, dairy

- rice cakes
- pancakes
- crepes
- frozen pizza
- small sandwich
- avocado toast
- crackers
- corn bread

- biscuits
- muffins
- cold frittata
- bagels
- string cheese sticks
- crackers
- yogurt (as it comes or frozen)

- raisin bread
- cereal (plain or with milk)
- wedges of hard-boiled egg
- cheese slices
- noodles
- cheese sticks

Other food matters

Tips for teaching your toddler to drink from a cup

Note: The definition of a cup is any container that does not have a nipple on it—a small cup, a spout cup, or a cup with a straw. A "training" cup with a nipple on it is a ridiculous concept and no different from a bottle.

Sometimes parents are under the impression that their toddlers are still using bottles because they can't drink from a cup yet. The parents are perhaps waiting for a sign from above. Drinking from a cup is a skill that has to be taught and encouraged and is possible from almost any age—six-month-old babies learn to drink from cups.

Once the bottle goes, toddlers start to drink good amounts from cups quite quickly. As long as they still use the bottle, they may resist a cup. Some toddlers, however, do drink efficiently from both.

You may need to experiment to find out what suits your toddler best—a small cup, a spout cup, or a cup with a built-in straw. A small cup is often the most successful to start with. Naturally, you have to hold the cup! Allowing a toddler free rein with the cup in the early days is asking for trouble. Begin with a small amount of fluid only. If you fill the cup, your toddler will get drenched and you will quickly lose patience. The main aim in the beginning is to gently teach your toddler what to do, not to try and get him to drink the same amount he has from the breast or a bottle.

Offer him a small amount in a cup at morning or afternoon snacks or after one of his meals. Use milk, water, or juice. The more opportunity he has to practice, the better he will become at drinking. The amount he drinks steadily increases. It takes a few weeks for a toddler to learn to drink a few ounces in one sitting.

Once he has the idea, move on to a cup with a lid and a spout or a straw cup. If you are going to use a straw cup, you will have to teach your toddler how to use a straw. Show him what to do then put the straw to his lips and encourage him to suck on the straw. With regular short practices each day you will find he's soon mastered the art.

When should he feed himself with a spoon?

Sometimes there is no choice about this because a number of toddlers from nine months onward won't eat unless they can feed themselves. If your toddler is an independent eater and you don't mind the mess, let him use a spoon and his fingers to feed himself mushy food as well as the less messy finger foods.

If your toddler is happy to let you be in charge of the spoon, there is no urgency about teaching him to do it himself until he is older and has better coordination. Most toddlers can use a spoon reasonably neatly around eighteen to twenty months.

Eating with the family

It is often recommended that toddlers eat with the family to encourage good eating habits and develop their pleasure for food. It also gives them the opportunity to see their parents enjoying a variety of nutritious foods (we hope). Solitary mealtimes without supervision, irregular meals, and tense mealtimes all contribute to eating problems in toddlers.

Many families enjoy eating with their toddlers at every mealtime, but others find that at the end of the day having an evening meal with a messy, tired toddler is a bit much to bear. It can become very tense, which negates the positives of sharing the meal. I think it is reasonable for parents to give toddlers under three an early dinner, bath, story, and bed before having their own meal. Sometime between three and five, toddlers reach a developmental stage where dinner with the family becomes an enjoyable (mostly) experience for all.

Cows' milk, juice, and water

Cows' milk is a useful source of calcium, protein, and fat and preferable to soy drink as it has more naturally occurring ingredients (fat, calcium, and iron). If your toddler will not drink milk, you can try a calcium-fortified soy drink, but unless your toddler has an intolerance or allergy to cows' milk, there is no advantage to using soy drink if he is happy to drink milk. Milk does not "make mucus." Mucus is a common feature of the toddler years, especially if the toddler is in group childcare, and is a result of viral infections, not milk consumption.

Many toddlers will not drink milk once they stop breastfeeding and using bottles. This does not mean that the bottles have to be continued (or the breast if you want to wean). As an alternative to drinking milk, try yogurt and/or cottage cheese with fruit, grated cheese on veggies, and as a snack, cheese sauce and macaroni cheese. Put milk in mashed potato or pumpkin and on cereal.

A smoothie (milk and yogurt blended with fresh fruit) or flavored milk can be offered in a cup once a day. Flavored milk and smoothies should not be given in bottles, as a huge amount can be consumed, which interferes with appetites for other food. And the slower removal of the liquid by sucking bathes the teeth in liquid sugar, which increases the risk of tooth decay.

Fruit juice is not an essential part of the diet. Unless your toddler needs extra juice for constipation, limit it to once a day (squeeze an orange); give water for all other drinks. Offer him fruit to eat rather than drink.

On the matter of veggies

Vegetables tend to be an acquired taste and many toddlers are indifferent to or refuse vegetables.

- Fruit is not a perfect equivalent for veggies, but it does compensate to some extent for the nonveggie eater.
- Stir-fry veggies tempt some toddlers.
- Allow him to feed himself veggies as finger food (as opposed to you mashing them up and trying to feed him with a spoon).
- Disguise veggies in soup, hamburgers, meatloaf, spaghetti sauce, risotto, and pasta.
- Try hot potato wedges.
- Above all, don't stress. Check out page 282 for information on the noneating healthy toddler.

Toddlers in the kitchen

Involving toddlers in safe food activities helps them discover more about food than just what is presented to them at mealtimes.

Here are some ideas

- Helping pack groceries away.
- Peeling bananas and adding to a smoothie.
- Spooning things out of packets.
- Counting (eggs, spoons, and so on).
- Holding pitchers and bowls while you mix.
- Mixing while you hold pitchers and bowls.
- Remembering ingredients for familiar recipes.
- Licking cake bowls.

Funny food behavior

1. Gagging

Gagging in healthy toddlers is a way of refusing food. It is often very successful as it has the potential to frighten the wits out of the parents, who confuse it with choking. Sometimes it's such a convincing performance that parents worry about the possibility of their toddler having a deformity of the throat. Strangely, chips, rolls, and anything else he feels inclined to eat go down without a problem.

A FRAMEWORK TO WORK WITHIN

- Gagging in babies is often involuntary while they are starting to learn to eat solid food. Most babies overcome this in the greater interest of getting the food down, but some start to gag voluntarily in response to being presented with food they don't want, and the gagging becomes a habit that persists into the second year. Toddlers who gag a lot at mealtimes are usually still drinking many bottles and will only eat pureed food.

- It is not easy to change the habit, but stopping the bottles and replacing meals with finger foods is the best strategy. Stopping the bottles will improve your toddler's appetite. Trying to give him lumpy food from a spoon will only result in gagging, even vomiting. It is better to put a choice of finger foods on his plate, give him a limited time to play with them or eat them, then remove the food. Follow the meal with water or milk in a cup.

- The more drama and attention given to the gagging, the longer it will stay around. Try to give positive reinforcement for drinking from the cup and eating food with fingers.

2. Hooked on commercial food

Nutritionally, commercial food in jars or cans is equivalent to home-cooked food, but it does not give the same variety of tastes. Prolonged use of commercial food does not help the toddler broaden his concepts of food or expose him to new eating experiences.

A FRAMEWORK TO WORK WITHIN

- This, too, is not an easy habit to change and takes time and persistence. Again, it is important to reduce fluid intake (yes, stop those bottles) so that the toddler is hungry.

- If your toddler will eat mush off a spoon, mix the canned food with the home-cooked food and gradually decrease it over a few weeks.

- If this is not feasible, give commercial food for one meal and offer finger foods at the other mealtimes.

3. Throwing food

Food throwing refers to the deliberate throwing of uneaten food, not the messiness that comes with self-feeding. Messy eating has to be tolerated. Put a cover on the floor under the highchair and accept it until age brings better coordination and neater eating.

Throwing food is attention-seeking behavior indulged in by many toddlers, usually between twelve and twenty-four months. Food throwing only persists beyond this age if the thrower is given plenty of attention and rewarded for his efforts.

A FRAMEWORK TO WORK WITHIN

- A toddler throws food on the floor instead of eating it because he is not hungry or because it guarantees a major response from his parents.

- A toddler's hunger is diminished by bottles of milk and snacks throughout the day, so he might not be hungry at the start of the meal. Or he might have eaten what he wants and is now entertaining himself.

- Put a small amount of food down to start with. If that gets eaten, give him some more.

- The minute the food throwing starts, the meal ends. Resist the temptation to fill him up with a big bottle of milk. Offer some milk or water in a cup. Wait until the next mealtime. He will be so hungry next time, the food throwing will more than likely be a nonevent. But if it reoccurs, repeat the procedure.

- Remove the interest in the food throwing and give warm acknowledgment of meals eaten efficiently. "I do like it when your food goes into your mouth instead of onto the floor."

4. The noneating healthy toddler

Fussy toddler eating is the bane of many parents' lives. If you are experiencing this, try to see it as a phase of normal development.

WHY IS FUSSY EATING AND FOOD REFUSAL SO COMMON?

- Once the first year has passed, toddlers' growth rates decrease quite dramatically and, for many of them, so do their appetites. Others continue eating with gusto.

- Eating and potty training are the two ideal areas for toddlers to test limits, to exercise some personal control, and to attract attention.

- Toddlers are busy exploring, experimenting, finding out about cause and effect, and practicing their increasingly proficient motor skills. For many of them, food comes a poor second in the interest stakes.

- Parents often have unrealistic ideas about how much should be consumed and allow the toddler's food intake to take over family life. As the battle escalates, the attention to meals and food gets way out of proportion. The toddler remains indifferent while the parent gets increasingly distressed—a difficult situation. To get back on balance, the parents must lose the distress and act indifferent.

HERE ARE SOME TIPS

- Try to look at the big picture rather than the day-to-day issues. For most toddlers this is only a passing phase. As long as the family diet is well balanced and your toddler has access to a variety of healthy foods, he will be fine.

- As a rule, healthy toddlers *will* eat when they are hungry. By the time they have consumed endless quantities of milk, juice, and

282

water and many little snacks, toddlers are often not hungry at mealtimes.

Cut down on fluids, stop the bottles, and avoid fluids one hour before meals. Resist the temptation to replace meals with bottles of milk.

If healthy snacking helps you both through the day, that's fine—but don't expect much interest to be shown at mealtimes.

- Many toddlers will only eat one good meal every day or two, and pick at bits and pieces the rest of the time. Try not to expect your toddler to eat the way you do yet.

AND A FRAMEWORK TO WORK WITHIN

- Limit mealtimes to twenty minutes, snacks to ten.

- Be relaxed about fads and what seems like a limited diet.

- Avoid hovering and offering immediate alternatives to food that is refused. The next meal or snack is not next week but in a few hours. Let him wait until then.

- Keep offering new foods (without nagging) even if they are initially refused. Research has shown that many toddlers will eat a previously rejected food if it is offered often enough; for example, up to ten times.

- Offer choices of two items: "Would you like brown bread or white?"

- Use a positive focus. "I'd like you to sit at the table until you have finished, Ella" rather than "Don't run off." "Can you manage that, James, or shall I cut it into smaller pieces?" rather than "Stop making a mess with the banana."

(Hmm—it does make me blush when I see these nice little conversations I compose in the peace and quiet of my cosy den, miles away from the reality of toddlers hurling food around kitchens. I must assure you that I did not always speak to my toddlers in such a civilized, positive manner. Remember that there is always going to be a discrepancy between the way we would like to respond and the way that we actually do. The thing is to keep trying . . . never give up.)

WHEN TO WORRY

Parents with noneating toddlers become a little weary when they are constantly told "Don't worry, it's normal" by cheerful health professionals. Occasionally an underlying problem needs help.

Seek advice for the following:

- If your toddler is constantly unhappy, lethargic, and uninterested in the world around him. Or if he is doing what you consider to be a lot of strange poo.

- If you feel angry, depressed, inadequate, and overburdened all the time.

- If he loses weight or does not gain weight over a period of a few months and this cannot be explained by an acute illness (such as gastroenteritis).

- If there are ongoing social or emotional family problems you can't resolve, which may be affecting your toddler's appetite.

- If you need help with any of the above, talk to your nurse practitioner, family doctor, or pediatrician.

Breastfeeding

Many variations on the breastfeeding theme are possible during the toddler years. It is fine to continue to breastfeed into the second year and beyond for as long as you care to. The advantages of breastfeeding for toddlers are well documented. Nutritional benefits, continued immunological benefits, and contraceptive protection are cited (continued contraceptive protection being dependent upon the number of breastfeedings every twenty-four hours and whether menstruation has recommenced). However, the major benefit in the toddler years is probably more to do with the emotional security that comes with the continued breastfeeding relationship.

In my opinion, the advantages are not significant enough to justify breastfeeding beyond twelve months when toddlers are healthy and living in a loving environment where there is plenty of fresh food and reliable contraception is available—if the mother wishes to wean.

My reason for making this point is not to make women who are committed to breastfeeding and are happy to continue feel that they should wean. Rather it is to reassure other women that weaning anytime from nine months onward is a perfectly acceptable option. Weaning at this time does not compromise a toddler's emotional development, nutrition, or future health.

For the sake of your mental health, follow whichever path you wish without feeling pressured by outside forces. And learn to ignore unwanted advice. For example, "It's time you weaned—it's disgusting still breastfeeding a two-year-old." Or, "You should keep breastfeeding until the toddler decides to stop; otherwise the attachment will be put at risk. Women in *other cultures* breastfeed for at least three years—it's what nature intended."

Breastfeeding into the second year and beyond

Women who continue breastfeeding for as long as their toddlers want usually do so when the night waking is not an issue for them and when they feel the rewards outweigh any disadvantages. Many also feel that leaving their toddlers to cry at night to teach them to sleep is unacceptable.

If this is your choice, continue to enjoy your toddler, your breastfeeding, and sharing your bed. Learn to shrug off negative comments—some view your approach as optimum.

Feeding a new baby and a toddler (called tandem feeding) is also the choice of some women, which is fine.

Unplanned weaning

A number of toddlers take themselves off the breast anytime from nine months onward. Some women find this upsetting; others feel relieved. Either way it is usually something you have to accept unless the breast refusal is because your toddler is unwell, in which case he might go back to the breast when he is better.

When it's permanent, talk about it to someone sympathetic, have a good cry if you need to, and the sad feelings will pass.

There is no need to start bottles, which your toddler is likely to refuse anyway if he has never had them. Give him small amounts of milk, juice, or water frequently throughout the day. The amount he drinks will gradually increase.

You will need to express your breasts—for comfort only—two or three times a day (depending on how many breastfeedings you have been doing), gradually diminishing that number over a week or two depending on how your breasts feel. If necessary, take acetaminophen for discomfort in the early days.

Mastitis is still a possibility, so see your family doctor if:

- Your breasts becomes inflamed and painful.
- You experience flu-like symptoms—headaches, chills, hot flashes.
- You have a fever.

Weaning toddlers between nine and fifteen months

If your toddler is breastfeeding a lot day and night and you wish to do fewer feedings or wean, here are some guidelines to follow.

Address the night waking first

Toddlers who are breastfeeding frequently around twelve months of age are often still feeding twice or more through the night. This does not hurt the toddler in any way, but a number of women find they are frustrated and depressed by the constant night waking.

If this is the case for you, waiting for your toddler to decide by himself to feed less or wean might mean waiting until he is a lot older. It's fine for you to make the decision to wean or stop night feeding rather than leaving it up to your toddler if that's what you want to do.

Stopping breastfeeding at night involves teaching your toddler to go back to sleep without the breast. Swapping the breast for something else, is not the answer—it simply teaches him to rely on something else and it will probably take even longer to get him back to sleep. Trying to make toddlers take bottles if they don't want to is a catastrophe. Trying to encourage unwilling eaters to eat more food to stop them from breastfeeding at night is also a waste of time and stressful to boot. None of these strategies will stop your toddler from waking at night for the breast.

Teaching your toddler to sleep involves letting him cry at night instead of feeding him; this is never easy, but by following some structured guidelines you can do this in three to five nights. Please see my information about "control crying" on page 237.

It will take three to five nights for your breasts to adjust to not being used, so ***don't forget to hand express for comfort once***

or twice a night for up to a week (depending on how many night feedings you were doing).

Daytime—diet and fluids

Once your toddler sleeps all night without needing the breast to go back to sleep, only breastfeed him three times during the day after meals. Be firm and consistent and don't give him the breast at sleep time. Changing your daily activities helps until he forgets about the breast.

Offer your toddler three meals a day and gradually replace each breastfeeding with milk from a cup. Once your toddler is not drinking all night and only having a few breastfeedings during the day, you will find he will drink more and more from the cup.

FLUID INTAKE

Some mothers worry about their toddler's fluid intake when cups are used instead of bottles, as it seems so much less than the amount consumed by toddlers who still have bottles. Try not to let this bother you—toddlers who drink from bottles drink more than they need.

When the weather is hot extra fluids can be given as fruit gels, fruit popsicles or by putting extra fluid in your toddler's food. Letting your toddler sit in the tub and suck the washcloth is another way of giving extra fluid in hot weather.

Once you decide to breastfeed less or wean, be consistent so that your toddler gets a clear message. If you do one thing one day and something else the next, he won't know what's going on. If weaning is your aim, never reintroduce a breastfeeding once it's gone.

Weaning toddlers from fifteen months onwards

As there is usually no easy way to persuade toddlers to stop breast-feeding, it is important to ask yourself why you want to wean. Unfortunately prolonged breastfeeding is viewed negatively in our culture and you may find you are being pressured to give up the breastfeeding by people around you. If you are perfectly happy to keep going, ignore the comments and continue.

If you are only breastfeeding once or twice a day, it may be easier to carry on until your toddler loses interest.

If you do want to wean, it is best to stop all feedings on a given day.

Gradual weaning usually doesn't work with older toddlers who are still having multiple breastfeedings because they find it difficult to understand why the breast is available at some times and not others. If you do try, you will probably find that you go around in circles because you keep reinstating feedings when your toddler's nagging and whining gets the better of you. You will find it difficult to stick to a set number of feedings if he gets sick, or if, when you are trying to talk to someone, he's whining and climbing all over you wanting the breast.

Most things in life work better with a little planning, so talk it over with your partner before you stop. It's best to stop at a time when your partner is available to help distract your toddler by taking him out in the day, putting him to bed at night, and getting him up in the morning.

Tell your toddler in simple language what you plan to do, then stick to that plan.

Change his breastfeeding routine. For example, don't bring him into bed with you in the morning and don't let him see you bare-breasted for a while.

It's tough for three to four days, but if you are confident and consistent, he will come to the party. If you act as though you are guilty and unsure, he will continue to nag and whine for the breast. Keep him busy, stick to your decision, and practice pretending to ignore. Praise him for using a cup and acknowledge meals eaten well.

Remember you are the parent and it's perfectly reasonable to wean—you are not committing some terrible sin.

Night waking for the breast from fifteen months onward

No easy answers—strategies are the same as weaning toddlers from nine to fifteen months. See page 287.

Taking care of your breasts when you stop breastfeeding

You will need to express (for comfort only) three times a day for a week, then twice for a few days, then once a day if necessary. When your breasts are comfortable, stop expressing. If you need to, apply cabbage leaves for the first few days and take acetaminophen. See your family doctor if you experience symptoms of mastitis (see page 286).

Your toddler's diet

Three meals a day and milk and/or water from a cup (spout or straw cup) is the way to go. Most toddlers preoccupied with breastfeeding start to eat more once they are off the breast. There is no need to consider starting up the breastfeedings again if your toddler won't drink milk. Put what dairy products you can into his diet and give him water to drink.

Two other suggestions for weaning (not for the faint-hearted)

I'm not recommending the following—rather, supplying information—use it or not as you will.

Weaning reluctant toddlers and children is a universal dilemma experienced by women of all cultures, not just the wicked women of the west. Women of *other cultures* sometimes apply chili pepper to their nipples by way of aversion therapy. I have known women here who have used the preparation available in pharmacies to discourage thumb sucking—with the desired result.

Or, disappear off the scene for a week. When you return, no more feeding.

Bottle feeding

Bottles and/or formula are not required for healthy toddlers after the first year except in those cases where they are appropriate for medical reasons. Generally it is better to dispense with the bottles as soon as you can, as the longer toddlers use them, the more dependent upon them they become and the harder it is to give them up.

Problems associated with prolonged bottle feeding

- Bottles become a quick fix to replace uneaten food, which does not encourage toddlers to learn to chew or try a range of food.
- It is easy for toddlers to consume large volumes of fluid

from bottles (which they don't need), which dulls their appetite.

- Excessive volumes of cows' milk via the bottle are a proven cause of iron deficiency anemia.

- Bottles of anything other than water are associated with black teeth. Not all bottle-addicted toddlers end up with dental caries, but a significant percentage do, especially when the bottles are used through the night for several years.

- An unlimited amount of juice in bottles exacerbates toddler diarrhea.

Difficulties associated with giving up the bottles

Many parents continue the bottles with the best intentions as a direct result of the mixed messages about nutrition that come via commercial and government bodies.

For example:

– "Toddlers should drink 600 mls of milk a day." (*The only way my toddler will consume this much is in a bottle.*)

– "Milk is the most important part of the diet for the first twelve months." (*If that is so, then it is probably wise that I continue, especially as my toddler is so reluctant to eat food.*)

Any information that specifies exact amounts of individual nutritional components required by toddlers (e.g., calcium, iron, protein, zinc, and so on) is potentially worrying for parents. (*The only way I can be sure that my toddler is getting the right diet is by using toddler formula, and if I don't put it in a bottle, he won't drink it.*)

Other parents keep the bottle going for behavioral reasons:
It's the only way I can get him to keep quiet in the car.
He won't go to sleep without it.
He has a tantrum if I don't give him the bottle.
It keeps him in bed for another hour in the morning.

How important is it really to stop the bottles?

I acknowledge that it would be difficult to pick out from a group of twenty-one-year-olds those who kept their bottle until they went to school (except the ones with dentures, of course—joking). And that the drama of removing the bottle can seem to be far worse than any potential benefits, but I can't help noticing how quickly and easily the bottle disappears when the first faint line of tooth decay appears.

It also bothers me that the drive to continue bottles and formula is, to a significant extent, commercially driven by companies with vested interests in encouraging the practice for as long as possible. Their sales pitches subtly exploit the normal anxieties parents experience when their healthy toddlers won't eat from the five food groups.

Here is a framework to work within

- If you are keeping the bottles going for nutritional reasons only and it is relatively easy to stop them, stop even if your toddler is not eating huge amounts and is not very good at drinking from a cup.
- If you are keeping the bottles going for behavioral reasons, limit them as much as possible (one or two a day at the most).

- Avoid putting your toddler to bed at night with a bottle. If it proves too difficult, you can try diluting the milk and gradually replacing it with water. Needless to say, I prefer direct action (remove the bottle and face the drama), as the above plan usually goes astray when the toddler will not accept the water.

- Give water and milk in a cup rather than a bottle during the day.

- Refusing to drink milk unless it's in a bottle is not a reason to continue the bottles. Give your toddler water to drink in a cup and put as many dairy products into his food as you can (yogurt, cheese, milk on cereal, and so on).

- Set a suitable time in the future (not when the new baby arrives) for the last bottle (for example, at fifteen months or eighteen months or on the second birthday).

- If you take your life into your own hands and bid the bottle farewell in one swoop, congratulations. If your toddler is very dependent upon the bottle, guidelines for managing his post-bottle behavior are similar to those for weaning a reluctant toddler. See page 289.

chapter **ten**

Play

What is play?

Play to an adult usually means to do something enjoyable just for
fun. Something relaxing and perhaps not in earnest, although I
guess it's easy to get intense about a game of golf or chess.

Play for babies, toddlers, and children is a vital part of their
development. Many experts refer to it as a child's "work," which
sounds very serious, but you are bound to have noticed that a lot
of the time your toddler is very serious when he is involved in puzzles, building, hammering in pegs, making mud pies, feeding his
teddy, drawing, and so on. At other times, play is fun and laughter—jumping on the bed, swimming, climbing, and making messes
and loud noises.

Through play a child finds out about himself—what is inside
and outside his body and where he is in relation to the world
around him and the people in it. Play teaches him what he can or
can't do, and what his strengths and weaknesses are. Playing helps
him learn new concepts such as up and down, hot and cold, and
shapes and how they fit. Play helps your toddler relive experiences
and work out what is real and not real. It teaches him how to
express feelings, acquire a wider use of language, and experiment
with social relationships. It is an opportunity for him to experience
a wider form of communication. While your toddler is playing, he

Much of your toddler's play is for the sheer pleasure of sensation . . .

is strengthening his muscles, improving his coordination, and letting off excess energy.

Much of your toddler's play is for the sheer pleasure of sensation—touching, feeling, and the thrill of moving his arms, his legs, his fingers and toes. Many play activities involve tasting, smelling, and listening, which hone the senses and heighten the enjoyment of the game.

Types or stages of play

Different types of play have been observed in toddlers—you might be interested to know what they are so that you can smile knowingly at playgroup and say, "Ha, parallel play." Here they are:

Solitary play

The toddler does his own thing, oblivious to anyone else's presence (if only, I hear you sigh). It is recommended that adults do not interrupt this kind of play—as if you would. However, if the play involves fascination with squeezing the contents of a toothpaste tube over the couch, you may decide interruption is the best course of action.

The onlooker

The toddler doesn't actually participate in play but shows interest in what is going on.

Parallel play

The toddler, not yet ready for group play, plays happily alongside other children of varying ages.

Cooperative play

As they move toward three years, toddlers start to play together in a cooperative way to achieve a result.

Common concerns about play

Play is something many parents in previous generations didn't give a lot of thought to. I'm sure that toddlers just scampered around using whatever playthings were available, and if we go back in time far enough, children probably started taking part in family chores from a young age.

The modern emphasis on play has led to a few concerns about some aspects of it.

A common unrealistic expectation of many adults today is that relatively large groups of children under three can spend hours with each other playing happily and cooperatively. Toddlers are often expected to have the social skills of the average forty-year-old, and adults get upset when their toddlers bite, don't share, push, throw sand, and so on.

It also seems to be widely believed that such group activity is necessary to encourage the development of social skills. For more information on the social development of toddlers, see page 315.

We (particularly the first time around) also tend to think that, ideally, play should be constructive with the aim of teaching our toddlers something. And that if we provide appropriate toys for the job, he will spend hours happily engaged in educational, constructive play while we go about our business.

The reality?

The reality is that toddlers actually spend much of their day touching, wandering about doing nothing much, whining and clinging, exploring in places we'd rather they didn't, wanting our attention, throwing food, and asserting themselves.

Interest in educational toys may be brief and intermittent. More sustained interest is likely to be shown in the kitchen cabinets, the contents of the garbage and the fridge, and any water anywhere but especially in the toilet.

Many toddlers will play with their educational toys if an adult sits with them and gives them undivided attention.

How often is this necessary?

Most of us only have limited time and capacity to sit and play with toddlers, and those times are likely to vary depending on what sort of a day we are having and what other things need our attention. Healthy toddlers in loving homes do not need endless stimulation and entertaining.

However, life with a toddler is more enjoyable and generally easier if some of the day is centered on activities for him. Getting out of doors to go to playgroup, for walks, trips to the park, or swimming is essential. As he gets older, outings to the zoo, to see trains, planes, ships, garages, stores, building sites, and the library are all possibilities.

What about when you are at home?

Obviously you can't spend all day, every day, out on the town. Being available to provide assistance and encouragement to your toddler while you are at home together does not require that you spend the day down on the floor with him. The toddler years are a time when he needs to start to learn that although he is very important and valued, your needs are as important as his. This is also a time when he needs encouragement to use his own resources, which are considerable.

Try to encourage him to play alone some of the time, even if it means putting up with whining and some lying around being bored while he learns how to do this.

Here are some tips for encouraging your toddler to play alone

- Check that the room is safe (see page 226) and as much of the house as possible is toddlerproof. You may need to have a gate (or gates) at the kitchen entrance, on stairs, or in the doorway of his bedroom to prevent him from hurting himself or breaking equipment.

- Make sure there are a few toys or household items around that he enjoys.

- Pick the right time. Toddlers who are tired, hungry, or restless are not going to be too happy left to their own devices.

- Be confident and optimistic in your expectation that he will play alone for a while. If you are hesitant and act as if you think you are doing the wrong thing, your toddler is not going to feel comfortable being away from you.

- As long as he is reasonably happy, leave him and do a quick check every ten minutes or so (remembering that long periods of absolute silence usually indicate that some interesting exploring and experimentation has been going on).

- The length of times toddlers are happy to be alone varies from five minutes to about thirty, which will increase in his third year, so don't have too many unrealistic expectations. Persistence pays off, so stick with it. Praise him when he has entertained himself for a while. Tell him what you have been doing while he has been doing "his work."

- I am aware that some toddlers are unrelentingly clingy and will not be left to play alone for a second. They spend the day wound around their mother's legs like seaweed and insist on accompanying her to the toilet, to the shower, and so on. It's not easy . . . See page 142 for a few tips.

- He can also spend time listening to music appropriate for his age or maybe watching some suitable TV or a video in short bursts.

Playing together

Whenever you can, spend ten to twenty minutes once or twice a day doing some one-on-one playing and reading. Obviously if you feel like spending more time than that, do so, and if there are days where it just doesn't happen, fine.

Toys

Toys only contribute to a part of a toddler's development. Most adults have unrealistic ideas about the entertainment and educational value of toys. We all become quickly aware that a toy telephone is not going to take the place of a real one and that a plastic bunch of keys is not the same as the ones that operate the car and open the front door. And that pretend wallets with make-believe credit cards are no substitute for getting sticky hands onto the genuine article.

Toys can be manufactured or they can be any objects that children find and play with. Toddlers and children often invent their own use for toys and objects that is quite removed from the intended one. It can be just as educational for a toddler to build a house out of cardboard cartons and various items around the home as it is to put an age-appropriate puzzle together.

Between twelve and fifteen months, most toddlers are at the height of learning to master their body movements—walking, running, climbing. With this new sense of power comes a need to explore and be on the move. Toys at this age are not likely to generate a lot of sustained interest unless they relate to movement and sensation (a swing, for example), as toddlers tend to be too distracted by what is going on both inside and outside their bodies.

Between fifteen months and two and a half years, toddlers are starting to come to terms with their emerging skills and power and are becoming more involved in the social aspects of daily life. They are interested in what their mothers and fathers are doing as well as all the other people they encounter (store owners, bus drivers, the doctor, pets and other animals, other children, babies, and so on).

By the age of two, toddlers are starting to use toys and other objects in an imaginative way as they develop fantasy and an imaginative life.

Between the ages of two and three, progress in all areas of development means that toys start to have more meaning and hold their attention for longer.

Toy safety

- Choose toys that are suitable for your toddler's age. Toys for older children may be dangerous for toddlers. Check labels carefully, especially when your toddler receives toys as gifts.

- Be aware of choking and inhalation hazards such as stuffing from old soft toys, beads used for eyes and noses on dolls and soft toys, small batteries, long strings, buttons, small plastic construction blocks, and marbles.

- Make sure there are no sharp edges, brittle plastic, or small parts that can snap off or be pulled off. Also make sure toys do not contain hazardous substances that may be found in colorants, coating material, plastics, paints, modeling material, and printed material (comics, magazines, fabric books).

- Check stability of play equipment such as swings, slides, and climbing apparatus. Make sure swings are constructed to prevent falls. Look at the potential the play equipment or toy has for pinching and crushing fingers, stabbing or inflicting other nasty injuries.

- Check flammability of fabrics used in toys and dressing-up costumes.

- Take care with packaging, as toddlers often enjoy the packaging as much as the toy. Plastic bags and staples are the main hazards to look out for.

- Store toys down low so that your toddler can reach them safely.

- Throw away broken or grubby toys.

Buying toys

The perfect toy that will keep your toddler entertained and busy for hours on end does not exist. When you buy the toy he loves to play with in your friend's house, you are likely to find that he quickly loses interest once it belongs to him.

Plenty of useful play materials are not what are commonly referred to as toys; for example, a box of Band-Aids, measuring cups, plastic spoons, old sets of keys, old telephones, balls, pots and pans, egg cartons, big boxes, old magazines, cellophane paper, ice-cream containers, and so on.

A few sturdy toys made by a reputable manufacturer that will last a long time and do what they are supposed to do are better than a never-ending flow of delicate novelties that break easily and don't work. Toys that are potentially multifunctional like blocks, little cars, balls, a wheelbarrow, a dump truck, a pail and shovel, and a small table and chairs will be both useful and entertaining for a longer period than a battery-operated puppy.

Buying toys works better with a little planning. Think about what you already have, your toddler's temperament, strength, age, and stage of development. Remember, too, that toys are often sucked, chewed, pulled apart, jumped on, and thrown around.

Some things to consider when buying toys

- *The safety and suitability of the toy:* Read the labels and instructions. When buying, look for toys that meet the specifications of the Toy Manufacturers of America's voluntary safety standard, ATSM F963 that incorporates the United States Consumer Product Safety Commission's safety regulations for toys.

- *The age range it is designed for:* The midpoint of the age range on the box is the best guide. For example, if the range is from two to four years, then the optimum age for that toy is two and a half to three years. There is no advantage buying, toys with an age range years ahead of your toddler's age. Toys labeled "not suitable for children under three years" contain small parts which a younger child could swallow. It has no bearing on the level of intelligence required to use the toy.

- **The function and appearance of the toy:** Is it colorful? Does it move? What kind of texture does it have? Will your toddler be able to use it himself or will he need help?

- **The maintenance required to keep it safe and functioning:** Look at the need for batteries and parts—many toys end up rusting in a corner.

- **The variety this toy will offer:** How different is it from everything else he already owns? Does it contribute to his special interests? Is it going to add to his pleasure and experience of life for longer than the first two minutes that he sees it?

Spaces to play in

Inside

Arrange places where toys can be used safely in your home. Depending on what space you have available, the usual place for play is likely to be your toddler's bedroom, but if the play area spills out into other rooms, you may have to relocate low coffee tables and other furniture.

The bedroom is also likely to be the place where most of the toys are stored. A set of shelves where toys are arranged so that the toddler can see them and reach them without having to climb is ideal but hard to maintain unless you are a saint. Most of us seem to end up with a big box full of toys that get thrown out onto the floor, then not played with. I can remember how my children would see all their toys anew when we arranged them nicely on shelves according to their type and function. But it never seemed to last . . .

However, it is usually easy enough to separate blocks and building equipment from cars, puzzles, and so on. Small plastic buckets work well to store categories of little things (long may it last). Some toys are best put away for playing with under supervision, and a special box of toys is a good idea for use in certain circumstances. Putting toys away, then recycling them, also helps children see them again in a different way.

A small table and chair, while not essential, is a great asset and can be used for a wide range of activities including eating meals (or perhaps I should say "offering meals," remembering that whether they get eaten or not is another matter altogether).

Toddlers should be encouraged to help put toys away and tidy up as soon as they are mobile. This is a long-term project, but it's worth persevering with as they do gradually become more helpful after a few years—don't expect miracles in a week!

Outside

Ideally the outside space should be arranged so that the toddler can have time there unsupervised; however, this is not possible for a lot of families until their toddlers are three or older.

Outside is for jumping, running, climbing, and making noise and mess. Good things to have outside are a sandbox, climbing equipment (or somewhere to climb), a swing, balls, things to ride on, and a place to play around with mud and water.

Books

Owning books is as important as owning toys. Board and vinyl books can be included with other toys. Older babies and toddlers between twelve and fifteen months will suck and chew them and practice their hand–eye skills by separating the pages. Your toddler will gradually start to look at the pictures and bring the books to you to look at with him. The vinyl ones are fun in the tub and it's handy to take a book or two with you when you go out.

Other, more easily damaged books are best kept separate until your toddler is old enough to take care of them. And then it's a good idea to have all the books together, separate from the other toys, in a special place for books and reading.

Reading

The benefits of reading are unlimited. Encouraging a love of books from a young age will help your toddler want to learn to read and eventually to use reading as a way to have fun, relax, and be entertained. Reading is a particularly self-sufficient form of entertainment, which is a great bonus for parents. (I still remember the dramatic difference it made to our vacations once our kids could read and swim.)

Books also help develop concentration, attention span, thinking and imagination. Reading is a cozy and intimate way to spend time together and an excellent bedtime ritual which can be a part of establishing good sleep routines. Books can also be a useful potty-training aid.

Initially you may feel that you aren't getting far because toddlers have a very short attention span and until about eighteen months they are often more interested in jumping around and exploring than sitting quietly looking at a book, but persevering is well worth the long-term rewards.

Here are a few tips

- Use books with big bold pictures about things he is familiar with (toys, pets, dolls, and food). Apart from books, try simple catalogs, magazines, and perhaps family photo albums. Books with jingles and rhymes are good too.

- Sit close together or hold him on your lap. Point to the pictures and tell stories about what is happening or what the people are doing. Show him how to turn the pages (he might like to help). Let him point and call out. Carry on as long as he is happy, even if he doesn't seem to be paying much attention. At this stage you may be sowing the seeds for future interest and enjoyment rather than capturing his immediate interest.

- When he doesn't want to stay with you, stop reading and let him go (unless it's bedtime, in which case settle him down for the night).

Fantasy, imagination, and make-believe

The capacity for fantasy and imagination increases significantly from the second year onward as the toddler's thinking abilities expand.

Fantasy and make-believe are aspects of early childhood that bring a lot of joy and laughter to families, even when parents are

up at unthinkable hours because of the chipmunk on the win-
dowsill (or the dinosaur under the bed).

From about two years, toddlers start to invent ways to use
objects and materials for simple make-believe play about things
they are familiar with (little dolls and animals, pretend stores, play
clay, mud, sticks, pebbles, and so on). Also, from two, toddlers are
transferring ideas from books into scenarios that feature themselves
and the people they are close to in the leading roles.

Make-believe play becomes increasingly elaborate from age
three onward. Between three and six, pretending to be adults in a
variety of roles, dressing up, and using props (mothers and fathers,
doctors, pilots, nurses, teachers, and so on) is very common.

Imagination is the link between the toddler's inner and outer
world. It is important for the following reasons:

- Pretending is a way for children to learn about things and solve
  problems.

- It is a way for them to deal with fears and anxiety by being able
  to make things the way they would like them to be, thus giving
  them some control.

- It helps them learn what is and isn't real.

- It helps develop a sense of humor.

- It also helps them start to develop consideration for other people
  by putting themselves in someone else's place.

- A well-developed imagination gives children (and adults) inner
  resources to ward off boredom.

- Make-believe allows toddlers to become someone else (a girl or
  a boy, a father or a mother, or a hero or heroine—Robin Hood
  [an old favorite of mine], Batman, Peter Pan, or Princess Leia).

Toddlers love their parents participating in their make-believe even
if it's only for a short time, and they especially like it when they

(the toddler) stay in charge and in control of the game. Even a distant involvement is appreciated—for example, by keeping up a running commentary from the kitchen or your office as your toddler reports in with the next episode.

Children need time to develop their imaginations. Too many structured activities (toddler gym, musical appreciation, dancing classes, formal learning of a foreign language) and too much TV rob them of the time and energy they need to explore the world on their own.

The imaginary friend

An imaginary friend is a normal part of many children's developing imagination and not an indication that something's wrong. Imaginary friends often make their first appearance late in the third year and may stay around on and off until school starts. It is much more common with oldest or only children, as imaginary friends like fairies tend to melt away when siblings make fun of them.

The imaginary friend can be anything the toddler wants him or her to be (and any age, any sex). The friend can take the blame for the toddler's misdeeds and accompany him on scary missions. The toddler can boss this friend around and use him (or her) as a sounding board for trying out new ideas and games. Imaginary friends are great—we could all do with one.

It's best for adults to welcome the friend but to respect the privacy of the relationship and let the toddler choose when to include the adult (sometimes the friend will be asked to dinner, but it's best not to preempt the request). Obviously it's also not in the friend's best interest to laugh about him or talk about him to others, especially within the toddler's hearing range.

Toddlers are aware that imaginary friends are just that – imaginary. They still need to play with real children and participate in activities with parents and real people.

Television

A toddler's interest in television grows from age two onward. Television has had a very powerful impact on society as a whole and most families in Western cultures today are exposed to it. Even when there is no television in the home, it is such an intrusive means of communication that one way or another a child will eventually become aware of it.

Overall it's better to learn to live with and teach children to use television constructively than to go out of your way to eliminate it. This does not mean that you should rush out and buy a television if owning and watching one is not a part of your lifestyle. The benefits of television (yes, potentially, there are a few) can easily be acquired by other means. But if you already own a TV and enjoy what it has to offer, it is not necessary to make a grand gesture and donate it to your favorite charity.

What are the benefits?

The benefits are only benefits in the context of a vigilant approach to what the toddler watches and limits set on the hours spent watching.

The risks of television watching far outweigh the benefits when toddlers or children are allowed to have unlimited hours of unsupervised viewing and when television is used as an anesthetic to avoid family interaction.

Bearing this in mind, here are some benefits:

- Television can give the parent a welcome short break to get a few things done and so help preserve his or her sanity at certain times of the day.

- Television can bring peace and diversion on rainy days when the parent has run out of ideas and the tension is building.

- It can expand the toddler's horizons by exposing him to different people, countries, ideas, activities, and music.

- It can help build number and letter skills, recognition of colors and shapes.

- Appropriate content and the right amount of exposure can motivate reading.

- Television stories can demonstrate effective ways to resolve conflict and healthy ways to express emotions.

- It can also reinforce values such as kindness, good manners, taking turns, and tolerance for others.

Potential risks and disadvantages when it is overused

- As previously noted, television can rob toddlers of the time they need to explore the world and find out things for themselves.

- Television depletes the toddler's natural energy.

- It interferes with the development of fantasy and imagination and the ability to read and play.

- It contributes to obesity.

- Many television stories oversimplify (in a major way) the ease of solving complex problems happily—in thirty minutes.

- Television exposes toddlers and children to violence in ways that positively reinforce violent, aggressive behavior.

- Research says (I don't know what writers of self-help books would do without that phrase) that watching four or more hours of television a day interferes with reading, social and physical skills, as well as creativity and forming other hobbies and interests. I'm sure there are many individual variations on this four-hour figure and that other factors relating to the toddler's family life will also impact on his development in these areas.

- Television (and videos) is particularly confusing for toddlers who think the world is a magical place and who are learning about cause and effect and what is and isn't real. Television can contribute in a negative way to the normal fears and anxiety that are a part of their development.

Minimizing the negatives

It is easy to blame the *television* for the negative effects it has on toddlers and children in general. Television and associated technologies (videos and computers) are tools that have brought a great deal of pleasure and improved the quality of life for many people, but the responsibility for how they are used lies in the home.

A FRAMEWORK TO WORK WITHIN

- Set firm limits about the number of hours of television permitted each day. Put the limits in place from a young age and stick to the rules as often as possible. Remember that toddlers will follow their parents' lead when parents stay firm about what it is they want to happen. A maximum of two hours a day is recommended for toddlers. Delay regular viewing for toddlers as long as possible. Most toddlers are not that interested until around two or even older unless the home is a place where the television is never turned off and/or where it has been used as a babysitting mechanism for extended periods since birth.

- Be a role model. Limit your own viewing. Let your toddler see you reading, listening to music, and taking part in other activities.

- Look for quality shows (for example, "Barney and Friends,"'Teletubbies," "Sesame Street"). Videos have the advantage of no advertisements, they can be watched at a time that suits, and you and your toddler can choose together exactly what he watches. It's also handy to be able to tape favorite television shows and replay them.

- When you can, watch together and encourage some discussion. Ask your toddler questions to see if he understands what is happening. Encourage guessing: "I wonder what he is going to do with that balloon." Connect what is happening with your toddler's own experiences: "He has a bed just like yours."; "Remember when we went on the plane to see Grandma?"

- When the show is over, turn the television off. Chat for a minute about what you saw. Redirect your toddler's activities. Give him something concrete to do. Try not to leave him in limbo, whining to have the TV turned back on.

Socializing and playgroups

Ways of arranging social contact for toddlers

- Part of an organized activity (swimming lessons, toddler gym).
- Informal time with extended families and friends.

- A regular taking-in-turn arrangement with one or more other families at a set time each week.
- It can be in a more formal setting such as playgroup, occasional care, daycare, or preschool.

The development of their toddler's social skills means a lot to parents. Parents want their children to have friends and to enjoy social activities. It is an area of childhood development that provokes strong feelings and unrealistic expectations, especially during the toddler and preschool years. Most toddlers find extended contact with other toddlers difficult up until age three.

Why?

Between twelve months and two years, a toddler prefers being with the adults he sees the most and who care for him, because they are predictable and he knows what to expect from them. Even allowing for individual temperaments, most toddlers show few niceties when they are in prolonged contact with other toddlers. There's often great joy and delight when toddlers greet each other, but the happy feelings tend to evaporate within a short space of time as children of this age simply do not have the experience to consider the feelings of others or deal with the unpredictable responses of other toddlers. They also believe that everyone sees the world in exactly the same way as they do, and their main concerns are for themselves—how *they* feel, where *they* are moving, and what *they* are doing. This is not conducive to easy social interaction with others at the same stage of development.

What works best?

Toddlers do need to be with other toddlers but for limited times under close supervision. Until they are closer to three years of age,

315

small groups or one-on-one works best, with a flexible time limit so that they can be taken home if they start to lose interest.

Toddlers actually do very well when they are with older children who, like adults, are more predictable and are prepared to make allowances for them. The combination of being with people who have the attributes of adults but are actually *children* is very appealing to toddlers—as their behavior with older children often indicates.

Toddlers will learn from their own families the social skills they need to help them get the idea of taking turns, sharing, and starting to be aware of the needs of other people. And most of them are only starting to get the hang of these sorts of concepts by their third birthday. It's not easy—think of all the adults you know who still haven't grasped them!

Informal playgroups

A playgroup is simply a small group of parents and toddlers who meet regularly. The toddlers play under their parents' supervision. The parents usually take it in turns to hold the playgroup in their homes but playgroups can also take place in the park, at the beach or in a community settings (a church hall for example). Playgroups are often an extension of mothers' groups formed in the early months after birth. Individual playgroups structure the group to suit the people involved. Some have arrangements where parents can take it in turn to leave their toddlers and so have some free time.

Playgroups allow toddlers to be able to see each other on a regular basis and start forming friendships. It is also a good way for toddlers to get to know other adults well.

Finding a playgroup depends a lot on where you live. Some areas are highly organized and have facilitators who advertise in local newspapers, community newsletters and the phone book. In other areas you'll have to check with childcare centers, libraries, universities, pre-schools, churches or any parenting community organizations. If you are on the web, visit http.www.google.com. Go to advance search, keyboard in "playgroups" and up will pop playgroup choices from all over the country.

Playgroups don't necessarily suit everyone, but even if the parents don't love it, it can be tolerable if their toddler does. Sometimes it's worth trying one or two different groups if a few are available to find one that suits you. Most importantly, if your toddler lives in a loving home with opportunities in his day-to-day life for spending some time with other children, there is no need to go out searching for optimal socialization opportunities for him if you don't feel the urge to do so.

Swimming

I love swimming and feel as if it is something I was born doing, so I am certainly in great favour of encouraging toddlers to enjoy the water as preparation for a lifetime of swimming.

Swimming is a wonderful family affair and a cozy one-on-one experience for parent and toddler as well. A morning swimming session also tires toddlers out and helps them sleep soundly.

Between ages two and four, start formal swimming lessons with an accredited instructor.

Introducing toddlers to swimming should be done at the toddler's pace with respect for any reluctance or anxiety. It is not about turning him into Ian Thorpe.

Constant ear infections associated with swimming should not be taken lightly. Sadly, they may preclude some toddlers from regular swimming until they are older and out of the time zone for ear infections.

Here are a few swimming tips

- Make sure your toddler is well protected from the sun.
- Sadly, many of our city beaches and natural pools are often polluted, so avoid them following heavy rain or if you have any concerns about the cleanliness of the water.
- Inflatable water wings are not safety devices and do not replace adult supervision. Water activities for toddlers under two should be on a one-to-one basis with a responsible adult. Never leave your toddler with an older child.
- Swimming lessons should be conducted by qualified instructors who are certified in pediatric heart–lung resuscitation. Learning or updating your own skills is very worthwhile.

Never forget that while water play and swimming lessons give babies and toddlers confidence and enjoyment, they do not give them skills that prevent them from drowning, even if they learn to float or dog paddle from a young age. Constant vigilance is vital.

Stimulating activities

For the last twenty years or so, an increasing obligation has been placed on parents to stimulate their children's natural development by enriching their environment and keeping them busy, busy, busy . . .

From the moment babies are born, there seems to be a rush to get them to achieve as much as possible in as short a time as possible. Toddlers and children are hurried from one activity to another in an effort to make sure they have a rich, full life and every possible advantage for optimum development so that they can become a doctor or a lawyer.

The pressure seems to start in babyhood. "How can I best stimulate my baby?" is a commonly asked question in the first six weeks. A lot of the time it is not necessarily because mothers want to accelerate their baby's development but because it is now a commonly held belief that the more we do for our children the more successful they will be.

Parents are bombarded with ways to provide optimum development. They are constantly advised that toddlers must have gym, swimming, and musical appreciation lessons, and endless other advantageous, stimulating activities.

Some of this advice seems to be more about helping adult lifestyles and egos than about giving children things they positively need.

Why the pressure?

- Affluence and the wish to give our toddlers the advantages and opportunities we think we didn't have.

- Competitiveness, guilt associated with both parents working, and guilt associated with broken families. In many ways it seems that it is easier for parents to arrange for a toddler to learn the violin than it is for them to be available and to keep his home stable.

- The explosion of research into human development, with the associated range of experts all putting in their opinions, also makes parents feel that they need to be urging their toddlers along by providing constant stimulating interaction and physical activities.

- Optimum child development is now a commercial growth industry, much of which is driven by profit rather than what is actually necessary for the well-being of toddlers.

- It's all over after the first three years: Currently, there is a huge emphasis on the first three years, which is fueling the parental obligation panic. Doors slam, we are told, never to reopen. If an opportunity is missed, the future is irredeemably compromised.

  Really?

  As John Bruer says so eloquently in his book *The Myth of the First Three Years*: *"For most learning, particularly learning culturally transmitted skills and knowledge such as reading, mathematics and music the windows of experience-dependent opportunity never close. You and your children can benefit from exposure to complex, enriched environments throughout your lifetimes. Based on the research, earlier is better only because enrichment that starts earlier can—odds are—last longer."*[5]

Who really needs help?

It seems to be forgotten that many of the recommendations to help or accelerate toddlers' development and enrich their environments relate originally to toddlers who have special needs or who have been emotionally or socially deprived.

So relax about the enrichment and the activities.

Your toddler is part of your family, not a research project. Being part of a family involves times when housework has to be done, when each family member has time to themselves, and when everyone is together. Extra activities for your toddler are fine when you have the money and it's convenient or when it provides a social outlet that you both enjoy.

Mostly toddlers need to observe, to witness the actions and interactions of those around them. They need constant, available parents who love them dearly and have enough self-confidence to provide what their toddlers need in order to develop in their own way at their own pace.

Play is not about fast-tracking your toddler to adult success (What do we mean by success anyway?); it's about gradually encouraging him to understand and enjoy the world he lives in.

chapter eleven

Safety and Immunization

An enormous amount of information is available about child safety. It is impossible to cover the area in its entirety, so I will focus on some of the basic issues that relate to toddlers. Other information on safety is to be found throughout the book when relevant.

Toddlerproofing your home—is it really necessary?

Toddlerhood is an intensely physical time. As toddlers climb, run, explore, examine, experiment, and frighten the wits out of their parents, accidents, or more correctly, unintentional injuries are common. A certain number of *minor* unintentional injuries, are to be expected—accidents have the capacity to teach toddlers more about life and the consequences of their actions.

But sadly, *serious* unintentional injury is the leading cause of disability and death during childhood. The greatest number of deaths and injuries occur in the one-to four-year-old age group and

are caused by motor vehicle/pedestrian accidents, drowning, choking, suffocation, falls, burns and scalds, poisoning, electrocution,
and dog bites.

Most of these serious injuries are avoidable.

And home is the most common place for the injuries to happen.

Toddlers are vulnerable to injury for the following reasons

- They have great mobility but lack experience to know their limits or understand the potential hazards of their environment.
  They have little understanding of cause and effect.

- Their limited vision—toddlers do not make use of their periph-
  eral vision (vision from the sides of their eyes).

- Their concentration is limited—they are easily distracted.

- Their actions are spontaneous—they do not think ahead.

- Their size in relation to everything around them means that
  they can't see potential dangers. Nor can they be seen easily
  by others.

- Their coordination and balance are still developing—they tend
  to be clumsy in many situations.

- Their intense curiosity and drive to explore lead them into dangerous situations.

- Their negativity and limit testing put pressure on parents whose
  attention may be diverted at the wrong moment. Most parents
  find the constancy of keeping toddlers safe exhausting—at least
  some of the time.

As we are all aware, toddlers and their parents are all different. Some parents do not feel the need to toddlerproof their homes because their toddlers can be taught to stay away from danger or precious objects. However, I think that for most parents, modifying their homes to make them as safe as possible, both *for* and *from* their toddlers, helps diminish stress and nagging and minimizes the chances of serious injury.

A guide for making your home safe

- Install safety gates where appropriate (on stairways, perhaps into the kitchen).
- Put childproof locks on doors where necessary (the bathroom, the laundry).
- Remove as many forbidden objects as possible. Some parents prefer not to do this because they believe that their toddlers should learn to treat things with respect right from the beginning. While this may be feasible for some families, it is usually easier to manage the toddler years by having as little around for them to damage as is practicable.
- Use the Home Safety Checklist on the following pages to make sure your home is safe.

Home safety check list

General home environment

Do you have a safety switch to prevent electrocution?

Yes ❏   No ❏

Can your hot water system be turned down to 120°F to prevent scalds?

Yes ❏   No ❏

Do you have a smoke detector located outside each bedroom area?

Yes ❏   No ❏

Are safety plugs fitted in spare electrical outlets?

Yes ❏   No ❏

Do you have a fence that restricts access to your driveway and the street?

Yes ❏   No ❏

Kitchen

Do your appliances have short cords that do not dangle over the kitchen counter?

Yes ❏   No ❏

Do you use the back burners and turn pot handles around to prevent pots from being pulled from the burners?   Yes ❏   No ❏

Are knives and other sharp objects stored out of reach of children?

Yes ❏   No ❏

Are cleaning products, chemicals and medications stored in a locked cabinet at least 4' 11" above the ground?   Yes ❏   No ❏

Do you have a multi-purpose fire extinguisher within reach of your stove?   Yes ❏   No ❏

Can you restrict access to the kitchen?   Yes ❏   No ❏

Bathroom

Does the bath have nonslip mats or hand rails?   Yes ❏   No ❏

Are medicines and sharp objects kept in a locked cabinet out of the reach of children?   Yes ❏   No ❏

Are any electricals (hairdryers, electric shavers) stored safely and away from water when not in use?   Yes ❏   No ❏

Is the bath water temperature always tested before putting toddlers into the tub?   Yes ❏   No ❏

Are hot water faucets unable to be operated by toddlers?   Yes ❏   No ❏

Laundry

Are cleaning products, bleaches and detergents stored out of reach, in a child-resistant cabinet?   Yes ❏   No ❏

Is the diaper bucket used with a lid and kept out of the reach of toddlers?   Yes ❏   No ❏

Can you restrict access to the laundry?   Yes ❑   No ❑

Living areas

Is the furniture located safely (e.g., away from the windows)?

Yes ❑   No ❑

Are sharp edges on tables and furniture covered?

Yes ❑   No ❑

Are blind and curtain cords out of reach?   Yes ❑   No ❑

Are glass doors protected by safety film, colorful stickers, or made of safety glass?   Yes ❑   No ❑

Is alcohol stored in a child-resistant cabinet?   Yes ❑   No ❑

Are toys kept away from the main walkway?   Yes ❑   No ❑

Are rugs and mats secure to prevent a fall?   Yes ❑   No ❑

Are there any low-level tables that dangerous items could be placed on (for example, watch batteries, tea and coffee, peanuts)?

Yes ❑   No ❑

Child's bedroom (see page 226)

Is the space between vertical crib railings between 2"–3" wide?

Yes ❑   No ❑

Are toys suitable for the toddler's age?   Yes ❑   No ❑

Is the furniture located safely (not near electrical switches, windows, or ceiling fans)? Yes ❏ No ❏

Garden shed/outdoors

Can your garden shed be locked at all times? Yes ❏ No ❏

Are pesticides, paints, and other poisons stored in tightly covered, labeled, original containers out of the reach of toddlers?
Yes ❏ No ❏

Is the outdoor play equipment damaged or potentially dangerous?
Yes ❏ No ❏

Does your pool have a fence at least 4 foot high around all four sides of the pool that cannot be climbed by children and has a self-closing, self-latching gate? Yes ❏ No ❏

General safety considerations

- Stay abreast of normal toddler development (there's plenty of information in this book). Toddlers rapid development during these years means that they are developing new skills all the time, which exposes them to new hazards.

- Learn or update the skill of CPR (cardiopulmonary resuscitation). CPR classes are available at local YMCA's, hospitals, community centers or local chapters of the American Red Cross or American Heart Association. It is becoming more common now for groups of parents to arrange for Red Cross personnel to conduct classes in private homes. If you are interested, call your local chapter (in the White Pages).

- Once you have taken a course it is also advisable to update your skills regularly.

- Make sure you have an emergency number for paramedics by the phone. Check the inside of your phone book to find the best number for your area. In some areas the number is 911 (or another number). In other areas the fire department handles paramedic services making it faster to call there directly.

- *Make a list of emergency numbers to keep near the telephone; for example:*
  POLICE
  POISON CONTROL CENTER
  PARAMEDICS
  FIRE DEPARTMENT
  LOCAL HOSPITAL
  FAMILY DOCTOR/PEDIATRICIAN
  CHILD ABUSE PREVENTION NUMBER
  AN ALL-NIGHT PHARMACY
  MOTHER'S WORK
  FATHER'S WORK
  NEIGHBOR
  RELATIVE

- *Assemble a first aid kit*
  Dressings
  A roll of gauze
  Elastic bandages in various sizes
  Non-stick pads
  Adhesive tape, sterile adhesive strips
  Gauze pads
  Cotton balls

Triangular bandage to use as a sling

Clean non-fluffy cloth or clean plastic to cover burns until seen by a doctor

Creams, lotions, and medications

Antiseptic solution

Calamine lotion

Saline eye wash

30+ sunscreen

Acetaminophen tablets and liquid with child resistant lids

Syrup of ipecac (only if you live more than thirty minutes from medical assistance. Ipecac should only be used on advice from a doctor or a Poison Control Center as it is dangerous to use it for some poisons (for example, kerosene). Ipecac needs replacing every three years.

First-aid equipment

A thermometer

Safety pins of various sizes

Scissors with one sharp end and one blunt end

Tweezers

Flashlight

Specific safety hazards for toddlers

1. Drowning

Drowning kills silently and is the number one killer in the first five years. Most toddlers drown in their own pool or a pool owned by friends or family. Swimming lessons do not make toddlers "drownproof." Constant vigilance is essential when toddlers are anywhere near water.

Some general guidelines for water safety

- Swimming pools should have five-foot high fencing on all sides with vertical posts no more than four inches apart and a self-closing, self-latching gate. Swimming pool barrier laws are increasing throughout the U.S. Contact your local governmental offices to find out the regulations in your county, city or town. •

- Never leave younger toddlers in the care of older children at bathtime or near any water. Flotation toys and swimming aids are not lifesaving devices and do not replace adult supervision.

- Alcohol increases water hazards. If you are taking your toddler to a pool party, it is a good idea to decide beforehand which parent is going to drink and which parent is going to drive and take care of the toddler.

- Always drain wading pools after use and remove the access ladder from above-ground pools when swimming is over for the day.

- Other drowning hazards for toddlers are diaper buckets, spas, fish ponds, pets' drinking bowls, and toilet bowls.

- When visiting, ask about any drowning hazards such as pools, spas, and ponds.

First-aid tips for drowning

Learn how to give resuscitation or take a refresher course.

In an emergency, take the toddler to the phone and call 911. Directions will be given to you over the phone.

2. Poisoning

Every year thousands of toddlers swallow dangerous substances in and around the house, such as medicines, household cleaning agents, petrochemicals, pesticides, and weedkillers.

The greatest number of poisonings occur in the toddler's home, but care must be taken when visiting, especially in homes where no children are living (for example, when visiting grandparents).

Some guidelines to protect toddlers from poisoning

- Lock all poisons away when not in use. Seventy percent of poisonings happen when a substance recently used is not closed and returned to its normal place out of the reach of toddlers. When using a poisonous substance, place it up high as a temporary safeguard.

- Dispose of old medicines and other poisons promptly.

- Install child-resistant latches on cabinets where you store poisonous products.

- Keep poisons in their original containers.

- Use products that come in child-resistant containers.

- Use a lockable medicine cabinet installed out of the reach of children. Avoid leaving contraceptive pills or other medication on bedside tables. Take medication when your toddler is not watching you.

- Take extra care when moving or in a new environment (for example, on vacations).

First-aid tips for poisoning

If you live more than thirty minutes away from medical help, keep a bottle of syrup of Ipecac in your first-aid kit. Ipecac induces vomiting but should only be used on advice from a doctor or a Poison Control Center, as it is dangerous to use it for some poisons (for example, kerosene). Ipecac needs replacing every three years.

If you think your toddler may have swallowed a poison, take the container with you to the phone and call the Poison Control Center.

3. Choking

Choking occurs when food or other small solid objects get caught in the throat and windpipe, obstructing the airway and preventing air from getting into the lungs. When it is a small soft item (a crumb or a soft lump), the toddler will usually cough, which removes the object from the airway.

Hard foods like peanuts, raw carrot and apple, and chunks of celery are the main causes of serious obstruction in toddlers. Coins and tiny batteries are other choking hazards.

Choking is different from gagging, but it's easy to confuse the two. Gagging is a common behavioral ploy of toddlers when they do not wish to eat certain foods. It quickly turns into a habit, and frightened parents unwittingly encourage the behavior because they fear that the toddler is choking. With gagging the toddler is very much in control. He is likely to make distressed facial contortions and even hold his breath, but eventually he spits or vomits the food out. When a toddler is choking, he will usually have a sudden fit of coughing and his face will become red or turn purple.

Some guidelines to protect your toddler from choking

- Constant supervision and monitoring of bits and pieces left around the house is essential, especially if there are older children living in the home.
- As much as possible encourage your toddler to sit down to eat.

- Grate apples and carrots. Avoid raw chunks of apple, carrot and celery until age three.

- Never force a distressed toddler to eat.

- Buy toys from recognized manufacturers and check them regularly for parts that may come loose. Check all toys regularly for wear and tear. Hair, noses, buttons, jewelry and other accessories on stuffed toys and dolls are often small enough to choke toddlers.

First-aid tips for choking

Allow your toddler to cough. Coughing is usually sufficient to clear the airway. If coughing does not clear the airway, the toddler will try desperately to breathe and will become very distressed.

If the toddler is coughing and wheezing but can breathe and speak, take him immediately to a hospital.

Emergency steps if the toddler is unable to speak or cry and is turning blue:

i. If there are two adults, one should call an ambulance immediately.

ii. If you can see the object, remove it using your finger as a hook. If you cannot see the object, do not try to remove it.

iii. If the choking continues, lay the toddler over your knees with his head downward and give three to four light blows on his back between his shoulder blades, using the heel of your hand.

iv. If choking continues, stand behind the toddler and wrap your arms around his middle. Grip the fist of one hand (placed over the toddler's stomach) with the other hand. Make three to four quick and firm thrusts, squeezing upward.

v. If breathing has still not occurred, start resuscitation.

4. Falls

Falls are a part of life for toddlers, especially around age two when they try to climb on everything around them. Injury from falls is the most common cause of toddlers needing medical attention. Falls are not often fatal, but broken bones, bruising, and head injuries can be distressing, so it's worthwhile trying to prevent as many as you can. Most toddler falls take place at home. They fall from furniture (tables, beds, and chairs), out of nursery equipment (highchairs), off steps and stairs, and from speeding tricycles.

Some guidelines to help prevent injury from falls

- Use gate barriers to keep toddlers away from dangerous areas and stairways. Teach younger crawling toddlers to come downstairs backward.
- Make sure there is no furniture the toddler can climb on to get to open windows.
- Decks need vertical railings with gaps between 2½"–3½" apart. If your deck has horizontal railings, attach netting from the floor of the deck to the top rail to prevent climbing.
- Avoid slippery surfaces (highly polished floors, scatter floor rugs).
- Use corner protectors on benches, coffee tables, and other sharp furniture, particularly when it is low.
- Use an H-shaped harness on toddlers when they are in strollers, carriages, highchairs, and supermarket carts.
- Toddlers should not sleep in top bunks of bunk beds.

5. Burns and scalds

Toddlers are at great risk of being burned or scalded. Here are some common ways that burns and scalds happen:

- From food heated in microwave ovens.
- From bath water that is too hot and from turning on hot faucets.
- From hot drinks and hot water in teapots.
- From exposed heating vents, open fires, and barbecues.
- From cigarettes, hot irons, and the metal fixtures in the interiors of hot cars.

Some guidelines to prevent damage from burns and scalds

- Don't hold or play with your toddler while you drink a cup of tea or coffee. Nearly half of all scalds are the result of hot drinks being spilled or from the toddler pulling hot liquid onto himself.
- Keep hot food and liquids out of reach until they are cool enough to use. Take special care with food that has been heated in a microwave—hot spots burn toddler mouths.
- Have a fire extinguisher in the kitchen.
- Use stove guards to avoid toddlers pulling down hot liquids.
- Put irons up high to cool after use.
- Keep a close eye on toddlers near barbecues and campfires and dress them in low fire-risk clothes.
- Use child-resistant taps or mixing valves to prevent toddlers from turning on the hot water. Keep a close eye on toddlers while they are in the bathtub. Never leave them alone in the bathtub with an older child.

First-aid tips for burns

- The general aim when treating a burn or a scald is to cool the area quickly, prevent infection, relieve pain, and minimize shock.
- If it is a scald (caused by hot liquid), remove all *wet* clothing quickly because clothing retains heat. For other burns, immerse the burned area in cold water; do not remove burned clothes that are stuck to the skin.
- Apply cold water for thirty minutes to reduce the heat in the skin, preventing deeper burning.
- Never use any oils, butter, or ointment to cover the burn.
- Never use ice or icy water, as toddlers can get dangerously chilled.
- Keep the toddler warm with blankets or adult coats.
- Remove any tight clothing from around the burned area before it starts to swell.

    Seek medical advice for anything other than a small burn.

6. Suffocation

Suffocation occurs due to a lack of oxygen being supplied to the body. The main suffocation hazards for toddlers include:

- Plastic bags
- Airtight enclosures such as old refrigerators, freezers, car trunks, and wardrobes
- Being left in cars, especially in hot weather or when the engine is running
- House fires

Some guidelines to protect your toddler from suffocation

- Do not allow your toddler to play with plastic bags of any sort, ever. Tie knots in plastic bags before storage or disposal.
- Avoid using a pillow until your toddler is around two years old.
- Check on the accessibility to toddlers of old fridges, freezers, and wardrobes. Arrange for their disposal if they are not being used.
- Never leave toddlers in cars without an adult being present.
- Install smoke alarms in your house and make a point of finding out what steps to take to minimize the risk of house fires and know what to do should one happen.

7. Dog bites

Sadly the family dog can be a hazard for toddlers. The one- to four-year-olds are the ones who have the highest rates of injuries from dog bites, the most serious of which are to the face and head. The family dog or a dog belonging to friends nearly always causes the injuries.

Some guidelines for protecting your toddler from dog attacks

- Always be aware that any dog may bite.
- If in any doubt at all, ask friends and family to keep their dogs away from your children.
- Always keep watch from within grabbing distance when a dog is near your toddler, especially when there is a new baby on the premises.

- Train your dog to obey commands. For example, "sit," "come," and "stay."
- Have your dog treated promptly if it is sick or in pain.
- Discourage your toddler from playing with your dog when the dog is eating.
- Teach your toddler how to deal appropriately with strange dogs and when to leave dogs alone.

Basic treatment for dog bite

- Clean immediately and thoroughly with antiseptic.
- A doctor should see extensive bites or puncture wounds immediately.
- Make sure your toddler's tetanus immunization is kept up to date.

Immunization

Immunization is safe, simple, and effective and has saved millions of children and adults worldwide from death and disability as a result of infectious diseases.

High levels of childhood immunization in a community protect not only the children who are immunized but those vulnerable others who are too young to be vaccinated, the rare baby who can't be vaccinated, and those few who do not respond to the vaccine.

Eleven diseases—hepatitis B, diphtheria, tetanus, whooping cough, poliomyelitis, measles, mumps, rubella, Hemophilus influenzae type B (HIB,a bacterial meningitis), chickenpox, and Pneumococcal disease—that cause serious complications and sometimes death can be prevented by routine childhood immunization.

Immunization procedures, recommendations and vaccines are

339

constantly being revised and it is impossible in a book to keep the information absolutely up to date. The information provided here is based on the best information available at the date of publication. If you are ever in any doubt about aspects of your baby's immunization please talk to your pediatrician, nurse practitioner, or your family doctor.

Benefits and risks

No vaccine is completely free of the possibility of side effects, but the unpleasant side effects experienced by some babies and toddlers are relatively minor and reversible. Serious adverse reactions to vaccines are not only extremely rare but are significantly less common and less severe than the diseases they are preventing.

Does immunization always work?

Most vaccines are not totally protective and become less protective if national immunization rates fall. Illnesses are usually shorter and less complicated in vaccinated babies.

Why do babies and toddlers have to have so many doses?

The immune system in babies and toddlers is immature and does not work as well as the immune system in older children and adults. Therefore, more doses of vaccines are required in the first five years of life to protect this age group from the most serious infections of childhood.

When should my toddler be immunized?

Most vaccines need several doses to be effective. Please refer to the schedule on page 344 to see when your toddler needs his immunization.

What about homeopathic immunization?

Homeopathic vaccines are not put to the stringent safety tests recommended vaccines have to undergo to show that they work and are safe. There is no proof that homeopathic immunization protects toddlers from disease.

The Council of the Faculty of Homeopathy, London, issued a statement in 1993 that reads: "The Faculty of Homeopathy, London strongly supports the conventional vaccination program and has stated that vaccination should be carried out in the normal way, using the conventional tested and proved vaccines, in the absence of medical contraindications."

What if he's not well?

Instances when immunization cannot be carried out are virtually non-existent but unfortunately sometimes healthcare professionals are nervous about being blamed for times when toddlers do experience adverse reactions and may unnecessarily delay or withhold immunization. Immunization can still be given when toddlers have snuffles, colds, ear infections or a mild fever.

Treating side effects

- If necessary, give a dose of acetaminophen (Tempra, Feverall, Tylenol). The dose is 7 mg per pound (15 mg per kg) and the dose can be repeated in four hours.
- Give extra fluids
- If side effects following immunization are severe and persistent, for example, a fever higher than 103°F, high pitched and prolonged crying, or if you are worried for any reason contact your pediatrician, family doctor or your nearest local hospital.

Vaccine Adverse Event Reporting System (VAERS)

VAERS is a system for reporting injuries suspected of being caused by vaccines. In the rare event your child has a vaccine-associated injury or even if you think a medical problem your child has might have been caused by a vaccine ask your doctor to file a VAERS form. You can also report a vaccine reaction to VAERS yourself. The toll-free information line is 1-800-822-7967.

Is vaccination compulsory?

All states require proof of vaccination before children can enter school; most private schools and daycare centers also require proof of immunization before they will accept your child. However, not all schools and centers require every shot.

Medical exemptions to vaccination will allow entry to schools, for example leukemia, cancer, or AIDS. And all states except Mississippi and West Virginia also accept religious exemptions. In some states, qualifying for an exemption from vaccination is a complicated process that may require hiring an attorney.

What about low cost or free vaccines?

You can get low-cost or free vaccines at U.S. public health service clinics. To find one near you call 1-800-232-2522. Every child up to 18 years of age who is enrolled in Medicaid, who lacks health insurance, or whose health insurance does not cover vaccines is eligible. All American Indian and Alaskan Native children are also eligible.

National Vaccine Injury Compensation Program

This is a federal program that offers compensation for the care of anyone believed to have been injured by vaccines. For more information you can call the program toll-free at 1-800-338-2382 or go to http://www.hrsa.gov/bhr/vicp

Immunization—is it a choice?

I am only going to touch on this briefly as readers of my information will know that I am one hundred percent in favor of immunization and believe that it is one area of baby and toddler care that is not optional. I acknowledge that a minuscule number of babies have significant reactions to vaccination, which may make other parents very wary of immunization. However, serious adverse reactions clinically proven to be solely related to immunization are rare whereas it is a proven fact that one in two hundred otherwise perfectly healthy, normal babies who suffer whooping cough die from pneumonia or brain damage. Babies and toddlers who are unimmunized because of parental choice are protected because the majority of babies in the U.S. are immunized, not because the unimmunized have healthy lifestyles and eat the right food.

Please see the Resources section for other reliable sources of information.

STANDARD RECOMMENDED CHILDHOOD IMMUNIZATION SCHEDULE UNITED STATES, 2001

At birth	Hept B#1
2 months	Hep B#2, DtaP, Hib, IPV
4 months	DTaP, Hib, IPV, PCV
6 months	DTaP, Hib, IPV, PCV
12–15 months	Hep B#3, Hib, MMR#1, Varicella, PCV
15–18 months	DtaP, IPV
4 years	DtaP, IPV, MMR#2

Hep B=Hepatitus B vaccine
DTaP=Combined diptheria, tetanus, pertussis (whooping cough) acellular vaccine
HiB=Hemophilus influenzae type B conjugate vaccine
IPV=Inactivated polio vaccine
MMR=Measles, mumps, rubella vaccine
Varicella=chickenpox vaccine

part **four**

WHY IS HE ALWAYS SICK? TODDLER MEDICAL CONDITIONS AND ILLNESSES

chapter twelve

Coughing, Mucus, and Poo

Why is there so much of it?

The toddler years are renown for snotty noses, ear infections, loose poo, strange rashes, and the never-ending cough. The natural immunity that babies are born with wears off by the end of the first year, leaving toddlers to venture out into the world with little resistance to common infections.

The number and severity of illnesses experienced varies tremendously from toddler to toddler. Some toddlers sail through this period with a minimum of sickness. Others seem to catch anything that's going around, and as they lurch from one to the other, they leave their parents despairing that they will ever be healthy and happy again.

Childcare and infectious diseases

It is estimated that when toddlers are in care with other toddlers the rate of illness they experience increases by about thirty percent, and parents quickly notice the sudden rise in the levels of mucus, poo, and so on once their toddler starts daycare. For most toddlers in care, the illness dramas subside between six and twelve months, but a few experience such debilitating ongoing symptoms that consideration has to be given to other options for their care.

The likelihood of illness is decreased in childcare situations where there are smaller groups of toddlers, where there is a low toddler–caregiver ratio, and where caregivers have a knowledge of the best practices to avoid the spread of disease and are motivated to use them.

Even when toddlers are not going to childcare, most of them will have episodes of infectious illnesses after contact with others at playgroup, preschool, birthday parties, the supermarket, and anywhere else there are large groups of humans. This does not mean that they should be kept in a bubble, as exposure to the vast range of bugs in the environment is essential to develop the immunity that children need to fight disease.

All very well, but when you are in the thick of it you may wonder how so much illness can possibly be normal. It is estimated in various studies that the average number of infections/illnesses experienced by toddlers is six to ten per year. By the time most toddlers reach the magic age of three, their immunity is developed enough to ward off common bugs and the constant round of illnesses diminishes.

Helping to minimize infectious diseases

While it is true that catching common infections helps toddlers to build up their immunity, no parent wants their toddler to catch a life-threatening disease which may have a serious impact on his future health and development.

The best way to minimize the chance of this happening is to make sure that your toddler is fully immunized and that he attends a childcare center that requires all attendees to be fully immunized. Vaccination is the single most effective way of preventing the spread of serious diseases. For more on immunization see page 339.

Other ways of helping to minimize recurrent illnesses include:

- Breastfeeding for the first six to twelve months.

- Making sure that your toddler is offered a healthy diet.

- Having a smoke-free home.

- Keeping him away from group settings with other toddlers when he has diarrhea, coughs, and colds or other infectious illnesses.

- Giving him the opportunity to have plenty of fresh air and out-door activities.

- Teaching him to wash his hands after using the potty, before meals, and before bedtime. Wash your own hands often and thoroughly so that he gets the idea. Handwashing is obviously a long-term project which is likely to be resisted initially by the limit-testing two-year-old, but stick with it. Eventually you will find that your efforts are rewarded. Many toddlers grow into meticulous handwashers by the time they are three or four (which can have its own irritations).

When to consult your family doctor

Many parents feel as if they live at their doctor's office during the toddler years. However, an understanding pediatrician will sympathize with the frequent dilemmas that beset the parents of toddlers (especially if he or she has a few themselves), so do not hesitate to make a visit if you are worried.

Here is a general list of situations when it is a good idea to contact your pediatrician:

- Apathy, lack of energy, pale and sweaty skin
- Any abnormal sleepiness or floppiness
- Sudden refusal to eat, lack of interest in food or fluid
- Bloated or tender tummy
- Simultaneous vomiting and diarrhea
- Any sign of blood in vomit, urine, or poo
- Thick, smelly urine
- Green or greeny/yellow stained vomit
- Persistent diarrhea
- A constant fever 101°F (38.4°C) that doesn't respond to acetaminophen and removing some of the toddler's clothes
- Difficulty breathing
- A persistent cough
- Any abnormal discharge, especially from the ears
- Any abnormal behavior that may indicate an ear infection (sudden night waking, unusual whining, shaking of head, unusual head banging)
- A convulsion or fit
- Neck stiffness
- Redness or discharge of pus from the eyes
- A sudden outbreak of a strange rash that you can't identify
- Any unusual swelling or lump, especially if it is hot and/or painful to touch
- Swallowing or insertion of foreign bodies into body cavities which can't be removed safely at home (coins, beads, stones, and so on)

Common nonprescription medications for toddlers

For relief of fever and pain

Acetaminophen and ibuprofen relieve the symptoms of pain and fever. They do not cure the disease that is causing the symptoms. Ibuprofen is an anti-inflammatory drug that is increasingly being used for symptoms of pain and fever in babies, toddlers and children. Like acetaminophen, it is available in a pediatric suspension.

Both drugs are equally efficient in relation to pain relief and fever reduction.

The safety of both drugs *depends on them being used correctly.* There is now a multitude of acetaminophen preparations available, all with their own individual strength and dose. It is very important to calculate and measure the dose correctly according to the manufacturer's instruction. If in doubt, check with a second person. Neither acetaminophen nor ibuprofen should be given more than once every four hours, and it is always a good idea to know exactly why you are giving it. Constantly giving acetaminophen or ibuprofen to toddlers for vague teething or gas problems or as a panacea for night sleep problems is risky.

Avoid medications containing aspirin for children under the age of twelve unless prescribed by a doctor for a specific medical reason. Aspirin is very effective but is not as safe for babies and toddlers as acetaminophen. In older children, aspirin has been linked to a nasty disease—Reye's syndrome—when given to children with influenza or chicken pox.

351

Coughs, colds, and all that mucus

A multitude of medications for relieving cold symptoms is available, from cough suppressants to mucus removers, from nose drops to chest rubs. These drugs treat the symptoms, not the cause of coughs and colds, which is usually a virus. They do not contribute to making the cold get better quicker.

Cough suppressants should not be used for toddlers and children, as inhibiting the coughing may mask other conditions needing medical attention. Medications to dry up the mucus may help when the cold is at its peak, but the feedback I get from parents suggests such preparations are mostly a waste of money. Some have a mild sedative effect, which can give everyone a little relief at night if the medication does not hype the toddler up (always a risk).

Overall the best medication for the discomfort and fever associated with colds is acetaminophen and lots of tender loving care.

Teething gels and medication (herbal or otherwise)

I do not recommend treatments for what is commonly known as teething.

Sedatives

Sedatives have a place occasionally. Their long-term use for a behavioral reason such as night waking is ineffective and potentially dangerous.

The use of sedatives for toddlers on long plane trips and to help them get over jet lag can be helpful and as long as the dose is carefully calculated, not dangerous. The common medication used is an antihistamine such as Benadryl (diphenhydramine), which is not strictly speaking a sedative but has a sedative effect. Benadryl should not be used for toddlers with croup as it dries the air passages. Other sedatives are available—if you feel you need to use a sedative for a particular purpose it's wise to talk it over with your pediatrician. Bear in mind too that antihistamines can have the reverse effect on some toddlers and cause over-stimulation rather than sedation.

Medicine safety

- Store all medicines in a locked cabinet out of reach, bearing in mind toddlers' climbing abilities.
- Take particular care with adult medications and preparations taken on a daily basis (for example, contraceptive pills, vitamin and iron supplements, and blood pressure tablets).
- Always read the label on the bottle before giving your toddler his medication, especially in the middle of the night.
- Make a point of regularly checking medications and dispose of those that are out of date or no longer needed (down the sink).

Prescription medication

Medication can be prescribed by your pediatrician or advised as treatment by a whole range of other health professionals, including alternative practitioners and pharmacists. When any medication is advised (herbal, homeopathic, or otherwise) or prescribed, don't hesitate to ask a few questions.

Here are some suggestions

- Why is it being prescribed?
- Is it really necessary?
- Is it treating the disease or the symptoms?
- Will the toddler get better without it?
- How soon am I likely to see an improvement?
- Are there any side effects?
- What should be done if the toddler vomits or spits it out?
- And if you are really unsure about what is being offered, ask what evidence is available to support the use of the medication (or treatment).

Giving medications

Giving toddlers medication is usually easy, but some toddlers manage to turn it into a nerve-racking ordeal.

Here are a few tips

- Avoid unnecessary medications. Medication is frequently used when the benefits are dubious. For example, teething medication, sedatives, cold remedies, cough mixtures, dietary supplements, anti-nausea preparations for vomiting, and antibiotics (when they are prescribed for viral infections).

- When possible, use medications that can be given in fewer doses every twenty-four hours. Ask your doctor if it is possible to fit the medication into daylight hours to save having to wake the toddler up during the night.

- Approach the task with firmness and optimism. Make it clear that taking the medicine is not optional. Give positive acknowledgement when the medicine has been taken. Follow up with a drink of water or juice or a popsicle (sugar-free of course).

- Most medications designed for young children come in palatable forms and unless your toddler is the sort who will eat and drink anything, it is advisable to use flavored preparations.

- If necessary, disguise disagreeable-tasting medications in a small amount of honey, jam, or fruit puree. Avoid putting medication into bottles of milk or juice or into the toddler's meal, as he may not get the full dose and it may make him suspicious of all food and drink forevermore.

- If your toddler is agreeable, giving the medication from a spoon or small cup is fine. If there is likely to be a spillage, a plastic disposable syringe is a useful way of getting the correct dose down with a minimum amount of mess (especially for younger toddlers). Sit your toddler on your lap, place the syringe along the inside of his cheek, and gently squirt the liquid into the side of his mouth.

- If your toddler resists despite encouragement and a friendly but firm approach, it may be necessary to use a little (eekk) force. Every effort should be made to work out why the toddler is resisting. If it proves to be impossible to get his cooperation, explain why you now have to do what you are going to do so that he doesn't think he is being punished, then carry out the procedure quickly and carefully. Stay as calm as you can. Whenever possible it is best to have two adults available for medicating an uncooperative toddler.

  Sit on a chair with the toddler in your lap. Place his inside arm behind your waist.

  Support his head (tilted forward) and neck with your arm, and hold his outside arm firmly with your hand to prevent his upper body and arms from moving.

  The other adult can then pop the medicine in and, if necessary, briefly hold his nose to help it go down.

  Give lots of comfort after the event.

- Sometimes chewable pills or capsules work for some toddlers, but most need liquid medication, which means crushing tablets and mixing them with water.

- Occasionally in times of great stress when it is vital for a medication to be given, it is easier to use a suppository if the medication is available in this form (as acetaminophen is, for example).

chapter thirteen

Skin Problems

Atopic dermatitis or eczema (the same thing)

Eczema or atopic dermatitis is a dry skin condition which affects some toddlers in varying degrees. The exact cause is unknown but is strongly affected by hereditary influences. Eczema is more likely to occur when there is a family history of allergic conditions such as asthma, hay fever, and eczema. However, about one toddler in five who has eczema has no family history of allergies.

Eczema in toddlers is rarely caused by an allergy to one particular thing, so it is usually not possible to "cure" the eczema by removing a specific substance.

Most toddlers outgrow their eczema before the age of five.

Eczema can be mild, moderate, or severe. Treatment is aimed at keeping the skin supple, relieving inflammation and itching, treating infections if they occur, and avoiding things which make it worse.

Common irritants for people with eczema

- Sand
- Soap, detergent, bubble baths, perfumed and medicated products

- Wool and acrylic materials found in clothes, carpets, furniture, and car-seat covers
- Chlorinated swimming pools
- Dry air (air-conditioning and heating)
- Increased sweating due to heat or exercise

Eczema appears as a dry rash, which may become red, moist and itchy. Often the first place it is noticed is around the ankles. The other main areas are the neck, behind the ears, on the upper chest, and in the elbow and knee joints. The most common places for toddlers are the insides of the wrists and the fronts of the knees and ankles.

The more severe the eczema, the more widespread and itchy it becomes. Mild eczema often presents as a round, dry patch which is frequently confused with a ringworm infection. However, a ringworm infection has to come from somewhere, and if your baby has not been in contact with a person or an animal with ringworm, the round, dry patches are more likely to be mild eczema.

Using moisturizers, the occasional application of a mild cortisone cream, and avoiding the common irritants usually keeps mild to moderate eczema under control.

It may be advisable to consult a skin specialist for more severe eczema, as the treatment is more complicated. Sometimes the skin becomes infected and needs oral antibiotic treatment. If an infection occurs, it is important not to use disinfectant preparations as this will irritate the skin further.

Research into the relationship between food and eczema is conflicting, and the success of dietary measures varies tremendously with individual toddlers. When they work, the eczema is improved but not cured. Toddlers should be kept away from people with cold sores, as they are particularly susceptible to the cold sore virus. These toddlers are also more prone to the contact dermatitis lots of toddlers get from time to time which causes diaper rashes, red cheeks, rashes around the mouth or eyes, cracking behind the ears, and red moist areas under the chin and in between the joints.

Cracking behind ears

This may be related to eczema or simply to moisture behind the ears causing irritation to the skin. It tends to be an on-again off-again little problem which, for most toddlers, gradually decreases throughout the second year.

Here are a few tips

- Always dry well but gently behind your toddler's ears every day and check to see what's happening.
- Frequent applications of a hypoallergenic moisturizing cream help keep the area supple, so apply a little whenever you can throughout the day and before bedtime.
- If the area becomes very inflamed, cracked, and weepy, see your pediatrician. A combination of a mild cortisone and anti-fungal ointment will clear it. Continue with the hypoallergenic moisturizing cream when it is clear.

Cradle cap

Cradle cap is the name given to a form of dandruff common in babies during the first six months. In babies it appears as crusts on the scalp, eyebrows, and behind the ears. The precise reason for cradle cap is unknown, although there is some evidence to suggest that in young babies it may be related to stimulation of the sebaceous glands by hormones passed from mother to baby during pregnancy.

Sometimes cradle cap on the scalp persists past the first year and continues to occur on and off indefinitely.

Treatment

As the underlying cause can't be addressed, treatment of cradle cap involves softening the crusts as they form so that they can be painlessly removed. Suggestions for doing this are many and varied, but it is not easy to treat as toddlers often do not even like their heads being washed, let alone someone scratching around trying to remove debris from their scalps.

It's tempting to let it accumulate; however, it does get smelly, sometimes itchy, and occasionally infected, so it's advisable to try to keep it under control.

As toddler skin is not as sensitive as baby skin and as the crusts are often harder to remove, treatment for toddler cradle cap is different from treatment in the first six months.

• Tar shampoos are effective for toddlers who will lie still while having their heads washed. If there is any chance that the shampoo will get into the toddler's eyes, it is best not to use it. Try Head and Shoulders, or Selsun Blue.

- A milder preparation for toddlers who cannot use either of the above is a hypoallergenic moisturizing cream.

    Massage in and leave overnight. Wash out the next day, removing softened crusts. Continue to use as crusts reappear.

- Softened crusts have to be manually removed—they do not just disappear or float out. They can be combed or brushed out or removed with your fingernails (trimmed, of course).

    Good luck!

Goosebumpy skin (Keratosis pilaris)

This is a very common skin condition where numerous tiny whitish hard bumps cover the outer upper arms and thighs (like goosebumps). It is more common in toddlers who have eczema, but it can occur without eczema being present. Occasionally it is all over the chest and (rarely) on the face as well.

It is a harmless condition of uncertain cause and in its milder forms does not worry the toddler or child at all. It often disappears spontaneously in adolescence, although it can persist into adulthood, finally disappearing in the late twenties.

In its more severe forms it can be upsetting for older children and adolescents as the bumps can look and feel unattractive. When treatment is appropriate, a prescription-only moisturizing preparation can be used to soften the skin and loosen the plugged ducts. A mild hydrocortisone preparation can help reduce redness and inflammation.

Heat rash (prickly heat)

Heat rash is caused by an overproduction of sweat clogging the sweat glands. It is very common in the first three years because of the immaturity of the heat-regulating center in the brain.

Many toddlers break out in a heat rash as soon as the hot weather arrives or if they are overdressed.

Heat rash in toddlers looks like separate little reddish dots and appears mainly at the back of the neck, on the tummy, and on the top of the chest. It is sometimes itchy, particularly around the base of the hairline and the back of the neck, where the toddler will sometimes scratch so much that he damages the skin.

It helps to move him into an environment where the temperature and humidity are lower (not always possible, of course). Cool baths and light, loose clothing are also useful in keeping him comfortable in hot weather.

A light coating of zinc and starch powder, for example, Desitin powder, (applied with your hands—shaking it into the air is an inhalation risk) is useful to help absorb the sweat and relieve the itch. If scratching is persistent, a mild hydrocortisone cream is helpful.

Hives

Hives are very common. Ten to twenty percent of the population will have a hive attack at least once in their lifetime. Hives usually disappear within a few days to a few weeks.

They look like fluid-swollen bumps that sit alone or pop up in clusters. Food, infections, and insect bites are the most likely causes.

Egg white, tomatoes, fish, nuts, strawberries, pork, and season- ings such as those in tomato sauce and mayonnaise are the main offenders in the food line—not the dreaded cows' milk.

Upper respiratory infections, chicken pox, and drugs such as aspirin, penicillin, sulfur and codeine may trigger hive attacks.

For many toddlers the bout is acute and it is relatively easy to work out the trigger. For example, the hives appear right after eating a tomato, then disappear within a few days—no more tomatoes, no more hives. Some toddlers, however, have chronic bouts that last for weeks and it is difficult to know what the trigger(s) is.

Treatment

The best treatment for hives is to find the cause and eliminate it, but this is easier said than done a lot of the time, particularly in chronic cases.

While possible causes are being investigated or when the cause cannot be found, oral antihistamines provide some relief. A variety of antihistamines are available, but sometimes it can take a while to work out the best combination for individual sufferers.

Infantile acne

Occasionally during the first year, a baby develops inflamed pim- ples and blackheads on his face, which look very similar to a mild form of teenage acne. It is an uncommon condition called infantile acne and tends to occur in babies from families with a strong history of teenage acne, although this is not always the case.

Although this condition is associated more with the first year, I am including it here because the blackheads and pimples often continue into the second year and the condition is frequently misdiagnosed.

While there is no wildly successful treatment, it is useful for parents to have some information about the condition to avoid launching into a range of ineffective "natural" treatments and dietary restrictions (it is not affected by diet). Dermatologists prescribe a liquid form of Retin A to be applied locally, which has mixed results.

As the toddler is too young to look into the mirror and agonize over his complexion, it doesn't bother him at all. Infantile acne disappears sometime in the second year, maybe to return in the adolescent years.

Mosquito bites

Mosquito bites look like a flat tiny red spot almost like a dot from a red felt-tip pen. Mosquito bites disappear without incident unless the toddler has a sensitivity to them, in which case the bites produce large hives and severe itching that lasts for a few days.

If your toddler is uncomfortable, apply ice packs and calamine lotion or some anti-itch ointment.

Diaper rash

Diaper rash is a general term referring to the variety of red, blotchy, and sometimes spotty skin conditions toddlers get in the diaper area. It may appear on the genitals, around the anus, on the buttocks, on the lower part of the tummy covered by the diaper, in the groins, and on the thighs.

Sometimes the whole diaper area is affected. Sometimes it only appears on one of the above areas.

What causes diaper rash?

The combination of wetness, friction, and heat that is generated inside a toddler's diaper makes the risk of a diaper rash ever present. The chafing and sogginess damage the protective layer of the skin, causing an area of rough, red, hot blotchiness.

More specific causes include medication (in particular antibiotics), viral diarrhea, food, creams, laundry detergent, or disposable diaper liners.

Toddlers who have eczema (dry skin) are more prone to diaper rash.

Treatment

No miracle cream or powder exists to prevent or cure all rashes. Frequent diaper changing helps avoid red bottoms, but some toddlers are prone to diaper rash no matter how often the diapers are changed and will not be totally free of the rash until they are out of diapers.

Successful treatment is most likely when a correct diagnosis of the rash is made, so if your toddler's bottom doesn't respond quickly to simple measures, it's a good idea to seek help from your pediatrician before buying out the pharmacy.

Types of diaper rash

There are quite a few variations on the diaper rash theme, all with their own names and diagnosis. The majority fall into two broad groups—those without and those with a yeast infection.

Diaper rash without a yeast infection

This is the basic red bottom caused by skin contact with irritants such as poo, urine, the material of the diaper, liners, laundry detergents, water softener, and so on. The redness is around the inner thighs, buttocks, and lower belly and does not include the skin folds.

The rash varies from pale pink to bright shiny red according to the severity. A sudden bright shiny bottom is sometimes the result of food or medication. Common offenders include soy drink, cows' milk, or yogurt. Cutting down or removing the food clears the rash up.

Viral diarrhea can also cause shiny red, raw bottoms that are very tender and painful, especially when the bottom is being cleaned.

Red raw bottoms need a good barrier cream thickly applied to help them heal. Toddlers who are prone to diaper rash may need the constant application of a barrier cream until they are out of diapers.

HERE ARE TWO BARRIER CREAMS I FIND THE BEST

- Ask your pharmacist to mix 1% Ichthyol and 10% zinc in yellow soft paraffin.
- Desitin ointment made by Pfizer is a good barrier cream for toddlers with sensitive bottoms—it heals and prevents diaper rash.

SERIOUS SORE BOTTOMS WITHOUT A FUNGAL INFECTION

Occasionally toddlers suffer from excruciating, raw, weeping skin in the diaper area. This is usually because of a chronic or acute illness. The following preparation is useful to protect and help heal the area—compound zinc oxide paste: 90 g; aluminium acetate sol: 10 mls in white soft paraffin. Ask your pharmacist to make it up.

Diaper rash with a yeast infection

If the rash does not clear up with the use of the barrier creams mentioned previously, it is usually because it has become infected with yeast. Once the skin's protective barrier is damaged it is at risk of being infected. Most diaper rashes will acquire a yeast infection (usually *Candida albicans*) within a couple of days if the treatment to remedy the red bottom is not successful. This is usually unavoidable.

Once the rash is infected with candida it appears as clusters of red bumps usually surrounded by a sharp border involving the skin folds.

A diaper rash with a yeast infection needs a combination of a mild hydrocortisone cream and antifungal cream to clear it up, so it's best to see your pediatrician or nurse practitioner before wasting money on a host of other preparations. Using either an antifungal or a hydrocortisone cream on its own will not clear up a diaper rash with a fungal infection in a toddler. Use of a hydrocortisone cream on its own for any length of time will make the rash worse.

TIPS WHEN USING COMBINED HYDROCORTISONE–ANTIFUNGAL CREAMS

- When using these creams, it is important to stop all other powders, moisturizers, cleansing lotions, and barrier creams as their presence on the skin surface will prevent the prescribed cream from working.

- Avoid constant washing of your toddler's bottom, as the friction from the rubbing and the moisture interfere with the skin's healing. When his diaper is wet, simply pat the skin dry and apply

367

the prescribed cream. When he has done a poo, clean gently with a little warm water only and pat dry before applying the cream. Naturally, continue with normal bathing.

- Use only the prescribed cream for seven to ten days or until the rash is gone. Combined hydrocortisone–antifungal creams should be used sparingly, not spread thickly in the manner of barrier creams.

Some tips if your toddler is prone to diaper rash

- Advice to leave toddlers out of diapers for long periods before they are reliably potty trained is impractical and unnecessary.
- Some evidence exists to suggest that disposable diapers can help when treating persistent diaper rash. Good quality disposable diapers use modern materials that keep the skin dry and are also less likely to result in overheating because they are thinner than cloth diapers.
- Frequent diaper changing helps avoid prolonged skin contact with urine and poo and minimizes wetness, friction, and over-heating. If your toddler is prone to diaper rash, cloth diapers need to be changed as soon as they become wet.
- Constant washing of the skin in the diaper area to keep the skin scrupulously clean increases wetness, is irritating to the toddler's skin, and wipes away the natural protective secretions.

When changing a wet diaper, pat the skin dry with a tissue. If you are not treating a diaper rash with an antifungal hydro-cortisone cream the use of a moisturizer such as a hypoallergenic moisturizing lotion (for example, Moisturel) is recommended to both clean and moisturise the skin surface.

- When your toddler does a poo, clean using damp tissues or a hypoallergenic moisturizing lotion (for example, Moisturel). Dry the skin after cleaning.

- Pre-moistened wipes are convenient but avoid using them regularly if your toddler is prone to diaper rash. Always dry the skin after using baby wipes as they leave the skin very wet, causing extra friction.

Pigeon lice bites

Pigeon lice bites are often confused with chicken pox, as they appear as small, raised pink spots that form a blister and a crust. If your toddler gets a few lesions like this when he is otherwise well and has not been in contact with chicken pox, pigeons may the culprit—if you live where there are a lot of pigeons flapping around, of course.

Rash around the mouth

This is very common and caused by saliva, milk, and food constantly on the toddler's face. Using a pacifier contributes as the fluid gets trapped under the plastic shield that surrounds the teat. Certain food may make the rash worse (orange juice, tomatoes, eggs, or yogurt).

This is a frustrating rash, as it's often difficult to clear completely until the toddler stops drooling.

Try to keep the area as dry as possible. Apply a soothing barrier cream at night.

Experiment a little with food—don't get too uptight about it though or you may find your toddler's diet is very restricted and the rash is still there anyway.

Applying mild cortisone *ointment* helps.

Red cheeks

Again, very common in babies and toddlers until drooling stops and their cheeks stop coming in contact with clothes and food. Toddler cheeks are very soft and chubby and stick out, so they catch the wind and sun, easily becoming dry and chapped, particularly in the cold, dry winter months.

Red cheeks (or sometimes only one red cheek) are not related to ear infections, teething, or diet, although once the cheeks are red, acidic food such as oranges may irritate them further.

Red cheeks are often hard to clear up until the drooling stops, but they don't seem to bother toddlers as much as they bother their parents. Try to keep the skin around the area dry; apply a hypallergenic moisturizing lotion (Moisturel) whenever you can (which is difficult as toddlers usually resist having anything put on their faces). Apply a soothing barrier cream before bedtime. A mild cortisone *ointment* helps if the redness is very severe. Ointment always works better than cream on moist areas.

White patches (Pityriasis alba)

This refers to lightened patches of skin on the toddler's body and face. The cause remains unknown, but it is believed that it is a form of eczema. The white patches are thought to be the result of a faulty process of pigment transfer and tanning within the outer layer of the skin; consequently the patches first appear after a period of sun exposure. The condition responds well to a hydrocortisone cream, but it can take months for the skin color to return.

chapter **fourteen**

An
Ailment
or Two

Asthma

Asthma is a condition which affects breathing because the airways of the lungs are oversensitive. This oversensitivity causes the lungs to respond to minor irritants (for example, smoke, allergens or viruses) by producing mucus and constricting the bronchial tubes (airways). This causes obstruction of the flow of air to the lungs and results in the following symptoms:

- A dry irritating cough, particularly at night—which occasionally may be the *only* sign of asthma.
- Wheezing with perhaps a whistling noise when the child breathes out.
- Difficulty in breathing.
- Often a "fullness" (overinflation) of the chest.

What makes some lungs so oversensitive?

No one knows for sure exactly why certain people get asthma. Some seem to be born with more sensitive airways than others. There is a strong tendency for asthma to run in families, but it can occur in people without any family history. Having one child with asthma in a family does not necessarily mean the other children will develop it too.

Childhood asthma is common. Thirty percent of children will have asthma to some degree in childhood.

Patterns of asthma

Childhood asthma can be classified according to the pattern the condition takes:

- Infrequent episodic asthma (seventy-five percent of children)
- Frequent episodic asthma (twenty percent of children)
- Persistent asthma (five percent of children)

Within each group the signs and symptoms are diagnosed as mild, moderate, or severe during an acute episode.

Children with infrequent episodic asthma tend to lose the symptoms with increasing age. Sixty percent of children under three who fall into this group lose their symptoms by six years of age.

What can cause an attack?

Certain triggers can act on sensitive airways and cause an attack. Some common triggers include:

- Viral upper respiratory tract infections (colds and influenza)
- Cigarette smoke
- Exercise
- Cold weather or cold air
- Dust and air pollution
- Pollen
- Some foods and food additives
- Some types of animals
- Strong smells and fumes

The triggers vary from person to person. Some people know exactly what their trigger factors are; others are unable to identify them.

Management of asthma

If your toddler is diagnosed with asthma, your doctor will work out an asthma management plan with you to keep your toddler's asthma under control and to indicate what steps should be taken if an attack occurs. Details of your toddler's treatment should be given to your toddler's childcare center or preschool and taken to all doctor's appointments.

Asthma is treated with medication, so most children can lead a normal life.

There are two main types of medication

- **Preventers** work by reducing the sensitivity of the airways, which helps reduce the number and severity of attacks. Preventers do not have an immediate effect and thus are of no benefit if taken during an attack. They should be taken every day over a long period of time.

- **Relievers** act quickly to make your toddler feel better during an attack by opening up the airways and quickly reducing the symptoms. Their effect only lasts a few hours.

Most asthma medications are given via inhalers or puffers because they are more effective if inhaled. There are a number of devices on the market suitable for use according to the age of your toddler; for example, nebulizers, spacers, dry powder devices, and pressurized aerosols. At the time of writing, spacers are the preferred devices for toddlers and children. Other treatment measures may be used for more severely affected children.

Additional medications such as nasal sprays are occasionally used for allergic rhinitis.

Some children may be treated by excluding foods thought to trigger attacks. However, special diets should always be supervised by a nutritionist to ensure the diet is sound.

Diagnosis of asthma in children under two

The accurate diagnosis of asthma in this age group is difficult. Episodes of prolonged coughing are common in toddlers. The endless cough is usually associated with upper respiratory tract infections and is unlikely to be associated with asthma when there is no wheezing or history of allergic conditions such as atopic dermatitis, hay fever, and reactions to food. Some babies under twelve months have troublesome episodes of wheezing but are otherwise thriving and happy. Most of them lose the wheezing after the first year. Consult your pediatrician if you are worried.

The endless cough

Coughing accompanies many toddler illnesses; for example, asthma, head colds, croup, and whooping cough. Coughing can also be part of the general cold symptoms that precede infectious diseases such as measles and chicken pox. It can also be due to extra mucus trickling down the toddler's throat as a result of allergies (remember, though, that milk does not make mucus). Coughing can also be caused by dry, cold air.

Many of us parents have memories of sleepless nights caused by our toddler's endless coughing, especially in the early hours of the morning when the temperature drops.

Worrying coughs should always be investigated, but even in this grand technological age there does not always seem to be an answer for the endless cough in the otherwise healthy toddler. Cough suppressants should not be used for toddlers, and other oral medication for coughing seems to have only minimal success. Some parents report success with the use of humidifiers, but controlled studies suggest they are of little benefit. Naturally, however, if you find a humidifier helps, use one.

It is sometimes worth a trial of asthma drugs via a spacer or inhaler for endless toddler coughing. Success of such a strategy indicates that asthma is the cause of the coughing.

Croup

Croup is a form of laryngitis that follows a viral infection in the upper respiratory tract and affects the voice box and trachea. It is more common in toddlers than in older children and adults because toddlers have small, soft windpipes that collapse easily when they become inflamed. The toddler's cough sounds like a baby seal barking and is accompanied by a crowing noise as he breathes in. His voice may be hoarse and he may have trouble breathing.

Croup is more severe at night when the air is cooler, and the worst period usually lasts about two nights. Some toddlers have what is known as spasmodic croup—frequent attacks of short duration. These tend to occur at night, lasting for a few hours and occasionally recurring on the next night.

Treatment

The treatment of using steam to alleviate the symptoms is no longer recommended as the risk of burns and scalds far outweighs any benefits, which have been shown to be negligible.

Calm your toddler as much as you can by sitting him on your lap while the bout lasts.

Go to the hospital immediately if:

- Your toddler has difficulty breathing.
- He becomes pale, sweaty, or blue.
- He is sucking his chest right in.

Croup is usually mild, but it can get worse quickly. If you are worried, seek medical help.

Medication

As croup is caused by a virus, antibiotics are not appropriate. The only medications suitable for croup are steroids and adrenaline, which are administered in the hospital for moderate or severe episodes.

Ear infections

Ear problems in toddlers are very common and usually occur in the middle ear because the eustachian tube, which connects the middle ear to the throat, is short and straight at this age. This allows easy entry of mucus, milk, and germs into the chamber of the middle ear. Toddlers also catch a lot of colds until they build up some resistance to bugs. The extra mucus colds create blocks the eustachian tube, which stops the middle ear from draining properly.

The two most common ear problems are

1. An acute infection from infected mucus. This is painful, so the toddler's behavior may change dramatically. He may have screaming attacks, whine more than usual, or develop a sudden sleep problem. It's always worth having your toddler's ears checked when these things happen. Antibiotics and/or pain relievers may be prescribed.

2. A collection of uninfected mucus in the middle ear, called glue ear. Glue ear is generally not painful but causes transient earaches, especially at night, so a change in night sleep patterns may occur even when a toddler is happy during the day.

   Toddlers should not be left for long periods with untreated glue ear. The hearing loss that can occur may affect their speech and language development. It is important for toddlers to have hearing tests following episodes of glue ear.

   Treatment for glue ear ranges from none to medication to insertion of tubes, depending on the frequency of infections, the discomfort, and the amount of hearing loss.

Fevers

Toddlers are much more prone to running fevers than older children and adults. Fever is the body's natural defense against infection and so may accompany an illness such as a cold, a urinary tract infection, gastroenteritis, and an infectious disease like chicken pox.

A toddler's fever can also be caused by other things not related to an infection, such as overdressing, being kept too long in a hot car, a hot day, sunburn, following immunization, or crying for a long time.

Sometimes toddlers run fevers for two or three days and nobody knows why. Growing teeth do not cause fevers. Constant mild fevers, which come and go over a period of time, should always be investigated.

A fever is not the only sign of an illness. Some serious illnesses only cause a mild fever.

How do you know your toddler has a fever?

If your toddler's temperature is above 99°F (37.2°C) he has a mild (low-grade) fever. His temperature may be taken by placing a regular glass thermometer under his arm (less convenient, more accurate) or by using an ear thermometer (more convenient, less accurate).

Things to do if your toddler is hot

- Give an appropriate dose of acetaminophen or ibuprofen if your toddler's fever is over 101°F (38.4°C) and/or if he is miserable.

- While waiting for the medication to work, undress your toddler down to his vest and diaper.

- I don't recommend cool sponges or baths as they often prove to be counterproductive (too cool, too hot, too long) but if your toddler is very distressed and you think sponging his face and arms will help soothe him, go ahead. Try to give extra fluids or a popsicle to suck.

- See your doctor as soon as possible for a fever of 104°F (40°C) that does not come down quickly with medication and/or if your toddler is limp and unresponsive. (see page 350, when to call your doctor)

Fever fits (convulsions)

A fever fit is a convulsion caused by a high temperature. The most common age for this to happen is between twelve and twenty-four months, but overall it happens to about four percent of all toddlers and children between six months and five years.

Why does it happen?

Toddlers and young children have immature brains that are particularly sensitive to outside stress. Sometimes in response to a high body temperature, the brain gives off an abnormal electrical discharge that results in a fit. Having a fit means the toddler loses consciousness and twitches all over. It can happen out of the blue when it is not even obvious that the toddler has a fever. Needless to say, it is extremely scary for parents.

What do you do?

- Don't panic! Stay with your toddler. Babies and toddlers do not die or suffer brain damage from fever fits.
- Gently place him on his side and wait for the fit to stop.
- Don't put anything into his mouth or try to force his gums open.
- When your toddler comes around, take him to your pediatrician or go to your nearest hospital emergency room, since it is important to confirm it is only a fever fit.
- There is a chance this may happen again before your toddler grows out of it, so always try and control any fever.
- Fever fits are not a form of epilepsy and rarely occur beyond five years.

Nosebleeds

Nosebleeds are quite common in otherwise healthy toddlers. Dry air, viral infections, rubbing the nose, and finger up the nose are the main causes. Some toddlers have fragile small blood vessels in the lining of their noses which rupture and bleed easily.

Stopping a nosebleed

- Encourage your toddler to sit or stand to slow the bleeding.
- If he will allow you to, gently pinch his nose shut near its tip.
- Remind him to open his mouth and spit out any blood.

Avoid

- Tipping his head back or lying him down.
- Stuffing cotton swabs or tissues up his nose—when you remove the packing, the bleeding will start all over again.

Helping prevent nosebleeds

- If your toddler will allow you to, put a smear of petroleum jelly inside his nose to keep the lining moist.
- A humidifier at night may help when the air is very dry.

When to get help

- If the nosebleed is in association with a fall.
- If the nosebleeds are suddenly frequent and especially if they are associated with bleeding gums or bruising.
- If the nosebleeds are in association with a new medication.

Odd lumps

Consult with your pediatrician about any lump you are unsure of, especially if it is inflamed, tender, or hot to touch or is becoming larger.

Lump under nipple

It is quite common to be able to feel a small lump under your toddler's nipple. This is normal breast tissue.

Lumps around hairline on neck

Small, movable lumps like peas, behind the ears or on the back of the neck, are common for toddlers. They are enlarged lymph nodes and usually not significant in an otherwise healthy, happy toddler.

Small, movable lumps under the skin

These are usually sebaceous cysts and, again, not significant in an otherwise healthy, happy toddler.

Lump in the groin

Any lump in the groin should be investigated, especially if it is accompanied by pain and distress.

Poo problems (noninfectious)

1. Constipation

Constipation refers to the difficulty a toddler has passing a hard poo—not how often he goes. If he only goes every three days and it's soft, that's fine. If he goes three times a day and it's a little hard dry ball and he's distressed, it's constipation.

Toddlers often get constipated, and it can be very distressing not only for the toddler but also for everyone else in the family. Constipation varies from being temporary and mild to being chronic and severe. Most toddlers' constipation is not a sign of underlying medical problems. Nor is it likely to be because they have inherited Grandma's lazy bowel.

Why does it happen?

- Constipation commonly occurs in the toddler years because of the toddler's fussy food habits, the pressures of potty training with its associated attention-seeking opportunities, and the developmental stage the toddler is at (negativism, testing limits, egocentrism, and so on).

- Reluctance to part with their poo and forgetting to go because of being distracted by other things also contribute to constipation.

- Sometimes pooing is painful, which encourages toddlers to hold onto it. Damage from a previous hard poo (anal fissure) or excoriation in the anal area caused by eczema or the red raw type of diaper rash are possible causes of painful pooing.

- Occasionally constipation is caused by emotional events. For example, the arrival of a new baby, family turmoil, hospitalization, starting childcare or preschool, and so on.

Temporary, mild constipation

Most temporary constipation in toddlers can be helped by simple dietary measures.

A FEW GENERAL GUIDELINES

- Fluids help toddlers more than bulky food when they are

constipated, so give extra water or juice (not milk) or add more fluid to meals when possible. Prune juice is excellent—dilute with a little water.

- Milk and cheese do not cause constipation in themselves, but when toddlers are on very restricted diets—for example, five bottles of milk a day and very little other food—they are likely to become constipated because their diets are lacking in fibre. Stopping the bottles and allowing the toddler to get hungry enough to start eating a variety of food will help the constipation.

- A breakfast of oatmeal, with warm milk, undiluted prune juice, and brown sugar helps (if your toddler will eat it, of course).

- Lentils are very good for the pooing process. Lentil dishes can be tasty and easy for toddlers to consume. Lots of good lentil recipes are available. Baked beans are also poo-friendly food.

- Papaya is excellent. Serve mashed with freshly squeezed orange juice and a little sugar. If your toddler won't eat papaya, try a fresh orange.

- Try a yogurt, milk, and fruit smoothy.

NONDIETARY CONSIDERATIONS

Potty-training pressure contributes to constipation in toddlers. If your toddler's constipation is in association with attempts to get him to use the potty, it is advisable to take the pressure off immediately. The drama of a year of chronic constipation is not worth landing a poo in the potty. Some toddlers insist on using a diaper to poo in until they are between four and five. It is exasperating and messy for their parents, but trying to make them use the potty before they are willing to do so usually ends up with an ongoing poo problem that not only causes the toddler distress but takes over family life.

For more on potty training, see page 192.

Chronic and severe constipation

Constipation becomes chronic when simple measures do not resolve the problem. A large amount of hard poo accumulates in the toddler's rectum. Some toddlers have rectums big enough to allow them to successfully hold four or five days' worth of poo. Once the rectum is distended for any length of time, the urge to do a poo is lost, which compounds the problem.

HERE'S A COMMON SCENARIO (TWO YEARS AND OVER)

- The toddler has episodes of watery poo that may be mistaken for diarrhea.

- The big poo only comes once every four or five days. In between times, the toddler stands with crossed legs or runs off and hides whenever he feels the need to do a poo.

- Any attempt to encourage him to poo is met with screams of anger and fear.

- He may be anxious and pale with diminished appetite until the big poo comes, with great pain and drama, which may include bleeding from the anus. Sometimes the big poo comes during sleep. After the event, the toddler is a changed person . . . until the cycle starts all over again.

TREATMENT

It is advisable to seek medical help for chronic, severe constipation, as there are usually no easy answers and it is a good idea to check that there are no underlying medical problems (rare).

TREATMENT INVOLVES

- Emptying the rectum. This requires the use of suppositories and enemas.

- Replacing the enemas and suppositories with regular doses of medication to keep the poo soft as soon as the rectum is emptied.

386

- Treating any fissures or excoriation of the anus.
- Routine testing of urine.
- Removing any stress-related factors where possible.
- Putting in place dietary measures and potty-training regimes appropriate for the age of the toddler.
- Looking at any emotional or psychological reasons for the dilemma. Sometimes chronic constipation needs input from child psychologists or psychiatrists.

Hard poo therapy usually takes six months or longer to be effective. Great patience is needed from both the parents and the health professional. Relapses along the way are common, but the final outcome is successful for the majority of toddlers.

2. Diarrhea

Diarrhea means that there are a lot of loose, watery bowel actions. Sometimes this happens suddenly and is an indication of an infection. Sometimes individual toddlers (and adults) have loose poo as a normal condition.

Diarrhea in toddlers can be caused by

- An infection (gastroenteritis), which may be viral, bacterial, or parasitical
- A toddler's normal metabolism (toddler diarrhea)
- Food or medication
- Food allergy or intolerance
- An underlying medical problem (rare)

Teething does not cause diarrhea. Did you get diarrhea when you got your wisdom teeth? The most common causes of diarrhea in otherwise healthy toddlers are gastroenteritis and toddler diarrhea. For more on gastroenteritis, see page 393.

TODDLER DIARRHEA

Toddler diarrhea is very common. The poo often looks like vegetable soup and may appear up to ten times a day. He is full of energy and thrives (while his mother and father nearly expire from the diaper changes). At this time of his life, the food moves through his bowel faster than normal.

Here are some suggestions

- Try to cut down on fluids, bulk up his diet (rice and pasta) as much as possible, and make sure you include full-fat dairy products. A diet of fruit juice, fruit and veggies, and no fat or meat exacerbates toddler diarrhea. Elimination diets are neither required nor recommended for this normally occuring condition.

- Toddler diarrhea slows down sometime between three and four and improves when the toddler is potty trained—remembering that it is not a good idea to force the issue, much as you are longing for the end of the veggie soup days.

DIARRHEA CAUSED BY FOOD OR MEDICATION

- If you think something in your toddler's diet is causing diarrhea, obviously stop the food.

- If the diarrhea is caused by medication, let your family doctor know (antibiotics are the main offenders).

DIARRHEA CAUSED BY FOOD ALLERGY OR INTOLERANCE

Tricky . . . If you think that this might be the case, seek advice from a pediatric dietitian so that you do not unnecessarily restrict your toddler's diet.

DIARRHEA CAUSED BY AN UNDERLYING MEDICAL PROBLEM

When diarrhea is caused by a medical problem, the toddler does not thrive and has no energy. These toddlers need a thorough medical investigation to determine the cause and special care from an appropriate health professional.

Undescended testes

Normally there are two testes in the scrotum, which are quite easy to feel. The testes travel from the abdominal sac into the scrotum during late pregnancy. If the opening through which they travel doesn't close off, one of the testes can appear and disappear from the scrotum, especially when the scrotum is exposed to cold. Sitting the toddler in a warm bath will bring the testis into the scrotum. Eventually the opening from the abdominal sac closes and the testicle remains in the scrotum. These testes are called retractile testes, and sometimes don't settle permanently into the scrotum until adolescence.

Occasionally one or both testes never descend and so are never felt in the scrotum. The testis may be situated in the groin or higher up in the abdomen. Occasionally it is absent altogether.

The causes of undescended testes range from prematurity to a hernia in the groin causing a blockage to hormonal reasons. But often the precise cause is unknown. A doctor's opinion should be sought to confirm whether the testicle is retractile (pops up and down) or is permanently undescended.

Surgery is performed between six months and two years of age to bring the testicle into the scrotum and to secure it there.

Urinary tract infection (UTI)

A urinary tract infection is caused by a growth of germs, usually in the bladder but sometimes in the kidneys. It is common in babies, toddlers, and children. Approximately thirty percent of these infections occur because there is an underlying structural problem in the urinary system. It is routine for all babies and toddlers to have tests (special X-rays) and an ultrasound when a UTI is diagnosed so that such conditions, if they are present, can be treated to prevent chronic renal problems later in life.

Symptoms

Symptoms in babies and toddlers under three can be vague and confusing, which is why urine is routinely tested when the cause of a fever is not clear. Irritability, vomiting, failure to thrive, and chronic constipation can also be symptoms of a UTI.

Sometimes the parent will notice odd-smelling urine or urine that looks cloudy or thick. Older toddlers may complain of pain when peeing.

Treatment

A urine specimen is collected and tested and antibiotics commenced if an infection is present. Collecting urine from toddlers can be a challenge. An attempt is made to catch a clean sample in a specimen jar. If this proves too difficult, and particularly if the toddler is very ill, the urine may have to be collected in the hospital by inserting a fine tube or needle into the bladder via the abdomen.

The current infection will clear in five to seven days with the antibiotics, but the toddler may need to continue a smaller dose of the medication until the results of the tests are known.

Treatment for underlying problems of the kidneys and bladder ranges from protective antibiotics for a period of time to surgery, depending on what the problem is.

Vomiting

Vomiting accompanies many illnesses and it is a good idea to have any vomiting investigated if you are unsure of the cause.

The best way to manage vomiting when it is caused by an illness (for example, gastroenteritis) is to give small amounts of clear fluids frequently for twenty-four hours. Most vomiting will cease within this time.

Toddlers vomit much more easily than adults, and vomiting is not always necessarily a sign of illness. Some toddlers vomit at the drop of a hat. For example, when they are upset about something, after a good cough, when they are made to eat something they don't like, and even sometimes as an attention-seeking device. Occasional vomiting of this nature should be cleaned up with as little fuss and attention as possible.

Vomiting as an attention-seeking device

Healthy toddlers who use vomiting as an attention-seeking device or as a way of manipulating their parents usually persist with it because they are rewarded for their efforts.

A framework to work within

- Have a checkup to make sure that there are no medical problems.

- Stop all the bottles of milk (vomiting-on-demand toddlers usually drink many bottles of milk a day, which makes for bountiful vomiting).

- Give minimal attention to the vomiting. Avoid constant referrals to it within the toddler's hearing range. When a vomit occurs, clean it up as quickly as possible without any anger, exclamations, sympathy, or any other sort of major attention.

- If you find that you are unable to do what is needed to change the situation, consider consulting a psychologist for help.

chapter fifteen

Infectious Diseases

Gastroenteritis (acute diarrhea and vomiting)

Sudden diarrhea and/or vomiting is usually caused by an infection in the gut. It is usually a virus but may also be caused by bacteria or a parasite. As well as the diarrhea and vomiting, the toddler may also have a fever, tummy pain, and cold symptoms (runny nose and cough).

It's often confusing sorting out viral diarrhea from loose poo caused by food, medication, or an upper respiratory, urinary tract, or ear infection. If you are ever in any doubt about the cause of your toddler's diarrhea seek help from your nurse practitioner, pediatrician, or nearest children's hospital.

Treatment

- Medication is not a part of treatment for most infectious diarrhea. Antibiotics are only used occasionally for a specific, diagnosed bacterial infection.
- Drugs to stop vomiting cause a range of side effects, which include spacing out, strange behavior and rolling back of the eyes. Vomiting in gastroenteritis is usually of short duration, but if it continues, it needs to be assessed, not suppressed.
- Medications such as adults take to stop the diarrhea are dangerous for toddlers and should not be used.
- Most toddlers with diarrhea are not in danger and can be treated at home with simple dietary measures.

  Give small amounts of clear fluids only (2 ozs.–3ozs.) every fifteen to thirty minutes for twenty-four hours (no need to wake during the night unless you are instructed to). If you are still breastfeeding, continue breastfeeding.

SUITABLE FLUIDS

• A commercial preparation such as Pedialyte:	Make as directed.
• White grape juice	1 cup to 4 cups tap water
• Rice water:	Boil ¾ cup of white rice in 7 cups litres of water until the water is milky—not too thick! Strain the rice and add four flat teaspoons of sugar to every 32ozs. (4 cups) of rice water.

A few important points
- A commercial preparation such as Pedialyte is *not* a medication. It is a fluid replacement to prevent dehydration.
- Toddlers with simple diarrhea do not need commercial preparations. Any of the other suggested fluids are fine.

394

- Follow the guidelines for the addition of sugar closely. A small amount of glucose or sucrose helps the toddler absorb fluid more efficiently and makes the fluid more palatable, but too much causes more diarrhea. Do not give undiluted flat lemonade—the sugar content is too high.

- After twenty-four hours of clear fluids, start your toddler back on a normal diet as soon as possible, but continue to give food in frequent, small amounts for a few days. Make sure some fat is introduced during the second twenty-four-hour period (for example, breastmilk, milk, yogurt) as constant clear fluids, fruit and veggies alone aggravate acute diarrhea.

- Sometimes toddlers develop a temporary lactose intolerance following gastroenteritis, which means their watery diarrhea comes back once full-fat milk is reintroduced. When this occurs, lactose-free milk is required for two to three weeks until the bowel recovers.

- Most toddlers respond well to these simple measures, but unfortunately there are times when the correct advice is not given or parents and health professionals underestimate the severity of the illness.

Always seek help or a second opinion if

- You are worried.

- Your toddler keeps vomiting and cannot keep any fluids down or is vomiting and pooing simultaneously at an alarming rate.

- You see blood in your toddler's poo.

- Your toddler suffers from other illnesses such as diabetes, heart disease, urinary tract infections, or is on any medication.

- Your baby is lethargic, drowsy, has a dry mouth, and is passing less urine than normal.

- You are given a diagnosis of teething (growing teeth do not cause diarrhea).

Mild diarrhea with no burnt bottom, vomiting, weight loss, or fever

When this happens to a well, happy toddler, it is difficult to decide whether or not to start the diarrhea regime, as the toddler is likely to get very irritable and very hungry. It's usually best to wait one or two days and see what develops.

Endless poo

Continuing loose poo in an otherwise well toddler can go on for some time after an episode of viral diarrhea. It's inconvenient and messy but harmless and eventually stops.

Remember, continual bottles of juice and formula exacerbate loose poo. If your toddler is still having bottles, keep to two or less a day and juice only once a day. Try water at other times when he is thirsty. Better still, ditch the bottles.

Head colds

Head colds are caused by viruses, which damage the mucous membranes of the nose and throat. This is what causes the runny nose, the sore throat and eyes, the cough, and sometimes a headache and fever. Toddlers are likely to catch around eight colds a year.

Complications from head colds, such as ear or chest infections, are more common in toddlers. As well, the extra mucus generated by a cold and the cough often seem to hang around forever in toddlers, even after the cold gets better.

Medications

Head colds without a fever are not helped a great deal by any of the various medications commonly suggested.

Viruses are the cause of most head colds, so antibiotics (which fight bacteria) are unlikely to do a lot. Antibiotics can cause diarrhea and yeast infections, so their use often complicates head colds in toddlers rather than having any beneficial effect.

Over-the-counter drugs which dry up the mucus may help.

Other suggestions

Unfortunately there is no magic potion to make colds get better quicker. Treatment always involves relieving the symptoms.

- Try a vaporizer. Despite the fact that research shows vaporizers make very little difference, lots of the parents I talk to find they help.

- A little Vicks Vapor Rub rubbed onto your toddler's chest after a warm bath will make you both feel better (I can still remember my mother doing that).

- If your toddler has a head cold with a fever above 100.5°F and/or is feeling miserable, use one of the acetaminophen or ibuprofen preparations to help him feel better and bring the fever down. Dress him lightly, give extra fluids, and use the

above medication every four hours until the fever subsides or
he is feeling better.

- The mucus trickling down the back of your toddler's throat is
usually the cause of the coughing that accompanies a head cold.
If there is a lot of coughing, check in with your doctor to make
sure there is no chest infection.

- It's wise to consult your doctor if you are worried or if your toddler has breathing difficulties, wheezes, or suddenly refuses to
eat or drink.

Impetigo

Impetigo is a bacterial infection of the skin. There are two forms.
The most common in the toddler years occurs when a lesion on the
skin becomes infected, usually because the toddler scratches it. The
lesion has a crusty appearance, underneath which is a moist red
area. The lesion slowly enlarges and spreads. Often pus is present
and other lesions may start to appear.

Impetigo is more likely to appear on exposed parts of the
body (arms, legs, and face) and is often associated with itchy
eczema or with a graze or an insect bite that has been picked or
scratched.

Impetigo can also appear as large blisters which erupt, leaving moist areas with a brown crust that continues to expand
rapidly.

Impetigo is highly infectious but responds rapidly to oral and
local antibiotics. See your pediatrician immediately.

Pneumonia

Pneumonia is a viral or bacterial infection that causes swelling and blockage of sections of the lung. It is also often referred to as a chest infection.

Pneumonia occurs at all ages but is more common in babies and toddlers.

Symptoms

Pneumonia may follow a mild infection of the nose and throat. It can be tricky to diagnose initially as the symptoms vary greatly and can be very subtle. For example, neck stiffness, lack of energy and loss of appetite, fever and tummy pains. Other symptoms include rapid breathing, grunting while breathing, and a bluish tinge around the mouth. A chest X-ray is usually needed to confirm the diagnosis.

Treatment

Antibiotics are used when bacteria cause the infection. Serious pneumonia needs hospitalization for intravenous therapy to administer fluids and antibiotics (if appropriate). Acetaminophen is used for pain and fever. Recovery usually takes seven to ten days.

COMMON INFECTIOUS DISEASES

DISEASE	INCUBATION (TIME BETWEEN EXPOSURE AND ILLNESS)	SIGNS AND SYMPTOMS	
		GENERAL	RASH
Chicken pox **Cause:** Varicella-zoster virus	2 to 3 weeks	• Mild fever • Cough, runny nose • Miserable toddler	• Small raised pink spots which turn into blisters, then form crusts. • Number of spots varies from a few to the whole body being covered, including inside the mouth and ears and on the scalp and genitals.
Colds	See page 396		
Conjunctivitis **Cause:** Various—viruses, bacteria, allergies	24 to 72 hours	• Red, watery eyes • Crusty eyes • Yellow discharge • Itching and pain sometimes	
Diarrhea (gastroenteritis)	See page 387		
Epiglottitis (inflammation of the upper part of the voice box)	Uncertain	• Sudden onset • Fever, croupy cough, sore throat, difficulty breathing • Red, swollen epiglottis	
German Measles (Rubella) **Cause:** Rubella virus	2 to 3 weeks	• Swollen lymph glands around the hairline, behind ears (most reliable sign confirming diagnosis) • Sore throat, runny nose, slight fever • Miserable toddler	• Small, pink separate dots that rapidly spread over body, especially the trunk
Hand, Foot, and Mouth Disease **Cause:** Coxsackievirus	3 to 5 days	• Fever, loss of appetite • A miserable toddler who complains of a sore mouth	• Lesions in mouth which usually become blisters • Lesions on fingers, then maybe on soles of feet
Impetigo	See page 398		
Kawasaki syndrome **Cause:** Unknown	Unknown	• Fever for 5 or more days • Conjunctivitis in both eyes with no discharge and a white halo effect around the iris (colored part of the eye) • Dry, cracked red lips and bright red tongue • Swollen neck gland • May have a cough, irritability, and diarrhea	• Rash, often like a red stain that comes and goes • Red, swollen hands and feet with a woody feel • May be peeling of the skin in the groin and diaper area

TREATMENT	OTHER INFORMATION
Treatment aims to relieve the itch and fever. • Give acetaminophen every four hours and warm to hot baths for the first few days. • Add some anti-itch solution to the bathwater. • Apply calamine lotion directly to the spots. • Severe cases may need anti-histamine to help the toddler sleep the first few nights (e.g., Benadryl). • Call doctor if worried.	• Cold symptoms abate once spots appear. • Infected toddler should be kept at home until 5 days after the spots appear. • Immunization is now available for Chicken pox (see page 344 for details).
• Bacterial and viral conjunctivitis is highly infectious until treated. See your family doctor for appropriate ointment or drops. • Conjunctivitis caused by allergy, chemicals, or a blocked tear duct is not infectious. If in doubt, a smear of the discharge can be examined microscopically to determine the cause.	• Keep toddler at home until discharge has stopped. • Often occurs in conjunction with a head cold—toddler rubs mucus from nose into eyes.
• If epiglottitis is suspected, go immediately to the nearest hospital emergency room or call 911. • Keep toddler upright, leaning forward with mouth open, tongue hanging out. • Emergency treatment involves maintaining airway, breathing tubes, and antibiotics.	• Mostly caused by bacteria. • HIB immunization (part of standard immunization schedule) protects against disease.
• See health professional to confirm diagnosis if in doubt. • Relieve cold symptoms if necessary. • Contact doctor if nonimmune woman in early pregnancy is exposed to the virus.	• Often difficult to diagnose in toddlers and frequently confused with measles, viral rashes, or allergies. • Cold symptoms disappear when rash appears. • Keep toddler home for at least 4 days after the rash appears. • Rubella immunization part of routine immunization schedule. See page 344.
• Often very painful for a few days, especially in the mouth. Give soft food or just fluids if toddler is very miserable. • Acetaminophen for pain relief. • Allow blisters to dry naturally.	• Often goes through preschool, childcare, centers and playgroups like wildfire. • No complications from disease. • Adults can catch disease, but it is very mild and only appears on the fingers.
• Seek medical help immediately if signs of Kawasaki syndrome appear. • Diagnosis can be difficult and may require diagnostic tests (blood tests, etc) to differentiate KS from other infections, measles, and toxic shock. • Treatment is an infusion of Immune Globulin Intravenous (IGIV) given over 8 to 12 hours. • A low dose of aspirin is given daily for 4 to 6 weeks. • Evaluation of heart function is necessary during convalescence.	• Cause of KS is unknown. • It affects preschool children—mostly in the first year of life. • Untreated KS leads to complications—the major potential damage is to the heart.

401

COMMON INFECTIOUS DISEASES

Disease	Incubation (Time between exposure and illness)	Signs and Symptoms	
		General	Rash
Measles Cause: Measles virus	1 to 2 weeks	• Fever, runny nose, cough • Red, watery eyes	• Two days after cold symptoms, rash appears • Spots first appear on back, neck, and behind ears • Within hours, body is covered and often looks like one red, blotchy mass
Meningitis (inflammation of the lining of the brain and spinal cord) Cause: Bacteria (e.g., HIB) Viruses	2 to 10 days	• High fever • Headache • Loss of appetite • Drowsiness • Irritability • Light may hurt eyes • May have a stiff neck	• A purple rash that looks like bruises or dots is a sign of a meningococcal infection and needs medical attention urgently • Most forms of meningitis have no rash
Meningococcal infections (Meningococcus is a bacterium which can infect the blood or the lining of the brain)		• High fever • Diarrhea and vomiting (seek help immediately) • Symptoms as previous section	• Tiny red or brown pinprick marks that change into purple blotches or blood blisters. Seek help immediately.
Mumps Cause: Mumps virus	12 to 25 days	• Pain and soreness in jaw area • Ear pain • Swelling and tenderness below and in front of one or both ears • Fever, loss of appetite, miserable toddler • Sometimes there are no symptoms	
Nonspecific viral illness	3 to 7 days	Often vague, may include: • Fever • Irritability • Loss of appetite • Diarrhea	One of a variety of vague rashes may be present: • Separate pink dots • Blotchy rash • Bluish pink dots
Pneumonia	See page 399		
Ringworm	See page 404		
Roseola (6th disease) Cause: Human herpes virus 6	Uncertain ?10 days	• Sudden onset of high fever which lasts 3 to 5 days • In susceptible toddlers high fever may cause a convulsion (see page 380)	• Pale blotchy rash appears just after the height of the fever • Rash is on chest, arms, and legs—rarely on face • Rash fades quickly within 3 to 48 hours

Treatment	Other Information
• Give acetaminophen to bring fever down. • Encourage extra fluids.	• Keep toddlers away from others for 4 days after the rash appears. • Measles has potentially serious complications and measles vaccination is part of the routine immunization schedule (see page 344).
• Seek medical attention immediately if you think that your toddler has meningitis. • Meningitis may be bacterial or viral. Bacterial meningitis is treated with antibiotics and most toddlers recover. Bacterial meningitis is a more severe meningitis and has the potential to cause more serious side effects than viral meningitis. • Viral meningitis gets better on its own. Drugs may be used to treat the symptoms. • Immunization against HIB, measles, mumps, whooping cough, and polio are a vital part of the prevention of meningitis. (See page 344 for immunization info.)	• Bacterial meningitis caused by HIB has been reduced by ninety percent since the vaccine was introduced. • Side effects from bacterial meningitis include death, brain damage, and deafness. • It is unusual for serious long-term effects to occur from viral meningitis.
• Infection may be **meningococcal meningitis** (brain) or **meningococcal septacaemia** (blood). • The bacteria respond rapidly to intravenous antibiotic treatment. • Treatment needs to be started as soon as possible. Delays mean a significant increase in the chance of death or disability.	• For excellent information about meningococcal infections, go to: www.meningitis.org/index.html
• Treat symptoms with acetaminophen. • Encourage fluids, soft food.	• Keep toddler away from others for 9 days after the first swelling. • Immunization to prevent mumps is part of routine vaccination (see page 344).
• Tender loving care. • Seek medical help if symptoms persist for more than a few days, if they change, or if they get worse.	• "It's a virus" is a very common diagnosis during the toddler years.
• Treat high fever with acetaminophen.	• Caused by cytomegalovirus (CMV)—one of the herpes viruses. • **Here's some history.** The name Sixth Disease goes back to the turn of the 20th century when there were six childhood rashes recognized and documented. Roseola was the sixth and Slapped Cheek Disease was the fifth.

COMMON INFECTIOUS DISEASES

Disease	Incubation (time between exposure and illness)	Signs and symptoms	
		General	Rash
Scarlet fever **Cause:** Streptococcus bacteria	1 to 3 days	• Sore throat • High fever • Frequent vomiting • May have a bright red tongue	• Bright red rash appears within 12 to 36 hours • Rash appears first on neck and chest • Rapidly spreads over body, including legs
Slapped cheek syndrome (5th disease) **Cause:** Parvovirus B19	1 to 2 weeks	• Very red cheek or cheeks (no, it's not "teething") • Fever • Runny nose • Joint pains	• Itchy lacelike rash on limbs and body • Rash may appear and reappear after exercise or hot bath
Worms and nits	See chapter 16.		
Whooping cough **Cause:** Bacteria (Bordetella pertussis)	6 to 20 days		• Short dry cough that becomes more severe • Fever • "Whoop" develops as toddler tries to breathe • Vomiting • Blueness in face

Ringworm (tinea)

Ringworm is not actually a worm but a spreading area of infected skin. A fungus causes the infection. Ringworm can be found in different areas of the body (hair, skin, nails, torso, feet) and looks different depending on where it is located. A variety of fungi can be responsible for causing ringworm, including some that can be transmitted from infected animals (particularly cats, dogs, and goats). The two most common forms of ringworm in toddlers are of the skin or scalp.

Treatment	Other Information
• Contact family doctor. • Scarlet fever is caused by bacteria, so antibiotics are used to treat for 10 days to prevent complications. • Treat fever with acetaminophen.	• Infectious period only for 24 hours once treatment has commenced. • Uncommon among toddlers.
• Treat fever and aches with acetaminophen.	• Toddler is not infectious once rash appears. • Pregnant women in contact with slapped cheek syndrome should seek medical advice and have a blood test.
• Seek medical help immediately. • Antibiotics may be given if the disease is diagnosed early enough. • Attention to dehydration (frequent small amounts of fluid/soft food. Babies may need intravenous therapy). IMMUNIZATION IS THE BEST WAY OF PREVENTING WHOOPING COUGH AND THE POTENTIAL DEATH AND DISABILITY CAUSED BY THE DISEASE IN BABIES UNDER SIX MONTHS.	• Toddler should be kept away from others for 14 days from start of illness or 5 days after the start of antibiotics. • Unimmunized contacts (under 5) should be kept home for 14 days or 5 days after the start of antibiotics.

The skin

Ringworm on the skin tends to be oval-shaped (hence the name) scaly patches. The outer edge is usually reddish and clearly defined. The edges may contain pus or fluid or may be dry and scaly or moist and crusty (take your pick). The center of the patch is clear and may look as if it is healing.

On the scalp

The infection causes hairless patches of varying manifestations depending on the specific infecting fungus. There may be itching, redness, scaling, and pus or large pus-filled swellings.

Ringworm treatment

Correct diagnosis is crucial and diagnosis may require microscopic identification to detect the type of fungus involved. Ringworm of the skin responds to the application of a local antifungal preparation. Ringworm infections of the scalp usually need oral medication, as local preparations cannot get to the base of the hair follicles where the fungus is lurking.

Treatment also includes examination and treatment of household pets if appropriate.

chapter **sixteen**

Infestations

By the time toddlers are into the preschool era, most parents will have experienced two of the most enduring features of childhood—nits and worms.

If you have not yet encountered these minuscule but parent-plaguing parasites, do not be smug—your turn will come.

Nits (headlice or Pediculosis capitis)

Nits are more likely to be a problem once your toddler starts preschool or school but are certainly a possibility before then, particularly if he is in childcare.

Eeekk, what happens?

The hair and scalp gets infected when a female louse lays a small egg at the base of the hair shaft which sticks like glue to the hair. These eggs (nits) are most commonly found in the hair behind the ears, at the back of the neck, around the crown, and under the fringe (in other words just about everywhere).

The nits hatch in seven to ten days. They mature into adult lice, which are wingless insects that start laying eggs after ten days (now you know where the concept of *Alien* came from). The lice move very quickly around the scalp and are very difficult to see among the hair. The nits (eggs) often look like dandruff but unlike dandruff cannot be brushed out and on close examination have a waxy look (trust me, I spent hours peering into my children's hair).

The most common way headlice are spread is by direct contact. This is the one area where toddlers share nicely—head to head.

The first sign of headlice (unless you get the phone call from childcare or school) is likely to be intense scratching of the scalp by your toddler. Do not foolishly hope that it is dandruff, a dry scalp, or a nervous tic. The only reason toddlers scratch their heads a lot is because of an infestation. Be warned.

Treatment

Treatment centers on washing the infected head with insecticides that kill lice, excluding infected children from childcare, preschool, and so on until treatment is effective, and washing bed linen in hot water (I can't begin to tell you what a pain it all is).

The insecticides

I sometimes think that the lice might be winning because over the years various preparations that start out with great promise eventually become ineffective as the lice build up a resistance.

- Two groups of insecticides stand out as being the most effective. These are pyrethrins and lindane.

- It is important to follow the directions (if you are like me, you normally never follow directions, but in this case for any chance of a successful result it's essential). Change the insecticide if the one you're using doesn't do the trick.

- It is also recommended that pregnant women, parents of babies less than twelve months old, and people with sensitive skin consult a doctor before applying pediculicides (which is what the insecticides that kill headlice are called—an excellent word to have up your sleeve for Scrabble).

- It is best to treat twice, the second time within seven to ten days after the first.

    Good luck!

Threadworms (also called pinworms)

You'll be happy to know that compared to nits, worms are a breeze as long as you are aware of a few salient points.

- Threadworms, as the name suggests, are fine, threadlike, centimeter-long wrigglies that live in the gut of humans. All children will experience symptoms of threadworm infestation from time to time throughout childhood.

- Threadworms are a human parasite and not related to the worms that infect dogs and cats, so domestic pets are not a source of infection.

- As soon as the diaper days are over and toddlers have access to their bottoms and are mixing with other toddlers, infection with threadworms becomes a part of life. Threadworm infection is also occasionally seen in babies under twelve months. Many adults probably carry threadworms around inside their guts, but unless symptoms develop, adults are unaware of their presence.

What are the symptoms?

- Toddlers, young children, and girls in particular are very susceptible to the symptoms of threadworms, whereas older children and adults are not.

- Symptoms include an itchy bottom (especially at night), general irritability, uncharacteristic bed-wetting, and behavioral changes.

- Little girls often have a red, sensitive, itchy area around the vulva (the front area) that may wake them, distressed, at night. This is often the first symptom in girls and is caused by the threadworms migrating from the anus to the vagina (from the back to the front). Adults are often unaware of what the problem is and spend much time and money in consultation with health professionals and on antifungal preparations for the itch and the rash, which do nothing. Medication for threadworms cures the redness, distress, and itching in forty-eight hours.

- The worm cycle starts when the toddler scratches his bottom (usually in the night) where the threadworm lays its eggs, then puts his hands in his mouth.

- Threadworms spread as long as the worms live in the gut and the infection continues until the person is treated. Reinfection is common as immunity does not occur. Toddlers and young children may need treating once or twice a year.

- The *actual* worms may not be visible, although they can sometimes be seen in the anus or in the poo. You do not have to wait to view a worm before starting treatment, and in fact I recommend that you avoid drawing a lot of attention to the worms by going on flashlight searches and using unnecessary and invasive tests with Scotch tape.

Treatment

- Cut and clean fingernails—give them a good scrub in the bath.
- Put on clean pajamas.
- Make sure the toddler is put to bed in clean sheets.
- Pinworm infections are not serious, and easily treated with a single dose medication (for example Vermox). Unfortunately in the U.S. this medication is only available on prescription—see your doctor.
- The medication is usually well tolerated, but some toddlers may experience tummy pain, nausea, or drowsiness. If you think there are problems, try changing the brand.
- It is important to repeat the above procedure in two weeks even if there are no symptoms—the incubation period is approximately a month.

Should the whole family be treated?

I am going out on a limb here . . . Technically, yes, but a common experience for families is that it does not make any difference to the reinfection rate for the toddlers and young children, even when megabucks are spent dosing up everyone in the household. Many doctors do not insist on treating all family members.

Over to you . . . and good luck with the worms too.

part **five**

FOR PARENTS

chapter seventeen

Your Toddler's Fine—How About You?

Life with toddlers is one of extremes. As toddlers develop independence and autonomy, difficult times inevitably accompany the joy of fat cheeks, dimpled bottoms, and the pride and excitement that parents feel at their toddlers' amazing developmental feats.

Raising toddlers is widely acknowledged and supported by a considerable amount of research to be a stressful activity. The parent who is most responsible for the day-to-day care of the toddler (usually the mother) is likely to experience varying degrees of tension, fatigue, irritation, and dissatisfaction.

Why is it so stressful?

Caring for a toddler day after day more often than not involves getting up at the crack of dawn every morning to a vigorous bundle in a reeking diaper who is ready to go, now!

It includes bathing and getting a body squirming with frustration into pajamas for bed every night and changing a struggling toddler's diaper numerous times a day. This is especially gruesome when there's a big toddler poo—an event to be anticipated at least once a day.

Then there's the supervising of a couple of little toddler friends for play and managing to stay on good terms with the little visitor's parents when your toddler bites their child in an enthusiastic moment.

Managing temper tantrums at home, in the supermarket, in the doctor's office, and while he is being put into the car seat are all features of daily care (not just for one day but every day).

There are the constant anxieties about nutritional deficiencies, developmental progress, whether his behavior is normal, and the thought that maybe he is autistic or has attention deficit disorder. And the very real possibility that the person you once were has gone forever.

Then there's the daily guilt about the flare-ups of anger and irritation and the shouting. Not to mention the cookies used as bribery, those fleeting moments when you wish you had never had a child, and the fact that he is in daycare and always sick.

And now that we are getting warmed up, let's not forget the daily struggle to clean toddler teeth. Or the getting up night after night for nightmares, night terrors, and drinks of water. And the frequent changing of clothes after water and mud games, reading about Miss Mouse for the fifth time in an hour, and wiping the eternally streaming nose. When there's a spare moment, there's that mindless puzzle he needs help with one more time, the same questions to answer over and over again, and shoes and socks to replace.

And each day is full of unscheduled toddler events, such as the raisin poked up the nose, the finger jammed in the car door, the sudden attack of diarrhea, the mysterious fever that disappears the minute you get to the doctor's office, the flat tire and the lost blanky or teddy. Not to mention waking early from the afternoon nap or refusing to nap at all, and wanting to leave playgroup the minute you arrive.

Sharing the care

These daily activities should not all be one person's responsibility when there are two people who share a deep emotional investment in the health and happiness of their toddler. The participation of fathers during the early childhood years is nonexistent in some families and remains marginal in most, although there is a small but growing trend for men to participate more equally in the household and childcare chores.

It's understandable that some men would sooner stay at work and come home after the toddler is in bed and that some women find the thought of work and childcare increasingly attractive.

Sole parents who have no other adults to share the work and the joys with find it very difficult being father and mother, managing the household, and earning a living. But in some ways it's even harder when there are two people available and one not only has to do everything but take care of the other as well.

Many men feel guilty about this state of affairs and would like to change but find it difficult. This may be because they get so caught up in their commitment to the family's material needs that they lose sight of their own potential for emotional and practical involvement in their toddlers' lives. It may be lack of confidence from never having been exposed to small children before their own arrived and perhaps feeling less equipped to meet their toddlers' needs. Or it may be because they find the day-to-day care of a toddler tedious and boring and have avenues of escape not available to women.

Putting it bluntly, a father needs to do more than provide financial and/or emotional support and play with his toddler when he is in a good mood. Fathers are often able to do the bathing and dressing with much less of a struggle. Fathers are needed to back up discipline and help provide the all-important consistency (it's impossible for the parent who is with the toddler twenty-four hours a day to stay consistent unless the toddler or the parent is a saint).

They need to be available physically, emotionally, and mentally to share the burden of responsibility by providing practical and psychological strength. And to share the negative feelings, the anxieties, the laughter, and the joy.

Toddlers love to be with their fathers. Simply spending time with your toddler (instead of long hours at the office) not only gives your partner some much-needed time off but, no matter whether your toddler is a boy or a girl, contributes in a major way to his or her healthy development and enjoyment of life.

Ambivalent feelings

Ambivalent feelings are a normal part of being a parent. All parents have moments of doubt, anger, frustration, and resentment, usually on a daily basis during the toddler years. You may feel unhappy with the way your life has changed and sad when you realize you are not the naturally patient, totally self-sacrificing parent you thought you would be. Most new parents expect far too much of themselves. For others, the addition of more children brings more complications than were bargained for.

Toddlers love to be with their fathers

Many parents admit that they feel stuck in the toddler years forever and to having moments when they secretly wish that their toddler was grown up and living elsewhere.

It's easy to feel inept when you can't seem to do anything about the tantrums, when your toddler is the worst behaved at playgroup, when you can't get him to eat nourishing meals, or when you can't get him to poo in the toilet. This is particularly difficult to handle when you are used to being efficient, getting a desired outcome and receiving a tangible reward for conscientiousness ("A" for effort).

These feelings of course are just a part of the whole experience. Other parts are the moments of breathtaking love, wonderful times of sharing and connecting, and a sense of accomplishing something amazing.

As parents adjust to their new lifestyle and role, they are usually able to help themselves around the negative bits and ambivalent feelings, especially when they realize that the feelings they are experiencing are shared by the majority of other parents. Coming to terms with the fact that the perfect parent is as much a myth as the perfect toddler (although all parents secretly think that their children are perfect, including me) is also part of the process of becoming a parent.

Confidence is crucial

It is normal for all parents to have periods of low confidence when they are raising children, especially when they are doing it for the first time. This includes early childhood experts such as myself and, I can assure you, countless other psychologists, nurses, midwives, and doctors I have seen in the course of my work.

Confidence crises are understandable during periods of childhood illnesses and in the early months of a baby's life when there is a huge adjustment to be made. They are also equally understandable at other times when children are going through a particular developmental phase that results in what we adults see as strange or frustrating behavior.

It is unfortunate when lack of confidence is a constant, since there's no doubt toddlers respond much more positively to confident parents who know what they are doing. Or at least give the impression that they do.

A toddler senses when his parents feel confused and guilty, when they are not confident and positive about what it is they want him to do. This results in the toddler not being sure of himself. He is likely to become more demanding and more disruptive.

Here are some reasons for lack of confidence

1. Being made to feel inadequate by health professionals

Health professionals are supposed to be in the business of increasing your confidence to work things out, not depleting it. And while some are truly excellent, others leave a lot to be desired. If you find you need to consult a health professional, keep trying until you find the right person for you. If you are seeing a health professional for routine checkups and he or she is making you feel inadequate, why on earth are you still going? Particularly if your toddler is happy and healthy. Give it a miss. Routine check-ups are not essential.

2. Conflicting advice

Differences between health professionals and other parents about how to raise children have existed forever. Oddly enough, though, whilse at this stage of their lives the child-rearing differences can

421

appear to be monumental, by the time toddlers are twenty-one, enough water has passed under the bridge that the controversies have become vague, even ridiculous memories.

The crazy thing is that within a basic framework of being loved, wanted, respected, and cared for in a stable home as free as possible from unhealthy stress, children will thrive regardless of the finer details of their upbringing. So it's often difficult to see what the nitpicking is all about.

Childcare recommendations for parents which relate to health not behavior (for example, immunization, SIDS, child safety issues, breastfeeding, and dietary advice), are by and large based on concrete scientific evidence amassed over many years. And as such are likely to be of benefit, although even some of these recommendations can be taken to extremes by overly conscientious parents and health professionals.

On the other hand, claims of good and bad outcomes in adult life based on the behavioral theories of certain experts are usually just that—unproven theories, which are often more in the realm of political messages than what is actually essential for a future adult's well-being. Some of the theories may appeal to some health professionals and parents; other theories may appeal to others. In the end, it doesn't matter as long as parents and health professionals respect everyone's right to pursue their own personal adventure as they raise their children.

3. Being made to feel inadequate by other parents

The competitiveness of modern living is alive and well in the first three years of life. Comparisons are made and there are always going to be the parents who love to boast about *their* own toddler and *their* child-raising techniques while subtly suggesting that there is something wrong with your toddler and the way you are raising him.

422

Here's a pep talk

By the time your baby is a toddler, you know him and yourself much better than when he was a few days old. By now you almost certainly know what kind of parent you want to be rather than what kind of parent others think you should be or even the kind of parent you imagined you might be before you had children. You are now also aware of the multiplicity of opinions about child-rearing that exist and know how to ignore the sometimes uncompromising stand people take on certain matters ("control crying," bed sharing, breastfeeding, and childcare, to name a few).

It is unfortunate when competitiveness and uncompromising ideas on the best way to raise children disrupt adult friendships. The first three or four years of their children's lives is a time when parents need cooperative contact with other parents – after all, modern living dictates that there is not a lot of support to be had from anywhere else.

4. Isolation and loneliness

After children arrive, you need to extend your circle of friends to include other parents, as childless friends will to some extent drop out of your life and families may live far away. The more isolated you become, the more you start to feel that you are the only one suffering from fatigue and feelings of inadequacy and that your toddler is the only one who doesn't eat and sleep.

Being part of a congenial group of parents should allow for differences between toddlers and views about their care and should build on your confidence. It should give you opportunities to rethink ideas, confess to your latest stupidity, and weep or die laughing. Swapping care with someone else for a few hours and being able to call on others in an emergency are other invaluable benefits.

Mothers' groups, playgroups, libraries, and other activities that involve social contact (swimming classes, baby gym, and so on) are all ways to meet other parents. Or if these ideas don't appeal to you, try putting a notice in your family doctor's office and form your own parent support group, or post a notice on a local website or in a community newsletter.

5. The impossible expectation that good parent, always have to keep their child happy

Being anxious, sad, bored, depressed, and angry are valid and important feelings which we all experience from time to time, including toddlers. Learning when such feelings are appropriate and how to deal with them is a vital part of emotional development which starts in the baby and toddler years and continues throughout life. If parents step in too quickly to rescue their toddler from feeling bad, it becomes difficult for toddlers to learn how to regulate their emotions themselves. For example, frustration over not being able to do things is common in the toddler years – if parents keep doing the task for their toddler, it does not teach him how to manage frustrated feelings without disintegrating.

6. The idea that a child needs constant life-enriching experiences to ensure he reaches his full potential

Parents cannot hope to deliver such a package and stay confident, nice people. The stress the child is likely to feel living with anxious, irritated parents rushing him from place to place will negate most of the benefits of the enriching experiences. Having every moment accounted for does not recognize that babies, toddlers, and children have built-in resources to help themselves reach their own potential. And that they will do so at their own rate according to their own temperament and interests. Toddlers need to learn to create their own stimulation, using their imagination and initiative, without adults always providing it.

7. Diminished extended family support

Much has been made of the lack of extended family support available to parents in the last twenty years. Yet in Western society people have been raising their children away from their extended families for many generations now. In many ways this is not ideal, but nor is it the unmitigated disaster that everyone keeps saying it is. The extended family is not necessarily the answer to every parent's prayer or to the future of the planet. And quite apart from that, it's pointless to keep harking back to it because the era of the extended family built on generations of inescapable obligation (which may not be what most of us really want) is not going to be a reality for most families in our society today.

Perhaps it's time we started to try to accept this and think of ways around the problems instead of moaning so much about how neglected we suddenly feel when the babies arrive. We tend to conveniently forget the independence and freedom we have away from the obligations that extended family life brings. Suddenly when our children are babies and toddlers we want it back and start to wax lyrically about the joys of extended family life, forgetting about why we left home and hearth in the first place.

The vast majority of families in Western society today have raised and continue to raise their families very confidently and successfully as small family groups, with input from extended family members by phone, email, and visits. Having easy access to extended family members in times of illness and confidence crises is a great and valuable bonus, but modern living dictates that most of us have to learn to manage without it.

Although it would also help families immeasurably if the broader community provided more support, especially for families in crisis, the fact remains that unless something dramatically changes in the way we live, parents are to a large extent on their own. Which is a good reason for belonging to and contributing to your local community of parents and keeping your relationship solid.

8. Guilt about childcare

In relation to confidence, childcare is a mixed blessing. Many women feel much more confident when they are in a position to choose what sort of childcare they want for their toddler and how often the toddler will be in care, and when they are comfortable about the quality of care their toddler is receiving. For women in this happy situation their confidence is also boosted because they are returning, by choice, to work that they find enjoyable and stimulating. One could say that they have it all.

However, many women have boring jobs, childcare that is far from what is commonly referred to as "quality," and perhaps feel that they have no choice in either matter. For these women the thought that their toddler is spending considerable time each week in less than perfect surroundings is likely to be stressful and deplete their confidence. The guilt-producing material that pours forth telling them what an utter disaster childcare is is no help either. Nor, however, are mindless reassurances. The dilemmas faced by families in which both parents are in the workforce by necessity are here to stay and at this stage are not being well addressed by governments or the community at large. For more on childcare, see chapter eighteen.

In conclusion

It is easy for a parent's confidence to be undermined by bad days, health professionals, conflicting advice, well-meaning friends and family, and the torrential flow of information predicting doom and

gloom every step of the way. And the feeling of not really knowing what you are doing doesn't help either, especially when you
are dealing day to day with an unpredictable and emotionally fragile toddler (not to mention your own emotional fragility). However,
the bottom line is that *you are the parent*. In order to feel secure,
your toddler needs confident parents who will show him in as fair
and reasonable a way as possible that *they* are in charge, not the
neighbors, not the health professionals, not the experts—and certainly not the toddler.

Confidence in your abilities as a parent will encourage your toddler to want to please you even if he does protest wildly about
specific things you may want him to do—or not do—from time to
time.

Never forget, you are the best parent for your toddler and you
know more about him than anybody else. Believe it.

Bickering parents

It doesn't hurt children to see their parents argue and make up.
Having it out in front of them (within reason, of course), then
explaining what it was all about, is a valuable way for children to
learn about relationships and how their parents handle conflict.
Arguing about your toddler in front of him is unwise but not a
major disaster when it happens occasionally—as it does to most of
us. In general, it's best for parents to aim to maintain a united front
in relation to discipline and care of their children even if they disagree about other really important issues such as feminism, the way
to world peace, and whose turn it is to get the dinner.

However, living in a home where the relationship is a constant
round of major violent battles, or where the battles are hidden but

the tension seeps out of every floorboard and parents are constantly irritable and emotionally absent, is frightening and painful for children. It contributes in a significant way to insecure and unhappy feelings.

A relaxed, peaceful home with two adults who laugh a lot, care for and respect each other matters far more to children, their welfare, and their future than anything else I can think of.

Separation and divorce

About twenty percent of children in the U.S. now live with only one of their natural parents as a result of the high rate of divorce. It is not my intention in this book to cover this topic in all its complexity and diversity but to focus on some general information concerning the major issues surrounding divorce and how it impacts on toddlers.

When divorce was relatively uncommon (prior to the 1960s), significant stigma was attached to it. Much shame was involved and, rightly or wrongly, it was common to predict pessimistic outcomes for children of divorced parents. Since the 1960s, divorce has gradually become more common. It is now accepted by many as an inevitable part of the reshaping of family life as the result of social changes. Changing attitudes about a whole range of behaviors that were once considered unacceptable, if not illegal, means that there is now a higher expectation of personal freedom and fulfilment. Adults today are much more inclined to take steps to escape from conflict and unsatisfactory marital relationships than adults of previous generations.

As with childcare, every "expert's" view on divorce is different, depending on their background. There does seem to be a tendency for some professionals in the field to be overly optimistic about the impact divorce has on children. Sometimes to the extent of suggesting that children of families where divorces takes place have advantages that children in nondivorcing families miss out on!

Other experts are depressingly pessimistic.

Either way, much time and effort is spent looking at *outcomes,* and this tends to gloss over the pain the toddler or child suffers around the time of the divorce and for up to the next two years. Two years in adult time is a drop in the ocean. In child years it is a long time indeed.

However, it is generally acknowledged that

- Some marriage breakups are necessary to protect children from especially unhealthy environments; however, most divorce arrangements are made because the parents wish to improve their life situations. Without wishing to minimize the pain, fear, and guilt a parent may go through for years before making the break, the concerns of the child and the pain that it will potentially cause him or her are a secondary consideration a lot of the time.

- While there is a good argument to support divorce as a better alternative for children than living in a home filled with anger, hostility, or aloofness, few children wish their parents to divorce and the majority are initially unhappy, anxious, and resentful.

- Most children do not suffer enduring *adverse* effects from divorce. After a period of crisis, most recover, as long as they are not continually exposed to new adversities and family turmoil. Depending on the temperament of the child and the issues surrounding the divorce, a small number continue to have problems, and some have a delayed reaction in adolescence or early adulthood.

- Many counselors believe that the crucial element for children is not so much the divorce as the way it is handled. Cooperation between parents minimizes the pain and protects children from it.

- Ongoing parental conflict in which the child is caught in the middle of two warring parents has a greater negative impact than the actual divorce.

Divorce is almost seen as a normal event these days, and because quite a lot of research does show that the majority of children from divorced homes don't end up with serious problems, the negatives of divorce are often not spelled out. Glossy magazines often feature cooperative, happy, blended families all sharing the care of well-balanced children, so it is easy to be lulled into the cozy feeling that divorce is really . . . a piece of cake.

It is rarely easy, and while for many families the negatives can be overcome with time and patience, they should never be underestimated.

Impact of divorce on adults

- A significant decline in income.

- Potentially an overload for one parent in relation to household tasks and childcare (depending on how housework and childcare were shared prior to the separation).

- Psychological upheaval—for example, intense emotional swings, deep-seated burning anger that won't go away, depression, anxiety, abnormal impulsive behavior.

- Physical symptoms—for example, an increase in infections, accidents, and allergies.

- A diminished ability to fulfill, the parental role because of a pre-occupation with him or herself and all the associated problems that separation and divorce bring.

- Even if the old life was in many ways unsatisfactory, it is now a way of life that is gone and there is usually a great sense of loss for the adult as well as the child.

Impact of divorce on children

- Changes in lifestyle due to decline in the family income.

- Great sense of grief caused by the loss of a family member, loss of the security and rhythm of family life, and loss of the every-day family interaction.

- Anxiety caused by fear of being abandoned, fear of being punished, and fear by the child that his or her actions caused the problems.

- Anger.

- Greater conflict between siblings.

- An increase in both academic and social problems for many children.

   The negative stresses are most marked in the first two years after the divorce. For most families these gradually decline with time.

Toddlers and divorce

It is easy to think or even hope that toddlers do not know what is going on around them, particularly before they can express

431

themselves; however, they are able to form ideas long before they can speak. It is a mistake to believe that they are unable to understand at least some of what is happening. They do not need to know the intimate details of the conflict, but they need to know what impact the family breakup will have on their life.

It is also essential for them to have their feelings recognized and to be encouraged to express those feelings in whatever way they are able. Respecting the toddler's reaction as important and valid will help him make sense of what is happening and give him comfort. Assuming that the separation won't affect him in the same way it will affect the adults involved means that his anxieties will go underground. Eventually they are likely to surface as one or more of a host of behavior problems that are in fact cries for help. For example, nightmares, regression in areas such as potty training, sleeping, and feeding, intense temper tantrums, and extreme separation anxiety.

Considerations for toddlers involved in divorce

- Toddlers learn how to trust other humans specifically through their experiences with their parents. They are in the midst of learning how control and predictability work and where their boundaries are. They rely on a predictable routine and on the predictable behavior of the adults in their lives to know how to respond to a variety of situations and to learn how others will respond to them. Divorce has the potential to pull the rug out from under them just when they are beginning to get a grip on things.

- Their limited life experience means that they view the world and those in it entirely from their own perspective (egocentrism). They believe that they are the center of the universe and that everyone in their world exists solely for them. Egocentrism also gives them an inflated view of their own capacity to make things happen (Daddy went away because I threw the doll out the window). It is difficult for toddlers to believe that people have their own reasons for their actions which may have absolutely nothing to do with them. If their world falls apart, they believe that something they did has caused it.

- Toddlers are at the very early stages of mastering communication, so it is easy for an adult to think that they are coping because they may not give any overt signs that they are aware of what is happening. However, the toddler may rely on games, facial expressions, body language, a change in demeanor, or a single word or sound to get his message across. A parent needs to be responsive to the tiniest of clues.

- It is a normal part of a toddler's development to experience a range of fears and phobias as well as a certain amount of anxiety. These subside as they learn how their world works. Routine, ritual, and predictability are important ingredients in this process. Disruption to the toddler's source of security as he overcomes fears, phobias, and anxieties has the capacity to interrupt normal emotional development.

- The development of fantasy and imagination from the second year may contribute to toddlers imagining circumstances far more frightening than those that are actually happening.

Concerns that toddlers are likely to experience

- They will worry about what is going to happen to them.
- They will miss the absent parent (even if the parent wasn't around much beforehand).
- They may be angry with both parents.
- They will remember past events and wonder why things have changed.

- They may think they have done something wrong. Or that the separation is somehow their fault.

Some ways to help your toddler

- Tell the truth insofar as it affects your toddler's day-to-day life. Give him a calm explanation in as simple a way as possible while avoiding negative comments about your partner and any inappropriate details; for example, "Daddy [or Mommy] is leaving because he or she loves someone else."

  Remember that your toddler needs to know that (if possible both) his parents (or parent) love him and will never leave him.

- The negative impact of divorce is greatly decreased when parents are able to put aside their personal grievances and work together for their toddler's best interests. If it is impossible to maintain a cooperative consensual relationship with each other, try for a noninterfering relationship where both partners, in front of the toddler at least, are positive about each other and avoid criticism. This makes great demands on parents, but it is ultimately the best way to avoid pain and ongoing distress for your toddler.

- Both parents need to acknowledge the importance of the other parent in their toddler's life and do their best to facilitate this relationship, regardless of how they feel about each other.

- Try as much as possible to remain available to your toddler. It is difficult when you are distraught and burdened, but he needs the reassurance of his daily routines, the comfort of his rituals, and your attention to his messages of distress.

- Talk about past events both good and bad, especially if by actions or words he brings them up. Reassure him as much as possible that new routines will take the place of old if there are to be changes in his life. Let him know of any changes before they happen.

- Be prepared for behavioral changes and perhaps an increase in illnesses. He may start throwing tantrums. There may be an increase in his negativity, clinginess, or sleep disturbances.

- Support from extended family and friends whom the toddler knows well will help you and will make a positive contribution to his adjustment.

Avoiding the breakup

Sometimes the conflict between couples is of a low level and the advantages, to themselves and their toddler, in trying to resolve their differences may be greater than going through the stressful experience of divorce. After all, the rate of breakdown of second and subsequent marriages is as high, if not higher, than first marriages, so it is reasonable to assume that going around again may have just as many pitfalls as the first time.

Unfortunately the option of staying put and sorting things out is often not considered, but sometimes the upheaval to everyone's lives can be avoided by having marriage counseling that includes looking at the issues from the child's point of view rather than concentrating solely on the parents' needs. It's well worth thinking about . . .

Managing the breakup

Seek counseling as early as possible. The earlier you take action, the more likely it is that you will resolve the major problems. Counseling and/or mediation help couples reach practical agreements about the separation, contact arrangements for the children, and arrangements about money and property without going to court. These services are available from and private mediators.

Try to come to an agreement on arrangements for the care of your children as cooperatively as possible. Court battles are emotionally draining, costly affairs that should be avoided as they prolong the suffering of the children and deplete the emotional and financial reserves of both parents.

Sole parents

In the U.S. about 20 million children now live with only one parent. Mothers overwhelmingly make up the majority of sole parents. Some women choose to have a baby and raise it alone, but for most, doing it on their own is not their first option but the result of an unplanned pregnancy or a relationship breakdown. Most one-parent families are a result of separation or divorce.

The large number of sole-parent families reflects the great changes that have taken place in our society in the last twenty years and the diversity that now exists in the way that families are shaped.

It is tempting to suggest that one-parent families have the same potential as two-parent families to reach the ideals of happiness, security, and fulfillment in family life which most of us strive for. However, the truth is that it is usually a tougher road for one-parent families.

One-parent families tend to be disadvantaged financially, socially, and emotionally. Children in one-parent families are often deprived of a gender role model, depending on which parent is absent (more often the father). They also miss out on observing how two adults live together, make decisions and compromises, and resolve conflicts.

Although this sounds extremely negative, there are of course many one-parent families that are not disadvantaged at all. Crucial aspects appear to be things like financial security and a loving network of friends and family with one or two male (or female) role models who are willing to spend some time with the children. As with two-parent families, a peaceful, stable environment and an available, emotionally strong parent make a huge positive difference to family life and the outlook for the children of one-parent families.

One-parent families are now a part of mainstream American society, not some sort of strange variation on the family theme that will disappear in time. More positive acknowledgment and support from the rest of the community, as well as assistance in material ways from governments and employers, would help reduce the disadvantages they face raising their children and so, in the long run, benefit us all.

Needing help is not a sign of weakness

Everyone needs a little help sometimes. Often you will find you can help yourself, given some guidance. At other times it may be beneficial to seek professional help, even if it is only for some reassurance.

Let's look at the main avenues for seeking help and when it might be advisable to try one of them.

Self-help

While the needs of your toddler must be met, in order to care for him in a wholehearted and constructive way you must also help yourself. Being aware of your own needs does not mean that your needs are more important than his. And being aware of your toddler's needs doesn't mean that his needs are more important than yours.

This requires talking with your partner about specifics, not generalities. For example, "I'm so tired all the time. I wish you'd help more," is better expressed, "Bathing James and getting him ready for bed is truly exhausting now, he's so big. I'd like you to do it on Monday, Wednesday, and Friday nights," (or whatever).

If you take the time to think about things and do some planning, it is often possible to structure your life together so that more of both your needs are met, at least some of the time.

Here are some suggestions on ways to achieve that:

Communicate effectively

It's essential to communicate effectively with your partner so that you can work out some sort of a schedule together. Just sitting around hoping he will notice that you need a haircut or an hour to do some exercise doesn't work. You might also find your partner has a few gripes that need some attention as well. When men are in the provider role, they can feel used, bossed around, useless, and marginalized. They often feel an increased responsibility to work harder, which in turn widens the gulf between them and their families.

If you are both working, it is vital to come to specific arrangements about domestic work and childcare. Sadly, it is still the norm for women to be responsible for most of the domestic work. Sharing the load equally is a reality in only a minuscule number of families.

Make a list of your basic needs

Here are some ideas:

- A healthy diet.

- Adequate rest. This involves making sure it isn't the same parent who gets up every night and at the crack of dawn each morning.

- Time off from toddler chores. Taking turns with the dressing, the diaper changing, the potty training, the supervision of meals, the bathing, the bedtime story reading, and the visits to the park means toddler burnout is much less of a risk. Men sometimes want to contribute more but are made to feel inadequate about things that don't really matter (odd socks, funny food combinations, too much water in the bathtub, and so on), so stay cool about irrelevant details. Partners should only intervene in each other's care of their toddler if they are concerned that what is being done will put the toddler at risk of being hurt.

- Some exercise.

- Some time away from your toddler—with your partner.

- Some time alone.

- Contact with other adults—as a couple and separately.

- Some time to do something you enjoy.

Look at your expectations

A big reason for feeling inadequate, irritated, and wornout is having quite unrealistic expectations of yourself, your toddler, and your family life. It's often hard to feel in control and confident with babies and toddlers. Things frequently take longer than anticipated, sudden illnesses hover incessantly on the fringes of daily life, and longed-for vacations often end up as disasters. Weekends may seem to be more stressful than the working week, often because there's no agreement about domestic and childcare duties and there's no sleeping in (for one parent at least). It's difficult to get to a movie or even to work in the garden. Old friends without children who initially promised unlimited babysitting disappear and even your mother is not around as much as you thought she would be.

Stop and think about things more realistically if you can. Good planning and communication will certainly help you enjoy family life more, but not all problems can be solved. Even the best planning and communication skills are not going to find time that isn't there and change vacations and weekends to how they were before you had a baby.

Time spent with babies and toddlers is much more about *being* than *doing*. The aim is to live with them—not in spite of them. Try not to see your toddler as an obstacle preventing you from participating in the main event of life. Being with babies and toddlers is an end in itself and often a time in life when the *doing* has to go on hold. It is honestly not for long.

Knowing something about normal development and the range of normal toddler behavior is also necessary to avoid a lot of agonizing over things that seem strange but are in fact perfectly normal. It also helps you understand the difference between the way toddlers and adults view the world. Expecting your toddler to see things the way you do will put you both under great pressure.

Accept that you won't always find the answer you are looking for in books or by consulting the experts. For example, it is unrealistic to expect a magic solution that will suddenly make the temper tantrums stop. Or to expect to find an easy way to stop your toddler from coming into your bed at night. Or to imagine that there is secret information somewhere that's going to make him suddenly start eating three nourishing meals a day. Bear in mind that books and advice come from people who in all probability have had the same range of difficulties you are having—that certainly includes the author of this book.

As your toddler learns to do things more efficiently and to understand the world around him, he will experience less frustration and lots of the exasperating things he does will fade.

Emergency self-help

Most parents have times when they feel very angry, even violent, toward their toddler. Times when you just reach the end of your rope. Maybe you are very tired from disrupted sleep, your toddler has been sick yet again and won't stop whining, or you have just had enough of the unremitting nature of parenthood. Angry or irritated feelings may range from a fleeting sensation to the odd unintentional spanking to feelings so intense that you feel you could do something truly damaging. Sometimes the angry feelings can take the form of emotional abuse. For example, constant shouting, threats of leaving, or threats of withdrawing affection.

The following factors influence the way parents respond to their toddlers:

- The temperament and expectations of the parents (particularly the one who is with the toddler the most—usually the mother). For example, an anxious nature, a need to control, and a desire for perfection all have the potential to contribute to a stormy passage through the toddler years.

- The temperament of the toddler or how the toddler's temperament is *perceived* to be; for example, easy, active, difficult, cooperative, uncooperative, moody, persistent, and so on.

- The health of the toddler. Ongoing illnesses or a disability have the potential to deplete the parents' reserves of patience and goodwill.

- The number of young children in the family and the age gap between them. It is sad but true that caring for two or more closely spaced babies or toddlers is very hard work and puts much more pressure on parents than just one toddler or two children widely spaced.

- How much contact time the parent has. Being alone day after day with the toddler without a break (especially if the toddler doesn't have a daytime nap, is up until late at night and surfaces very early in the morning is extremely draining).

- The amount of company, moral support, and practical help the parent receives with the day-to-day care of the toddler.

- The opportunity the parent has to have time to him or herself, to pursue other interests, and to make contact with other people.

- Increased pressure due to employment concerns, relationship difficulties, and financial worries.

Many parents recognize that factors such as these influence the way they feel and they are able to do something constructive to minimize their outbursts and regrettable behavior. Most of the time angry feelings are transient and the parent has no intention of acting upon them.

Nevertheless, you may need a plan for times when you fear physical damage is a real possibility.

SOME SUGGESTIONS

- Put your toddler somewhere safe (a good reason to have a safety gate or two in appropriate places; use his crib if that is still an option). Go as far away from him as you can.

- Scream into a pillow, punch a beanbag, cry, take a shower, or make a cup of tea.

- When you are feeling a little calmer, think about how he looks when he's sleeping. Or look at a cute photo of him (have one available for such times).

- Call someone—a friend, your partner, your mother (even if she does live on the other side of the continent). If they do not answer, call your local helpline for support or freecall 1-800-688-009. It is a good idea to have this number on your emergency phone number list beside the phone.
- If possible, get your toddler and yourself out of the house.
- Try to arrange some time for yourself (hire a babysitter, enlist your partner's or a friend's support).

If these feelings are happening more than occasionally, it is time to have a serious discussion with your partner about the reasons why and work out some strategies between you to take off some of the pressure. If this is not possible or doesn't work, seek professional help.

Getting professional help

Admitting that you need help can be daunting, especially if you view it as a sign of failure or if you are apprehensive about what may be uncovered. I find in my work that men in particular tend to find it very difficult to ask for help or to even acknowledge that they, their partners, or their toddlers need help.

However, being prepared to ask for help is a sign that you are taking responsibility and doing something constructive to remedy the situation. One of the pluses about being a parent today is the range of help available. And the easy acceptance that parents and children often need a little assistance.

What sort of help do you need?

Talking to others can be very helpful. Counseling with a professional gives you the opportunity to discuss issues with someone who is supportive but not emotionally caught up in the day-to-day turmoil you are experiencing. There are a number of avenues depending on what the problems are.

COUNSELING, PSYCHOTHERAPY, AND FAMILY THERAPY

These are all methods used to help with depression, anger, anxiety, and family relationships. You might be finding that your toddler's negative behavior is beyond your problem-solving skills. Often there is a sense of being stuck in a never-ending struggle which is making you feel increasingly anxious and depressed. Sometimes in order to resolve things and move on, it is necessary to look for other reasons behind your toddler's behavior and your responses to it.

Counseling and *psychotherapy* aim to help you identify the various factors contributing to this situation. You are then in a better position to resolve issues and increase your options about how you respond to difficult toddler behaviors and other life stresses. Some approaches encourage you to talk about issues in your past as well as the present which might be affecting the way you and your toddler are relating to each other.

Cognitive behavior therapy looks at how our thoughts, our self-talk and our actions affect the way we feel. Cognitive behavior therapy helps change inappropriate expectations and ways of thinking so that they are more realistic and positive. It is particularly helpful during times of intense anxiety and depression when things may seem worse or more hopeless than they really are. Cognitive behavior therapy looks at your expectations and assumptions and helps you sort out the forest from the trees. This in turn leads to changes in the way you respond to situations and helps you feel better about yourself and more in control.

Family therapy is suitable when the problem lies with the parents' relationship and is affecting their ability to communicate and cooperate, which in turn is causing problems between themselves and their toddlers. Or alternatively when the toddler's behavior is affecting the way the family functions and the way the parents are relating to each other.

All of the above are available from psychologists, psychiatrists, social workers, some family doctors, some nurse practitioners and other qualified counselors.

Depression

Everybody gets depressed from time to time. However, depression can also be a complicated mood disorder that varies in intensity from mild to severe. At its extreme, depression seriously impairs the sufferer's ability to function from day to day. No one knows exactly what the causes of clinical depression are, but they are thought to range from a chemical imbalance in the brain to life events to hereditary factors to occupation or lifestyle. Misuse of alcohol and drugs, stress, and modern living are thought to be other reasons, but there is also still a big unknown factor involved.

Clinical depression occurs in varying degrees in all age ranges (including children), in both sexes, and in people involved in a diversity of lifestyles and occupations. A full discussion encompassing the total experience of depression is outside the scope of this book. Rather, I shall look at the depression commonly related to childbirth and the care of babies and toddlers.

1. Mild (occupational) depression

It is common for women at home with small children to suffer from mild to serious depression. The risk of this is higher if the woman has a history of depression, but many women who do not have a past history become depressed during the early years of their children's lives. If it happens to be the father who is the one at home, then he is equally at risk. Most depression suffered by people at home with young children seems to be caused by the demanding nature of the job—occupational depression.

Why?

It can be lonely, unrelenting, and unacknowledged work. It's often stressful because of the continuous small conflicts that take place with the toddler throughout the day and, when there is more than one child at home, there are the squabbles and the inescapable level of noise to contend with. Lack of personal space, fatigue, and feelings of being unappreciated and unrecognized all contribute.

Hmmm, who wouldn't feel down—at least some of the time?

Mild occupational depression like this tends to come and go at various times in the first two to three years, and is often exacerbated by things such as the particular developmental stage the toddler is going through, toddler sleep problems, ongoing minor toddler illnesses, or financial, occupational, or relationship problems. It is so common it is thought by many to be a normal part of adjusting to parenthood and a natural consequence of being at home with babies and toddlers if there is very little in the way of support and company. This does not make the feelings of depression any less unpleasant or distressing. Nor should it deter you from seeking help if you feel yourself sinking.

Help for mild depression

Mild depression usually responds to counseling with the right person, some company (joining groups), solving toddler sleep problems, some regular time out for the parent, moving on past trying developmental stages in the toddler, and, for some, going back to work.

2. Serious (postnatal) depression

Postnatal is the name given to the depression some women suffer following childbirth and is more debilitating and severe than mild occupational depression. *Postnatal* is misleading in many ways because it implies a condition that occurs directly following the birth of a baby. It is not usually mentioned in toddler books because the perception (and hope) is that women who suffer from this distressing condition will have been identified, treated, and cured in the first three to six months after their child's birth. However, I am aware from my work that some women are missed and battle on throughout the toddler years without proper help. For others the depression develops further down the track when the excitement and the novelty of the baby wears off and much of the support they had gradually diminishes.

The following information is to help you if you are feeling depressed, especially if you have not told anyone so far or if you have tried but not found the treatment you need.

About ten to twenty-five percent of women suffer severe depression during the first months after birth, although it may take a lot longer to identify the problem. This type of depression is known as postnatal depression, and a part of getting help and treatment is to differentiate it from milder depression as discussed in the previous section.

What causes severe (postnatal) depression?

Severe depression relating to childbirth and caring for babies and toddlers affects women from across the whole spectrum of society – those living in poverty, the middle class, the educated, the uneducated, the disadvantaged, and the wealthy. The causes are innumerable; as well as all the occupational reasons previously mentioned, other causes may include:

- A family history of depression and/or a previous history of mental health problems and emotional difficulties.

- Women who do not have a close relationship with the father of their toddler are more susceptible, as are women who do not have a circle of friends or relatives they can confide in and express negative feelings to.

- Women who like to live a highly organized lifestyle and who are used to being in control may be more at risk.

- Disappointment and feelings of failure following a forceps delivery or a cesarean section sometimes play a part.

- A constantly crying baby or a "difficult" toddler.

- Life events such as moving house and relationship difficulties.

- The role hormone imbalance plays is unclear, but it seems unlikely to have a major one. Hormone imbalance does not account for the number of women who become seriously depressed months after the birth.

- A biological vulnerability to feeling highly emotional under stress.

An exact cause that is the same for every woman does not appear to exist. Some women spiral into depression when none of these things are present in their lives. Other women may experience all these things yet not suffer from serious depression.

What are the symptoms of depression?

Here are the recognized warning signs:

- Feeling out of control.

- Low confidence, low self-esteem, and a sense of loss of self.

- Feelings of hopelessness, self-doubt, and indecisiveness.

- A continued inability to get anything organized or done so that there's a feeling of being a prisoner and unable to leave the house.

- Feelings of frustration, anger, and resentment which do not go away. Women I talk to often mention feeling envious of women without toddlers or women who have older children.

- Alternatively, feelings of numbness.

- Physical symptoms such as constant headaches, palpitations, sweaty hands, sleeping difficulties (even when the toddler is sleeping well), or loss of appetite.

- Constant feelings of guilt and shame.

- Fear of going crazy.

- Frightening delusions and fantasies about harming yourself or your baby.

- Panic attacks.

Help for serious depression

It is important not to try to carry on in the hope that the distressing symptoms will go away. The first step on the road to recovery is to **tell someone**. Discuss your feelings with your nurse practitioner, or your family doctor. If you feel you do not get the help you need, try someone else.

OPTIONS FOR HELP

- Sympathetic one-on-one counseling from a skilled health professional who can help you help yourself is a vital first step.

Helping yourself involves things like learning to nurture yourself, learning how to take a break, and setting long-term and
short-term goals. With the help of the counselor, you can slowly
regain a sense of self and start to take control of your life again.

- Many women find joining a support group where they can talk
  in confidence to other women who are having the same experience helps a great deal.

- Reading books on the subject is helpful for you and your
  partner.

- Your partner requires support too. Men often try to solve the
  problem quickly rather than validate their partner's feelings and
  often end up feeling unappreciated and depressed as well.

  Your partner needs to understand it is not his fault and the
  power to fix the problem does not lie with him. Listening,
  accepting how you feel, and supporting whichever road to
  recovery you are taking are ways in which he can help, as well
  as sharing the physical tasks of caring for the toddler and running the home.

- At times psychiatric help and drug therapy is appropriate.
  Women understandably may not like this idea, but psychiatrists
  skilled in the area do not load women up with unnecessary
  medication and in fact often do not medicate at all. Medication
  takes the edges off the symptoms, but it is not effective on its
  own and should always be used in conjunction with counseling
  and the other supports mentioned above.

Recovery

Recovery is slow and can take up to twelve months, sometimes
longer. A lot of patience is needed from you and your partner, as
well as commitment from your healthcare worker, because time is
an essential part of the recovery process.

Although recovery can take a while, the result is positive for most women. Obviously, given a choice, no one would choose to suffer from depression as a part of caring for their babies and toddlers, but many women acknowledge that in hindsight, positive things do come from the experience. By working through the pain of depression, women and their partners learn more about themselves and about relating to others, which can add a new, positive dimension to their lives.

chapter eighteen

The Vexed Topic of Childcare

The topic of childcare for babies and toddlers is not a vexed one for all parents. Many parents are confident and comfortable with their decision to return to work and to use nonparental care. Others are sure that their decision not to use nonparental care during the first two or three years is right too.

This section is not meant to solve the problems that face parents today as they decide how they are going to meet their children's needs, the economic needs of the family, and their own personal needs both as parents and as adults. It is a basic guide to the childcare situation as it exists in the United States at the present time, warts and all, and I promise neither bland reassurances nor exaggerated predictions of doom.

Childcare—the nuts and bolts

What is available?

Childcare covers a range of possibilities.

One-on-one care at your home with a nanny

Nannies range from people who have completed a short nannying course to people who have qualifications in early childhood or enrolled nursing to university graduates of nursing, midwifery, and child and family health. Like any other area of childcare, the quality of care provided by nannies varies tremendously from person to person.

This is the most expensive option and has many advantages. Your toddler doesn't have to compete with others for attention. He stays in his own familiar surroundings and doesn't have to be up, dressed, and out of the house early in the morning. He is at far less risk of illness and doesn't have to be part of a large noisy group for hours each day.

Negatives include the cost (although like all workers in childcare, nannies' wages are not high for the job that they do), arrangements if the nanny is sick or leaves suddenly, and the possibility of an unsuitable personality or that the nanny might be someone the toddler doesn't take to.

Sharing a nanny with one or more other families

A more economical option with the same advantages and disadvantages plus the need for the families to communicate and cooperate. The possibility for parents falling out for a variety of reasons is quite high.

Commercial daycare centers

This is childcare provided in a center that is open for ten to twelve hours per day. Some cater to shift workers and so are open longer. These centers are mostly run as private businesses but may also be parent co-ops or sponsored by an organization (for example a church, the military) or run by employers for their employees. There are obvious advantages to having childcare available at the workplace or nearby, but unfortunately the numbers of workplaces where childcare facilities are provided remain fewer than the numbers of families who need them.

Daycare centers are regulated. In most states, centers that care for more than 12 children have to be licensed. Licensing is not necessarily a criterion for quality. It simply shows that a center has met the minimum health, safety, and teacher training standards set by the state. Accreditation by the National Association of Family Child Care is a definite sign of quality, but to date few daycare centers have this accreditation (more are being added regularly). Staff/child ratios differ from locality to locality. Recommended baby and toddler/staff ratios vary from one caregiver to three babies and one caregiver to four toddlers to one caregiver to four babies and one caregiver to five toddlers. Obviously, the lower the toddler/staff ratios the better however the low staff ratio required for this age group can make it difficult for many parents to find places for babies and toddlers under two.

Daycare staff may or may not have previous childcare experience; however they are generally supervised by someone who has childcare experience and is trained in early childhood education.

The main advantages of daycare centers are the affordability (in comparison to nanny care) and the assurance that the care is always available and not at the whim of an individual. Disadvantages include an increase in childhood illnesses and the lack of one-on-one care by an adult with a parent-like commitment, thought by some experts to be highly desirable for babies and toddlers in the first two years of life

Family daycare (also called Home daycare, Family child care providers)

Family daycare provides caregivers who look after an agreed number of babies, toddlers or children in their own homes. Requirements vary from state to state, however, most states require that family daycare providers be licensed if they care for more than four children. Many states have a voluntary regulation process for caregivers caring for four children or less. All states set minimum health, safety and nutrition standards for providers and require the caregivers to have criminal checks, child abuse clearance, and to be safety certified in either CPR, First Aid or both. Most states inspect family daycare homes annually or on a random sample basis.

Family daycare appeals to parents because they like the idea of their toddler being in a home atmosphere with fewer children; however family daycare does depend a lot on the individual personalities of the caregivers, their energy levels and the environment they provide. Licensing is no guarantee of quality in these areas. It can also be tricky matching personalities of caregivers with those of parents. There may be other family members around (adolescents and partners) who may add or detract from the service. Backup when the caregiver is sick is also a potential problem (in some states Family daycare programs provide this back-up.)

Preschools

The line between preschools and daycare centers has become blurred since childcare has become such an important part of recent times. Preschools are not necessarily solely for children whose parents work, but have historically been based on social and educationally focused programs for children aged three to six as a precursor to nursery schools and kindergartens. Nowadays, however, many daycare centers offer similar programs to preschools. If the daycare center your child attends is fulfilling his educational and social needs, there is no requirement to change to a preschool once he turns three. For children who are at home with a parent, preschool is an option any time from two and a half onward, an age when it is recognized that children benefit from social contact with other children.

Hours vary according to the age of the child and the structure of the program. Some have morning and afternoon sessions; others operate from nine to three. Most children do not attend preschool full-time unless the preschool offers extended hours and is thus also fulfilling the function of a daycare center. If your child needs care outside preschool hours, that will have to be arranged.

Preschools are often staffed and run by people who have completed a university graduate course in early childhood education. And like daycare centers, they generally have an educational component, encourage creativity, and build on the child's development.

Preschools are now viewed as an almost essential prerequisite to school.

Preschool is not compulsory, however. While it provides plenty of interesting experiences for the children who enjoy it and offers a welcome break for parents, it does not give children any *lasting* advantages educationally or socially, apart perhaps from children who may have specific disabilities (for example, Down's syndrome). For the majority of children, there is no evidence to show that preschool attendance has any advantages in relation to long-term academic and social success.

Assessments of the benefits are mostly based on evidence that children who have been to preschool adjust more quickly to school. I do not think it is necessary to persist in pushing children into preschool when they keep resisting, are miserable, and do not settle happily after an agreed time (perhaps a month). Many three-year-olds will settle happily at preschool by the time they are four if they can take their own time about it.

Most preschools concentrate on creating a positive social experience rather than trying to produce the infant Archimedes. However, there are a small number of preschools around that offer their own brand of educational experiences; for example, Montessori, preschools that teach a second language, and so on. It is yet to be determined whether such input has a long-term beneficial effect. If the children enjoy the equipment, routines, and the other

456

children, it does not really matter as long as parents don't get too carried away with the notion of turning their small child into a doctor or a lawyer.

Occasional care

Occasional care provides short periods of care for an agreed time, for example three or four hours. Occasional care centers should have at least one person who has formal training in a child-related area administering and coordinating the service. Local government, universities, or community groups may run occasional care centers. The centers are to be found in shopping malls, gyms, indoor pools, sometimes attached to childcare centers, and in churches. Sometimes home-based carers will also mind toddlers for short periods.

Occasional care centers are invaluable in allowing parents to have a break, shop, or attend to appointments.

The hourly rate for occasional care varies from around $3 to $7 an hour.

Informal care with extended family or friends

Informal is from the bureaucratic dictionary and means childcare that is provided without formal licensing and guidance regulations provided by the state child care and licensing agencies. Arrangements are by personal agreement between the parents and the caregivers. Many babies, toddlers, and preschool-aged children are cared for in this manner.

Caregivers may be family members, friends, or other people who mind children. Most of the time it is quite satisfactory, especially when it is for short periods. When friends and relatives undertake the care, it is free and flexible. Parents find it very reassuring to know that their toddlers are with someone who loves them and has a parent-like commitment to them.

Problems arise when unsuitable people are undertaking the care,

457

when the children are being cared for in dangerous and/or unhealthy environments, when parents have unrealistic expectations of the people doing the caring, and when the caregivers don't respect the parents' views. Many families combine formal with informal care, which works well provided the care is stable and consistent and not a mishmash of arrangements that keep changing. Personally, I think that a calm day spent one-on-one with grandma is potentially welcome restorative therapy after a busy day in a daycare center.

The fees and government assistance

Childcare center fees across the U.S. at time of writing vary from $85–$200 per week depending on the area the service is in, the age of the baby/toddler/child and what is provided. Many centers have fee structures based on family income and family size (offering discounts for siblings). Universities and colleges offer lower fees for students.

Fees vary widely for Family daycare, but overall it is usually less expensive than childcare center care. A rough guide is $90–$120 per week depending on the age of the baby or toddler.

The fee for a nanny is from $8–$15 an hour.

There are various sources of federal and state subsidies to help parents pay part of the cost of childcare. Eligibility is based on family income, the reasons for needing childcare and your child's age. To find out about financial assistance for child care, call a local Child Care Resource & Referral (CCR&R) agency. Call Child Care Aware, toll free at 1-800-424-2246 to locate CCR&R agency. Alternatively contact your state child care subsidy agency via the National Child Care Information Center (NCCIC) at 800-616-2242 or at http://nccic.org/statepro.html.

You can obtain a tax credit for a portion of your child care expenses by using the Child and Dependent Care Credit (CDCC).

The credit can reduce your federal, and in some cases state income taxes, and you are eligible for this regardless of your income. For some low-income families, the Earned Income Tax Credit (EITC) is also available and may involve a refund, even if you don't owe taxes. You must file a tax return in order to get the credit. For questions about tax credits and refunds call the Internal Revenue Service at 1-800-829-3676.

Finding care

Call your local CCR&R agency (call the Child Care Aware hotline at 1-800-424-2246 to find the number) for help in finding child care providers in your area. Put your name on the waiting list of every program that would suit you should openings come up unexpectedly.

Talk to friends and neighbours. Look in the local library, church or community centers. Try senior citizen organizations, hospital auxilliaries, La Leche League and the local newspapers.

If you have access to the Internet go online:

http://www.babycenter.com has a range of websites listed to help your search for childcare.

Look in the phone book. The Yellow Pages will have lists.

Bear in mind that lists on websites and the Yellow Pages are unscreened and not comprehensive.

What to look for

You will need to ask about the following; ideally the caregiver can supply written information as well:

- What qualifications and experience does the staff (or caregiver) have?
- What is the toddler/staff ratio?

- What happens if the caregiver is sick or is unable to mind your toddler for other reasons.

- How are accidents and illnesses, arrivals and departures, infectious diseases, and records dealt with? How is confidentiality assured? What are the arrangements for arriving and departing? Are parents able to drop in at any time?

- Have the correct steps been taken to provide a safe environment? Check out the sleeping facilities and behaviour management policies.

Here are some things to consider

THE CAREGIVER (HOME-BASED CARE) OR CAREGIVERS (DAYCARE CENTERS).

Caregivers need to be people of warmth, energy, and imagination. They need to be reliable with appropriate skills for the age groups they care for. They need to demonstrate good practical skills such as diaper changing, organizing meals, sleeps, attending, to potty training and so on. They need to respect your wishes and be willing to take time to tell you about or keep a log of the details of the day's events, especially about exciting new developmental leaps; for example, walking, talking, new drawing expertise. Find out the number of babies, toddlers and children being cared for and what other obligations the caregiver(s) has apart from looking after the children. How are emergencies handled? Does the caregiver(s) allow for flexible routines that accommodate the individual needs of babies and toddlers?

THE ENVIRONMENT (IF IT'S NOT YOUR OWN HOME)

Get a feel for the atmosphere and surroundings. What are the arrangements for hygiene (diaper disposal, washing hands, food storage, and so on)? Are the premises well maintained? Check out the indoor and outdoor playing areas, the toys that are available, and the state they are in. Take note of safety issues such as large areas of glass, electrical sources, gates on stairs, and heating vents. There should be a special area for sleeping and resting. What about smoking? And how often is the TV on? Is it a place where you would like to be each day?

Childcare—the debate

Nonparental care during the first three years of life remains one of the burning issues regularly aired with great passion in the media. The subject is usually framed as a debate, but with everyone having their say it's easy to lose sight of what the debate is actually about.

It *could* center on a number of things.

- The right of women to have a family and a career.
- Whether it is essential for babies and toddlers to be cared for solely by their mothers in order to ensure healthy emotional development.
- Whether tax revenue should be used to pay one parent to stay at home rather than having two parents in paid employment and toddlers and babies in group care.
- The relevance of attachment theory (see page 468) to childcare and whether it is appropriate to use the theories of predominantly male researchers from another era to justify anti-childcare views today.
- For many women the thought of staying at home full-time with babies and toddlers is anathema. This is understandable, but is it an acceptable reason to put little ones into nonparental care?
- The level of contribution governments should provide to help all families reconcile the needs of the parents with the needs of the children.

And so on . . .

© Cathy Wilcox

Reams could be written about any of the above, but I believe what most parents are concerned about is the following:

- Is nonparental care harmful?
- If it is, at what age and in what ways?
- And under what circumstances?

Whenever these issues are aired in the public arena, the zealotry, smugness, and shrillness of the voices from either side of the debate make me feel very sympathetic toward parents in America today, especially those who have limited choices about how they conduct their lives. It seems that there is an unlimited amount of analysis and research to draw upon in support of whatever claim is being made. "Research shows" that childcare is beneficial. "Research shows" that childcare is harmful. Take your pick.

The issue of childcare has been the source of much controversy and guilt for families (read mothers) for the last twenty-five years and even longer. I am now probably about to add to it as it seems impossible to write on the subject without causing grief to someone.

A veritable mountain of research on all sorts of aspects of childcare exists around the world. It is extensive, expensive, and conflicting. However, in my opinion, issues surrounding childcare are less clear and more polarized than they were fifteen years ago, despite the increase in research and the number of babies, toddlers, and children in care, and the greater acceptance of women's right to work. The rapid changes in the last thirty years in employment, family structure, the economy, the culture, and the environment have left us all gasping. And perhaps not quite sure what to do about the children. One thing is for certain though—nonparental care is here to stay.

Let's look at those three concerns

- Is nonparental care harmful?
- If it is, at what age and in what ways?
- And under what circumstances?

As discussed in "Childcare—the nuts and bolts," nonparental care covers a wide range of possibilities. The concerns of parents and those who have an interest in the subject are mainly focused on the effect childcare might have on babies and toddlers under three who spend long hours in daycare centers. The number of families using this type of care is rising.

One reason that daycare centers are the settings most open to scrutiny is because they are much more visible and accessible. They are easier to study because they are accountable to county govern-ment bodies. Another reason they attract criticism is because of the concern that there may be negative effects on babies and toddlers when they are cared for in groups by caregivers who change from time to time. A fuzzy feeling exists that family daycare or home-based care is "better" because of its homelike atmosphere, and while this might be true in some cases, this type of care can also be vari-able.

Many health professionals, childcare experts, and researchers are of the opinion that *quality* care, regardless of the setting, decreases the possibility of negative effects from extended periods in nonparental care.

So what exactly is "quality" care?

Well, on one level quality care refers to the training and experience of the caregiver, the ratio of the number of children per caregiver, and the health and safety characteristics of the environment. But note that there is no reference here to the emotional or develop-mental needs of the baby, toddler, or child.

If we consider the complexity of the development of a young human, quality care is a lot more than a safe, clean environment, good food, and a nice place to sleep, important though those things might be. I venture to suggest that there are many homes with much loved and well-cared-for toddlers that do not meet the standards required in daycare centers for space, hygiene, and safety.

And while the qualifications of the caregiver are also important, think of all the first-time mothers who have never held a baby before, let alone fed one, bathed one, and changed a diaper. Or soothed a screaming baby. Or all the people with super qualifica-tions who fall apart when their own toddlers won't sleep or poo in the potty. So qualifications are good, but may not necessarily be an indication of quality care.

The first three years of human life are a highly vulnerable time not only because of the physical dependency on others for survival but also because of the dependence on interested adults for emotional, cognitive, and social development. Optimum development relies on the response babies and toddlers receive from adults who have an intense emotional involvement in their progress. They need interested people to witness their achievements, which in the first two years of life occur almost on a daily basis. The majority of parents are totally absorbed in their children in a way that friends or other acquaintances will never be. I am always amused when checking developmental milestones to hear parents say, "Oh, do they all do that?"

The first three years are also a time when children need constant attention and supervision. Most parents who love them to bits find they can get stressed after spending days on end with their one or two toddlers (let alone triplets or more). So one wonders why childcare workers who don't have an emotional investment in their charges would find it any different? Or, if it comes to that, nannies who might be caring for babies and toddlers for long hours in isolated circumstances.

Quality care is primarily about the relationship the toddler has with the caregiver and the likelihood of his individual needs and emotions being met and acknowledged rather than being swept away in the routine of the day. This increases in importance the longer the toddler is in nonparental care—when a toddler is in full-time care the caregiver is the one who will be taking his parents' place for a great deal of the time.

The staff-to-child ratio in daycare of one caregiver to three to four babies and one caregiver to four to five toddlers is the official standard for *quality* care in the U.S. at the current time, but many centers operate outside this standard. Although a caregiver

465

has a certain number under her care, there are frequently large groups of toddlers being cared for in the same space. The official staff–toddler ratio in the U.S. is viewed by many experts to be a licence for neglect rather than an indication of quality care.

It is also widely acknowledged that there are many licensed and nonlicensed childcare services operating in the U.S. under the banner of "quality care" that fall short of this essential ingredient. Staff burnout and turnover is high among caregivers whether based in centers or in their own homes, which makes it difficult for the toddler to form a relationship with one person. In many childcare settings the staff-to-toddler ratio is affected by sick leave or the necessity for one caregiver to attend to tasks not directly related to being with the toddlers.

The commitment and emotional involvement expected from the caregivers is way out of proportion to the wages they earn and the conditions they work under. Many will, understandably, choose to avoid the emotional side of the business and concentrate on efficiency and routine. Common sense tells us that a caregiver's enthusiasm for a toddler's developmental achievements cannot match that of the toddler's parents when it is something seen every day as part of the job. Expecting anything else is unrealistic.

In the case of daycare center care as it is currently conducted, other disadvantages for toddlers include no privacy, no escape, and no place of one's own. Group care also lacks the flexibility to cater to individual temperaments and the daily variations in behavior that are so common in the toddler years (good days and bad days). Toddlers with "easy" temperaments may fit in with little stress, but others may find it distressing being part of a noisy group day after day. A thirty percent increase in childhood illnesses is also a part of life at daycare for most toddlers until they build up their immunity.

How depressing. Are there any benefits?

Yes, a huge benefit that seems to be overlooked by the opponents of childcare is the opportunity for greater financial support for the family when both parents are employed. As well, the availability of childcare is a crucial part of many families' lifetime goals for achieving the resources they need to take care of not only their children but also themselves beyond the child-rearing years.

Childcare has a number of advantages for adults which have the potential to indirectly benefit their toddlers and children. It gives women the opportunity for the self-fulfilment and career opportunities that traditionally only men have had. It alleviates the need for one adult to have to depend on another's income for the necessities of life. One of the arguments in favor of accessible quality childcare, especially in the first two years, is that a self-fulfilled happy mother is better equipped to care for her baby and toddler than a depressed, unfulfilled mother moping around the homefront day after day.

Other claimed benefits of group childcare include helping toddlers to become self-sufficient and to learn to share and cooperate. And there is no doubt that some toddlers love the interaction and the social opportunities. However, these are things that are normally met in the course of being cared for at home and in my opinion cannot be viewed as advantages. They are only of particular advantage for children who are living in homes where they are at risk of neglect and/or abuse.

Do babies need to be in childcare in order to learn to socialize?

It is common in the great childcare debate for people from both sides to overstate their case. The case for childcare which blossomed in the late seventies and eighties somehow swung around to the notion that not only was childcare advantageous but it was

467

even essential for development. And that children who remained at home were in fact disadvantaged!

Hmmm . . . A case of overkill.

This has left the impression that even if it is not needed for employment purposes, babies and toddlers should be in childcare anyway for social development. If you are concerned about this, be assured that babies and toddlers are not well adapted to social groups, which is obvious if you read the development and behavior sections of this book. The normal social interaction that goes on between families and friends is all the socializing they need. While other babies and toddlers fascinate them, they are far too young to spend hours every day socializing. By the time they are two or three (depending on the toddler), most are ready for some limited time in a group setting for play and social purposes.

So is childcare in the first two years harmful?

Given that a baby or toddler is being cared for in a safe environment and by a responsible carer, the main concern relating to harm has historically centered on attachment theory. Psychoanalyst John Bowlby developed this theory in the 1950s. The basic premise is that during their first three years babies and toddlers must be in the constant, predictable presence of a loving, responsive person and one or two other beloved adults in order to develop into emotionally healthy, competent children. In other words, if they are away from their primary caregiver for long periods of time (that is, for example, placed in childcare), this developmental process will not take place the way it should and will potentially cause a range of problems, some of which may continue into adult life. The problems relating to attachment security are things like difficulties relating to others, increased aggression, a damaged sense of trust, social withdrawal, manipulative behavior, and increases in depression and anxiety. Scary stuff . . .

WHEW! IS THAT REALLY TRUE?

I don't think that anyone knows. On the balance of the evidence, probably not. Certainly not for the majority. From my point of view, I deplore the often smug predictions of lifelong problems made by some experts and others associated with the debate. The prospect of this possibility should not be used to scare the wits out of parents when the evidence either way is so ambiguous. As all people involved in the childcare debate tend to support their gut feelings with research of their choice, I choose to use these two publications to support mine.

1. In her excellent book, *The Emotional Life of the Toddler,* Alicia Lieberman states that "two decades of research have failed to yield reliable findings that early child care has substantially negative effects on the relationship between mother and child. The majority of infants and toddlers with early daycare experience are securely attached to their mothers."[4]

2. *The Myth of the First Three Years* by Dr. John Bruer quotes a study in the United States undertaken by the National Institute of Child Health and Development on the effects of childcare on infant–mother attachments.[5]

   The study cost $88 million and looked at over a thousand families of diverse backgrounds and included both children who were cared for at home and in various forms of childcare. The children were followed from birth to first grade.

   The following are the relevant findings in the context of the possibility of harm from daycare:

- Overall their data revealed that there were no significant differences in attachment security related to childcare outside the home, regardless of the quality of the care and the age of the baby.

- Mother–child attachment depends more on the interaction between the mother and the child rather than features of the

469

childcare setting. Their conclusion was that the mother–child and father–child attachment is an extremely resilient bond.

- This study found that the most powerful influences on child development lie in the genes, the home, the neighborhood, friends, and socioeconomic status.

In my work, I see only a small number of toddlers who have unresolved problems settling into group childcare. Signs of emotional disturbance that should not be ignored are things like ongoing sadness, withdrawal, lack of energy and curiosity, or exaggerated clinginess even when the parents are around. I am also aware of a small number of babies and toddlers who become seriously debilitated with constant illnesses. It is hoped that the situation of the family is such that if either of these things occur the toddler can be removed from group care until a later time.

The main issues

I believe that one of the two main issues to do with childcare relates to the quality of life some babies and toddlers in nonparental care experience at this particular time in their lives, not the possibility of emotional or psychological problems when they are twenty-one. Mediocre childcare is not necessarily a concern because of the toddler's future but because of the quality of life the toddler is experiencing *right now*. Toddlers are not interested in outcomes—they live very much in the present. So the question has to be asked, what is the quality of their day-to-day lives in mediocre nonparental care?

The other main issue centers on the inadequacies of the system currently in place. The problem is that if the quality factors (the two main ones being the ratio of caregivers to babies and toddlers and the wages of the caregivers) were to be improved (that is, fewer children per carer and higher wages), the cost of childcare would be even more prohibitive for most parents than it is now.

At the current time, even mediocre quality care is outside the range of many families. There is no sign that the general community is prepared to sanction the massive increase in taxes needed to subsidize the high costs of true quality childcare or to introduce other schemes to replace daycare for the first eighteen months. Employer-sponsored childcare facilities are increasing, but still unavailable to many families. Flexible hours, job sharing, and paid maternity leave for the first year are only available to a privileged group of professional women in flexible employment.

Everyone was a child once, but childcare is viewed as an issue only for parents when they are in the thick of it all. Surveys repeatedly show that about sixty to seventy percent of Americans believe babies and toddlers should be cared for at home by one of their parents. However, people generally give no thought to or show any interest in the subject prior to having children, and then once their children are at school, most parents heave a sigh of relief and move on, glad that it's something they no longer have to worry about.

It is remarkable that provisions for even minimal childcare have to be begged for, despite the fact that nearly half of all wage earners contributing to tax revenue are women. And the fact that we need people to keep having children for the sake of our humanity and the future of the country.

Childcare—the practicalities

Preparing yourself

All children respond differently to being with unfamiliar adults for any length of time, whether it's at home or elsewhere. Some adapt very quickly, others take a while, and a few never do. The most difficult time to leave toddlers is between eight and eighteen months. Most mothers (and let's face it, it's mothers who bear the emotional burden of childcare—for some extraordinary reason it seems to be taken for granted that if anyone is going to return to work, it'll be the father) find it much harder than they anticipate to leave their babies or toddlers with people they are not emotionally connected to.

It is normal to feel anxious and sad and maybe even envious of the caregiver who is now going to be such a big part of your toddler's life. Alternatively, there is nothing wrong if you feel a sneaking sense of relief and joy at getting back into the world. When women are confident of the care their toddlers are receiving and enjoy their work, they find that the anxious feelings pass with time. Often the thought of leaving the toddler and the organization necessary to get everything into place turns out to be more stressful than the actual event.

Babies and toddlers have lots of minor illnesses, especially when they are in care with other children. As they grow older, this is less frequent, but it is very common in the first two years, so you need to establish a network of friends and family who are prepared to help in times of emergencies.

Women in paid employment do get very tired, as few ever seem to receive enough help to manage two jobs, either from their partners or their employers. Make time to have a good talk with your partner concerning sharing tasks and come to definite arrangements about day-to-day activities. For example, picking your toddler up and delivering him to the caregiver's, getting up at night, sharing care when your toddler is sick, and sharing the housework evenly.

Preparing your toddler

If your toddler is going to be cared for by someone he doesn't know, and especially if he has had minimal time away from you, arrange for the two of you to spend some time with the caregiver before you start work. It is very important that the caregiver and the environment are familiar to him before you leave him. This might mean staying with him for an hour or two at the daycare center or the caregiver's home, which also gives you an opportunity to get a feel for the way the caregiver responds to him and the environment he will be in.

If you think that your toddler's temperament means that he is going to find it difficult to separate from you, go back to work part-time if possible while he settles in. Part-time care and shorter hours of care are easier for toddlers to manage while they are adapting.

Preparation also means explaining to him exactly what will be happening, who will be with him, where he will be going, when and how you will drop him off, and when you will pick him up. Remember that he can understand a lot more than he can say from a young age.

It's important to take time when dropping him off and picking him up (as often as you can). Try not to leave in a great flurry. Make a point of talking to his caregiver and settling him in. But don't hang around for too long. When it's time to go, say goodbye, give him a big hug, tell him you will miss him and leave decisively. Don't stop and start and hang around. If your toddler gets upset when you leave, resist the temptation to sneak away when he's not looking. This will only make him more anxious. Painful as it is to go off to work with his shrieks ringing in your ears, it is much better for him to learn to trust you and know that when you go, you will always come back. Many toddlers seem to be very upset when their parents leave, recover and enjoy themselves, then get upset all over again when their parents return.

Make sure he has his security blanket, teddy, or whatever. And perhaps a photo of you.

When you arrive to collect him, it's also a good idea to allow a little time to do it in a relaxed manner instead of a rush in, grab toddler, rush out sort of way, although I am very much aware there are times when this is unavoidable.

Try and keep the rest of his life as stable as possible, especially during his settling-in period. It's very reassuring for toddlers to know what's going to happen next.

Relationships

Your toddler with other toddlers

Toddlers form close friendships with other toddlers from quite a young age when they are in care together even if they do grab, bite, and punch each other. They miss their little friends if they suddenly leave. It is thought that these friendships help toddlers adjust to being away from their parents for long periods. Toddlers in care interact with each other, learn each other's names, and play pretend games together from a younger age than toddlers who are at home.

Your toddler with his caregiver

A good relationship with a stable caregiver is at the heart of quality care. When the caregiver is someone your toddler grows to like, trust, and enjoy being with, it helps him understand that he can be comfortable with and trust someone other than his parents. Naturally, if this is the case, it makes the world of difference to how you feel about leaving your toddler when you go to work. It is a huge relief and you can start to see the good side of all this childcare business. But it also means that to some extent you have to share your toddler's love with another adult who is in a parent-like situation with him. Sometimes it might even seem as though he prefers being with her rather than you!

It is normal to have fleeting feelings of jealousy about your toddler's relationship with his caregiver and moments of insecurity about your relationship with him. Most parents feel a little disconcerted when their toddler calls his caregiver "Mom."

Accept that you may feel this way from time to time. Remember that there is very strong evidence to show that loving a few different adults does not undermine a toddler's love for his parents. The fierce emotional connection that exists between parents and toddler is very clearly etched into the toddler's mind and heart, and no one else can take that place. He knows the difference between you and his caregiver and the relationship that he has with you both.

You and the caregiver

The relationship you have with the caregiver is another essential component of quality care. Good communication is vital, as is your thoughtfulness and interest in the caregiver as a fellow human being providing a vital service for you. Many caregivers report feeling used and abused by parents, as well as underappreciated. Becoming familiar with the routines and getting to know the staff at a center means you can talk to your toddler about the day's events and the people he is involved with.

It's important to come to arrangements with the caregiver about discipline, food and eating habits, potty training, and a host of

475

other things about which there are conflicting opinions. If you are happy with the care overall and particularly if you are happy with the caregiver, it is not worth making a big issue of small things that don't matter too much, even if they are different from what happens on the homefront. Toddlers will adapt to minor differences and are able to learn without a big drama that what happens with the caregiver is not necessarily what happens with mommy and daddy. However, if it is something that is becoming an area of ongoing tension it is better to make a convenient time when neither of you are rushed and stressed in order to discuss it.

Contact your state childcare licensing agency. To obtain contact information, call the National Childcare Information Center (NCCIC) at 1-800-616-2242.

Problems

Difficulties settling

Many toddlers have difficulties settling happily into care, particularly between the ages of nine months and two years, a time when they are reconciling their feelings of being mighty with their feelings of still being a baby. For many, separation anxiety is at its height during this time.

When it's just for a few hours or so while you take some time to yourself, I do not think that you have to make other arrangements as long as the caregiver can handle the situation. Everyone needs a breathing space, and if your toddler is not particularly happy about it, too bad. A few hours a week is not going to hurt him. Eventually he will learn that you always come back and he might even start to enjoy himself in your absence.

If it is for a considerable time each week, your toddler will need a lot of help from the caregiver to acknowledge his distress and comfort him rather than just encourage him to eat his lunch or play with the other children. You also need to know the extent of his distress. Is he upset all day? Or just in the mornings and evenings when you drop him off and pick him up?

In my experience it can take up to eight weeks for toddlers to settle into care. I suggest continuing for this period as long as the caregiver is happy and your toddler is not showing signs of continuing deep distress at home (sadness, withdrawal, or exaggerated clinginess even when you are around).

Constant illness

As well as problems settling into care, many toddlers immediately come down with a range of minor illnesses such as diarrhea, coughs and colds, and ear infections. Toddlers are prone to these things anyway in their second and third years as they build up antibodies, but being in close contact with other children hastens the arrival of common childhood bugs, and there is a tendency for toddlers in childcare to go from illness to illness in rapid succession.

The combination of an unhappy toddler and never-ending mucus and poo can be very stressful. It sounds depressing, but it is a reality, which is why a little flexibility is advisable if possible (backup care with a family member, for example).

A small number of toddlers never settle and situations do arise with a constantly sick, miserable toddler where it may be advisable to reconsider your plans and put work on hold for another six months or a year.

Differences in behavior

You might find that your toddler naps nicely for his caregiver, poos in the potty and even eats all his veggies for her, while at home with you he will do none of the above without a fuss. You might also find that when you come to pick him up in the evening he behaves appallingly at times, even acting as if he hates you. This can be upsetting, but it is his way of showing you that he knows exactly who his mother is—there is no confusion in his heart or mind. It can also be the result of tiredness, or it might be because you arrive tired and stressed with a cross face after a bad day, the thought of the evening routine foremost in your thoughts.

He knows that even if he behaves badly, you will still love him in a way that no one else does. It is best not to overreact to these sorts of behaviors because they will pass. The more attention you give them, the more important they will be in his mind and the more they will endure.

Fear of abuse and mistreatment

This is every parent's nightmare and sadly is a possibility even when toddlers are cared for by close relatives. Concerns may range from the toddler being spanked by grandma to serious neglect by the caregiver to the real possibility of physical or sexual abuse. It is easy to overreact and misinterpret toddler behavior, but the following is a guide. (If you are concerned it is advisable to remove your child from care and, if appropriate, contact the correct agency in your State for further help with the matter. (See page 476)

- A sudden dramatic change in behavior. Bear in mind that there is a range of things that can cause behavior changes; for example, ear infections, moving to a new house, divorce and excessive stress on the homefront, a new baby, or a sudden change in his childcare (a caregiver leaving suddenly or even a little friend moving on). Scary events on TV can also cause fears, sleep disturbances and other strange behavior.
- Regression in areas like potty training, night sleeping, self-feeding, and playing alone may have a relationship to events at childcare.

478

- Refusal to eat, accompanied by weight loss, withdrawal, lack of energy, and a half-hearted approach to life are serious concerns that need investigating. As do continual bruises or injuries for which there are increasingly suspect explanations.

- Toddlers can misinterpret events, but once they have some command of language, they do tend to report accurately what they see. It is advisable to follow up any strange stories that seem to implicate inappropriate behavior by an adult in as tactful a manner as possible.

- A sudden adamant refusal to go to childcare after the toddler has been settled in for some time might be caused by mistreatment, although it could equally be related to someone leaving or to being bullied by another child or because he's decided he's simply had enough of going to childcare. It is certainly necessary to investigate. A caregiver who is overly defensive rather than genuinely concerned is a worry.

Childcare—a summary

- The demand for good, quality childcare that is flexible and affordable for all families is not going to diminish.

- The childcare issue of most relevance to parents centers on the question of potential harm to babies, toddlers, or children in nonparental care during the first three years.

- *Full-time* nonparental care, particularly center-based daycare, or family daycare, or care for babies and toddlers under two is the focus of the debate.

- There are problems associated with groups of babies and toddlers in full-time nonparental care. But in my opinion the issue is the diminishment of the quality of life they may experience at that time of their lives rather than the largely unsubstantiated claims of permanent emotional and psychological damage that "experts" keep scaring parents with.

- You will have noticed I have not made any recommendations regarding childcare. I believe that parents need to read as much information as they can and make their own decisions based on their own research, the resources available to them, and the requirements of their individual families.

chapter **n i n e t e e n**

Room for More?

While it's common now for young people to delay having babies or even to decide not to have them at all, those who do decide to have them tend to have more than one.

It's interesting to ponder why. The planet is seriously over-populated. I doubt that anyone in our culture has children with a view to having someone to support them and take care of them in their declining years. Children in Western societies do not make valuable contributions to the family income; rather the reverse. Infant mortality is such that the odds of a child not making it into adulthood and beyond are few. And even if the unthinkable happens, the grief of losing a child is not necessarily assuaged by the presence of another.

Some reasons why parents have more than one

- Some parents find that the experience the first time around was so positive, rewarding, and fulfilling that they can't wait to do it all over again.

- Some pregnancies sneak in the back door, unexpected or earlier than planned. Even when babies arrive in the midst of less than favorable circumstances, it is not necessarily a calamity. Many parents have tales to tell of wonderful outcomes arising out of disastrous beginnings.

- Some parents have a secret wish to have a baby of a different gender from the one that is already at home. This is a risky business and most parents claim happiness anyway when a healthy baby of the same gender as his sibling(s) arrives.

- Most parents' stated reason for having second and subsequent babies is so that the first baby will have a companion. The first child may not necessarily be grateful for this lovingly bestowed gift.

- Other parents base their decision on a mixed bag of memories from their own family experience. Only children want six children. Someone from a family of six only wants one child. The oldest child from a family of eight doesn't want any children—she saw enough by the time she was twelve. And so on.

But perhaps the deciding factor is that the dream of a family is still at the core of human lives. The dream may be changed and battered, but it remains incredibly dear to us, and, for many, the dream means having more than one child.

For some parents the decision is easy—yes, we want another baby, or, no, we are going to be a one-child family. Others feel unsure, especially if they found that the first baby changed their lives and stretched them emotionally, physically, and financially much more than they had anticipated. If you are thinking of having another baby but are unsure, here are some things to think about:

- The basics are things like the age of the parents, their relationship, their state of health, and the temperament of the parents and of the child they already have. Finances, career plans (particularly the mother's), lifestyle, support available, and sometimes religion are other considerations. How the parents see themselves managing the lengthy intensive and personalized care that human babies and children need is perhaps the most vital factor and one that many people seem to underestimate. The levels of energy and tolerance required increase with the number of children there are to love and care for.

- ***The following are not good reasons to have another baby***
    - As company for the first child.
    - Out of fear of having a spoiled only child. (There is no evidence to support the theory that only children are more disadvantaged or overindulged than any other children.)
    - As a chance of getting a baby of a preferred gender.
    - To hold a faltering relationship together.
    - In case something happens to the first child.

        The only sound reason to bring a life into the world is because of an overwhelming feeling that another child is wanted for him or herself. And because the circumstances of the parents' life are such that they and the baby will get pleasure from the experience. Any benefits that evolve from this in relation to siblings, relationships, or the gender of the baby are spin-offs and are in no way guaranteed.

- On the other hand, fears about the first child's reaction and guilt over loving another child are not good reasons to give up on the idea of another baby if the time, your feelings, and the circumstances are right. Love does not have to be divided – like breastmilk, the more you express, the more there is. Enough for one child or six.

- It is true that it is easier mentally to care for second babies. The agonizing that goes on the first time is dimmed by experience, and on the whole, parents find that they are much more relaxed. However, it is more physically demanding looking after two children than it is looking after one. The old saying that once you've had one the rest is a breeze is not the reality for the majority of people. The more you have and the closer they are in age, the harder it is during the first four or five years.

- While you are making a decision, have realistic ideas about the potential relationship between the new baby and the toddler. A new baby is a joyous event, but an extra person in the family means there are now more needs to be balanced and more tension to deal with.

- If you swing from longing for another baby one day to thinking it would be a disaster the next, it is better to wait a while. Let a natural decision evolve. You may be surprised by what it is.

What about only children?

The only child is a child like any other. Lack of effective contraception and the necessity to produce many children for biological and economic survival meant families of the past were much bigger than they are today. These days our views about the structure and purpose of families are in many ways different from those of previous generations. Oddly enough, though, feelings that there is something inherently wrong with the concept of only children are still around.

The percentage of adults who have only one child is rising, and in relation to the overpopulation issue, can be seen to be a worthy choice. Much research and conjecture has taken place about characteristics of the only child (as well as the oldest child, the middle child, twins, and so on), and if you are interested, there is plenty of reading material available. Only children, like eldest children, tend to be more conservative, high achievers, and closer to their parents.

Parents with one child need to work out ways to make sure that their child has frequent social contact with other families and, where possible, with their extended families. They also have to think harder about creating a space separate from themselves for their child. It is easier for two or more children to form a group and set themselves apart from their parents. An only child has no peer to gang up with and may at times feel that he is swamped by the adult world. The chance of him being included in all family discussions and decision making, some of which may not be appropriate, is higher when there is only one.

Negative aspects of being an only child, however, are no greater than negative aspects of being a twin, the oldest, the youngest, the middle child, or anything in between.

Twins or more

Advances in treatment for infertility and the higher incidence of older women having babies has increased the number of multiple births in the last fifteen years.

Parents of twins find the rewards of looking after and loving two babies a positive and wonderful experience, despite the exhaustion and challenges involved. The negatives are counterbalanced by feeling unique and special and of accomplishing something amazing.

The twin toddler years present the usual range of ups and

downs that parents of single toddlers experience. Advantages for parents of twins include the fact that the twins have someone around to keep them occupied and can keep themselves entertained for longer periods of time. There's often less squabbling between twins than other siblings too.

But of course the negatives tend to be magnified. The doubling up of typical toddler behaviors and illnesses, particularly in areas like sleep, not eating, the constant limit testing, the endless runny noses and diarrhea, can put a strain on parents' emotional and physical resources. Keeping twins safe also tests parents' ingenuity. Supervising two toddlers requires even more vigilance than it does for one, and most parents of twins find this a demanding aspect of their care until age brings more sense and less likelihood of danger.

If you are looking for some enlightened information or help on issues relating specifically to twins, you are most likely to find it through other parents with twins and through the National Organization of Mothers of Twins clubs. There are also many books around that deal in depth with multiple birth and life with twins or more.

Toddler twins—some general information

- Encourage your twins to be themselves. Give them plenty of opportunity to act, look, and be different.
  For example:
  Dress them differently.
  Try to avoid referring to them as "the twins."
  Allow them to keep their own special toys separate from each other.
  As they grow older, give them the opportunity to get involved in separate activities and have separate friends if they want to.

- Expect differences in temperament, the achieving of milestones, and in areas like sleep, potty training, and eating. For twin tips on sleep, potty training, and eating, refer to the appropriate sections in this book.

- Twins and particularly triplets are hard work in the first three years. It is advisable if you are finding the going tough to consider regular use of occasional care or childcare. Parents of triplets may choose to split the care between the toddlers so that each toddler has a day alone with his or her parent. Regardless of how you choose to use such facilities, it is not in any way a sign of weakness. Extra help in whatever way you choose to arrange it can help smooth out some of the rough times and bring more enjoyment to the experience.

- It is often difficult for a single older sibling to adjust to the arrival of twins. Parents are usually very much aware of this and go out of their way to compensate; however, with the best will in the world it can still take an older sibling quite a long time to come to terms with the attention and clutter that constantly surround twins. It's also easy for busy parents to expect too much from the older sibling too soon. His ongoing needs must still be met and you may have to keep reminding yourself of that.

Spacing babies

The decision has been made to go ahead. The next consideration is how close in age should the babies be.

Again, everyone has their own ideas, and spacing decisions are centered on similar things to those mentioned above—the age of the parents, their relationship, their state of health, support available, finances, career plans, and so on.

Some people don't care. Others have to deal with surprise events; for example, a multiple birth or an unplanned pregnancy.

Eighteen months is thought to be the ideal minimum interval between babies in order to give a woman's body the chance to recover from the previous pregnancy and birth. Many people feel that two babies so close would be too much for them, preventing them from giving both babies the time and attention needed, and would not consider an interval of less than three years. Not many parents *choose* to have babies twelve to fourteen months apart, although some women who are older mothers feel the need to do so.

Some things to think about if you are deciding how close your babies should be

- Caring for toddlers from twelve months to around two and a half is not only labor intensive because of their emerging skills, but in terms of their emotional, social, and cognitive development it is hard for them to understand what is going on when a new baby suddenly materializes. It is difficult for toddlers of this age to have to share their parents' affection and almost impossible for them to understand why their mothers now have less time available for them. The younger they are, the more difficult it is, which makes life harder for the parents.

- Generally by the time toddlers are close to age three, they are more accustomed to waiting for attention and can handle being denied things that they want from time to time. They are starting to respond to limit setting and have good physical skills (getting up and down stairs, in and out of cars, and so on). They have a well-developed short-term memory, can communicate feelings, and usually feel sure of their place in their parents' affections.

- Individual personalities and temperaments of both parents and toddlers make a big difference. Some toddlers are relatively calm, easygoing little people, as are some parents, which makes closer spacing easier to manage. You know your own situation and your own resources.

Preparing for the new arrival

A great deal has been written about this topic, and most parents are very conscientious about preparing their toddlers for the big event in their lives. But, as previously noted, even with the best will in the world, things can be difficult for a while. Most parents have unrealistic expectations of their toddler's reaction and their own, and may find to their surprise that they have unexpected feelings of resentment toward their toddler when he behaves badly.

When the toddler is two years or younger, it is almost impossible to prepare him for the changes that will occur in his life after the baby arrives. However, there are some things you can do (or not do) to help.

- Make any big changes well before the baby arrives. Your toddler's limited understanding of causality will mean that he will associate the arrival of the baby with any changes that might appear to him to be negative. It's very helpful to sort out sleep problems, the giving up of bottles and pacifiers, potty training, the changing of bedrooms, and the moving from bed to crib before the baby arrives, but do it well in advance.

Starting childcare, preschool, or even regular occasional care may be other useful changes, but ideally they need to be in place at least a few months before the birth. Sometimes it is impossible to plan and execute things to such a degree, especially in relation to potty training. If you don't get around to doing everything you would have liked, you will probably find they are best left until at least six months after the baby comes home (depending, of course, on the temperament of your toddler).

- Talk in a general way about families and how they usually have more than one child—use your own or your partner's family as an example. Photograph albums and books are handy for this.

- Wait until your pregnancy is obvious before telling him about the new baby, but make sure you tell him before anyone else does. Let him feel the baby and talk to him about babies and what they do, as well as telling him some funny, positive stories about him when he was a baby.

- Try not to make unrealistic promises about the baby, such as: "You will love having a baby in the house" and "You will have a playmate." Chances are he won't love the baby or the changes the baby brings to his life, and until the baby gets much older, she certainly won't be a playmate. Help him to understand that the baby won't be an instant playmate because babies can't walk, talk, and so on.

- Expand his life outside the home. Organizing a social life for him means he has other houses to visit and places to go. It's also a way of showing him that he's different from the baby. If this is done in advance it also avoids the toddler feeling that he's being pushed off because he's a nuisance.

- Plan the arrangements for his care during the birth well in advance so that he knows what's happening and, ideally, knows and loves whomever is responsible for his care.

- Show him the hospital or the birth center where you will have the baby. Tell him you will only be gone for a short while and he will be able to visit. Let him help you pack your bag. When he's not looking, put in a surprise for him to find when he visits.

After the birth

Things often get off to a smooth start until the toddler realizes it's a permanent arrangement, at which time negative behavior is likely to surface. Most negative behavior in toddlers at this time is not directed against the baby but against the huge adjustment that has to be made, so he might be very loving to the baby and horrible to you.

What sort of behavior?

A lot depends on the age and temperament of the toddler, but all the normal toddler behaviors may be exacerbated—whining, clinginess, tantrums, not eating, and sleep disturbances. Older toddlers may deliberately test your reaction by touching things you'd rather they didn't while you are busy breastfeeding.

Attention-seeking behavior is normal—shouting, interrupting, making noise, throwing toys around, climbing, and jumping off forbidden objects and wanting more of your time. You might find that your toddler regresses in areas such as potty training, feeding himself, dressing himself, wanting to be carried, and he may want to breastfeed or use a bottle or a pacifier again.

Parents too . . .

Once the high of the first few weeks after the birth passes, parents also go through an adjustment period when they may feel varying degrees of resentment and guilt for a whole range of reasons.

Ill-feeling toward the baby, the toddler, and each other is not uncommon. The mother may resent the toddler's intrusion during the time when she is trying to settle into a relationship with the baby, particularly while she is breastfeeding. There is not an easy answer to the breastfeeding dilemma. Standard advice suggests that toddlers will settle with a treat, special activities, or a favorite TV show while the breastfeeding is underway, but the reality in many homes is that the toddler is not going to settle for anything. He somehow knows that this is a time when he has quite a deal of power to disrupt and make his presence felt and may do so with great determination. Second babies often get their best feedings when someone else is around to occupy the toddler or during the night. They thrive nevertheless.

The mother feels guilty because she is not spending as much time as she used to with her toddler and because no one has taken any photos of the new baby yet. The new baby is in second-hand clothes and is not getting anything like the attention the first baby got.

Mother and father both feel guilty because they are neglecting each other and are now letting the toddler get away with murder because their guilt is making them feel that they have to make life easier for him. In the meantime, the toddler senses that not only has the baby interrupted his life but that his parents no longer know what they are doing, and he starts testing his limits, which makes the parents angrier and guiltier.

Naturally this scenario is not everyone's experience, but most parents will relate to some aspects of it to some degree.

What's the best thing to do?

- Try to keep to your toddler's routine as much as possible. Be understanding and allow for some flexibility, but keep to the same limits that were in place before the baby arrived.

- Involve your toddler with the care of the baby in ways that are suitable for his stage of development. Toddlers need a lot of supervision and reminders to be gentle, but they can hold the baby, fetch diapers, make the baby smile, let the baby hold their fingers, put an extra cuddly on the baby, and so on.

- Make sure the house is as toddlerproof as possible so your toddler can roam around while you are breastfeeding or busy with the baby and not get into dangerous situations. Staying relaxed about the state of the house (within reason—living in total disarray is extremely stressful for most people) is the only sane approach when you have babies and toddlers around.

- Accept that your toddler might regress temporarily in some areas and might want to be a baby at times. If he knows that he's free to behave like a baby sometimes without being disparaged, he'll stop doing it after the novelty wears off. Help him recognize the benefits of being older by emphasizing the things he can do that the baby can't.

- Above all, stay confident. Everyone gets torn in many directions in the course of family life, especially with the arrival of a new member. Give your children the message that you feel right about what you are doing and they will not feel neglected—in any permanent sense at least.

Here are some other tips

- Any time you can spend with your toddler without the baby helps enormously. This doesn't have to be for lengthy periods. Some short but reliable private time together on a regular basis is what's needed.

- When you can't do something he wants to do, try not to make the baby the excuse all the time—it's unavoidable some of the time, of course.

Toddlers need a lot of supervision and reminders to be gentle,
but they can hold the baby . . .

- Fathers can help a lot by minding the baby while you do something with the toddler or by doing something interesting with the toddler when you are busy with the baby.

- If he is old enough to understand, prepare him for the fact that babies attract a lot of attention—remind him that he did when he was a baby. Let him know he can be with you if he is feeling lonely or jealous.

- Help him not to feel guilty about jealous feelings by talking to him about feelings, how strong they can be, and the best ways of handling them.

- Obviously the baby has to be protected from physical harm, which means avoiding situations where the toddler may harm her. It also means that you have to teach your toddler that aggressive behavior toward the baby will not be tolerated. However, in doing so, you can still let him know that you understand why he's being mean.

- Try not to leave the baby's belongings all over the house under the toddler's nose.

- Avoid talking about the baby in ways that could hurt your toddler's feelings—things like "Thank goodness we have a girl this time" or "She's a much easier baby" and so on. Remember that toddlers can understand much more than they can say.

- It's also advisable to avoid talking about the baby in negative ways in front of the toddler. For example, "The baby is driving me nuts, she screams all the time," "Life was much easier before the baby came; now, it's impossible to do anything," and so on. Even when it's not serious, negative talk about the baby within his hearing range gives the toddler permission to be negative too, which is not good for his adjustment to the new situation.

- It's unrealistic to expect your older child to automatically love the new baby—this will probably happen in time. Encouraging the idea that the baby likes him will help him feel special to his new sister or brother.

- When the age difference between the baby and the toddler is between one and three years, try to synchronize meals and bedtimes once the baby is around twelve months (if not before). You will find it makes a huge difference to your day and your workload.

- Remember that you are only human, and looking after babies and young children is one of the hardest things anyone can do. Blowing your stack sometimes or finding it difficult to manage is completely understandable.

- As time goes by, it all gets easier. It takes about six months for the family to orient themselves after the birth of the second child. Sometime between three and seven months, the initial jealousy passes and your toddler will forget what life was like when he was the only one.

Sibling bonds and rivalry

This refers to the fluctuating love and hate, cooperation and competitiveness that has gone on between siblings since the world began. The ways that siblings relate to each other are diverse, ranging from intense affection to intense hostility. These feelings vary tremendously from family to family and from sibling to sibling and tend to wax and wane over time. Some sibling relationships are very durable and last a lifetime; others have little importance once children leave the home and move out into the world.

It is common for most parents to have unrealistic expectations of how well their children are going to get along, and it can be unsettling for them when the inevitable conflict surfaces. Sometimes this is not evident until the younger child is mobile and begins to learn how to hurt the older child. Young children start to learn about each other's weak spots and how to predict each other's behavior, not only in the course of competing for their parents' attention but because they also enjoy the sneaky pleasure derived from the forbidden satisfaction of getting the better of someone. Living with, loving, and learning about one another's strengths and weaknesses is a valuable experience for children. It teaches them a lot about compromise, competitiveness, and conflict.

Family life with two or more

Sibling rivalry, or, putting it another way, squabbles, teasing, meanness, and uncooperative behavior toward each other are inevitable unless you only have one child or two with a huge age gap in between. The amount and intensity vary enormously depending on the temperament of the children. It is true that in some families the extent of sibling rivalry is minimal. I notice in my work that conflict between twins, particularly of the same sex, seems to be a lot less than between other siblings. However, sibling rivalry in one form or another tends to surface in most families at some stage. It is better to expect it and deal with it than to waste a lot of energy constantly trying to avoid it.

It is not possible to treat all children equally all the time. Circumstances, ages, personalities, individual talents and characteristics dictate parent responses. Preference for one child is a reality for most parents, but the preference is likely to vary according to the particular stage of development, the day of the week, the time of the year, and the mood the parent is in. Normally most parents are aware of this and treat all their children with a basic goodwill and affection even when one of the children is going through a stage that is particularly irritating.

Favoring one child starts to be destructive if the parents' attention is constantly centered on that child and he is also allowed privileges denied to his sibling(s).

Drawing unfavorable comparisons between siblings is something most parents do from time to time, but it's advisable to try to avoid this as much as possible—either directly or in conversations with other adults which children may overhear.

It's always tempting to try to persuade one child to do something by comparing his stubbornness with the sweet cooperation of his sibling. This is likely to make the stubborn child even more stubborn and foster tense relations between the children. It also puts pressure on the cooperative child to maintain her sweet persona, which is not in her best interests, especially when it all falls apart as it is bound to somewhere along the line.

Regular one-on-one time with each child as they grow is a wonderful way of building a positive relationship with your children. It's like adding credit to his or her emotional bank. It does not have to be for long periods, but research has shown that children remember happy times spent with their parents more clearly than anything else in family life. As children grow and become closer developmentally, time spent with all the children in a positive way as a family is also important.

Dealing with the strife

There's a strong tendency for parents to take the disputes more to heart than the children do, and this can add to the conflict. Sometimes this goes back to memories of their own relationships with their siblings or because of unrealistic expectations of how family life should be. If you find yourself getting very distressed by your children's attitudes toward each other, it can be helpful to think through some of these things and perhaps change the way you are perceiving and handling the situation.

Parents are usually advised to ignore and stay out of as many squabbles as possible, but there are times, especially during the toddler years, when this is not necessarily the best plan. A toddler may be at risk of being hurt. One child might be continually persecuting another, and to keep ignoring that gives the child permission to continue. Parents need to have a flexible but consistent strategy for living with and dealing with their children's disputes (see below for some ideas). More importantly, they need to agree about the strategy, refuse to take sides, and show their children that they are united and cannot be divided. It is more difficult if you are a sole parent, but again, have a strategy, communicate it clearly to your tribe, and be as consistent as you can.

I am aware that all of this is easy to write and difficult to do. Fights among siblings are universally acknowledged to be an irritating feature of family life that regularly drives most parents batty.

Here are some ideas

DRAW UP SOME FAMILY RULES

For example:

- No hurting each other (biting, hitting, pinching, and so on).
- No screaming.
- No grabbing toys from each other (toddlers).
- Respect each other's belongings (older children).

Family rules need changing as children grow and develop.

GIVE ADEQUATE SUPERVISION

Toddlers and preschoolers need close supervision and more intervention than older children, especially if there is a baby crawling around as well.

HAVE REALISTIC EXPECTATIONS

Toddlers have a limited capacity to play together for long periods without a drama. Have realistic expectations and a backup plan for distraction purposes when things get tense.

A guide to dealing with conflict between siblings

- Make allowances for each child's temperament, age, and development. The main aim is to keep the conflict at manageable levels. Continually trying to prevent any conflict at all will waste a lot of your energy and will probably only result in accelerating disputes.

- Communicate a few rules clearly and consistently so that your children know what to expect and what is expected of them.

- Acknowledge the times when they are being nice to each other.

- As long as no one is being physically hurt or victimized, ignore as much of the negative stuff as possible.

- When there are rumbles escalating, distract your tribe with new interests or, if possible, a change of venue.

- Avoid taking sides or spending hours finding out who the guilty party is. Intervention and firm action is needed for deliberate physical injury or continued victimization of one toddler or child.

- When you intervene, do so decisively without agonizing about justice and listening to long tales of woe about who did what to whom. Act firmly.

Examples of firm action

1. Depending on the situation (the intensity of the aggression and the extent of injury inflicted), start with a firm verbal request to stop the behavior and a short simple explanation of why it is unacceptable.

2. Remove the toy the argument is about or stop the game and redirect them to another activity.

3. Administer some sort of timeout (see page 117) for one or both children depending on your rapid assessment of the situation and the age of the toddlers or children.

One scenario that is so common it is worth a specific mention

Parents are often floored by a sudden show of nastiness by the older child who has appeared to date to love his little brother or sister. It's usually when the little brother or sister has reached an age when they can be thought of as a child rather than a baby (typically around fifteen to eighteen months). The older child (age three to four) usually starts doing something horrid (punches or takes toys away) very deliberately on a regular basis. Naturally the younger child protests dramatically and noisily. The parents' sympathies tend to be with the younger child because there's an expectation that the older child should be behaving in a far more sensible and restrained manner. Parents tend to overestimate the maturity of the older child.

Distressing though this is for the younger child who needs his or her share of sympathy, the older child also needs some help to make his life happier. Simply drawing his attention to the distress

501

of his sibling in an attempt to make him feel guilty is not going to do a great deal.

Here are a few suggestions

- Remember that it is normal for the older child to have some ambivalent feelings about his younger sibling even if they have not surfaced until now.

- The nasty behavior probably gives him some feeling of control, even power, which is probably worth risking your displeasure for.

- How often are the children together? Try to arrange for some time away for the older child, doing something he enjoys (playgroup, preschool, or playing at a friend's house).

- A regular short private time each day with his mother or father is extremely helpful. In a casual way, encourage him to talk about how he feels or read a book and talk about how the characters feel. Perhaps play a game with him in which you take turns or share something of yours with him.

- Let him keep a few precious things that are for his use only. Of course, the younger child should have the opportunity to do that too. Make sure it's only a few things and that the rules regarding them are very clear.

- When the older child deliberately takes toys away from the younger one or mistreats her, minimal but serious attention is best. Concentrate on how you don't like the behavior rather than how mean he is being or going on at length about how upset the younger child is. Parents often unconsciously favor the younger child because he or she seems so vulnerable.

- If the negative behavior continues, timeout is the next option.

- Make a point of acknowledging his behavior when he's being good. Reward him with words and smiles. It's important to show him that you notice when he's being cooperative and friendly.

In conclusion

Life with two or more has its ups and downs, and no doubt there will be times when you wonder—why?

However, like most parents, once the initial disruption a new baby brings settles down, you will go on to find immense pleasure in seeing your children growing and developing together. Continuing to balance all your children's needs takes considerable time and effort throughout their childhood. Make it clear you love them all as individuals and try not to compare them or hold them up as examples to each other.

And take comfort in the fact that the moment of panic you experienced when you saw your toddler stuffing his peanut butter sandwich into the baby's mouth will become a treasured part of family folklore.

The Last
Word . . .

Like all parents, you will have many a toddler tale to tell.

It's tempting to reveal my own experiences to counterbalance the fear I have of sounding prescriptive, smug, unrealistic, and preachy from time to time and to let everyone know that I too fell into big holes. However, I have tried not to let my own mighty toddler tales wriggle their way onto the pages of this book because, in the manner of toddlers, they would probably take over. Besides, my children might never speak to me again.

I am keenly aware that it is relatively easy to sit undisturbed in a calm environment far away from the day-to-day turmoil and joy that toddlers bring and compose dot points about temper tantrums. And it is easy to write about discipline with the wisdom of hindsight when the two most beautiful toddlers ever born are no longer around to pull the plug out of the computer and make me lose not only my composure but also all my dot points.

Time spent with toddlers is not neatly packaged as discipline, potty training, and sleep but is a blur of chaotic experiences all running into each other throughout the day (and often the night as well). I remember it only too well and found it just as hard as you.

Yet I eventually learned that meaning comes from the chaos. Toddlers force us to become more flexible, more tolerant, more patient, and more self-disciplined. Above all, toddlers encourage us to learn to be resourceful in the face of daily uncertainty, disorder, and confusion.

Perhaps toddlers are a gift. A gift of humbling unheralded love bestowed upon adults to help us see the world and ourselves as having infinitely greater possibilities and far wider horizons than the small, safe, predictable space we inhabited before they arrived.

A mighty gift indeed . . .

SOURCES AND RESOURCES

Resources
and Helping
Organizations

America has many resources available for families, although there never seems to be quite enough. Some are constant, others wax and wane according to funding available and how much voluntary support is around to keep them going. In the U.S. resources for parents vary tremendously between urban and rural areas, from state to state right down to individual communities.

Resources come and go as do phone numbers, websites and name changes so it is not practical to have detailed resource lists in books as it is impossible to keep such lists up to date and relevant. The aim of the following is to let you know the main services that are available. The internet is an invaluable source of information but I am aware that it is still not available to many so I have included phone numbers and/or addresses as often as possible.

Use the following resources to find out what is in your area:

Your family doctor/pediatrician

Your nearest children's or local

Hospital

Your local library

A church or synagogue

The phone book

Here are some specific resources to give you an idea of what's around. Bear in mind there are many more resources available than those listed here.

Breastfeeding Education, Information, Advice, and Support

La Leche League International (LLLI).

1400 N. Meacham Road
Schaumburg, IL 60173-4048
Telephone: 847-519-7730 or 1-800-525-3243
Website: **http://www.lalecheleague.org**

Childcare

National Childcare Information Center (NCCIC)

Telephone: 1-800--616-2242
TTY: 1-800-516-2242
Website: **http://www.nccic.org**

Child Care Aware

Telephone: 1-800-424-2246
Website: **http://www.childcareaware.org**
To find your local Child Care Resource and Referral (CCR&R) organization. Local CC&Rs provide information on local financial assistance, child care providers and guidelines for choosing quality child care.

National Association for the Education of Young Children (NAEYC)

NAEYC is dedicated to improving the quality of services for children and their families. Amongst other things this organization helps parents find accredited childcare in their areas.
Telephone: 1-800-424-2460 or 202-232-8777
Website: **http://www.naeyc.org**

International Nanny Association

Membership Services Office
900 Haddon Avenue, Suite 438
Colingswood, NJ 0810
Website: **http://www.nanny.org**

National Association for Family Child Care

Parents can call NAFCC's offices to find accredited family daycare in their area.
Telephone: 801-269-9338
Website: **http://www.nafcc.org**

Sick child resources

A list can be found on **http://www.bluesuit.mom.com**
ChildCareAware and NCCIC (see above) have information about sick-child and backup care.

Child Safety

U.S. Consumer Product Safety Commission (CPSC)

CPSC is an independent federal regulatory agency created to protect the public against unreasonable risk of injuries and deaths associated with consumer products. The CPSC covers a wide range of baby and child consumer products.

Telephone: 1-301-504-0990.

Toll-free consumer hotline: 1-800-638-2772, 1-800-638-8270 (TTY)

Web site: **http://www.cpsc.gov**

U.S. Consumer Gateway (Consumer.gov)

Consumer.gov is a resource for consumer information from the federal government and has a category for children with information ranging from childcare to immunization to product recalls.

Telephone Federal Information Center: 1-800-688-9889

Web site: **http://www.consumer.gov/children.htm**

National Highway Traffic Administration (NHTSA)

NHTSA, under the U.S. Department of Transportation was established to carry out safety and consumer programs in all areas relating to traffic and motor vehicle safety. NHTSA has a wide range of valuable information about baby/child motor vehicle passengers that includes a list of child safety seat recalls.

Telephone nationwide toll-free number: 888-327-4236.

TTY number is 800-424-9153.

Web Site: **http://www.nhtsa.dot.gov**

National SAFE KIDS Campaign

SAFE KIDS is dedicated to the prevention of unintentional childhood injury and has 300 state and local SAFE KIDS coalitions in all 50 states. SAFE KIDS provides information on all aspects of baby and child safety including a product recall list.

Telephone: 202-662-0600

Web site: **http://www.safekids.org**

Juvenile Products Manufacturers Association, Inc (JPMA)

JPMA is a national trade organisation of over 400 companies that manufacture and/or import infant products such as cribs, car seats, strollers, bedding and a wide range of accessories and decorative items. JPMA developed an extensive Certification Program to help parents select baby/child products that are built with safety in mind. Parents can look for the seal on product packaging.
Telephone: 856-638-0420
Web site: **http://pwww.jpma.org**

Consumer Reports

Consumer Reports Magazine and Consumer Reports Online is an independent, nonprofit testing and information organization that tests products, informs the public and protects consumers. The organization has a comprehensive Babies and Kids category that includes detailed ratings and reports for hundreds of products.
Address: 101 Truman Avenue, Yonkers, NY 10703.
Telephone number and email address is only given to subscribers.
Web site: **http://www.consumerreports.org**

Safety Belt Safe Ride Help Line

(Provides guidelines for proper infant/child car-seat installation as well as information on booster-seat and airbag safety).
Telephone: 1-800-745-7233
Website: **http://www.carseat.org**

Immunization

National Immunization Program Hotline: 1-800-232-2422
National Immunization Website: http://www.cdc.gov/nip

National Vaccine Injury Compensation Program

Telephone: 1-800-338-2382
Website: **http://www.hrsa.gov/bhpr/vicp**

Low-cost/free vaccinations

Telephone: 1-800-232-2522

Multiple Birth

National Organization of Mothers of Twins Clubs (NOMOTC)

PO Box 231188
Albuquerque, NM 87192-1188
Telephone: 800-243-2276 or 505-275-0955
Website: **http://www.nomotc.org**

Postpartum Depression

Depression after delivery

A postpartum delivery clearinghouse that has information on causes, symptoms, treatments as well as resources for women suffering from depression after the births of their babies.
Telephone: 1-800-944-4773 (4PPD)
Website: **http://depressionafterdelivery.com** (the website has links to other resources for postpartum depression).

Sole Parents

Parents without partners

Telephone: 1-800 637-7974
Website: **http://www.parentswithoutpartners.org**

Support for Parents who Think They Might Hurt Their Babies

Parents Anonymous

Dedicated to breaking the cycle of child abuse. Don't be afraid to call.
Telephone: 90 9621-6184
Website: **http://www.parentsanonymous.org**

Recommended Reading

Toddler development

Alicia F Lieberman, PhD, *The Emotional Life of the Toddler*, Simon & Schuster, USA, 1995.

Highly recommended for absorbing, moving, and amusing insights into the minds of toddlers—how they think and how they feel. Lieberman's many hours of observation are recorded in minuscule detail, giving the reader entertaining examples of toddler behavior and the reasons behind it.

Burton L White, *The New First Three Years of Life*, 2nd, Simon & Schuster, USA, 1995.

Psychologist Burton White, his work, and his books have been a part of the early childhood development scene in America since the sixties.

There are aspects to his style, language, and some of the information that some might find unappealing. But his painstaking account of child-hood development in the first three years in all areas (cognitive, emotional, social, gross motor, and so on) contains details of development based on years of close observations of infants and toddlers in their own homes which I have never read anywhere else. You may well disagree with his ideas on the overindulged baby and discipline, but this book is well worth reading for the gold to be found throughout. Available by order through bookstores or through **www.amazon.com**

John T Bruer, *The Myth of the First Three Years: A new under-standing of early brain development and lifelong learning,* Simon & Schuster, USA, 1999.

This book is not an easy read but is essential for parents who feel anxious about the frequently quoted "new" brain science research that claims optimum human development is only possible at certain times (the first three years) and under certain conditions ("proper" attachment and enriched environments). And the even more worrying claims that the baby or toddler brain may in fact shrink if parents handle these two factors improperly. The claims being made impact on the day-to-day care of babies and toddlers, particularly in areas such as "control crying" and childcare.

John Bruer reviews and analyzes all the evidence to date which purports to support current hype about early childhood brain development, revealing the flimsy foundations the theories are based on. He shows us how so often well-intentioned theorists, researchers and health professionals confuse what they want with what is actually true.

Childcare

Children First: What Society Must Do—and is Not Doing—For Children Today, Penelope Leach, Random House, U.S.A., 1995.

The Emotional Life of the Toddler, Alicia F. Lieberman, Ph.D., Simon & Schuster, 1995.

518

Seperation and divorce

The Emotional Life of the Toddler, Alicia F. Lieberman, Ph.D., Simon & Schuster, 1995.

Sleep

Solve Your Child's Sleep Problems, Richard Ferber, Fireside, revised edition, USA.
Three In A Bed, Deborah Jackson, Bloomsbury, U.S.A., 1999.
The Family Bed, Tine Thevenin, Avery Publishing Group, USA, 1987.

Endnotes

1. A. Gopnik, A. Meltzoff & P. Kuhl, *How Babies Think: The science of childhood*, Weidenfeld & Nicolson, UK, 1999.

2. Peter Williamson PhD, *Good Kids, Bad Behavior*, Simon & Schuster, USA, 1993. (Unfortunately this book is out of print at the time of writing.)

3. John T. Bruer, *The Myth of the First Three Years: A new understanding of early brain development and lifelong learning*, Simon & Schuster, USA, 1999, pp. 189–191.

4. Alicia F. Lieberman PhD, *The Emotional Life of the Toddler*, Simon & Schuster, USA, 1995, p. 220.

5. John T. Bruer, op. cit.

Bibliography

Rothenberg, B. Annye, Hitchcock, S., Harrison, Mary Lou & Graham, M., *Parentmaking: A practical handbook for teaching parent classes about babies and toddlers*, Banster Press, USA, 1983.

Sheridan, Mary D., Frost, Marion & Sharma, Ajay, *From Birth to Five Years: Children's developmental progress*, (rev.), Australian Council for Educational Research, Australia, 1998.

Singer, Dorothy G., Revenson, Tracey A., *A Piaget Primer: How a child thinks*, rev., Penguin, USA, 1996.

Walsh, Froma (ed.), *Normal Family Processes*, Guilford Press, USA, 1993.

White, Burton L., *The New First Three Years of Life*, rev., Simon & Schuster, USA, 1995.

Wyckoff, Jerry & Unell, Barbara C., *Discipline Without Shouting or Spanking: Practical solutions to the most common preschool behavioral problems*, Meadowbrook Press, USA, 1984.

Acknowledgments

Some extraordinary toddlers have magically found their way onto the pages of this book. Thank you, Gabriel, Indigo, Edward, James, Samuel, William, Isabella, Bronte, Emily, Isabel, Sophie, Ben, Oscar, Grace Pearl, Ella Bella Boo, Natasha, Matthew, and Jack.

Clinical nurses are the backbone of the health system. Thank you to the following expert clinical nurses:

Kate Watson, Clinical Nurse Consultant Child Development, for your advice and encouragement and for so generously sharing your expertise.

Irene Mitchelhill, Clinical Nurse Consultant, for your advice and information regarding toddler growth.

Lorraine Young, Clinical Nurse Consultant at the Public Health Unit, South Eastern Sydney Area Health Service, for your input into the immunisation information.

Pediatric nurse practitioner Carol Sutton, Jann Zintgraff, Donna Walsh, and Marianne Nicholson for always being available to listen to my ravings, for happily supplying information when requested, and for your belief in the value of expert clinical nursing knowledge.

I am delighted to acknowledge the following people for reading early drafts of the manuscript—sometimes at stages when they, like me, perhaps wondered where it was all going:

Psychologists Kerry Gee, Marion Kovari, Frances Gibson, and

Jillian Ball, who provided input and expertise into development, separation and divorce, depression and getting help. Carolyn Parfitt, who also contributed to divorce and separation.

Speech-language pathologist Hassia Lichtman, who set me straight on speech and language development, but I hasten to add that the view taken on normal stuttering is my own.

Pediatrician Dr Karen O'Brien, who read and commented on the medical section.

Glynn Feldman, Cathy Burke, and Susan Hely who helped me find my way through the childcare maze.

Michelle Maxwell who knows everything there is to know about child safety.

Jane Phillips and Megan and Nelson Contador—all parents of one or more toddlers and who read the entire draft.

Thank you to you all.

Writing hardens the ribs, collapses the sternum, freezes the shoulders, and stiffens the back. Without Annie Cocksedge, the best yoga teacher in the world, I would now be in a wheelchair.

To Kate Llewelyn, one of my favorite authors and poets, thank you for your permission to use "The Flames." And to Cathy Wilcox too for the use of your perceptive cartoon about childcare—ain't it the truth!

I am fortunate indeed to be surrounded by generous and talented friends who have so willingly contributed their craft and skills to my endeavors. Tim Snowdon, friend and gifted artist whose illustrations tell the toddler story with such feeling.

Jane Curry, publisher, thank you for your gentle persistence in getting the show on the road. And for your cheerful support through sticky eyes, slapped cheek disease, the endless cough, mucus galore, and a range of debilitating viruses.

To Julia Stiles, editor and dear friend, my deep appreciation not only for your enthusiastic support from beginning to end but for removing the dross (those theorists and more), talking on the phone for hours in between breastfeedings and toddler shenanigans, and pulling it all into shape. During the writing of *The Mighty Toddler,* we have shared a birth, several confidence crises as writers and mothers, and many hilarious moments. May there be many more books in the years ahead.

I am also grateful to another editor, Cath Proctor, who, out of the goodness of her heart, read and commented on the entire draft manuscript in between the mania of toddlerdom and work. Thank you, Cath, for your interest and astute suggestions.

A special mention to Garry Wells and Linda Bingham, inspired dentists, and to Fiona Hutton for spreading the word in the north. Thanks, too, to Margaret O'Sullivan, friend and agent.

Of what value is a book about toddlers without the ingredient of love? It is present in this book, on the pages and wound around the words, courtesy of a long and loving association with two erstwhile toddlers, Adam and Kate, and their father, Roger, my partner and soulmate in all things.

BOYS: BIRTH TO 36 MONTHS PHYSICAL GROWTH PERCENTILES

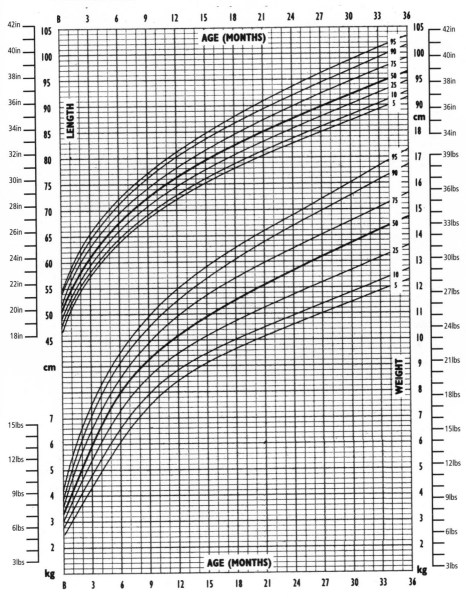

GIRLS: BIRTH TO 36 MONTHS PHYSICAL GROWTH PERCENTILES

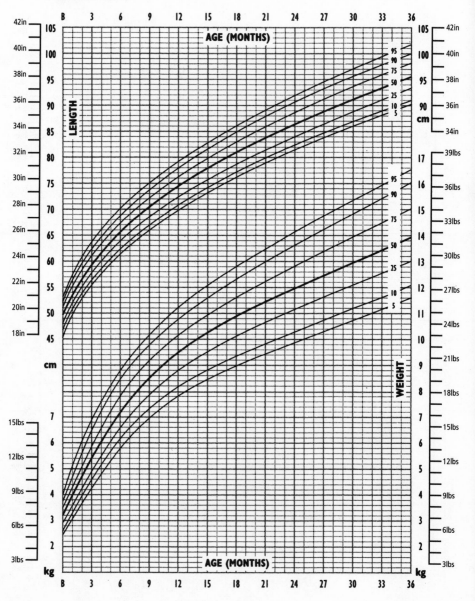

Index

abstract thought, 89–90
abuse
    childcare and, 478–79
    emotional, 13
    physical, 13, 516
acetaminophen
    for colds, 352
    for coughs, 352
    for fever, 351, 379
    for mucus, 352
    for pain, 351
acknowledgment
    praise vs., 110
acne
    infantile, 363–64
activity bag
    traveling and, 214–15
ADHD (Attention Deficit Hyperactivity
    Disorder), 83
adrenaline, 377
advice
    in parenting, lack of confidence and,
    421–22
aggressive behavior, 131–37
    alternatives for, 134
    biting and, 135–36
    boredom and, 132
    consequences of, 134–35
    of eighteen-month toddlers, 131–37
    experimentation with, 132
    of fifteen-month toddlers, 131–37
    hunger and, 132
    overstimulation and, 132
    overtiredness and, 132
    prevention of, 133–34
    reprimanding in, 134
    of thirty-month toddlers, 131–37
    of thirty-six-month toddlers, 131–37
    with toys, 137
    of twelve-month toddlers, 131–37
    of twenty-four-month toddlers, 131–37
ailments. See also infections
    asthma, 372–375
    constant illness and, 225, 477

convulsions, 380–81
croup, 376–77
ear infections, 378
fever, 379–80
fever fits, 380–81
lumps, odd, 382–83
nosebleed, 381–82
allergy, food, 266-69
    diarrhea and, 389
alternatives
    for aggressive behavior, 134
ambivalent feelings, 418–20
antibiotics
    for urinary tract infection (UTI), 391
antifungal cream, 367–68, 406
antihistamine, 353
anxiety, 95–98
    harmful, 96–97
    unhealthy (chronic), 97–98
artificial coloring
    behavior and, 271
aspirin
    for fever, 351
    for pain, 351
asthma, 372–375
    attack, causes of, 373–74
    diagnosis of, 375
    management of, 374–75
    oversensitive lungs and, 373
    patterns of, 373
    prevention and, 374–75
    relievers and, 375
atopic dermatitis. See eczema
attention, attracting
    head banging and, 158
attention, attracting of
    head banging and, 158
Attention Deficit Hyperactivity Disorder
    (ADHD), 83

B12 supplement
    vegan diet with, 262
babysitting, 190–91
    safety, 191

basic food routine plan, 273
bathing
    refusal of, 150–51
bathroom
    home safety check list for, 326
bed
    crib to, 250–51
bedroom safety, 226–27
bedtime
    consistency at, 230
    routine for, 227–28
    temper tantrums and, 244
behavior, aggressive, 131–37
    alternatives for, 134
    biting and, 135–36
    boredom and, 132
    consequences of, 134–35
    of eighteen-month toddlers, 131–37
    experimentation with, 132
    of fifteen-month toddlers, 131–37
    hunger and, 132
    overstimulation and, 132
    overtiredness and, 132
    prevention of, 133–34
    reprimanding in, 134
    of thirty-month toddlers, 131–37
    of thirty-six-month toddlers, 131–37
    with toys, 137
    of twelve-month toddlers, 131–37
    of twenty-four-month toddlers, 131–37
behavior. See also *behavior management
        techniques*
    artificial coloring and, 271
    differences in, childcare and, 477–78
    help for, 129
    power struggles, 130–31
    siblings and, 491
behavior management techniques, 107–27
    consequences for misbehavior in, 114
    consistency, 113
    encouraging desirable behavior in, 123–24
    ignoring undesirable behavior in, 115–17
    negative reinforcement, 111
    positive reinforcement, 108–10
    reprimands, 117
    spanking, 121–23
    timeout, 117–21
    warning v. threats, 112
Benadryl (diphenhydramine), 353
bickering parents, 427–28
biting, 135–36. See also *aggressive behavior*
    nail, 161
blanket
    security object, 167–68
blue attack, 139
books, 307–8
    benefits of, 307
    destroying of, 145
boredom
    aggressive behavior and, 132
    screaming and, 166

bottle feeding, 291–94
    giving up, 292–93
    prolonged, 291–92
bottom shuffling, 46
bow leg, 49
bowel movement. See *poo*
Bowlby, John, 468
breastfeeding, 284–91, 422
    care of breasts after, 290
    daytime feeding, 288
    diet and, 12
    La Leche League International (LLLI), 510
    night waking for, 287–88, 290
    in second year and beyond, 285–86
    unplanned weaning and, 286
    weight and, 9
breath holding, 138–40
    blue attack, 139
    white attack, 139–40
bribes, 416
    rewards vs., 108–10
    temper tantrums and, 182
Bruer, John, 469
burns, 336–37
    first-aid tips for, 337
    prevention of, 336

calcium
    essential nutrients, 263–64
Candida albicans, 367
car-seat refusal, 140–42
car trips, 217
carbohydrates
    essential nutrients, 261
care
    of breasts after breastfeeding, 290
    sharing, of toddler(s), 417–18
    of teeth, 209–11
    of toddlers, 189–220
    of uncircumcised penis, 192
caregiver
    of childcare, 460
    of home daycare, 460
    qualifications of, 464–65
    "quality" care by, 464–66
    relationship with parent, 475–76
    relationship with toddler, 474–75
causality, 85–86
chest rubs, 352, 397
Child and Dependent Care Credit (CDCC),
        458
Child Care Aware, 458, 511
Child Care Resource and Referral (CCR&R)
        agency, 458
childcare, 452–80
    abuse and, 478–79
    availability of, 452–58
    behavior differences and, 477–78
    benefits of, 467
    caregiver of, 460
    Child Care Aware, 458, 511

commercial daycare centers and, 453–54
concerns with, 463–64
constant illness and, 225, 477
debate over, 461–63
difficult settings and, 476–77
environment of, 460–61
family daycare, 454–55
family daycare as, 454–55
fees for, 458–61
finding, 459
government assistance for, 458–61
guilt about, 426
informal, 457–58
International Nanny Association, 511–12
mistreatment and, 478–79
nanny and, 453
National Association for Family Child
Care, 512
National Association for the Education of
Young Children (NAEYC), 511
National Child Care Information Center
(NCCIC), 458, 511
occasional, 457
practicalities of, 472–73
preparing parents for, 472–73
preparing toddlers for, 473–74
preschool, 455–57
problems with, 476–79
"quality" care in, 464–66
recommended reading for, 518
sick child resources in, 512
socializing and, 467–68
what to look for in, 459–60
for zero to twenty-four months, 468
child's bedroom
home safety check list for, 327–28
choking, 333–34
first-aid tips for, 334
protection from, 333–34
cholesterol
food diet with, 259
chronic (unhealthy) anxiety, 97–98
clinginess
excessive, 142–44
cognitive behavior therapy
for parenting, 444
cognitive development, 20–21, 25
of eighteen-month toddlers, 52–53
of fifteen-month toddlers, 43
object permanence and, 87–89
of thirty-month toddlers, 62
of thirty-six-month toddlers, 66–67
of twelve-month toddlers, 40–41
of twenty-four-month toddlers, 58
colds
head, 396–98
nonprescription medications for, 352
commercial daycare centers, 453–54
commercial food
hooked on, 280–81
communicating effectively

in parenting, 438
concrete thought, 90
conductive hearing loss, 32, 33
confidence, lack of
advice in parenting and, 421–22
childcare and, guilt about, 426
keeping child happy and, 424
life-enriching experiences for child and,
424
other parents and, 422–23
in parenting, 421–27
conflict, dealing with, 104–7
anticipating problems in, 106
distraction in, 106
minimizing unnecessary, 105–7
problem with behavior in, 105–6
realistic expectations in, 105
rituals in, 106–7
routines in, 106–7
consequences
for aggressive behavior, 134–35
for misbehavior, 114
consistency
at bedtime, 230
in behavior management, 113
constipation, 383–87
cause of, 384
chronic, 386–87
severe, 386–87
temporary mild, 384–85
Consumer Reports, 514
"control-crying," 232
harm of, 232
success rate of, 232
conversation
interruption of, 158–59
convulsions, 380–81
cooperative play, 298
cortisone ointment, 370
cosmetic tooth appearance, 212
fluoride and, 211
cough(s)
endless, 376
nonprescription medications for, 352
counseling
for parenting, 444
cow's milk, 277–78
cracking behind ears, 359
cradle cap, 360–61
treatment of, 360–61
creams
antifungal, 367–68, 406
first aid kit and, 330
croup, 376–77
medication for, 377
treatment of, 377
cup
drinking from, 275–276

daycare. See also childcare
disadvantages of, 466

family, 454–55
family child care providers, 454–55
home, 454–55
daytime sleeping, 252–54
tantrum on waking from, 253–54
death, understanding, 217–20
developmental issue in, 218–19
parent role in, 219
routines after, 219
decay, tooth, 210
depression, 445–51
mild, 446–47
parenting, 447–51
postpartum, 516
serious, 447–51
dermatitis, atopic. See *eczema*
Desitin ointment, 366
development, 18–37
cognitive, 20–21, 25
emotional, 34–35
gender awareness in, 35–37
of hearing, 31–33
of language, 23–24, 25–27, 28–30
of memory, 21–23
milestones in, 18–20
recommended reading for, 517–18
of sexuality, 35–37
of speech, 23–24, 25–27, 28–30
toys and, 301–5
of vision, 33–34
diaper rash, 364–69
causes of, 365
tips for, 368–69
treatment of, 365
types of, 366–69
without fungal infection, 366–67
without yeast infection, 366–67
with yeast infection, 367–68
diarrhea, 387–89
acute, vomiting and, 393–96
causes of, 387–88
food allergy and, 389
food and, 388
intolerance and, 389
medication and, 388
mild, 396
teething and, 204
toddler, 388
underlying medical problems and, 389
viral, 12, 396
diet, 12, 422
breastfeeding and, 12
hyperactivity and, 269–71
vegetarian, 265–66
diphenhydramine (Benadryl), 353
discipline, 99–127. See also *conflict*
anticipating conflict problems in, 106
beliefs on, 99
consequences for misbehavior in, 114
consistency with, 113
dealing with conflict, 104–7

definition of, 100
distraction, conflict and, 106
encouraging desirable behavior in, 123–24
feelings about, 99
ignoring undesirable behavior in, 115–17
minimizing unnecessary conflicts in, 105–7
negative reinforcement, 111
positive reinforcement, 108–10
problem with conflict behavior and, 105–6
punishment and, 100–101
realistic expectations in, 105
reprimands, 117
rituals, conflicts and, 106–7
routines, conflicts in, 106–7
spanking, 121–23
timeout, 117–21
for toddlers, 104
warning v. threats, 112
divorce, in parenting, 428–36
avoidance of, 435
impact on adults, 430–31
impact on children, 431
management of, 435–36
toddlers and, 431–435
dog bites, 338–39
basic treatment for, 339
protection from, 338–39
dressings
first aid kit and, 329–30
drooling, 207–8
drowning, 330–31
first-aid tips for, 331

early morning waking, 254–55
Earned Income Tax Credit (EITC), 459
ear(s)
cracking behind, 359
glue, 378
infections, 12, 32, 225, 347, 378
eating
fussy, 282
healthy but non, 282-84
with family, 277
eczema, 357–59, 370
impetigo and, 398
irritants with, 357–59
egocentrism, 84–85
sharing and, 168–70
eighteen-month toddlers, 51–54
aggressive behavior and, 131–37
breath holding by, 138–40
car-seat refusal by, 140–42
cognitive development of, 52–53
emotion development of, 53
fine motor skills of, 51–52
gross motor skills of, 51
hearing of, 52
help for, 54
language of, 52

pacifiers and, 145–47
play of, 53–54
social development of, 53
speech of, 52
toys for, 54
vision of, 51–52
emergency numbers, 329
emergency self-help in parenting, 441–43
emotional abuse, 13
emotional development, 34–35. See also
    feelings
of eighteen-month toddlers, 53
of fifteen-month toddlers, 43–44
of thirty-month toddlers, 62–63
of thirty-six-month toddlers, 67
of twelve-month toddlers, 41
of twenty-four-month toddlers, 58–59
Emotional Life of the Toddler, The, 469
emotional problems
weight loss and, 13–14
environment
of childcare, 460–61
essential nutrients, 260–65
carbohydrates, 261
minerals, 263–64
protein, 261–62
vitamins, 262
expectations
in parenting, 439–41
experimentation
aggressive behavior and, 132

falling, 335
prevention of, 335
family child care providers, 454–55
family daycare, 454–55
fees for, 458
family support, lack of
in parenting, 424–25
family therapy
for parenting, 444–45
fantasy, 308–11
developmental issues and, 226
fat
food diet with, 258
fathers
responsibility of, 417–18
favoritism of one parent, 162–64
fears, 93–95, 148–57
bath refusal, 150–51
hair-washing refusal, 151–52
potty training and, 198
of separation, 152–57
separation and, 152–57
sleeping and, 248–49
support through, 95
feces. See *poo*
feeding
general guidelines for, 257–66
problems, 9
feelings

about discipline, 99
ambivalent, 418–20
toddlers and, understanding others, 91–92
fees
childcare and, 458–61
feet
flat, 49
turning in of, 48
turning out of, 48–49
fever, 379–80
acetaminophen for, 351
aspirin for, 351
diagnosis of, 379
nonprescription medications for, 351
treatment of, 379–80
fever fits, 380–81
fifteen-month toddlers, 42–44
aggressive behavior by, 131–37
breath holding by, 138–40
car-seat refusal by, 140–42
clinginess by, 142–44
cognitive development of, 43
destruction of books by, 145
developmental concern at, 46–50
emotional development of, 43–44
fine motor skills of, 42–43
gross motor skills of, 42
hearing of, 43
language of, 43
pacifiers and, 145–47
play of, 44
social development of, 44
speech of, 43
toys for, 45
vision of, 42–43
fine motor skills, 19
of eighteen-month toddlers, 51–52
of fifteen-month toddlers, 42–43
of thirty-month toddlers, 61–62
of thirty-six-month toddlers, 66
of twelve-month toddlers, 40
of twenty-four-month toddlers, 57
fine motor skills. See *motor skills, fine*
finger/snack foods, 274–75
firm action, 501
first aid kit, 329–30
first-aid equipment in, 330
first-aid tips
for burns, 337
for choking, 334
for drowning, 331
for poisoning, 332–33
flame resistant sleepwear, 252
flat feet, 49
fluid
gastroenteritis and, 394
fluoride, 211
food, 257–94
allergy, 266–69
commercial, 280–81
diarrhea and, 388

gagging on, 279–80
hooked on commercial, 280–81
intolerance to, 266–69
refusal of, 282
routine and, 199
throwing, 281
variety of, 258
food allergy, 266–69
diarrhea and, 389
forty-eight month toddlers
breath holding by, 138–40
endless questions by, 148
pacifiers and, 145–47
forty-two month toddlers
car-seat refusal by, 140–42
endless questions by, 148
pacifiers and, 145–47
free vaccines, 343, 515
fruits, 259
fungal infection
diaper rash without, 366–67
fussy eating, 282

gagging
on food, 279–80
garden shed
home safety check list for, 328
gastroenteritis, 393–96
treatment of, 39496
vomiting and, 391
gender awareness, 35–37
general home environment
home safety check list for, 325
genitals, 192. See also *penis*
masturbation and, 159–61
undescended testes, 389-90
glue ear, 378
Good Kids, Bad Behavior, 103
goosebumpy skin, 361–62
government assistance
childcare and, 458–61
grains, 259
grinding teeth, 212
groin, lump in, 383
gross motor skills, 19
of eighteen-month toddler, 51
of fifteen-month toddler, 42
of thirty-month toddler, 61
of thirty-six-month toddler, 65–66
of twelve-month toddler, 39–40
of twenty-four-month toddler, 55–57
gross motor skills. See *motor skills, gross*
growth, of toddler, 9–17
boys, 525
girls, 526

habit
head banging, 158
nails biting, 161
nose picking, 162
screaming, 166–67

hair
pulling of, 131
pulling out, 164
washing, refusal of, 151–52
hairline, neck
lump around, 383
handedness, 47–48
harmful anxiety, 96–97
head banging, 157–58
attract attention and, 158
habit and, 158
sleep technique and, 158
temper tantrum and, 157–58
whining toddler and, 158
head colds, 396–98
medications for, 397
headlice. See *nits*
health professional
parenting and, lack of confidence in, 421
hearing, 19
development of, 31–33
of eighteen-month toddlers, 52
of fifteen-month toddlers, 43
loss, 32–33
of thirty-month toddlers, 62
of thirty-six-month toddlers, 66
of twelve-month toddlers, 40
of twenty-four-month toddlers, 57–58
height, 10
growth disorders of, 16–17
increase in, 9
premature baby and, 17
help in parenting, 437–445
helping organizations, 509–17
herbal teething medications, 352
hitting, 131
hives, 362–63
treatment of, 363
home daycare, 454–55
caregiver of, 460
home safety check list, 325–28
bathroom, 326
child's bedroom, 226–27, 327–28
garden shed, 328
general home environment, 325
kitchen, 325–26
laundry, 326–27
living areas, 327
outdoors, 328
homeopathic immunization, 341
humidifiers, 376
hunger
aggressive behavior and, 132
hydrocortisone cream
for diaper rash, 367–68
for white patches, 371
hyperactivity, diet and, 269–71
Hypoallergenic Moisturizing Lotion/Cream, 200

ibuprofen

for fever, 351, 379
for pain, 351
ignoring, undesirable behavior, 115–17
temper tantrums and, 180–181
illness, constant, 225, 477
imaginary friend, 310–11
imagination, 308–11
developmental issues and, 226
immunization(s), 339–44, 422
age for, 341
benefits of, 340
choices and, 343–44
doses of, 340
effectiveness of, 340
homeopathic, 341
National Vaccine Injury Compensation
Program, 515
risks of, 340
sick children and, 341
side effects of, 342
standard recommended childhood schedule for, 344
Vaccine Adverse Event Reporting System
(VAERS), 342
impetigo, 398
infantile acne, 363–64
infections
ear, 12, 32, 347, 378
upper respiratory tract, 12
urinary tract, 12
infectious diseases, 347–48, 393–406
common, 400–5
consulting family doctor for, 349–50
gastroenteritis, 393–96
head cold, 396–98
impetigo, 398
minimizing of, 348–49
pneumonia, 399
ringworm, 404–6
infestations, 407–11
nits, 407–9
threadworms, 409–11
informal childcare, 457
informal playgroups, 316–17
injury. See also toddlerproofing
falling with, 335
vulnerability to, 323–24
inside play, 305–6
intellectual development, 20–21
International Nanny Association, 511–12
intolerance
diarrhea and, 389
iron supplement, 263–64
isolation
in parenting, lack of confidence and, 423–24

jet lag, sedatives and, 353
juice, 265, 278
Juvenile Products Manufacturers Association,
Inc. (JPMA), 514

keratosis pilaris, 361–62
kicking, 131
kitchen
home safety check list for, 325–26
knock-knees, 49

La Leche League International (LLLI), 510
labial fusion, 192
language, development of, 23–24, 25–27,
28–30
of eighteen-month toddlers, 52
encourage, 27–28
of fifteen-month toddlers, 43
of thirty-month toddlers, 62
of thirty-six-month toddlers, 66
of twelve-month toddlers, 40
of twenty-four-month toddlers, 57–58
laryngitis. See croup
laundry
home safety check list for, 326–27
toddlers, 200
legume, 259
Liberman, Alicia, 469
life-enriching experiences for child
and parenting, 424
lindane, nits and, 409
living areas
home safety check list for, 327
loneliness
in parenting, lack of confidence and,
423–24
long-term memory, 22
lotions
first aid kit and, 330
low cost vaccines, 343, 515
low-salt foods, 260
lumps, odd, 382–83
groin, 383
movable, 383
neck hairline, 383
under nipple, 383
lungs, oversensitive
in asthma, 373
lying, 174–75

make-believe, 308–11
manipulation. See fine motor
man's responsibility
in parenting, 417–18
masturbation, 159–61
medical conditions
causing obesity, 15
medical illnesses
low weight in toddlers and, 11–12
medication(s). See also creams; nonprescription medications; sedatives; specific
drugs
antihistamine, 353
antibiotic, 391
aspirin as, 351
for asthma, 374–75

for colds, 352, 397
for coughs, 352
for croup, 377
diarrhea and, 388
for fever, 351, 379
first aid kit and, 330
giving, 354–56
for head colds, 397
herbal teething, 352
for jet lag, 353
for mucus, 352
for pain, 351
prescription, 354
medicine safety, 353
memory, development of, 21–23
long-term, 21
sensory, 21
short-term, 21
mild depression, 446–47
help for, 447
milk. See *bottle feeding*
cow, 277–78
minerals
essential nutrients, 263–64
misbehavior, consequences for, 114
mistreatment, childcare and, 478–79
moisturizers, 200
mosquito bites, 364
motor skills, fine, 19
of eighteen-month toddlers, 51–52
of fifteen-month toddlers, 42–43
of thirty-month toddlers, 61–62
of thirty-six-month toddlers, 66
of twelve-month toddlers, 40
of twenty-four-month toddlers, 57
motor skills, gross, 19
of eighteen-month toddler, 51
of fifteen-month toddler, 42
of thirty-month toddler, 61
of thirty-six-month toddler, 65–66
of twelve-month toddler, 39–40
of twenty-four-month toddler, 55–57
mouth, rash around, 369–70
mucus
ear infections and, 378
head colds and, 397, 398
nonprescription medications for, 352
muscle tone, 9
Myth of the First Three Years, The, 469

nails
biting of, 161
cutting of, 165–66
nanny, childcare and, 453
fees for, 458
napping. See also *sleep*
resting and, 253
tantrum after, 253–54
National Association for Family Child Care, 512
National Association for the Education of

Young Children (NAEYC), 511
National Child Care Information Center (NCCIC), 458, 476, 511
National Highway Traffic Administration (NHTSA), 513
National Organization of Mothers of Twins Clubs (NOMOTC), 515
National SAFE KIDS Campaign, 513
National Vaccine Injury Compensation Program, 343, 515
neck hairline
lump around, 383
negative reinforcement, 111
negativism, 92–93
nerve deafness, 33
newborn
pacifiers and, 145–47
night-light, 249
night terrors, 247–48
night waking, 228
dealing with, 229–30
teaching-to-sleep and, 231–42
nightmares, 225, 246–47
nine-month toddlers
car-seat refusal by, 140–42
clinginess by, 142–44
destruction of books by, 145
pacifiers and, 145–47
nipple
lump under, 383
nits, 407–9
lindane and, 409
pyrethrins and, 409
treatment of, 408
noncrawler, 46
nonprescription medications, 351–53
for colds, 352
for coughs, 352
for fever, 351
for mucus, 352
for pain, 351
sedatives, 353
teething gels, 352
nose drops, 352
nose picking, 162
nosebleed, 381–82
avoidance of, 382
prevention of, 382
stopping of, 381–82

obesity, 14–16
medical conditions causing, 15
parents and, 14–15
object permanence, 87–89
play ideas in development of, 88–89
occupational depression. See *mild depression*
onlooker, 297
only child, 484–85
outdoors, home safety check list for, 328
outside play, 306
overseas traveling

sedatives for, 213
overstimulation
  aggressive behavior and, 132
overtiredness
  aggressive behavior and, 132
overweight, 14–16. See also *obesity*

PABA, 203
pacifiers, 145–47, 239, 369
  prolonged use of, 146
  sanity and, 146
  sleeping problems and, 146
pain
  medications for, 351
parallel play, 298
parenting
  advice in, 421–22
  ambivalent feelings about, 419–20
  bickering parents and, 427–28
  childcare and, guilt about, 426
  childcare preparation for, 472–73
  cognitive behavior therapy and, 444
  communicating effectively in, 438
  confidence in, lack of, 421–27
  counseling for, 444
  death and, 219
  depression and, 445–51
  divorce and, 428–36
  emergency self-help in, 441–43
  expectations in, 439–41
  family support in, lack of, 424–25
  family therapy for, 444–45
  father's responsibility in, 417–18
  favoritism of parent and, 162–64
  health professional and, lack of confi-
    dence in, 421
  help for, 437–445
  isolation in, lack of confidence and,
    423–24
  keeping child happy and, 424
  life-enriching experiences for child and,
    424
  listing basic needs in, 439
  loneliness in, lack of confidence and,
    423–24
  man's responsibility in, 417–18
  mild depression in, 446–47
  other parents and, lack of confidence by,
    422–23
  professional help for, 443–45
  psychotherapy for, 444
  self-help in, 438–43
  separation and, 428–36
  serious depression in, 447–51
  sleep-deprivation in, 233–34
  sole, 436–37, 516
  stressfulness of, 415–17
  woman's responsibility in, 417–18
parent(s)
  favoritism of one, 162–64
  obesity in, 14–15

sleep-deprived, 233–34
Parents Anonymous, 516
Pediculosis. See *nits*
peek-a-boo game, 88–89
penis, uncircumcised
  care of, 192
percentile charts, 10–11
pets
  ringworm and, 406
phobias, 93–95
phone calls
  interruption of, 158–59
physical abuse, 13, 516
pigeon lice bites, 369
pinworms. See *threadworms*
pityriasis alba, 370–71
plane trips, 216, 353
play, 19, 295–321
  books and, 307–8
  buying, 303–4
  concerns about, 298–301
  cooperative, 298
  of eighteen-month toddler, 53–54
  fantasy and, 308–11
  of fifteen-month toddler, 44
  imagination and, 308–11
  inside, 305–6
  make-believe and, 308–11
  necessity of, 299
  outside, 306
  parallel, 298
  playgroups and, 314–17
  reading and, 307–8
  reality of, 299
  routine and, 199
  socializing and, 314–17
  solitary, 297
  stages of, 297–98
  stimulating activities and, 318–21
  swimming and, 317–18
  television and, 311–14
  of thirty-month toddler, 63
  of thirty-six-month toddler, 68
  tips for encouraging toddler to, 300–1
  together, 301
  toys and, 301–5
  of twelve-month toddler, 42
  of twenty-four-month toddler, 59–60
playgroups, 314–17
  arranging of, 314–16
  informal, 316–17
pneumonia, 399
  symptoms of, 399
  treatment of, 399
pointing, 47
poisoning, 332–33
  first-aid tips for, 332–33
  protection from, 332
poo
  endless, 396
  smearing of, 170–71

poo problems, 383–89
  constipation, 383–87
  diarrhea, 387–89
positive reinforcement, 108–10
  praise v. acknowledgment, 110
  rewards v. bribes, 108–10
postnatal depression. See *serious depression*
postpartum depression, 516
potty training, 192–99
  constipation and, 385
  night training, 198–99
  right time for, 193–94
  signs of readiness for, 194
  of twins, 197
powder, talcum, 200
power struggles, 130–31
praise
  acknowledgment vs., 110
praise v. acknowledgment, 110
premature baby
  height of, 17
  weight of, 14
preschool, 455–57
  benefits of, 456
  daycare and, 455
  hours for, 455–56
  social experience of, 456–57
  staffing at, 456
prescription medication, 354. See also
  medication
preservatives
  behavior and, 271
professional help, for parenting, 443–45
  cognitive behavior therapy, 444
  counseling, 444
  family therapy, 444–45
psychotherapy, 444
protein
  essential nutrients, 261–62
psychotherapy
  for parenting, 444
punishment, discipline and, 100–101
  spanking in, 102
pyrethrins
  nits and, 409

"quality" care
  in childcare, 464–66
questions
  endless, 148

rash, diaper. See *diaper rash*
reading, 307–8
  benefits of, 307
red cheeks, 370
reprimanding, 117
  for aggressive behavior, 134
resources, 509–17
respiratory tract infection, upper, 12
resting, 253. See also *napping*
rewards

bribes vs., 108–10
  temper tantrums and, 181
Reye's syndrome, 351
ringworm, 404–6
  on scalp, 405
  on skin, 405
  treatment of, 406
rituals, 106–7, 228
role models
  for toddlers, 4–5
routines, 106–7, 199–200
  after death, 219
  bedtime, 227–28
rules
  family, 499

safety, 322–39, 422
  babysitting and, 191
  burns and, 336–37
  choking and, 333–34
  Consumer Reports, 514
  dog bites and, 338–39
  drowning and, 330–31
  emergency numbers and, 329
  falling and, 335
  first aid kit and, 329–30
  general considerations about, 328–30
  hazards, 330–39
  Juvenile Products Manufacturers Associa-
    tion, Inc. (JPMA), 514
  medication, 353
  National Highway Traffic Administration
    (NHTSA), 513
  National SAFE KIDS Campaign, 513
  poisoning and, 332–33
  Safety Belt Safe Ride Help Line, 514
  scalds, 336–37
  suffocation and, 337–38
  toddlerproofing home, 322–28
  U.S. Consumer Gateway, 513
  U.S. Consumer Product Safety Commission
    (CPSC), 512
Safety Belt Safe Ride Help Line, 514
salt foods, low, 260
scalds, 336–37
  prevention of, 336
screaming, 166–67
screeching, 166–67
security objects, 167–68
security rails, 251
sedatives
  nonprescription medications and, 353
  for sleeping, 243–44
  for travel, 213–14
self-help
  in parenting, 438–43
sensorineural hearing loss, 33
sensory memory, 21
separation
  anxiety, developmental issues and, 226
  fear of, 152–57

temper tantrums and, 181
separation, in parenting, 428–36
   recommended reading for, 519
serious depression, 447–51
   causes of, 448
   help for, 449–50
   recovery for, 450–51
   symptoms of, 449
sexuality
   curiosity of, 159–61
   development of, 35–37
shampoo, 200
sharing
   refusing to, 168–70
shoes, 50
short-term memory, 22
shyness, 80
   as inborn trait, 80
   living with, 80–81
   as part of development, 80
siblings, 481–503
   advantages of, 481–83
   behavior and, 491
   bonds between, 496–503
   dealing with strife and, 498–501
   disadvantages of, 483–84
   family life with, 497–98
   preparing for, 489–96
   rivalries between, 496–503
   spacing of, 487–89
sick child resources, 512
side effects of immunizations, 342
single parents
   sleep and, 240–41
skin problems, 357–71
   atopic dermatitis, 357–59
   cracking behind ears, 359
   cradle cap, 360–61
   diaper rash, 364–369
   eczema, 357–59
   goosebumpy skin, 361–62
   hives, 362–63
   impetigo, 398
   infantile acne, 363–64
   keratosis pilaris, 361–62
   mosquito bites, 364
   pigeon lice bites, 369
   pityriasis alba, 370–71
   rash around mouth, 369–70
   red cheeks, 370
   white patches, 370–71
sleep, 221–56
   basic routine and, 227–28
   bedroom safety and, 226–27
   constant illness and, 225
   in daytime, 252–54
   deprived parent, 233–34
   developmental issues and, 225–26
   head banging and, 158
   interruption of, 253
   nail cutting and, 166

   night-time attention-seeking devices and,
     249–50
   night waking and, 228
   patterns, 224–25
   recommended reading for, 519
   routine and, 199
   single parents and, 240–41
   teaching to, 231–34
   teething and, 204
   twins and, 240
sleepwear, safe, 251–52
   flame resistant, 252
snug-fitting, 252
snack box
   traveling and, 214–15
snack/finger foods, 274–75
snug-fitting sleepwear, 252
soap, 200
social problems
   weight loss and, 13–14
social skills, 19
   childcare and, 467–68
   of eighteen-month toddlers, 53
   of fifteen-month toddlers, 44
   of thirty-month toddlers, 63
   of thirty-six-month toddlers, 67–68
   of twenty-four-month toddlers, 59
socializing, 314–17
sole parenting, 436–37, 516
   sleep and, 240–41
solitary play, 297
spanking, 102, 121–23
   effectiveness of, 122–23
speech, development of, 19, 23–24, 25–27,
   28–30
   of eighteen-month toddlers, 52
   encouragement of, 27–28
   of fifteen-month toddlers, 43
speech-language pathologist, 29
   of thirty-month toddlers, 62
   of thirty-six-month toddlers, 66
   of twelve-month toddlers, 40–41
   of twenty-four-month toddlers, 57–58
SPF, in sunscreen, 203
spoon feeding, 276
standard recommended childhood immunization schedule, 344
steroids, 377
stimulating activities, 318–21
stress
   parenting and, 415–17
stroller refusal, 171–73
stuttering, 30–31
suffocation, 337–38
   protection from, 338
sugar, 259–60, 271
   natural, 261
sun protection, 202–4. See also *sunscreen*
sunlight
   avoiding, 202
sunscreen

about, 203
choosing of, 203–4
PABA, 203
SPF in, 203
superactive toddler, 82–84
suppressants, cough, 352, 376
swear words, 173–74
swimming, 317–18
symbolic thought, 22

talcum powder, 200
talking. See *speech*; *language*
tantrums. See *temper tantrums*
teaching-to-sleep, 231–34
teeth
brushing of, resistance to, 165–66
care of, 209–11
cosmetic appearance of, 212
decay of, 210
dietary risk factor of, 210–11
fluoride and, 211
grinding of, 212
teeth, growing of, 204–12
discomfort in, 207
drooling and, 207–8
teething. See *teeth, growing of*
telephone calls
interruption of, 158–59
television, 311–14
benefits of, 311–12
disadvantages of, 312–13
risks of, 312–13
temper tantrums, 175–84, 416
avoidance of, 179–80
bedtime and, 244
bribery and, 182
from daytime nap, 253–54
developmental reasons for, 176–79
head banging and, 157–58
ignoring of, 180–81
intervention of, 180
lengthy explanations and, 182
losing control and, 182
positives of, 184
in public, 182–83
rewarding and, 181
separation and, 181
threats and, 182
timeout and, 181
temperament, 77–84, 152–53. See also
temper tantrums
car travel and, 141
childcare and, 466, 473
head banging and, 157–58
modification of, 79
personalities and, 78–79
recognizing of, 78
sharing and, 169
types of, 80–84
terrible twos, 3
testes, undescended, 389–90

thinking. See *cognitive development*
thirty-month toddlers, 60–64
aggressive behavior by, 131–37
breath holding by, 138–40
car-seat refusal by, 140–42
clinginess of, 142–44
cognitive development of, 62
emotional development of, 62–63
endless questions by, 148
fine motor skills of, 61–62
gross motor skills of, 61
hearing of, 62
help for, 64
language of, 62
pacifiers and, 145–47
play of, 63
social development of, 63
speech of, 62
toys for, 63–64
vision of, 61–62
thirty-six-month toddlers, 65–69
aggressive behavior by, 131–37
breath holding by, 138–40
car-seat refusal by, 140–42
cognitive development of, 66–67
emotional development of, 67
endless questions by, 148
fine motor skills of, 66
gross motor skills of, 65–66
hearing of, 66
help for, 69
language of, 66
pacifiers and, 145–47
play of, 68
social development of, 67–68
speech of, 66
toys for, 68
vision of, 66
threadworms, 409–11
symptoms of, 410–11
treatment of, 411
threats
temper tantrums and, 182
warning vs., 112
throwing food, 281
throwing up, 239–40
thumb sucking, 185
timeout, 117–21
after, 120
length of, 120
place for, 119–20
temper tantrums and, 181
tinea. See *ringworm*
tiptoe walking, 46–47
toddlerproofing home, 322–28
guide for, 324
safety check list, 325–28
toddler(s). See also *specific ages of toddler*
anxiety of, 95–98
basic needs of, 4–5
behavior of, 73–98

behavior, description of, 73–75
being only child, 484–85
being twins, 486–87
caring for, 189–220, 415–51
causality of, 85–86
childcare preparation of, 473–74
classifying, cataloging, and sorting by, 86–87
control of, 76
development of, 18–37
discipline of, 99–126
divorce and, 431–435
eighteen-month, 51–54
fears of, 93–95
fifteen-month, 42–44
foods for, 272–75
growth of, 9–17
immunizations for, 339–44
interests of, 76–77
in kitchen, 279
labeling and, 76
negativity of, 92–93
noneating but healthy, 282–84
other people and, 76
phobias of, 93–95
physical world and, 76
predictability of, 76
relationship between, 474
relationship with caregiver and, 474–75
safety of, 322–39
siblings, preparing for, 489–96
siblings and, 481–503
thirty-month, 60–64
traveling with, 212–17
twelve-month, 39–42
understanding feelings of others by, 91–92
toys, 301–5
and age range designed for, 304–5
aggressive behavior with, 137
appearance of, 305
for eighteen-month toddlers, 54
function of, 305
maintenance of, 305
safety of, 303, 304
suitability of, 304
for thirty-month toddlers, 63–64
for thirty-six-month toddlers, 68
throwing, 131
for twelve to fifteen-month toddlers, 45
for twenty-four-month toddlers, 45
variety of, 305
traveling, toddler and, 212–17
activity bag for, 214–15
car trips, 217
overseas, 213
plane trips, 216
sedatives, 213–14
snack box for, 214–15
trichotillomania, 164
twelve-month toddlers, 39–42

aggressive behavior and, 131–37
breath holding by, 138–40
car-seat refusal by, 140–42
clinginess by, 142–44
cognitive development of, 40–41
destruction of books by, 145
developmental concern at, 46–50
emotional development of, 41
fine motor skills of, 40
gross motor skills of, 39–40
hearing of, 40
language of, 40
pacifiers and, 145–47
play of, 42
social development of, 41
speech of, 40
toys for, 45
vision of, 40
twenty-four-month toddlers, 55–60
aggressive behavior by, 131–37
breath holding by, 138–40
car-seat refusal by, 140–42
clinginess by, 142–44
cognitive development of, 58
destruction of books by, 145
emotional development of, 58–59
fine motor skills of, 57
gross motor skills of, 55–57
hearing of, 57–59
help at, 60
language of, 57–59
pacifiers and, 145–47
play of, 59–60
social development of, 59
speech of, 57–59
toys for, 45
vision of, 58
twins, 485–87
National Organization of Mothers of Twins Clubs (NOMOTC), 515
potty training of, 197
sleep and, 240

underweight, 13
undescended testes, 389–90
undesirable behavior, ignoring, 115–17
appropriateness of, 116
inappropriateness of, 116–17
technique of, 115–16
unhealthy (chronic) anxiety, 97–98
urinary tract infection (UTI), 390–91
symptoms of, 390
treatment of, 391
urinary tract infections, 12
U.S. Consumer Gateway, 513
U.S. Consumer Product Safety Commission (CPSC), 512
UTI (urinary tract infection). See *urinary tract infection (UTI)*

vaccine. See also *immunization(s)*

free, 343, 515
low cost, 343, 515
National Vaccine Injury Compensation
    Program, 343
required, 342–43
Vaccine Adverse Event Reporting System
    (VAERS), 342
VAERS (Vaccine Adverse Event Reporting
    System), 342
vaporizer, 397
vegan diet, 262, 266
    B12 supplement in, 262
vegetables, 259, 278
vegetarian diet, 265–66
Vicks Vapor Rub, 397
vision, development of, 19, 33–34
    of eighteen-month toddlers, 51–52
    of fifteen-month toddlers, 42–43
    of thirty-month toddlers, 61–62
    of thirty-six-month toddlers, 66
    of twelve-month toddlers, 40
    of twenty-four-month toddlers, 57
vitamins
    essential nutrients, 262
vomiting, 391–92
    attention-seeking and, 392
    diarrhea and, 393–96

walking, tiptoe, 46–47
warning
    threats vs., 112
water safety, 64–65, 277–78, 331. See also
    drowning
weight, 9, 10
    concern about, 11
    low, reasons for, 11–14
    over, 14-16
    premature baby and, 14
    social problems of loss in, 13-14
whining, 185–86
    head banging and, 158
    teething and, 204
white attack, 139–40
white patches, 370–71
Williamson's, Peter, 103
woman's responsibility
    in parenting, 417–18

yeast infection
    with diaper rash, 367–68
    without diaper rash, 366–67